MEETINGS, EXPOSITIONS, EVENTS, AND CONVENTIONS

An Introduction to the Industry

SECOND EDITION

George G. Fenich, Ph.D.

PEARSON

Prentice Hall

Upper Saddle River, New Jersey 07458

Library of Congress Cataloging-in-Publication Data
Fenich, George G.
    Meetings, expositions, events, and conventions:
        an introduction to the industry/George G. Fenich.
        p.cm.
    Includes index.
    ISBN 0-13-234057-7
    1. Hospitality Industry.   2. Congresses and conventions.
        3. Meetings. I. Title.
    TX911.2.F455 2007
    647.94—dc22

                                            2007018276

Editor-in-Chief: Vernon R. Anthony
Senior Editor: William Lawrensen
Senior Marketing Manager: Leigh Ann Sims
Editorial Assistant: Lara Dimmick
Marketing Coordinator: Alicia Dysert
Marketing Assistant: Les Roberts
Managing Editor: Mary Carnis
Production Liaison: Jane Bonnell
Production Management: Janet Bolton
Manufacturing Manager: Ilene Sanford
Manufacturing Buyer: Cathleen Petersen
Senior Design Coordinator: Miguel Ortiz
Cover Design: Geoff Cassar, Koala Bear Design
Cover Image: Bruce Forster, Getty Images Inc.—Stone Allstock
Composition: Carlisle Publishing Services
Printer/Binder: Courier Westford
Cover Printer: Phoenix Color Corp.

Pearson Education LTD.
Pearson Education Singapore, Pte. Ltd.
Pearson Education Canada, Ltd.
Pearson Education–Japan

Pearson Education Australia PTY, Limited
Pearson Education North Asia, Ltd.
Pearson Educación de Mexico, S.A. de C.V.
Pearson Education Malaysia, Pte. Ltd.

10 9 8 7 6 5 4 3 2 1

ISBN-13: 978-0-13-234057-1
ISBN-10: 0-13-234057-7

Contents

PART 2   Key Players

PART 3   Important Elements in Meeting, Exposition, Event, and Convention Planning _____

Preface

The meetings, expositions, events, and conventions (MEEC, pronounced like *geese*) industry continues to grow and garner increasing attention from the hospitality industry, colleges and universities, and communities. This book gives a broad overview of this industry and is thus an introduction. It is not meant to provide a hands-on or step-by-step method for handling gatherings in the MEEC industry.

This book is being produced at this time for a number of reasons. One is the continued growth of this industry; in spite of the ebbs and flows of the economy and disasters such as 9/11 and Hurricane Katrina, the MEEC segment of the hospitality industry remains resilient. Communities continue to build or expand MEEC venues unabated, and the private sector has also become a player in convention center construction and operation. People still find a need for face-to-face meetings. The MEEC industry appears to be on a growth curve and is of interest to many people (not unlike the casino industry was in the early 1990s).

Also, college faculties have indicated a need for a book such as this. The author/editor has been teaching an introductory MEEC course for many years and has found himself having to continually supplement the existing books to make them both current and more complete in addressing the various segments of the MEEC industry. Therefore, he began to contemplate the development of a book on the subject. Then, at a meeting of the Convention Special Interest Group at the Council on Hotel, Restaurant, and Institutional Education (CHRIE) Convention in 2001, the need for a new text was discussed. The members of this group all noted the need, and the author/editor volunteered to spearhead an effort to put together a new book using faculty and industry experts to write various chapters. This book is a culmination of that effort. The result is a text where some of the best and most notable people in the MEEC industry have made contributions; as you will see, there is a fairly even balance between educators and practitioners among the chapter contributors.

The approach to deciding on topics was unusual. Rather than have a list of topics or chapters based on people's willingness to contribute, a more scientific method was used. The author/editor reviewed existing books, both theoretical and practical, to ascertain which topics to cover. Topics that appeared in more than one text were compiled into a list. Then a number of meetings were held with educators, and the relative importance of topics was discussed, which led to the development of a comprehensive list of topics. This list was sent to educators and practitioners, who were asked to rank the importance of each topic as critically important, important, or not important. Results were used to pare down the list, and this iterative voting procedure (Delphi technique) was used to reach the decision as to the topics to include in the book. This second edition not only has updated material and statistics but has relied on feedback from adopters and reviewers to make improvements to the previous edition.

Meetings, Expositions, Events, and Conventions should be of interest to practitioners, educators, students, and the general public. It is the most up-to-date book on the MEEC industry and will provide users with an overview of the industry; it is also comprehensive and covers a wider range of MEEC topics than any other book available. It can easily serve as the basis for an introductory college course on the subject or for orientation sessions for new employees in the industry. It should meet the needs of anyone interested in knowing more about the MEEC industry.

George G. Fenich, Ph.D.

Acknowledgments

I would like to thank Kathryn Hashimoto for her unabated support, patience, and encouragement; Michael Davidson, Ph.D., for his support and encouragement; and students everywhere for their interest in the MEEC industry. Also, thank you to the educators in the MEEC field for helping develop the concept for this book: Patti Shock, UNLV; Howard Reichbart, NVCC; Curtis Love, UNLV; Court Carrier, Mt. Hood CC; Tyra Hilliard, UNLV; M. T. Hickman, Richland College; and the Meetings/Conventions SIG of CHRIE. The following reviewers also deserve a special thank you: Linda Brothers, IUPUI, School of Physical Education and Tourism Management, Indianapolis, IN; Angelo Camillo, Ph.D., San Francisco State; Amanda K. Cecil, Ph.D., CMP, Assistant Professor, Indiana University, Department of Tourism, Conventions and Event Management, Indianapolis, IN; Raphael Thomas George, Associate Professor, Ohio State University; Tyra Hilliard, University of Nevada at Las Vegas, William F. Harrah College of Hotel Administration, Las Vegas, NV; Jeffrey P. Ivory, Associate Professor, St. Luis Community College at Forrest Park; and Brian Miller EdD, Assistant Professor of Hospitality, Department of HRIM, University of Delaware, Newark, DE. Finally, my thanks go to the chapter contributors in this second edition: Curtis Love, Howard Reichbart, Bob Cherny, Patti Shock, Elaine Rosquist, James M. Goldberg, James Spellos, Denise Michelet, and Kenneth Rayes.

About the Author

George G. Fenich, Ph.D., is a professor in the Hospitality Management Department at East Carolina University. Dr. Fenich worked in the hospitality industry for 15 years before joining academe in 1985. He teaches and researches in the area of conventions and meetings, has written over 30 academic articles, and has presented at almost 100 conferences—including the Council on Hotel Restaurant and Institutional Education, the Destination Marketing Association International, the Association for Convention Operations Management, the International Association of Assembly Managers, and the Professional Convention Management Association. He is on the editorial board of six journals—including associate editor for conventions and meetings for *HTL Science* and the *Journal of Convention and Exhibition Management*. He is also the co-founder of the consulting firm Trends Analysis Projections LLC.

CHAPTER 1

Introduction to the Meetings, Expositions, Events, and Conventions Industry

The Olympic Games are but one of the many aspects of the meetings, expositions, events, and conventions industry.
Getty Images Inc., Hulton Archive Photos

Chapter Objectives

This chapter provides the reader with an understanding of the following:

- History of the Meetings, Expositions, Events, and Conventions (MEEC) industry
- Where MEEC fits in relation to the hospitality industry
- Magnitude and impact of MEEC
- Careers in MEEC
- Different types of gatherings

Chapter Outline

Introduction
    What a Difference a Day Makes
Accepted Practices Exchange (APEX)
What Is a Meeting?
    Industry Terminology and Practice
Organizational Structure of the
        Hospitality Industry and How
        MEEC Fits In

Background of the Industry
Economic Impact
Scenario Planning
Why Have Meetings?
Employment in and around the MEEC
        Industry
    What Does a Meeting or Event
        Planner Do?

The box on the next page is meant to provide an example and insight into the field of meetings, expositions, events, and conventions (MEEC). This chapter concludes with the second half of this box, "End of the First Day."

Introduction

WHAT A DIFFERENCE A DAY MAKES

Planning for AAP's 35th Annual Congress began long before the previous year's program ended. The scenario in the opening of this chapter is only a brief glimpse of the multitude of complexities that support planning and management and of the jobs that employ those who work in and around the **meetings, expositions, events, and conventions (MEEC)** industry, all of which contribute to a meeting's success.

The Big Day

Picture this: The sun rises above the horizon, releasing rays of blue and pink light that whisk across the ocean and spill onto the beautifully manicured greens of the resort hotel's championship golf course. Against the backdrop of the crashing surf and pleas of hungry gulls, you can also hear the sounds of morning stirring at the resort hotel: car doors slamming, muffled voices sharing greetings and farewells, china and silver clashing, and squeaking wheels of fully laden carts, each heading off to its appointed area under the guiding hand of one of many hotel staff who have arrived before most guests are awake.

Today is a big day. The Association of Amalgamated Professionals (AAP) will open its 35th Annual Congress with an evening reception, and before the day is done, 1,900 guests and hundreds of vendors will have descended on this resort hotel.

Todd Cliver, **Convention Services Manager (CSM)** for the resort hotel, convenes a last-minute meeting for the hotel's team that is handling the Annual Congress. Todd has worked tirelessly for nearly nine months, coordinating all

A fully laden pastry cart ready to head to its appointed destination.
Courtesy of Wayne Sorce

(continued)

The Big Day (*continued*)

of the plans, wants, and needs of his client, the association's Senior Meeting Manager, Barbara Tain. Today represents the culmination of hundreds of faxes, e-mails, phone calls, and personal meetings between Todd and Barbara. Todd interacted with every department in the resort hotel. Barbara worked closely with AAP staff and volunteers and also worked with other vendors as well as supervised AAP support staff for the AAP's 35th Annual Congress.

Donna Miller, Director of **Sales and Marketing,** whose department was responsible for contracting this—the largest meeting the resort hotel will have ever managed—reports on her client's last-minute changes and concerns, all meticulously logged since her client, Barbara Tain, arrived two days ago. David Stern, Front Desk Manager, recaps the latest report on expected room occupancy and on the timing and numbers of anticipated arrivals. Throughout the day, he will continue to check with his staff to ensure that there will be adequate (and contracted!) numbers of front desk clerks to support the check-in flow, bell staff to manage the deluge of luggage and golf clubs, and door staff, valet parkers, concierge and guest services staff, and housekeeping support.

David Fenner, Director of Catering, provides his final status report, commenting on the readiness of the kitchen and serving staff to serve, over the next three days, the equivalent of almost 12,000 meals and untold gallons of juice, milk, coffee, tea, soda, and alcoholic beverages. In addition, the resort hotel's **outlets** (restaurants and lounges) expect a much higher than average volume and have planned for supplies and personnel accordingly.

Other resort hotel staff members report to the Director of Sales and the CSM. These include those involved with recreation (golf, tennis, health club, and pool), maintenance, security, and accounting. Even the animal handlers who work with the parrots, an attraction for guests as they enter the resort, want to ensure there are only healthy, well-behaved birds to greet the guests!

This one **convention** has already impacted and will impact every area of the resort hotel's operations. Armed with all this information, Todd leaves for his final preconference meeting (pre-con) with Barbara Tain, his client.

Meanwhile, on the other side of the country, Jane Lever steps onto Concourse B of the Philadelphia International Airport, her airline boarding pass, e-ticket receipt with its special "meeting discount" price, and photo ID firmly in her grasp. She has checked her luggage, making sure to leave it unlocked for a possible security search. She scans the bank of monitors for her flight information. Before her day ends, she will have touched down at two other airports, eaten one airline snack, grabbed a candy bar on her way through a change of planes at another airport, made numerous cell phone calls, bought a newspaper and a few magazines, and paid for a taxi to the resort hotel. Around the country, 1,899 other professionals just like Jane will do the same thing and travel to the same place, for the same purpose—a **meeting.**

In the resort hotel's **destination** (city), Kathy Sykes, the owner and president of Skylark **Destination Management Company (DMC),** is at her office reviewing final arrangements for ground transportation, event theme preparations, and entertainment for the AAP meeting. Kathy has already received two complaints from the manager of the headliner rock star booked for tonight's reception: He wants only chilled glasses for his orange juice—which he expects to be freshly squeezed in his suite—and can only get dressed if he is provided with navy blue towels for his after-shower rubdown. Kathy, of course, ensures compliance with these requests; she wants to avoid any problems before tonight's event.

With a thunderstorm threatening for tomorrow afternoon, Kathy's mind is also already racing through alternatives for the golf tournament. She knows the golfers can play in the rain, but a thunderstorm would endanger their safety.

Jack Ardulosky, a senior technical engineer for an audiovisual company, pulls into the hotel's delivery area while completing his mental checklist for final site review, satellite link integrity, picture clarity, and sound quality. With three global broadcasts and web casts, he will have little room for error. He sees the florist unloading the last of the fresh floral arrangements and makes a note to himself that leaves and petals can cause just as much of a viewing obstruction as meeting room columns. He scans the area around him for a parking spot: not too much available with all the trucks and vans unloading the trade show booths. Jack notices the rising temperature and expects a long, hot day. He will feel better as long as he can find parking in the shade, even if he has to walk a greater distance.

Barbara Tain, the Senior Meeting Manager for the association, wipes the beginning of fatigue from her eyes—she has already been on site for two days, and her constant checking of details has not allowed her to sleep as well as she would have liked—and continues her walk-through of the registration area, information center, and cyber café en route to a meeting with Todd Cliver and David Fenner. Having eaten just a few bites of her breakfast during a meeting with association executives and key committee members, she will still be late to her meeting with Todd and David because of

(continued)

The Big Day (*continued*)

last-minute details and concerns from the meeting with association staff and volunteers.

Only half glancing at the space around her, she again reviews her lengthy checklists: **banquet event orders (BEOs),** transportation schedules, badges, staffing, centerpiece design and delivery, phone lines, computers and printers, exhibitor booth setup, VIP procedures, concerns about tomorrow's weather, special check-in process, audiovisual equipment, opening production needs, PowerPoint files, handouts, arrangements for participants with disabilities, special needs for those with specified food allergies, amenities for VIPs . . . her mind is crowded with details.

With all this and more going through her mind, her most dominant thought is, "What could go wrong over the next three days—weather? Delayed arrivals? Delayed departures? The illness (or worse, death) of a participant? How prepared am I and the resort hotel to respond quickly and effectively?" The fact is, although it is almost never apparent to a meeting participant, some things may not proceed as planned. The meeting planner and CSM are never more important than at that moment when a crisis must be averted.

It is opening day at last, and everything is in motion.

By the time the AAP program is over, roughly 1,900 people (participants and exhibitors) will have flown on approximately nine major airlines and regional carriers on 200 different flights, covered 4 million air miles, and consumed 1,000 airline snacks and thousands of bags of candy or snacks grabbed on runs through airports; sat through 60,000 person-hours of presentations and education; played 4,000 person-hours of golf; and eaten approximately 12,000 catered meals. They will have made about 80,000 telephone calls, purchased and read 5,700 newspapers, transmitted and received more than 500 faxes, and injected about $5 million into the local economy. Their presence will generate about $500,000 in taxes for state and local coffers. Countless local business owners will make sales in everything from clothing to artwork to souvenirs. Dry cleaners, cab drivers, restaurateurs, sports facilities, attractions, and hotels will all see jumps in their average weekly revenue. There may also be a significant boost to the local underground cash-only economy, with contributions from the seamier side of this phenomenon such as gambling, drugs, and prostitution. In total, the convention-related activities for this single event will touch more than 250 local jobs.

Performing poorly at any of the hundreds of potential failure points of planning and executing a meeting or event can cause a dramatic and immediate financial loss to the geographic area. In addition, the financial impact could result in positive or negative impacts for years to come: A good experience by each attendee will result in praise to many others; a negative experience will result in even more people hearing the negative results of the stay in that destination. Each of these people can bring or deny more business to the destination and the resort.

Accepted Practices Exchange (APEX)

Throughout this book you will hear about the **Convention Industry Council (CIC)** and its **Accepted Practices Exchange (APEX).** The following is from CIC's Web site, http://www.conventionindustry.org/apex/FAQ_File.htm, and is meant to provide early insight into this initiative.

The CIC is at the forefront of efforts to advance the meetings, conventions, and exhibitions industry. It represents a broad cross-section with 32 member organizations representing more than 103,500 individuals as well as over 17,300 firms and properties involved in the meetings, conventions, and exhibitions industry. Formed in 1949 to provide a forum for member organizations seeking to enhance the industry, the CIC facilitates the exchange of information, develops programs to promote professionalism within the industry, and educates the public on its profound economic impact. By its nature, the CIC provides an impartial and inclusive forum for APEX and the development of accepted practices for the industry.

APEX is an initiative of the Convention Industry Council that is bringing together all stakeholders in the development and implementation of industrywide accepted practices to create and enhance efficiencies throughout the meetings, conventions, and exhibitions industry.

Some of the results of accepted practices implementation will be:

- Time and cost savings
- Eased communication and sharing of data
- Enhanced customer service

- Streamlined systems and processes
- Less duplication of effort and increased operational efficiencies
- Better-educated, more professional employees

Seven panels, each addressing key areas, will work to develop recommended accepted practices. Each panel has a formal charge, which serves as a guide to direct its work:

1. *Terminology.* The purpose of the APEX Terminology Panel is to develop accepted terminology that encompasses all aspects of the meetings industry.

2. *History/Post-Event Reports.* The purpose of the APEX History/Post-Event Reports Panel is to develop recommended industry accepted practices for collecting, storing, and retrieving accurate and thorough history/post-event report data on meetings, conventions, and events.

3. *Requests for Proposals (RFPs).* The purpose of the APEX RFPs Panel is to develop recommended industry accepted practices for consistent and thorough requests for proposals (RFPs) that address core information and unique needs.

4. *Resumes and Work Orders.* The purpose of the APEX Resumes and Work Orders Panel is to develop recommended industry accepted practices for preparing and sharing complete resume and work order instructions/details for meetings, conventions, and other events.

5. *Meeting and Site Profiles.* The purpose of the APEX Meeting and Site Profiles Panel is to develop recommended industry accepted practices for consistent and thorough profile formats for sites, as well as meetings, conventions, and other events, that include both core and unique information.

6. *Housing.* The primary purpose of the APEX Housing Panel is to develop recommended industry accepted practices for collecting, reporting, and retrieving complete housing data for meetings, conventions, and other events. A secondary purpose is to recommend industry accepted practices around housing issues such as housing providers, Internet issues, international housing, and disclosure.

7. *Contracts.* The purpose of the APEX Contracts Panel is to review all aspects of industry contracts and develop contract guidelines and, where appropriate, acceptable contract language. Additionally, the panel will develop an outline to format industry contracts.

What Is a Meeting?

What are these things called "meetings," "exhibitions," "symposia," "congresses," "events," and "conventions"? Why are they so important to the economy? Will these face-to-face gatherings be eliminated in the years ahead? Why have them at all? Are they all the same, or are they different, and if so, what are those differences, and why are they present? All of these questions are addressed in this chapter. Welcome to the fast-paced, tense, yet ultimately fulfilling world of MEEC.

The APEX initiative proposes the generic definition of "meeting": a gathering for business, educational, or social purposes. Associations often use the term to refer to a combination of educational sessions and exhibits. This can include seminars, forums, symposiums, conferences, workshops, clinics, and so on.

In various online tools, synonyms for "meeting" include the following:

Entry:	meeting
Function:	noun
Definition:	gathering
Synonyms:	affair, assemblage, assembly, assignation, audience, bunch, buzz session, call, cattle call, clambake, company, competition, conclave, concourse, concursion, confab, **conference,** conflict, confrontation, congregation, congress, contest, convention, convocation, date, encounter, engagement, gang, get-together, gig, huddle, introduction, meet, nooner, parley, powwow, quickie, rally, rap session, rendezvous, reunion, session, showdown, sit-in, talk, tryst, turnout
Concept:	business action

Source: Roget's New Millennium™ Thesaurus, First Edition (v. 1.3.1), edited by Barbara Ann Kipfer, Ph.D. Copyright © 2007 by Lexico Publishing Group, LLC. All rights reserved.

INDUSTRY TERMINOLOGY AND PRACTICE

We have always generically referred to gatherings of two or more people as "meetings." This term clearly could encompass meetings that are also called "conventions," "congresses," "symposia," and so on, some of which could have tens of thousands of people in attendance. If one adds displays of materials or products to a meeting, the meeting then has a **trade show** or **exposition** or **exhibition** component.

The following list of terms is important for anyone involved in MEEC to know. The terms were developed by the Terminology Panel of APEX and are a small sample of the thousands of words that apply to this industry. The complete glossary of terms used in the MEEC industry can be found online at http://glossary. conventionindustry.org.

- *Meeting.* An event where the primary activity of the attendees is to attend educational sessions, participate in meetings and discussions, socialize, or attend other organized events. There is no exhibit component to this event.
- *Convention.* An event where the primary activity of the attendees is to attend educational sessions, participate in meetings/discussions, socialize, or attend other organized events. There is a secondary exhibit component.
- *Exhibition.* (1) An event at which the primary activity of the attendees is to visit exhibits on the show floor. These events focus primarily on business-to-business (B-to-B) relationships. (2) A display of products or promotional material for the purposes of public relations, sales and/or marketing; same as Exposition or Trade Show.
- *Trade Show.* An exhibit of products and services targeted to a specific clientele and not open to the public.
- *Exposition.* A display of products and/or services; same as Exhibition.
- *Seminar.* (1) A lecture and dialogue allowing participants to share experiences in a particular field under the guidance of an expert discussion leader. (2) A meeting or series of meetings of ten or more specialists who have different specific skills but have a specific common interest and come together for training or learning purposes. The work schedule of a seminar has the specific object of enriching the skills of the participants.
- *Workshop.* (1) A meeting of several persons for intensive discussion. The workshop concept has been developed to compensate for diverging views in a particular discipline or on a particular

subject. (2) An informal and public session of free discussion organized to take place between formal plenary sessions or commissions of a congress or of a conference, either on a subject chosen by the participants themselves or on a special problem suggested by the organizers. (3) A training session in which participants, often through exercises, develop skills and knowledge in a given field.

- *Conference.* (1) A participatory meeting designed for discussion, fact finding, problem solving, and consultation. (2) An event used by any organization to meet and exchange views, convey a message, open a debate, or give publicity to some area of opinion on a specific issue. No tradition, continuity, or periodicity is required to convene a conference. Although not generally limited in time, conferences are usually of short duration with specific objectives. Conferences are generally on a smaller scale than congresses. See also Congress, Convention.

- *Clinic.* A workshop-type educational experience where attendees learn by doing.

- *Break-Out Sessions.* Small group sessions, panels, workshops, or presentations offered concurrently within the event, formed to focus on specific subjects. Break-out sessions are separate from the general session, but within the meeting format, and are formed to focus on specific subjects. These sessions can be arranged by basic, intermediate, or advanced information or can be divided by interest areas or industry segment.

- *Assembly.* (1) The process of erecting display component parts into a complete exhibit. (2) A general or formal meeting of an organization attended by representatives of its membership for the purpose of deciding legislative direction, policy matters, election of internal committees, and approval of balance sheets, budgets, and so on. Consequently, an assembly usually observes certain rules of procedure for its meetings, mostly prescribed in its articles and bylaws.

- *Congress.* (1) The regular coming together of large groups of individuals, generally to discuss a particular subject. A congress will often last several days and will have several simultaneous sessions. The length of time between congresses is usually established in advance of the implementation stage and can be either semiannual or annual. Most international or world congresses are of the former type, whereas national congresses are generally held annually. (2) A meeting of an association of delegates or representatives from constituent organizations. (3) A European term for convention. See also Conference, Convention.

- *Forum.* (1) An open discussion with an audience, panel, and moderator. (2) A meeting or part of a meeting set aside for an open discussion by recognized participants on subjects of public interest; also for legal purposes, as part of the proceedings of a tribunal, a court, or a similar body.
- *Symposium.* A meeting of a number of experts in a particular field at which papers are presented and discussed by specialists on particular subjects with a view to making recommendations concerning the problems under discussion.
- *Institute.* An in-depth instructional meeting providing intensive education on a particular subject.
- *Lecture.* An informative and instructional speech.
- *Panel.* A discussion with a moderator and two or more participants.
- *Incentive Travel.* A travel reward given by companies to employees to stimulate productivity; also known as an incentive trip.

Organizational Structure of the Hospitality Industry and How MEEC Fits In

MEEC is a part of and encompasses many elements of the hospitality and tourism industry. In order to understand how MEEC is related to the hospitality and services industry, one must understand the organization and structure of the hospitality and tourism industry itself.

There are six major divisions, or segments, of the hospitality and tourism industry: lodging, food and beverage, transportation, attractions, entertainment, and shopping.

1. *Lodging.* The lodging segment consists of all types of places where travelers may spend the night. These can include hotels, motels, bed-and-breakfasts, cruise ships, trailer parks or campsites, condominiums, and college dormitories. The important characteristics of this segment are that they are available to the public and charge a fee.

2. *Food and Beverage.* Obviously, this segment actually contains two subsegments: food service operations and beverage operations. Food service operations can include the following: table service facilities that can be further broken down by price—high, medium, and low; by type of service—luxury, quick service, and so on; or by cuisine—American, Asian, Italian, Chinese, and the like. Food service also embraces other types of operations including catering, chains, and institutional feeding. Beverage operations can also be broken down by price or type of service and even whether they serve alcoholic beverages or not.

3. *Transportation.* This segment includes any means or modality that people use to get from one place to another, including walking. The better-known elements include air transportation, water transportation, and ground transportation:

   Air transportation. This subsegment includes regularly scheduled carriers such as Delta or Southwest and charter air service that can involve jets, propeller aircraft, and helicopters.

   Water transportation. This subsegment includes cruise ships and paddle wheelers, charter operations, ferries, and water taxis.

   Ground transportation. This subsegment includes automobiles, taxis, limousines, jitneys, buses, trains, cog railways, cable cars, monorails, horse-drawn vehicles, and even elephants.

4. *Attractions.* This segment of the hospitality and tourism industry includes anything that attracts people to a destination and can be further divided into natural and man-made attractions:

   Natural attractions. This subsegment includes mountains, seashores, lakes, forests, swamps, climate, and rivers.

   Man-made attractions. This subsegment consists of things made or constructed by human beings, including buildings such as convention centers and hotels, monuments, museums, theme parks, and some restaurants.

5. *Entertainment.* This segment of the hospitality and tourism industry includes anything that provides entertainment value for a guest such as movie theaters, playhouses, orchestras, bands, and festivals.

Shopping, such as in a Disney store, is an important segment of the hospitality and tourism industry.
Courtesy of Getty Images, Inc.—Liaison

6. *Shopping*. This is an important segment of the hospitality and tourism industry and an area in which people spend considerable sums of money. Many attractions have developed products that carry their theme or logo and result in significant revenue streams for the operator. Probably the best known is Disney, whose products are sold not only at its attractions but also in stand-alone retail centers.

As you can see, the hospitality and tourism industry is multifaceted. Further, the framework offered in the preceding list is meant to help provide an understanding of the industry and is not intended to be a well-delineated typology. There are many overlaps between the categories: A hotel may be an attraction in itself, such as the Venetian or New York New York in Las Vegas. The same is true of some stores, such as FAO Schwartz in New York City and the Mall of America in Minneapolis. Hotels often have food and beverage outlets, retail stores, and even entertainment. Further, some of the businesses mentioned above cater to both the tourist and local resident, making it difficult (if not impossible) to determine how much business is derived from each constituency.

It would seem, then, that the MEEC industry is involved with all segments of the hospitality and tourism industry. Understanding the interactions and complexities of the hospitality and tourism industry, along with MEEC, helps explain why it is difficult to determine the size and scope of these industries. Until the late 1990s, the U.S. government, using its Standard Industry Classification (SIC) codes, did not even track many elements of these industries. For example, the government did not even list "meeting planner" as a recognized profession until the late 1980s.

BACKGROUND OF THE INDUSTRY

Gatherings, meetings, events, and conventions (of sorts) have been a part of people's lives since earliest recorded history. Archaeologists have found primitive ruins from ancient cultures that were used as meeting areas where citizens would gather to discuss common interests such as government, war, hunting, or tribal celebrations. Once humans developed permanent settlements, each town or village had a public meeting area, often called a town square, where residents could meet, talk, and party! Under the leadership of Alexander the Great, over half a million people traveled to what was then Ephesus (now Turkey) to see exhibitions that included acrobats, magicians, animal trainers, and jugglers. Andrew Young, the former U.S. ambassador to the United Nations, said at a **Meeting Professionals International (MPI)** meeting in Atlanta in the middle 1990s that he was sure there would have been a meeting planner for the Last Supper and certainly for the first Olympics. In Rome, the Forum was a type of organized meeting to discuss politics and decide the fate of the country. Ancient Rome had the Coliseum, which was the site of major sporting events such as gladiatorial contests—someone had to organize them! Through the use of excellent roadways, the Romans were able to establish trade markets to entice people to visit their cities. In Old England, there are stories of King Arthur's Round Table, another example of a meeting to discuss the trials and tribulations of the day. Religious gatherings of various faiths and pilgrimages to Mecca are examples of ancient religious meetings and festivals. The Olympics began as an ancient sporting event that was organized as similar events are today. World's fairs and expositions are still another piece of the MEEC industry.

The MEEC industry has also been a part of American culture and development. The white steeples surrounded by snow-covered ground seen in Currier and Ives prints actually depicted the town square of New England cities. In one of the oldest communities in North America, Santa Fe, the square not only houses the seat of government but also has been traditionally used as a festival marketplace. Even today, Native Americans can be seen around the perimeter of the square displaying their handicrafts for sale.

The First Continental Congress in Philadelphia is an example of a "formal meeting," in this case to decide the governance of the thirteen colonies. Political conventions have a long history in the United States and are part of the MEEC industry. Americans have also made festivals and celebrations of every sort, such as Mardi Gras in New Orleans, a part of their lives since the early days of this country, and events like these can also be part of the MEEC industry.

Today, structures supporting the MEEC industry are integral parts of major cities. It is a well-known fact that in order to be considered a "world-class city," a community must have a convention center and a stadium or arena for sports and events. The largest cities, including New York, Los Angeles, Chicago, London, Moscow, and Hong Kong, all have them. The hope is that these public facilities will attract out-of-town attendees for conventions and events who will spend money in the community.

In spite of its long history, meeting planning as a recognized profession did not develop until 1972, when MPI was founded. Only 120 planners and suppliers attended the first convention. The first board of directors was headed by "Buzz" Bartlow and led to the development of the first academic meeting planning program. This program, approved by the state of Colorado in September 1976, was implemented by Metropolitan State College in Denver. This initiative was closely followed by the meeting planning program at Northeastern Oklahoma University in Tahlequah. In 1979, Patti Shock started the convention service management (hotel perspective) and meeting

Native Americans have held their festival marketplace in Santa Fe for centuries.
© Danny Lehman, CORBIS

planning classes at Georgia State University (GSU). In 1983, trade show classes were added with the financial support of the National Association Exposition Managers (NAEM) (now the International Association for Exposition Management, or IAEM) and the International Association of Fairs and Expositions (IAFE). GSU was the first to implement trade show classes; therefore it was the first to cover the whole convention industry.

There were two factors that contributed to the rapid development of both industry workshops and academic programs during the 1980s. The first was the development and implementation of the Certified Meeting Professional (CMP) examination and designation by the Convention Liaison Council (CLC; now the CIC). This certification gives both status and credence to the person who achieves it. A second factor was the development of a "model" meeting curriculum by the Professional Convention Management Association (PCMA). Once PCMA had its model curriculum, it actively pursued the inauguration of its program in several colleges and universities.

Since its founding in New York in 1949 by four organizations—the American Society of Association Executives (ASAE), American Hotel and Motel Association (AH&MA; now the American Hotel & Lodging Association), Hospitality (then Hotel) Sales & Marketing Association International (HSMAI), and **International Association of Convention and Visitor Bureaus (IACVB)** (now Destination Marketing Association International, or DMAI)—the Convention Industry Council (then the Convention Liaison Council) has traditionally followed the lead of its constituent organizations, which now number 31 (http://www.conventionindustry.org).

> In 1895 the roots of present-day convention & visitor bureaus (CVBs) [were] planted when journalist Milton Carmichael suggest[ed] in *The Detroit Journal* that local businessmen band together to promote the city as a convention destination, as well as represent the city and its many hotels to bid for business. Two weeks later, what [became] the Detroit Convention and Businessmen's League form[ed] to do just that. Carmichael head[ed] the group, which . . . later evolve[d] into the Detroit Metro CVB.
>
> *Source: EXPO Magazine* at http://www.expoweb.com/expomag/BackIssues/2001/Apr/feature2.htm.

The role of convention and visitor bureaus (CVBs) has changed over time. As in Detroit, most began by trying to attract only conventions and business meetings to their community. Later, they realized that leisure visitors were an important source of business and added the "V" for "visitors" to their name. Today, virtually every city in the United States and Canada, and many cities throughout the world, has a CVB or convention and visitors association (CVA). The CVB or CVA is a membership organization that helps promote tourism, meetings, and related business for their cities. Most recently, the term "Destination Marketing Organization" (DMO) is being used in place of CVB. In this text the terms are synonymous and interchangeable.

ECONOMIC IMPACT

The MEEC industry is diverse. As a result, it is hard to estimate the size, magnitude, and impact of MEEC. According to the CIC's 2004 Economic Impact Study, the MEEC industry, along with associated incentive travel, generated $122.31 billion in direct spending, making it the twenty-ninth largest contributor to the gross national product of the United States. To put this in perspective, the industry contributed more than the pharmaceutical and medical manufacturing industries. In addition, according to the CIC study, the number of "full-time equivalent jobs supported by the direct spending of the industry is 1,710,000 and the direct tax impact is $21.4 billion" (from the Convention Industry Council at http://www.conventionindustry.org/aboutcic/pr/pr).

One of the most comprehensive accounts of the impact of the MEEC industry is published biannually in the "Meetings Market Report" in *Meetings & Conventions Magazine*. The August 2006 issue reports that in 2005 there were 1,020,300 corporate meetings, 210,600 association meetings, and 12,700 conventions, for a total of 1,243,600 meetings held during the year. The number of people attending meetings is also significant. In 2005, 79,700,000 attended corporate meetings, 37,900,000 attended association meetings, and 18,900,000 attended conventions, for a total meeting attendance of 136,500,000 that year. Total expenditures included $31.8 billion for corporate meetings, $41.8 billion for association meetings, and $33.6 billion for conventions. This is a total aggregate expenditure of $107.2 billion for all meetings in 2005. Readers are reminded that these figures are for direct spending and do not include the "multiplier effect." This is a term from economics and refers to the indirect effect of spending when the money circulates through the regional economy. When the latter is considered, the amounts above are doubled. Thus, the total impact of the MEEC industry sector studied is extremely significant. Based on those statistics, even the average corporate meeting has 77 attendees at an average cost of $31,167.

SCENARIO PLANNING

Another recent concern has been the effect of disasters such as Hurricanes Katrina and Rita on the meeting industry. How can meeting planners even hope to plan for such events? What can they do so far in advance about devastating events that can affect their business that they have no control over? How can they address the sense of uncertainty from communities such as New Orleans and the Mississippi Gulf Coast that have had a significant convention industry suddenly devastated and address those organizations that may be looking to return to those areas for future conventions? A July 2006 article in the PCMA journal *Convene* by Sarah Torrence addresses these questions by suggesting that meeting planners use scenario planning, "a dynamic strategic planning concept." The complete article is available at PCMA's

Web site, http://www.pcma.org/resources/convene/archives/displayArticle.
asp?ARTICLE_ ID=5359, and is excerpted here:

> For the past five years, the uncertainty of our times has certainly been played
> out in the meetings industry—with the after-effects of Sept. 11, the SARS
> scare, and raging hurricanes, such as Katrina, disrupting the normal flow of
> business.
>
> While new to many planners, scenario planning can help them assist their
> organizations as a whole—in addition to looking at their meetings in a new way.
> As Laura Jelinek, associate executive director of the American Association of
> Oral and Maxillofacial Surgeons said, "We are in business to provide benefits to
> our membership." Brad Kent, vice president–sales at AVW-TELAV, noted, "Our
> industry, in many ways, became a victim after Sept. 11. Scenario planning gives
> you a 35,000-foot view before getting consumed with the emotion of the situation.
> You can plan for the unexpected, rather than be a victim."
>
> "Scenario planning is best used for strategic planning in a world of uncer-
> tainty," explained Roch Parayre, Ph.D., senior fellow at the Mack Center for
> Technological Innovation at the Wharton School and managing director and sce-
> nario planning expert with Decision Strategies Inc. (DSI). "The world for most
> industries is becoming increasingly unpredictable today. Many are beginning to
> 'twist in the wind.' This is certainly true of the travel and hospitality industry,
> especially after Sept. 11," he emphasized.
>
> Indeed, the meetings industry seems to possess many conditions under
> which scenario planning should be used, as outlined by Dr. Parayre:
>
> - Uncertainty is high, relative to one's ability to adjust.
> - Too many costly surprises have occurred in the past.
> - Insufficient new opportunities are perceived.
> - The quality of thinking is deemed to be low.
> - A common language is desired, without stifling diversity.
> - Major differences of opinion exist, each having merit.
> - Your competitors use scenario planning.
>
> When implementing scenario planning, planners and executives alike should
> consider the forces that are shaping the future of their organization or industry
> and then build a scenario matrix relative to these forces. "There could be hun-
> dreds of forces facing an organization or industry," Dr. Parayre said. "Scenario
> planning is a systematic way of taking those forces into account when you plan."
> Dr. Parayre provided a six-step process for formulating strategies in uncertain
> conditions, and planners can easily use these steps to strategize for their meet-
> ings as well as for the direction of their department and association:
>
> 1. *Consider General Scenarios.* As an example, Dr. Parayre said if a group is
>   planning a meeting in a certain destination, think about what political or
>   other scenarios might play out there.
> 2. *Examine the Organization's Market.* "One size does not fit all," he said.
>   "There are individual strategic market segments. Conduct market research
>   and detailed needs assessments to understand each group," he advised.

3. *Assess the Organization's Internal Core Capabilities.* "It's better to stick to what you do well and look to a partner or third party to do the rest," he gave as an example. Too many planners try to do it all, so this is sound advice.

4. *Put the Pieces Together.* Looking at your information in the first three steps, analyze how different outcomes will be influenced by different scenarios.

5. *Identify Tactical Initiatives to Support Strategic Directives.* "For example, if you want to enhance certain capabilities, such as data mining, how will you make that happen? Through partnering?" asked Dr. Parayre.

6. *Implement.* Be sure to measure the initiation of strategies against preset developmental milestones, budgets, and time frames.

So scenario planning may be helpful for the meeting planner in preparing ways to address an uncertain environment. Today, the economic uncertainty in the United States and throughout the world, the reality of civil wars, the possibility of international war, and the disarray and financial woes of the airline industry have made the traveling public skittish about leisure and business travel. Hotel occupancy rates in all cities have fallen—more dramatically in what the industry calls "first-tier" cities, which are those that host large conventions and trade shows. Cities continue to build convention centers and new hotel projects that were planned before the economic downturn, and they hope to be able to fill them with meetings that will in turn bolster the local economy.

WHY HAVE MEETINGS?

In the early to middle 1980s, there were discussions (as there were immediately after September 11, 2001) that face-to-face meetings would be a thing of the past—that teleconferencing or other e-conferencing and learning would supplant face-to-face gatherings. The Foundation of MPI conducted studies in the mid-1990s that focused on what made meetings work for associations and corporations (http://www.mpiweb.org and http://www.mpiweb.org/resources/mpif/pdfs/whitepaper.pdf). These studies show that people prefer meeting face-to-face and that one of the most important values of gatherings is the ability to meet with and learn from peers. "Virtual" meetings in all forms (audio- and videoconferences, online learning and exchanges) do not yet create the desired effect. Further, face-to-face meetings have the added benefit of including all forms of communication, both verbal and nonverbal. For example, when you meet people for the first time and the palms of their hands are sweaty, are you concerned whether they are telling the truth or

Shaking hands is a form of nonverbal communication.
Dorling Kindersley Media Library

are nervous for some reason? What do the strength and style of a handshake tell you about people? Facial expressions can support a message or send one that is completely different from the verbal message. How do you feel if the people to whom you are speaking never look you straight in the eye? Nonverbal communication is a very important part of meeting with people.

When we meet, we build "communities of practice." Through these communities of practice, we are able to strengthen skills (at sales or association educational meetings or symposia), impact change (at political conventions or governance meetings), observe accomplishments (at incentive meetings and celebrations), renew acquaintances (at reunions), and learn about new products in our field (at exhibitions and trade shows).

Employment in and around the MEEC Industry

The MEEC industry is a subsegment of the hospitality industry, which itself is part of the larger services industry. It encompasses many areas of the hospitality industry. Thus, readers are challenged to conceptualize their personal ideal job and then determine how and where in the MEEC industry they could be employed doing what they dream of.

Some careers in MEEC include the following:

- *Event Planner.* This person puts together special events such as the Super Bowl in football, the Final Four in basketball, festivals, and celebrations.
- *Meeting Planner.* He or she organizes meetings and other gatherings for companies, corporations, and associations. These gatherings can include a small board of directors meeting, a stockholders meeting, new product introductions, educational seminars, and national conventions.
- *Wedding Planner.* Did you ever think that *someone* needs to organize all the weddings that occur each year?
- *Hotel Sales.* The majority of positions in hotel sales deal with groups, and MEEC covers most of those groups.
- *Restaurant Sales.* While most people think of restaurants attracting walk-in clientele, many rely heavily on the MEEC industry for business. Food and beverage (F&B) venues employ significant numbers of people on their group sales staff. In New Orleans, Arnaud's, Emeril's, and even lesser known restaurants such as the Crescent City Brewhouse have convention sales teams.
- *Entertainment Venue Sales.* Although these places primarily attract individual patrons, most also devote much time and effort to selling and producing events for groups. Further, groups have lots of money and can afford lavish productions.
- *Destination Management Companies.* DMCs function as the "local experts" for companies and associations in organizing gatherings and events. People employed in DMCs usually work in either sales or production.
- *Hotels.* Hotels are one of the primary locations where MEEC events are held, using ballrooms, meeting rooms, break-out rooms, etc., for their gatherings, along with sleeping rooms and F&B for their attendees. The two hotel departments that deal

with the MEEC industry are catering and convention services and sales.

- *Convention Centers.* These venues include dedicated facilities such as McCormick Place in Chicago, the Jakob Javits Convention Center in New York, and the Sands Expo in Las Vegas. Also included in this category are multipurpose venues such as the Superdome in New Orleans and the Astrodome in Houston. Once again, careers there are found in either sales or operations.
- *Conference Centers.* These facilities are akin to convention centers but often include specially designed educational facilities, sleeping rooms, and food service.
- *Exposition Service Contractors.* If you like to build things or have thought about being an engineer or architect, you should consider being an exposition service contractor (ESC). ESCs design and erect the booths, backdrops, staging, etc., for meetings and conventions. The decorations and backdrops for your school prom may have been done by an ESC. Again, career paths exist in sales and in production.
- *Destination Marketing Organizations (Convention and Visitor Bureaus).* DMOs serve to represent a wide range of MEEC companies and to market the destination to business and leisure travelers. DMOs have many departments and careers, including convention sales, tourism sales, housing bureaus, convention services, marketing, research, and member services.

As you can see, the MEEC industry is a vibrant, dynamic, and exciting part of the hospitality industry. It may also serve as an ideal work environment for someone who has tried or worked in many different areas and likes them all. Many careers in MEEC involve multiple aspects of the hospitality industry. For example, someone who works in convention or group sales in a hotel must interface with, and be knowledgeable about, hotel sleeping rooms, front desk, food and beverage, catering, and all of the meeting facilities. Furthermore, unlike front desk employees, hotel convention employees develop long-term friendships and relationships with their MEEC clientele. These hotel convention employees have been known to be invited to clients' homes, vacation retreats, birthdays, weddings, and so forth. In fact, one of the most important considerations for anyone involved in MEEC is the building of long-term relationships with clientele. In marketing jargon, this is called "relationship marketing." An example of this relationship building occurred after Hurricane Katrina devastated New Orleans. A CSM at one of the hotels in New Orleans had evacuated her family to Dallas. While she returned to the hotel within a month of the storm, the family had to stay in Dallas. When it came time to bring them home, the CSM happened to mention the planned trip to a corporate client whom she had known for a long time. The corporate client asked for details and then told the CSM that the corporate jet would be waiting in Dallas to fly her family home to New Orleans, free of charge. When the CSM got on the plane, there was an envelope on the seat with her name on it. It contained a check for $10,000 and a card explaining that the money was to be used for her family and was in appreciation of the stellar long-term service she had provided to the corporate client.

Think for just a moment about all the lives and jobs that could impact one of the meeting participants and the meeting organizers involved in the scenario for the Association of Amalgamated Professionals. They include the following:

The Meeting Sponsor

Association of Amalgamated Professionals

Meeting planner

Executive director or chief executive officer (CEO)

Staff specialists in departments including marketing, governance and government affairs, education, membership, information technology, and accreditation

Employees who staff call centers, copy materials, process registrations, manage human resources, control purchasing, and more

Board of directors

Committees

Sponsors

The Facility

Owners

Executive staff, including (but not limited to) general manager, revenue manager, resident or hotel manager, directors of sales, marketing, convention services, catering, housekeeping, engineering, maintenance, purchasing, human resources, food and beverage, front office operations, and security

Thousands of other full- or part-time year-round or seasonal staff, such as groundskeepers, animal handlers, housekeepers, food servers (for banquets, room service, and the resort's outlets), maintenance, security, and engineering

The Destination
DMO/CVB (president, directors of sales, marketing, convention services, membership, registration, and all support staff)

Restaurants

Attractions

Off-site venues

Theaters

Copy and printing companies

Transportation (buses, airport shuttles, taxicabs, limousines)

Airport concessions

Doctors and medical personnel

Pharmacies

Florists

Department and other stores

Destination management companies

Audiovisual suppliers

General services contractors

Specialty services contractors

Dry cleaners and tailors

City, county, and state employees

IT division and telecommunications department

All Others Providing Services for Meetings
Talent (entertainers, disc jockeys, bands, magicians)

Education (speakers, trainers, facilitators)

Sound and lighting

Transportation (air, rail, car, boat, travel agencies)

Printing

Shipping

Promotional products

Off-property food and beverage

An industry trade show.
Cindy Charles, PhotoEdit Inc.

Translators for American Sign Language and other languages

Americans with Disabilities Act (ADA) equipment

Carpentry

National sales (hotels, conference centers)

Third-party or independent meeting planners

Is there anyone who does not have some influence on the MEEC industry? A case can be made that every person has an impact, in some way, on each and every meeting—even those meetings of two or three that take place in an office or restaurant. Take a few minutes and add to the jobs or functions above that might affect a meeting. Then think again. Even the president of the United States and Congress impact our industry by determining what the trade regulations and security issues are and whether or not our country goes to war.

WHAT DOES A MEETING OR EVENT PLANNER DO?

When asked about a "typical day," there are few (if any) meeting professionals, whether they work in an organization or operate an external planning company, who could say that any day is "typical." The job of a planner is ideal for those who love to multitask, who have broad interests, who enjoy problem solving, and who care passionately about building community through meetings.

Doug Heath, Certified Association Executive (CAE) and Certified Meeting Planner (CMP), who was the second executive director of MPI, said many years ago, "Meeting planners have to be more than coffee-cup counters." When Heath said that, it was a time when most meeting planners were concerned only with logistics—ensuring room sets, coffee and refreshment breaks, meals, and audiovisual setups.

Today, the jobs of a planner are strategic. Planners are charged with supporting the work toward an organization's bottom line. To do that, in the course of planning a meeting or event, a planner may do any or all of the following (and more):

- Define meeting/event goals and objectives.
- Develop an RFP based on the meeting/event objectives, audience profile, budget, and program.
- Send the RFP to national sales offices of hotel and conference center companies, to DMOs, and to external meeting planning companies.
- Prepare and manage a budget and expenditures that can range from a few hundred dollars to hundreds of millions.
- Negotiate contracts with a facility, transportation providers, decorators, speakers, entertainers, and all the vendors and venues that will support a meeting/event.
- Market the meeting/event electronically and in print, and then track results.
- Invite and manage needs (travel, lodging, registration, room setup, and audiovisuals) for all speakers, trainers, and facilitators involved in delivery of information and knowledge for the meeting/event.
- Invite and manage contracts and needs for entertainers.
- Design food and beverage events, and negotiate contracts for these events. To do so, a planner must know the audience (age, gender, abilities, and allergies of participants, geographic location, and more), and timing for the program.
- Prepare a crisis management plan in conjunction with other staff, facilities, vendors, and emergency personnel.

- Register participants, ensuring data is accurately entered.
- Manage the multitude of changes that happen from first conceptualizing a meeting/event to the execution.
- Monitor industry and business publications for strikes and other issues.
- Calm others' nerves and remain calm.

The following are some questions you might answer in order to determine if you have what it takes to be a successful meeting/event professional:

- Do you like to plan parties, work schedules, your day, and so forth?
- Do you have a date book or personal digital assistant (PDA) that you update regularly and that includes everything you need to do for weeks or months into the future?
- Do you like to organize your bedroom, car, workplace, and so on? Is your idea of fun organizing a closet for someone?
- Are you very organized, almost to the point of obsession?

If you answered "yes" to all of those questions, you have the aptitude to be a good meeting/event professional.

To be prepared for short- and long-term change, meeting professionals—a term that encompasses those who plan and execute meetings/events, those who work for and in facilities in which meetings/events are held, and those vendors who supply services for meetings—must begin to anticipate changes that will occur as the nature of meetings changes. In the scenario at the beginning of the chapter, there is a designated vendor to work with satellite and other e-communication tools. In the future, meeting professionals will need a greater working knowledge and will be charged with selecting meeting destinations (cities) and sites that can facilitate distance learning and e-communications.

For meeting professionals, meetings never truly end. No matter how we define a "meeting," each meeting is a matter of intense planning and execution, evaluation, follow-up, and starting over. Our role is critical in ensuring outcomes, and from those outcomes, we contribute to a sound economy.

End of the First Day

It is the end of the first day of the AAP's 35th Annual Congress, which Barbara Tain, the AAP Senior Meeting Manager, refers to as the "Annual" or "Annual Meeting," and so far all has gone well.

Barbara will have had formal, prescheduled meetings with Todd Cliver, the resort hotel's CSM. Barbara will also have spoken with Todd and many others who work for the resort hotel via radio (sometimes referred to as a "walkie-talkie") and mobile phone and through chance meetings. These talks include a review of banquet checks with various departments, one of which will include accounting. She will have talked with those on the AAP staff and in volunteer leadership and with outside vendors. She will also check the weather many times using her PDA, television, radio, and the newspaper. Barbara will have eaten on the run, tried to find a few minutes to check office voice mail and e-mail, and kept a smile on her face through it all.

At the end of the day, she will review her notes and check room sets for the next morning's sessions and crawl into bed for a few hours' sleep before it all begins again.

When the final curtain closes on the AAP's 35th Annual Congress, Barbara Tain will be one of the last to leave the resort hotel. Before leaving for the airport to fly home, she will review all the master account charges, conduct a post-convention ("post-con") meeting with the property staff and her vendors, and make notes for next year's meeting.

Summary

In this chapter, you have been introduced to the world of MEEC. As we have seen, MEEC is multifaceted and exciting, and it offers diverse career opportunities. MEEC is also very large and incorporates many facets of the hospitality industry. It has tremendous economic impact. You are now prepared to continue with the remaining chapters in this book. They expand on and provide more details about the concepts and practices of MEEC that this first chapter only touches on.

Key Words and Terms _____

For definitions, see the Glossary or go to http://glossary.convention industry.org.

Accepted Practices Exchange (APEX)

Banquet event order (BEO)

Conference

Convention

Convention Industry Council (CIC)

Convention Services Manager (CSM)

Destination

Destination Management Company (DMC)

Exhibition

Exposition

International Association of Convention and Visitor Bureaus (IACVB)

Meeting

Meeting Professionals International (MPI)

Meetings, expositions, events, and conventions (MEEC)

Outlet

Sales and marketing

Trade show

Review and Discussion Questions _____

1. What are meetings?
2. Describe some events from the past that were "meetings."
3. Describe some current aspects of MEEC industry jobs.
4. Who attends meetings?
5. What can be accomplished by convening or attending a meeting?
6. What are five key jobs in a facility (hotel, resort, conference center) that contribute to the successful outcome of a meeting?
7. What is CIC?
8. What is APEX, and what does it hope to accomplish?
9. What is the impact on the U.S. economy of meetings?
10. What is the future of electronic meetings?

About the Chapter Contributor _____

Joan L. Eisenstodt, a facilitator, trainer, and meeting manager with thirty years' experience, is president of Washington, DC-based Eisenstodt Associates, LLC, a company she founded in 1981. Joan is moderator of the MIMList, an international online community. In her community, she serves on the Board of Governors of George Washington University–Hillel and on the Advisory Board of *Speaking from the Heart.* She has been recognized by hospitality industry organizations as Planner of the Year (MPI), Teacher of the Year (PCMA), and a "Pacesetter" (HSMAI). Joan has been included in the "One of the 25 Most Influential People in the Meetings Industry" list since its inception. She has also been recognized as one of the "Power Players" ("10 Women Who Are Changing the Industry") and appears in "The 'A' List: 10 Women Meeting Industry Leaders." Joan is the recipient of the Pyramid Award from the International Association of Conference Centers.

CHAPTER 2

Meeting, Exhibition, Event, and Convention Organizers and Sponsors

Corporations organize a significant number of MEEC events, such as this Shaklee company meeting.

Teri Leigh Stratford, Pearson Education/PH College

Chapter Objectives

This chapter provides the reader with an understanding of the following:

- Major types of organizations that hold gatherings
- Types of meetings held by the different categories of organizations
- Typical lead times for planning the various types of gatherings
- Differences between the marketing strategies used to build attendance
- Associations that support the professional development of those responsible for producing gatherings

Chapter Outline

Introduction

Who Holds the Gatherings

    Corporations

    Associations

    Government

Entities that Help Organize Gatherings

    Exhibition Management Companies

Association Management Companies

Meeting Management Companies

Independent Meeting Managers

Event Management Companies

Other Organizations Arranging
    Gatherings

Introduction

This chapter focuses on gaining an understanding of the entities that organize and sponsor different types of gatherings. Each segment of these entities creates gatherings to satisfy its unique needs and its constituent populations. Whether the organization is a nonprofit association or a corporation, a government agency, or a private company that produces exhibitions, it has goals that may require an MEEC gathering to commemorate an event. Our purpose here is to identify who these organizing/sponsoring organizations are, the types of gatherings they hold, how much time they have to plan the event, who their attendees are, and how they build attendance. The people who play a major role in producing the gatherings are identified, as are the professional associations that provide them with support and professional development.

Who Holds the Gatherings

Among the entities that organize and sponsor MEEC gatherings, the three most significant ones are corporations, associations, and the government.

CORPORATIONS

Virtually all businesses have needs that require them to plan and execute gatherings. Publicly held companies have a legal requirement to hold an annual meeting of shareholders. All companies have varying needs to hold a press conference or a ribbon cutting ceremony. They also have continuing needs to train key personnel in matters of company policy and procedures or development of new policies and procedures and to improve their effectiveness. Client groups may be brought together to capture their opinions in a focus group or to introduce them to a new product or service. Executive retreats may be held to improve communication or to develop long-term business plans. Gatherings are held to honor employees (for promotion or retirement), to celebrate holidays, and to build overall morale within the organization. Companies may also be involved with sponsoring a sporting event or entertaining clients in VIP areas at major sporting events such as the U.S. Open or Super Bowl.

Definition   Although there are numerous kinds of **corporations**, for the purposes of this chapter the term "corporations" will refer to legally chartered enterprises that conduct business on behalf of their owners with the purpose of making a profit and increasing its value. These include public corporations that sell stock on the open market and have a board of directors who oversee the affairs of the corporation on behalf of the shareholders (or owners) who elected them. Private corporations have the same fundamental purposes as public corporations, but their stock is not sold on the open market.

Number and Value of Corporate Meetings   When a corporation decides to hold a gathering, it determines what the budget will be, where the gathering will be held, and who will attend. Since the corporation typically pays for all expenses associated with attending the meeting, the corporation is in control. Attendance by corporate personnel is usually mandatory. Many corporate meetings are booked as needed, typically less than six months before the meeting will be held.

Decision Makers   The decision to hold a corporate meeting is typically made by persons in positions of key responsibility within the corporate hierarchy. Officers and senior managers in the sales and marketing area may call for a meeting of their regional sales managers to develop sales strategies for new product lines, or senior financial managers and controllers may call a meeting of their dispersed staffs to discuss budgets for the next year.

Types of Corporate Gatherings and Events (Their Purposes and Objectives)   Corporations have a variety of needs that can be satisfied by scheduling a gathering. The following should not be viewed as a comprehensive list but rather as an indication of the types of gatherings sponsored by corporations:

- *Stockholders Meeting.* Voting shareholders of a corporation are invited to attend the company's annual stockholders meeting. Attendees are presented with reports on the state of the corporation and have the opportunity to vote on issues of significance. While most stockholders do not attend this meeting, they do participate in the governance of the corporation by filing a proxy statement in which they identify how they want their shares voted. This is an annual meeting that is usually held in the city where the company is headquartered, although there is an emerging trend to move it to different locations to be more accessible to the stockholders.

- *Board Meetings.* The board of directors is the governing body of a corporation that typically meets several times a year, usually in the city where the corporation is located. While a **board meeting** may be held in the corporate headquarters, any overnight stays, dinners, and related activities are often held at local hotels.

- *Management Meetings.* There are numerous reasons for a company to hold management meetings. Every major division of a corporation may have a need to bring its decision makers and other important personnel together to develop plans, review performance, or improve their processes. While some of these meetings may occur on a scheduled basis, others may be called spontaneously to solve problems and address situations that require immediate attention.

- *Training Meetings.* As companies undergo change, it may be necessary to hold training meetings to bring their managers and

Qwest stockholders meeting.
Jack Dempsey, AP Wide World Photos

key employees up-to-date on improved methods of job performance or to gain skills needed to operate new systems and equipment. Also, companies may use the training meeting to introduce new managers to corporate procedures and culture. Some of these meetings may be held on a regularly scheduled basis, while others may be held when conditions dictate it.

- *Incentive Trips.* Many corporations offer **incentive trips** to reward their top performers based on certain criteria. Those winning these trips may be employees, distributors, and/or customers. While these trips are often to exciting and glamorous destinations, an emerging trend is to schedule a number of educational and social activities for the participants to provide an added value to the sponsoring corporation. Companies may bring together these top performers with their corporate leadership to create a more synergistic organization.

- *Sales Training and Product Launches.* These events are often held to upgrade the performance of the sales staff, distributors, and retailers and to introduce new products and services to distribution networks and the general public. These events are designed to educate and motivate those who have a significant impact on the success of the corporation.

- *Professional and Technical Training.* These meetings may be held to bring managers and others up-to-date on issues relevant to their role within the company and to enhance the knowledge of their service providers. For example, a company may have a meeting of its unit and regional controllers to discuss changes in tax law and company policies.

Attendees   Most of the attendees of a corporate gathering or event are members of the corporate family and persons who have a close business relationship with the company.

Need for Marketing to Build Attendance   While the purposes of corporate meetings should be carefully crafted, attendance at these meetings is mandatory for the majority of the attendees. Therefore, sending invitations or notices to those who will attend constitutes the majority of promotional activity. That it may be a command performance does not lessen the need to make the meeting informative, productive, and enjoyable for those attending.

Department and/or Individual Responsible for Organizing and Planning   Corporate planners are really a hybrid group. The majority of people who plan corporate meetings have responsibilities beyond or in addition to the planning of meetings. According to *Meetings & Conventions* 2006 "Meetings Market Report," in 2006 corporate planners spent about 53% of their time on meetings. However, only about one-third of those have job titles that would indicate that they have meeting planning responsibilities; the other job titles indicate that they are corporate executives or managers (23%), sales and marketing (17%), general administration (19%), and other (10%).

Therefore, since the typical meeting planner's job title does not specifically indicate "meetings" as part of their responsibilities, it should be no surprise that the majority do not work in a meeting planning department. They tend to work in the departments that hold the meetings (sales and marketing, finance) and have assumed meeting planning responsibility at the request of their supervisors. Of the 13% of corporate meeting planners who have earned professional certifications, about 11% earned the Certified Meeting Professional (CMP) designation and 2% the Certified Meeting Manager (CMM). According to Mary Jo Blythe of Masterplan, a company that provides meeting planning services for several major corporations, "Most large corporations have internal meeting planning departments." However, they do also "utilize outside meeting planning firms for specific projects, overflow, or on an as-needed basis."

Professional Associations Supporting the Corporate MEEC Industry   Many corporate meeting planners join associations to support their professional development. The associations that they most often join include Meeting Professionals International (http://www. mpiweb.org), the Professional Convention Management Association (http://www.pcma.org), the Society for Incentive & Travel Executives (http://www.site-intl.org), and the Society of Government Meeting Professionals (http://www.sgmp.org). However, according to the 2006 "Meetings Market Report," 61% of corporate meeting planners were not members of the aforementioned professional organizations.

The following are some links to specific corporate meetings:

- http://www.meetingsnet.com/corporatemeetingsincentives/
- http://office.microsoft.com/en-us/products/ FX011595271033.aspx
- http://www.businessballs.com/meetings.htm
- http://www.pointsebago.com/groups/groupscorpmeetings.html
- http://www.netscape.com/tag/corporate+meetings

ASSOCIATIONS

The name "association" implies the act of being associated for certain common purposes, whether for professional, industry, educational, scientific, or social reasons. Gatherings such as annual **conventions**, topical conferences, world congresses, and topical workshops and seminars are held for the benefit of the association's membership. Other gatherings need to be held for the betterment of the organization. Examples of these include board of directors meetings, committee meetings, and leadership development workshops. Many **associations** have an affiliated exhibition held in conjunction with their convention at which products or services of interest to the attendees are displayed. Besides providing value to the members of the association and potential recognition for the association, these gatherings also generate an important revenue stream for the organization. According to PCMA's *Convene* magazine "Meetings Industry Almanac

Corporate Meeting Planning

MARY JO BLYTHE, CMP
President, Masterplan, Inc.

Corporate meetings range from small VIP board of directors meetings to large sales meetings, customer incentive meetings, and lower-tiered staff training meetings. One common thread between them is that they are always paid for (hosted) by the corporation. The funds come from a department or individual budget, thus creating a VIP(s) "host(s)" at the meeting. This VIP(s) usually expects special treatment, and it is the planner's job to ensure that the VIP(s) is taken care of well.

The planner must also embrace the corporate culture and ensure that it is depicted in all aspects of the meeting, from hotel selection to airport transportation to menu choices to social activities. Flashy companies will have flashy meetings, and conservative companies will have conservative meetings. The planner is the ultimate controller of this element.

The meeting objectives will typically include motivation, camaraderie, brainstorming, and review of goals. There is also quite often an emphasis on the social events at a meeting. Although perceived as recreation, the opportunity for sidebar conversations at nonmeeting functions often will impact future corporate decisions. Social events should be strategically planned to ensure that the proper people are sitting together at dinner or assigned to the same foursome at the golf outing.

Corporate meetings, although a category of their own, can be as diverse as corporations themselves. Paying special attention to your VIPs, embracing the corporate culture, and knowing your objectives get the corporate meeting off to a successful start.

2006," associations derive about 33% of their annual income from conventions and exhibitions.

Number and Value of Association Meetings   A major difference between association and corporate gatherings is that attendance at association meetings is voluntary, not mandatory. Another difference is that the attendees are personally responsible for their registration, transportation, hotel, and related expenses. In some instances, employers may fund the attendance of employees at industry and professional association events that are work related.

The booths at the Global Gaming Expo (G2E) reflect gambling products.
Photo by George G. Fenich, Ph.D.

Association meetings, especially conventions, tend to be very large, ranging from several hundred to tens of thousands of attendees. This issue of size can eliminate many smaller cities and venues from hosting these events and can also create increased demand by larger associations for prime locations for their gatherings. It also increases competition among the larger destinations to capture the major association gatherings.

To adjust to these supply and demand factors, larger associations book their major gatherings five to ten or more years ahead of the scheduled date to ensure that they have the space needed for their event. Small associations have a broader selection of locations that can accommodate their gatherings and therefore require less lead time to secure needed accommodations and facilities.

According to the 2004 *Business and Convention Travelers Report*, a joint production of the Travel Industry Association of America, the National Business Travel Association, and the Institute of Business

Travel Management, the top 25 cities for convention/conference/seminar travelers are as follows:

1. Chicago, IL
2. Las Vegas, NV
3. Washington, DC (metro area)
4. Orlando, FL
5. Atlanta, GA
6. Dallas, TX
7. San Francisco, CA
8. Nashville, TN
9. San Diego, CA
10. New Orleans, LA
11. Denver, CO
12. San Antonio, TX
13. Phoenix–Mesa, AZ
14. Los Angeles–Long Beach, CA
15. Boston, MA (metro area)
16. Philadelphia, PA
17. Tampa–St. Petersburg/ Clearwater, FL
18. Austin–San Marcos, TX
19. New York, NY
20. Seattle, WA (metro area)
21. Detroit, MI
22. St. Louis, MO
23. Riverside–San Bernardino, CA
24. Minneapolis–St. Paul, MN
25. Houston, TX

Decision Makers   The decision-making process for association meetings is rather complex and goes through several distinct stages. Once it is decided that a meeting will be held (usually by the board of directors or as stated in the association's constitution or bylaws), the location needs to be decided. Some organizations rotate their meetings through their geographic regions, thereby dispersing hosting opportunities and responsibilities throughout their total membership. The specific city to host the meeting is decided by the board, based on the report of site visitations by the association's own meeting planner or by a contracted meeting management provider.

Once the choice has been narrowed to a specific city, the meeting planner, based on site visits and inspections, will locate a venue (e.g., hotel and/or convention center) that is both available on the desired dates and well suited to the needs of the meeting. Typically, the meeting planner makes the recommendation to the association's board and, if approved, negotiates the financial and meeting details with the facility, which results in a contract that is eventually signed by both the venue and the association's senior staff person (usually the meeting planner's boss).

Types of Associations

Local. Most members are located in the metropolitan area where the organization is located.

State. Most members are located within the state where the organization is located.

Regional. Most members are located within the region (e.g., New England) where the organization is located.

National. Most members are located within the same country where the organization is located.

International. Membership is comprised of people from several different nations.

Professional. Membership is comprised of persons from the same industry.

Not-for-Profits or Nonprofit Associations. **Not-for-profits** and **nonprofit associations** have a special tax-exempt status granted by the Internal Revenue Service (IRS). Although they do not have a profit motive, these associations need to be run efficiently and must have their revenues exceed expenses. Since all revenues are used to support the mission of the organization, excess funds (similar to profits in the corporate world) are allowed to stay with the organization, tax-free.

SMERFs. These are not the little blue people from Saturday morning television. **SMERF** refers to small associations with members who join for **s**ocial, **m**ilitary, **e**ducational, **r**eligious, and **f**raternal reasons. Persons attending these meetings tend to pay their own expenses; accordingly, this category tends to be very price sensitive.

Types of Association Gatherings and Events (Their Purposes and Objectives)

Conventions. These are assemblies of people for a common purpose. Depending on the type of association sponsoring the convention, it may attract attendees from state, regional, national, or international markets. Many conventions have an exhibition (or trade show) as an added feature. The exhibition may be a major source of revenue for the association. Exhibitors participate in these events because these events offer them an opportunity to show their products and services to a well-targeted group of potential buyers.

Board Meetings. The association's board of directors typically meets several times a year to provide collective advice and direction to the association. This meeting is usually the smallest association meeting held.

Committee Meetings. Many association committees will hold smaller meetings to discuss the affairs related to their purpose (e.g., government relations, convention host committee, national conference program committee, and publications committee).

Regional Conferences. Organizations with a regional structure often schedule one or more events each year to bring together members who are in the same geographic area.

Training Meetings. Associations often offer their members opportunities to upgrade their professional skills and knowledge through meetings targeted to specific topics. Many professions require continuing education (e.g., continuing medical education for different medical specialties). Some associations offer training meetings to develop the leadership potential of the association's elected national and regional officers.

Educational Seminars. This type of association meeting is led by an expert and allows participants to share their views and experiences.

Attendees   Since attendance at association meetings is voluntary, the meetings must offer appealing programs to draw members to the events.

Need for Marketing to Build Attendance   The marketing of association meetings is critical to the success of the gathering. All good association marketing should begin with an understanding of who the members are and what their needs are. This focus should be brought into the development of all meetings.

If the meeting provides genuine opportunities for the members to satisfy their needs, the promotional aspect of marketing the meeting becomes much less intense. Since the primary group of attendees includes members of the association, the key elements of the meeting promotion include providing advance notification of the date and location of the upcoming meeting along with information about the planned content, speakers, and special activities. Later, detailed registration information and a preliminary program will need to be provided.

The vehicle for communicating this information to the members has traditionally been through direct mail and notices or advertisements in the association newsletter and magazine. Technology and cost considerations have moved many associations toward the use of electronic media to communicate with their members. There has been a rapid growth in the use of broadcast fax and e-mails, which emphasize that recipients should visit the association Web site to seek out the details.

To expand the number of attendees at the gathering, many associations send promotional materials and notices to nonmembers who have been targeted as sharing an interest in the meeting's purpose. Since the nonmember fee is usually higher than the member fee, this effort (if successful) could result in attracting new members to the organization.

Department and/or Individual Responsible for Organizing and Planning   According to the *Meetings & Conventions* 2006 "Meetings Market Report," about 40% of the association planners who responded to their survey had the words "event," "convention," or "conference" in their job titles, while 26% held the title of president, executive director, or executive vice president. The respondents spent an average of 61% of their workday planning. Some associations, usually smaller ones, contract out some or all of their meetings to independent planners and association management companies. In the 2006 "Meetings Market Report," over 25% of the planners surveyed possessed an industry certification: 22% were Certified Meeting Professionals (CMPs), 4% were Certified Association Executives (CAEs), and 2% were Certified Meeting Managers (CMMs).

Professional Associations Supporting the Association MEEC Industry   Association meeting planners join professional associations in greater numbers than their corporate counterparts. Those associations include the American Society of Association Executives and the Center for Association Leadership (http://www.asaecenter.org), the Meeting Professionals International (http://www.mpiweb.org), the Professional Convention Management Association (http://www.pcma.org), the International Association for Exhibition Management (http://www.iaem.org), and the Society of Government Meeting Professionals (http://www.sgmp.org). There are also many local organizations of meeting planners that provide support and professional development opportunities for them.

The following are Web sites with examples of association meetings:

- http://www.pcma2007.org/home.asp
- http://www.mpine.org/newsletter/summer06.pdf

- http://www.restaurant.org/show/index.cfm
- http://www.natpe.org/conference/
- http://www.chrie.org/i4a/pages/index.cfm?pageid53330

GOVERNMENT

Governmental entities at all levels have continuing needs to hold gatherings, since they have continuing needs to communicate and interact with many constituent bodies. These meetings may involve the attendance of world leaders, with large groups of protestors and supporters, or a small group of elected local officials holding a legislative retreat. Government meetings are subject to many rules. The federal government and many state governments establish **per diem rates** that set limits on expenditures for lodging and meals. Facilities where federal meetings are held must be able to accommodate persons with certain physical limitations, as per the Americans with Disabilities Act (ADA), and must meet fire safety certifications.

Since the list of per diem rate tables are so extensive, it is recommended that those in need of the current federal domestic per diem rates go to the General Services Administration Web site at http://www.gsa.gov.

Decision Makers   Managers at government agencies are typically those who identify the need to hold a meeting and have the responsibility to provide funding through their departmental budget process or locate other sources of funding. Meetings, like other parts of an agency's budget, are very dependent on funding provided through the legislative process. Accordingly, as political interest in an agency's mission grows or diminishes, the budget will increase or decrease, as will its ability to sponsor gatherings.

Types of Government Gatherings and Events (Their Purposes and Objectives)   The purpose of many government meetings is the training of government workers. On the federal level, many of these meetings will be replicated in several areas of the country to minimize travel expenses for the employees of an agency's branch offices.

Other government meetings may involve both agency employees and those in the general public who may have an interest in the topic of the meeting. Meetings such as those to discuss prescription drug proposals or the future of Social Security are likely to go on the road to gather input from the public.

Association Meeting Planning

SUSAN REICHBART, CMP
Director, Conferences and Meetings
College and University Professional Association for Human Resources

Associations offer their members opportunities to enhance their professional development at conferences, seminars, and workshops. These events may combine structured educational sessions of several hours or days with informal networking events, such as receptions, golf tournaments, and dinners. These activities encourage collegiality and allow members to exchange information in a relaxed social setting.

Associations encourage their members to become involved so that meetings *for* members are planned with input *from* members. The meeting planner works with the member committees from the initial planning stage through the final production of the event. Committee members can suggest program topics and speakers that their colleagues will find appealing and, at best, compelling. Local committee members may suggest local venues for social events, tourist attractions and tours, entertainment options, and golf courses for a conference tournament. One particularly enterprising volunteer researched local options and put together a comprehensive notebook rivaling those found at hotel concierge desks. Working under the supervision of the meeting planner, volunteers perform a myriad of duties during the event, such as giving out badges at registration, monitoring recreational events, and hosting social events—all duties that save the association the cost of hiring temporary staff. Member assistance is a value-added and integral part of the planning that helps ensure an event's appeal and success.

Association events are a source of revenue for associations. The greater the number of paid attendees, the greater the revenue, and the more lucrative the event is to the association. However, since members must pay registration fees and spend additional funds for travel and lodging, the association must provide programs that its members will find too valuable to miss. The meeting planner develops a marketing strategy that promotes benefits to entice members and prospects. The marketing plan may feature keynote speakers, concurrent session programs, an appealing location, and exciting social and recreational events. This information may be posted on the association's Web site, highlighted in newsletters, mailed in comprehensive preliminary programs, and sent by fax and e-mail "blasts." In addition to promoting all facets of the event to all members and prospects, additional marketing emphasis may be directed at targeted groups, such as past attendees.

(continued)

Association Meeting Planning (*continued*)

Association meeting planners work with their member committees to develop worthwhile programs and then design effective marketing plans to maximize participation. The combined focus results in events that are beneficial to members and the association.

Attendees   Attendance by employees at government meetings would generally be mandatory, while attendance by the general public would be voluntary.

Security   There is no segment of the MEEC industry more attuned to safety and security than government. They work on a regular basis with the Department of Homeland Security since many of their attendees are high-profile leaders. PCMA held a forum entitled "Security Door to Door" where the following suggestions were made for implementing security:

- Plan and prepare.
- Refine the preconvention meeting to emphasize security issues.
- Be sure there is coordination of all parties involved.
- Establish a security team and its decision makers.
- Provide education on security for attendees.
- Be proactive rather than reactive.
- Stay informed and alert to incidents.

Source: Sara Torrence (Sept. 2004). "Security Door to Door." *Convene*, p. 22.

Need for Marketing to Build Attendance   Government meetings have characteristics typical of both corporate and association meetings. Mandatory attendance by government employees requires only that sufficient notice be provided so that participants can adjust their schedules in order to attend. Attracting voluntary attendees may require additional promotion.

Department and/or Individual Responsible for Organizing and Planning   Government meeting planners resemble their corporate counterparts, as they are located throughout their agencies. While some government meeting planners devote all their work time to planning meetings, others handle meetings as one of their extra assigned duties.

Many government agencies hire meeting management companies or independent meeting planners to handle meetings that fall beyond their internal capabilities. In the Washington, DC, area, there are several meeting planning companies that specialize in managing government meetings.

Professional Associations Supporting the Government MEEC Industry   Meeting planners who work for the government and/or independent meeting management companies are likely to join associations to support their professional development. These associations include the Society of Government Meeting Professionals (http://www.sgmp.org) and its local or regional chapters, the Professional Convention Management Association (http://www.pcma.org), and Meeting Professionals International (http://www.mpiweb.org). Those who have responsibility for organizing exhibitions are likely to join the International Association for Exhibition Management (http://www.iaem.org).

The following are Web sites providing examples of government meetings:

- http://en.wikipedia.org/wiki/2004_Republican_National_Convention
- http://www.state.gov/p/io/ipp/usgmeet/
- http://www.ofee.gov/whats/ggmt.htm
- http://www.mlive.com/news/aanews/index.ssf?/base/news7/1161355369235290.xml&coll=2

Entities that Help Organize Gatherings

There are a number of categories of organizations that are key players in aiding corporations, associations, and government in producing their meetings and events. They include exhibition management companies, association management companies, and meeting management companies.

EXHIBITION MANAGEMENT COMPANIES

There are a number of companies that are in the business of owning and managing trade shows and expositions. These companies both develop and produce shows that profit their companies as well as produce events for a sponsoring corporation, association, or government client. While trade shows and expositions are both events at which

Government Meetings Are Unique

SARA TORRENCE
President, Sara Torrence & Associates
Gaithersburg, Maryland

Meetings for the government are unique. They are different from any other type of conference. Why is this so? Because these meetings are bound by government regulations and operating policies that do not apply to other types of meetings.

First, consider rates for sleeping rooms. In an effort to save the government money, the General Services Administration (GSA) Office of Government-wide Policy sets per diem rates for lodging, meals, and incidental expenses for individual travelers for all locations in the continental United States (CONUS). In most cities, these rates are below those charged to conference groups, which take up a larger amount of a hotel's inventory of rooms than transient travelers. To offset this problem, GSA allows government meeting organizers to negotiate a rate up to 25% above the lodging allowance. Also, GSA's Federal Premier Lodging Program offers government travelers guaranteed rooms at guaranteed rates—right where the federal traveler needs to be—and enters into contractual relationships with hotels in the top seventy U.S. travel markets. Additionally, meetings may only be held in properties that comply with the Hotel Motel Fire Safety Act of 1990. Government regulations regarding travel are located at http://www.policyworks.gov on the Web.

Federal procurement policies also distinguish the government meeting. Bids for meeting supplies and services must be obtained from *at least* three vendors for all but the smallest purchases. Additionally, government meeting planners usually are not the people who commit federal funds. All purchases must be approved and contracted for by a federal procurement official. In some cases, meeting planners have been trained by their agencies in procurement practices, so they are able to commit a limited amount of money ($2,500, $10,000, or $25,000, for example). But private-sector meeting suppliers should be forewarned to determine who has the authority to commit funds and sign contracts.

Hotel contracts are not considered "official" by the government. A hotel contract may be attached to the paperwork submitted to the procurement official, but in all cases, the government contract—not that of the private sector—is the prevailing authority. This applies to all procurements for meeting services. Funds must be approved *before* the service is rendered, not after. In addition, the government *must* be able to cancel a contract without liquidated damages if funding for an event is withdrawn, if there are furloughs or closures of government facilities, or if other government actions make it inadvisable to hold the meeting. The government cannot pay for services not received. And the government cannot indemnify or hold harmless anyone who is not a government employee conducting official business.

Other characteristics that make government meetings unique include the following:

- *There is a short turn-around time for planning government meetings.* While associations plan their conferences with many years of lead time, most government meetings are planned only months—or even weeks—before the event. This is true for large multifaceted meetings as well as small gatherings.

- *Government meetings do not fit a particular mold.* They may be elaborate international conferences for high-ranking dignitaries or small scientific conclaves for eight to twelve researchers. Some meetings may be held only once and therefore have no history.

- *Government meetings often require a disproportionately large amount of function space relative to the number of sleeping room nights booked.* This may be because only a small percentage of attendees are coming from out of town.

- *Policies for meetings can vary from agency to agency.* Some agencies collect registration fees to cover expenses. Others will not allow appropriated fees to pay for lunches; collections often have to be made on site from attendees. In addition, as GSA allows each agency to implement the "up to 25%" allowance as they see fit, government lodging allowances may vary from agency to agency.

- *Government meetings frequently bring together representatives from the uniformed services and non-Department of Defense agencies.* Often, these groups share software applications designed for their *own* purposes, such as encrypted messaging and global directory systems that list only those with a "need to know" the information. Frequently, such meetings are classified and are required to be held in a "secure" facility, whether a government building or a public facility secured by trained personnel.

(continued)

Government Meetings Are Unique *(continued)*

Government-sponsored meetings are far more complicated than most private-sector conferences that are often planned by people who are not full-time meeting planners. They may be budget analysts, public affairs officers, scientists, secretaries, or administrative officers. And as government meetings are perceived to provide less revenue for a hotel, they may be assigned to junior members of the hotel sales staff.

All government meeting organizers are bound by a code of ethics that prohibits them from accepting anything from a vendor that is valued at more than $20. Those who work with the government should realize this and not put the planner in a compromising position.

Thankfully, there is an organization that specializes in providing education and resources to government planners and suppliers—the Society of Government Meeting Professionals (SGMP).

Note: Prior to her recent retirement, Sara planned special meetings for the federal government.

products and services are displayed for potential buyers, the **trade show** is generally not open to the public, while **expositions** are usually open to the public. The companies that operate these exhibitions are profit-making enterprises that have found areas of economic interest that attract, according to the purpose of the exhibition, either the general public (for example, an auto, boat, home, or garden show) or members of a specific industry (for example, high-technology communications networking). Exhibitions provide the opportunity for face-to-face marketing. Some associations hire **exhibition management companies** to manage all or part of their exhibitions. For their efforts, the companies are paid for the services they provide.

Among the largest exhibition management companies are Reed Exhibitions (http://www.reedexpo.com), which organizes over 470 events in 29 countries; VNU Expositions (http://www.vnuexpo.com), which creates, markets, and produces 50 trade shows and educational conferences; and George Little Management (http://www.glmshows.com), which markets and produces 49 shows. These three companies manage 40 of the top 200 shows, according to a 2002 study by Tradeshow Week Inc. Their shows serve a wide variety of industries, domestically and globally, including aerospace, art and entertainment, electronics, hospitality, security, sport and health, and travel. Other exhibition management companies include International Gem and Jewelry Inc., Cygnus Expositions, National Event Management Inc., and SmithBucklin.

Decision Makers   The owners and senior managers of company-owned shows decide where, when, and how often they will produce their shows. The decision is driven by the profit motive—offering too many shows could lead to a cannibalization of the market; offering too few shows creates an opportunity for the competition to enter the market with their own shows.

Types of Gatherings (Their Purposes and Objectives)

Trade Shows. Exhibits of products and services that are not open to the general public. Trade shows may be part of a convention or may stand alone.

Public Shows. Exhibits of products and services that are open to the public. They usually charge an admission fee.

Attendees   Depending on the nature of the exhibition, the attendees vary greatly. For trade shows, the market is well defined by the trade or profession. For **public shows**, the attendees are basically defined by their interests and geographic proximity to the show location.

Need for Marketing to Build Attendance   The exhibition management companies have a need to market to two distinctly different yet inexorably linked publics. One group that has to be targeted is exhibitors who need to reach potential buyers of their products and services. The other group includes the trade or the general public who have a need or desire to view, discuss, and purchase the products and services presented by the exhibitors.

The trade group only needs to be informed of the dates and location of the trade show. Direct mail and e-mail may be all that is needed for an established show. Shows appealing to the general public require extensive media advertising (newspaper, radio, and television) to communicate the specifics within the geographic region. Promotional efforts such as the distribution of discount coupons are common. In both cases, it is essential that the marketing effort results in a high volume of traffic at the exhibition to satisfy the needs of the exhibitors.

The exhibition management company really is a marketing company, since it is creating the environment in which need-satisfying exchanges can occur. The focus is on selling exhibit space and building buyer attendance.

Department and/or Individual Responsible for Organizing and Planning   In this case, the entire exhibition management company is dedicated to the organizing and planning of the exhibition.

Professional Associations Supporting the Exhibition Management Industry   The associations that support the exhibition management industry include the International Association for Exhibition Management (http://www.iaem.org) for the production side of the business, and the Trade Show Exhibitors Association (http://www.tsea.org) for the exhibitor side of the business. Other related associations include the Exhibit Designers and Producers Association (http://www.edpa.com), the Exhibition Services & Contractors Association (http://www.esca.org), and the Healthcare Convention & Exhibitors Association (http://www. hcea.org.)

Corporations plan and execute production of gatherings that often include a keynote speaker, such as this one. Management companies are often used to secure keynote speakers.

Used by permission of Paradise Light & Sound, Orlando, Florida

ASSOCIATION MANAGEMENT COMPANIES

As the name of this category implies, this type of company is contracted by an association to assume full or partial responsibility for the management of the association, based on its needs. A designated person in the association management company is identified as the main contact for the association and interacts with the board of directors and members to fulfill the association's mission. If the association is small and has limited financial resources, that contact person may serve in this capacity for two or more associations. Since they manage more than one association, association management companies were formerly known as multimanagement companies. Confusion as to who to target for their services necessitated this change.

Other employees of the association management company support the main contact and provide services as contracted (such as membership, finance, publications, government relations, and meeting management services). With this type of arrangement, the association office is typically located within the offices of the association management company. Examples of these types of companies include SmithBucklin of Chicago, Illinois, and the Association Management Group of McLean, Virginia.

MEETING MANAGEMENT COMPANIES

These companies operate on a contractual basis, like the association management company, but limit their services to providing either selected or comprehensive meeting management services. They may manage all aspects of the meeting or may be focused on on-site research, hotel negotiations, exhibit sales, on-site management, registration and housing, or any combination of these. The meeting may be held at the association's own location, or the function may be located elsewhere. Examples of meeting management companies include ConferenceDirect of Los Angeles, California, and Conferon Inc. of Twinsburg, Ohio.

INDEPENDENT MEETING MANAGERS

Experienced meeting professionals often use their expertise and contacts to set up their own business of managing meetings, or parts of meetings, for an association or several associations. An independent meeting manager may be called in to run a golf tournament that is an integral part of a gathering or to provide on-site management. In some instances, an independent is called in to handle crises in the meetings department. Personnel changes in the meetings department shortly before a meeting may require hiring a competent professional to pull the meeting together and bring it to a successful conclusion.

Professional Associations Supporting Independent Planners
The type of company that individuals are associated with will dictate the type of association that they would likely join to support their professional development. Many of them will join the Professional Convention Management Association (http://www.pcma.org) or Meeting Professionals International (http://www.mpiweb.org). Others will choose to join organizations such as the International Special Event Society (http://www.ises.com), the National Association of Catering Executives (http://www.nace.net), the American Rental Association (http://www.ararental.org), or the Association of Bridal Consultants (http://www.bridalassn.com).

EVENT MANAGEMENT COMPANIES

Within the context of the meetings industry, event management companies are usually brought in to manage a specific aspect of a larger gathering. They may be hired to plan, script, and supervise all aspects of the awards ceremony or the closing gala. Depending on their market and location, some of these companies may provide local event management, including the grand opening of a building or business; handle the arrangement for a parade; and do wedding and other party planning.

OTHER ORGANIZATIONS ARRANGING GATHERINGS

There are a number of other entities that organize or sponsor gatherings or events. They include the following:

- Political organizations
  - Republican or Democratic national parties
  - Local political organizations
- Labor unions
  - The Teamsters
  - Service Employees International Union (SEIU)
  - Pipe Fitters Union

- Fraternal groups
  - Kiwanis
  - Elks
  - University fraternities and sororities
- Military reunion groups
- Educational groups
  - Universities
  - For-profit education groups
  - Common interest groups
  - High schools

Summary

The types of organizations that sponsor gatherings are as diverse as the types of gatherings held and the people who attend them. Most of the U.S. population will participate in these gatherings at least once in their lives. For many, attending a meeting, convention, exhibition, or other event will be a regular occurrence. The gatherings they attend reflect their personal and professional interests.

People seeking career opportunities with sponsoring organizations will have to use targeting techniques to locate them, although these positions do exist throughout the nation. The greatest number of these positions can be found in locations where the organizations are headquartered. The metropolitan Washington, DC, area is considered to be the "meetings capital" of the world, with several thousand associations located there. Many national and international organizations are located in and around Washington, as is the federal government. State capitals are home to many state and regional associations, in addition to agencies of state government.

Major corporations tend to be located in large cities, although many may be located in smaller cities and towns. Their meetings are typically planned at corporate headquarters.

Employment opportunities with organizations and facilities that host gatherings are located in both major cities and small towns. The organization will select a location for its proximity to access by the attendees (near a major airport or the interstate highway) or for the purpose of the gathering.

With baby boomers (the largest age group in the U.S. population) approaching retirement age, it is anticipated that there will be an increasing number of employment opportunities in the coming years on both sides of the meeting, event, exhibition, and convention industry.

Key Words and Terms

For definitions, see the Glossary or go to http://glossary.convention industry.org.

Association	Incentive trip
Board meeting	Nonprofit association
Convention	Not-for-profit
Corporation	Per diem rate
Exhibition management company	Public show
	SMERF
Exposition	Trade show

Review and Discussion Questions

1. Identify the type of sponsoring organization that holds the greatest number of gatherings and the type that generates the greatest economic benefit.
2. Which type or types of sponsoring organizations have the greatest marketing challenges to ensure the success of their gatherings?
3. What changes are occurring with incentive trips to provide more value for the corporation sponsoring the gathering?
4. How do not-for-profit associations differ from for-profit organizations?
5. What type of organizations comprise the category of associations known as SMERFs, and what similarities do they share with each other?
6. How do government procurement officers view meeting contracts from their hotel suppliers?

7. Distinguish between the trade show and the exposition.
8. What efficiencies do association management companies bring to the management and operation of small associations?

About the Chapter Contributor

Howard E. Reichbart is an associate professor in the Hospitality Management and Meeting, Event & Exhibition Management Department at Northern Virginia Community College in Annandale, Virginia. Professor Reichbart developed his interests in the hotel and meetings industry as a youngster working in the family hotel business. These interests led him to earn a degree in hotel administration from the University of New Hampshire. He then worked in hotel management for Hotel Corporation of America/Sonesta International Hotels in Hartford, Connecticut, and Washington, DC. He served in the U.S. Army as the club officer/manager of the Ft. McPherson Officers Club in Atlanta, Georgia. Professor Reichbart has been a faculty member at Northern Virginia Community College for thirty-seven years, including almost twenty years as the program head. During his time as program head, he developed one of the first degree programs in meeting, event, and exhibition management in the United States. He has also taught at the University of Nevada–Las Vegas, the University of Maryland, and George Washington University.

CHAPTER 3

Destination Marketing Organizations (DMOs)

DMOs attend industry trade shows to promote their city.
Photo by George G. Fenich, Ph.D.

Chapter Objectives

This chapter provides the reader with an understanding of the following:

- Roles and functions of DMOs
- History of DMOs
- Ways to organize and fund DMOs
- Activities of DMOs relative to convention marketing and sales
- Overview and definition of DMO services for meeting professionals
- Destination Marketing Association International (DMAI) and its services to member bureaus and meeting professionals

Chapter Outline

Roles and Functions of Destination Marketing Organizations

What Is a Destination Marketing Organization?

Purpose of DMOs

Why Use a DMO?

What DMOs Can Do for Meeting Planners

Advantages of Using DMOs to Plan a Meeting

Activities of DMOs Relative to Sales and Marketing

DMO Services for Meeting Professionals

What Information Do DMOs Have vis-à-vis Hotels?

DMAI Services to Member Bureaus and Meeting Professionals

OfficialTravelGuide.com

Meetings Information Network (MINT)

Online RFP

Destinations Showcase

Professional Development Offerings

Certified Destination Management Executive (CDME) Program

PDM Certificate Program

Destination Marketing Accreditation Program (DMAP)

Industry Information and Research

DMAI Resource Center

DMAI Foundation

Introduction

"If a destination were merely a place, a dot on a map, a bump in the road or just another stop along the way, then the destination would not matter—nor would this guide be meaningful." But as we all know, destinations do matter. They are called destinations for a reason: People want or need to go there and visit. In many instances, people go to great lengths to get there; they are drawn to them. For a few, they may be the realization of some lifelong dream.

By boat, car, plane, or train, they go. Why? Contrary to the wise old proverb, it is not about the journey, but about the destination—and the reasons for making the journey are as varied as the people who are traveling. Whether for business or leisure, they come because of the expectation of an enjoyable experience.

> Somewhere along the way, this is exactly what the visitor believes. This is the appeal; this is the driving force behind the quest. This is the lure of the destination. This is the benchmark to be met at journey's end.
>
> *Source:* Michael Gehrisch, president of the DMAI (2005). *Destination Brand-Science.* Chicago (IL): Destination Marketing Association International, p. 1.

Roles and Functions of Destination Marketing Organizations

WHAT IS A DESTINATION MARKETING ORGANIZATION?

A **destination marketing organization (DMO)** is a not-for-profit organization supported by transient room taxes, government budget allocations, private memberships, or a combination of these three. The DMO in each city, county, or region has three prime responsibilities: The first is to encourage groups to hold meetings, conventions, and trade shows in the city or area it represents; the second is to assist those groups with their meetings and meeting preparations; the third is to encourage tourists to visit and enjoy the historic, cultural, and recreational opportunities the destination offers.

A DMO does not actually organize meetings, events, and conventions, but it does help planners and visitors learn about the destination and area attractions and make the best possible use of all the services and facilities the destination has to offer. The roots of present-day DMOs stretch back to 1895 when a group of businessmen in Detroit put a full-time salesman on the road to invite conventions to their city. Today, DMOs operate throughout the world.

Initially, DMOs existed to sell and service conventions. As the years passed, more and more of these organizations became involved in the promotion of tourism. DMOs are synonymous with convention and visitor bureaus (CVBs). In fact, the use of the term "DMO" began outside the United States but has now evolved to be commonly used worldwide. Some consider the acronym "DMO" to stand for destination *marketing* organization while others consider it to stand for destination *management* organization. Further, some experts in the field have suggested that an even better and more descriptive term would be **Destination Marketing and Management Organization (DMMO).** In this text, DMO and CVB as well as DMMO are interchangeable terms.

PURPOSE OF DMOS

DMOs are primarily not-for-profit organizations charged with representing a specific destination and helping the long-term economic development of communities throughout the travel and tourism business. DMOs are usually membership organizations bringing together businesses that rely on tourism and meetings for revenue. DMOs serve as the "official" contact point for their destination.

For visitors, DMOs are like a key to the city. As an unbiased resource, DMOs can serve as a broker or an official point of contact for: convention, meeting, and event planners; tour operators; and tourists. They assist planners with meeting preparation and encourage business travelers and tourists alike to visit local historic, cultural, and recreational sites.

There are a number of reasons why a DMO is valuable to a meeting planner. DMOs offer unbiased information about a destination's services and facilities. They save meeting professionals time and energy, as they are a one-stop shop for local tourism interests. Also, DMOs can provide a full range of information about a destination, and they do not charge for most of their services.

If DMOS Do Not Charge for Their Services, How Do They Make Money?   DMOs do not charge their clients—the tourist, the business traveler, and the meeting planner—for services rendered. Instead, most DMOs are funded through a combination of hotel occupancy taxes and membership dues.

Why Are Meetings and Tourism Important?   Travel and tourism enhance the quality of life for a local community. They provide jobs, bring in tax dollars for improvement of services and infrastructure, and attract facilities such as restaurants, shops, festivals, and cultural and sporting venues that cater to both tourists and locals.

Meeting Professional Awareness Program

The following is a summary of a meeting professional awareness program that the Boise, Idaho, CVB developed to educate meeting professionals on both the services available to them from the Boise CVB and ways to market themselves as an attractive and affordable meeting destination

Bureau

Boise Convention & Visitors Bureau

How Was This Program or Material Developed?

It was developed jointly by bureau staff and an outside consultant or agency.

Statement of Objectives

To create a campaign that would produce "top-of-mind" awareness of Boise as a sensory experience and an attractive meeting destination. The use of direct mail was designed to attract clients for the solicitation of meetings and conventions, enhancing the city's image as an attractive and affordable meeting location while increasing an awareness of Boise.

Implementation

The project was a hands-on, interactive three-part campaign spotlighting the sensory experiences of Boise and targeted meeting planners. The initial "door opener" piece was a quad-fold mailing featuring visual teasers of Boise that would invite the reader to "feel," "hear," "taste," and "see." The folder promised additional mailings for the recipient to anticipate. The second piece was a larger quad-fold mailer, which contained a brightly colored round Boise mouse pad with additional visual depictions of Boise's sensory highlights. The actual mailer contained testimonials from representatives of past organizations that had met in Boise. The third and final mailing continued the quad-fold design and contained a CD instructing the recipient to place it in a CD-ROM drive for viewing. The CD provided the viewer with a fast-paced musical presentation of Boise's sensory experiences. At the end of the CD, the planner was invited to log on to Boise's Web site.

Evaluation

Follow-up phone calls were made to all of the clients. The mouse pad received positive remarks. The CD proved very useful for planners, as it gave a good overview of Boise as a meeting site. Because Boise is a somewhat unfamiliar destination, it was helpful for the planner to be able to log on to the Web site and view the many ways Boise makes for a great meeting city. These kinds of direct-mail programs enhance marketing efforts and allow the sales staff an opportunity to further their relationships with clients. A result of direct mail may be a site visit, familiarization trip, or bid opportunities.

Source: Entry submitted by Boise DMO at the 2002 DMAI Idea Fair.

A New Look & Feel

The Baltimore Area Convention & Visitors Association (BACVA) has unveiled a new major branding and marketing campaign aimed at raising the awareness level of Baltimore with the traveling public. The marketing efforts of the campaign include a redesigned logo, a Web site, commercials, and an inviting tagline and call to action: "Get in on it." The initiative highlights the city as a unique, exciting, and desirable destination for visitors, meetings, and group tours. "Research shows that tourists who have experienced Baltimore love it because of its world-class attractions that are easy to get to and for its distinct personality, described as casual and fun," commented BACVA's interim president, Ronnie Burt.

The box on page 66 contains a profile of CVBs, as represented by a sample of 222 of these organizations that participated in the Destination Marketing Association International (DMAI) 2005 CVB Organizational & Financial Profile.

Why Use a DMO?

DMOs make planning and implementing a meeting less time-consuming and more streamlined. They give meeting planners access to a range of services, packages, and value-added extras. Before a meeting begins, DMO sales managers can help locate meeting space, check hotel availability, and arrange for site inspections. DMOs can also link planners with suppliers, from motor coach companies and caterers to off-site entertainment venues that can help meet the pre-requisites of any event.

2005 Profile of Convention and Visitor Bureaus

COMMUNITY PROFILE

Visitor Centers

- A destination has, on average, two official year-round visitor centers.
- CVBs operate the majority (77%) of these centers with 76% paid staff and 24% volunteer staff.
- Almost half (45%) operate a store in the visitor center.

Convention Centers

- For those destinations that have convention centers (67%), the vast majority (87%) are *owned* by a government-related entity (city, county, state/province, authority).
- Half (53%) are also *managed* by a government entity, while 40% are privately managed.
- Sales and marketing responsibility rests with the CVB (38%), the Center (28%), or a joint relationship between the CVB and the Center (23%). An additional 11% use the services of a private entity.
- For Centers where CVBs are responsible for sales and marketing, 41% have an 18-month window for dates they control, while 22% can book events anytime.
- Almost half the Centers have no booking criteria; an additional 38% have a room night criteria.
- The average size of the primary convention center is 268,000 gross square feet.
- Typically, there are 13 hotels and 2,800 rooms within a half mile of the primary convention center.

Hotel Rooms

- The average number of hotel rooms served by a CVB is approximately 13,600.

Average Tax Rates

- Total Tax on a Hotel Room (incl. hotel room tax, sales taxes, etc.): 12.2%
  - Average Hotel Room Tax: 6.7%
  - Average Sales Tax on a Hotel Room: 5.5%

- Total Tax on a Car Rental: (incl. rental tax, sales tax, etc.): 11.7%
- Special Restaurant Tax (excl. sales tax): 2.7%

Ways Hotel Room Taxes Are Used

- On average, 55% of the hotel room tax monies collected are allocated to the CVB.
- Slightly more than one-third of destinations use hotel room tax monies for convention center purposes (operations, construction, and debt service).
- About 11% of destinations allocate hotel room tax revenue to arenas and sport facilities.

Ways Special Restaurant Taxes Are Used

- For those destinations that have this tax (19% of all CVBs), the two common uses are convention center operations/construction/debt service and CVB funding.

ORGANIZATION PROFILE

Structure: The majority of CVBs are independent not-for-profits—61% are 501(c)(6) and 4% are 501(c)(3); 18% are government agencies (city, county, state/province, authority); and 5% are a chamber or a division of a chamber of commerce.

Membership: Almost half (49%) of CVBs are membership organizations, averaging 569 members. The following is a typical member composition: 23% accommodations, 17% attractions/cultural institutions, 17% event services/suppliers, 16% restaurants, 11% retail establishments.

Years in Operation: The average CVB is 39 years old.

Revenue: The average total gross revenue of CVBs is $4.4 million (excluding Las Vegas).

Relationship with Primary Funding Source: Around 60% of CVBs have a contract with their primary source. Almost one-tenth (8%) of these contracts are awarded through a request for proposal (RFP) process. Slightly more than half (54%) of the contracts are annual; the remainder are multiyear terms.

(*continued*)

2005 Profile of Convention and Visitor Bureaus (*continued*)

Board Composition: A typical CVB Board of Directors is comprised of 19 voting members with a six-person Executive Committee. Three-fourths of CVBs have bylaws that specify the composition of the Board.

Additional Corporations: About 17% of CVBs have an additional/affiliated 501(c)(3), or foundation.

Staff Size: The average CVB has 11 full-time and 3 regular part-time employees.

Out-of-Town Offices: Overall, almost one-third (30%) of CVBs have out-of-town/satellite offices (90% of CVBs with budgets of $10 million or more), primarily in Washington, DC, and Chicago.

FINANCIAL PROFILE

Funding

- The majority of CVBs (87%) receive *public* funding from hotel occupancy tax revenue. Additional key public funding sources include state/province (nontax) funding (26% of CVBs) and city (nontax) funding (18%).

- In terms of *private* funding, 52% of all CVBs receive membership dues. Other top private sources include donated (noncash) services (46%), co-op advertising (41%), Visitor Center sales (39%), promotion participation (38%), and print advertising (37%).

Expenses

- CVBs spend almost half (43%) of their budget on sales and marketing efforts, with media advertising the top activity (17% of total expenses). The remainder is spent on personnel (40%) and administrative expenses (17%).

- CVBs typically spend 24% of their entire budget (sales & marketing, personnel, administrative) on convention sales and marketing; 19% is spent on consumer leisure marketing efforts. An additional 10% is directed toward the travel trade sector. Communications/PR efforts receive 9% of the budget; Visitor Services receive 8%.

Source: 2005 CVB Organizational and Financial Profile Report, DMAI Foundation, April 2006.

Jacob K. Javits Convention Center.
Dorling Kindersley Media Library

WHAT DMOs CAN DO FOR MEETING PLANNERS

Consider a DMO to be similar to a meeting planner's Yellow Pages. Many people are aware of the existence of DMOs, but they are not aware of all the services DMOs have to offer.

Most DMOs are not-for-profit organizations representing a specific destination. Most are membership organizations bringing together businesses that rely on tourism and meetings for their livelihoods. A DMO has many responsibilities. It encourages groups to hold meetings in the city and assists groups with meeting preparations. DMOs also provide promotional materials to encourage attendance and establish room blocks, among other things.

Most importantly, DMOs serve as *the* official point of contact for convention and meeting planners. Meeting planners can access a range of services, packages, and value-added extras through a DMO.

Before going into the specifics of what a DMO can do for a meeting planner, let us examine a few common misconceptions about DMOs:

Misconception 1. DMOs solely book hotel rooms and convention space.

Fact. DMOs represent the gamut of visitor-related businesses, from restaurants and retail to rental cars and racetracks. Therefore, they are responsible for introducing planners to the range of meeting-related products and services a city has to offer.

Misconception 2. DMOs work only with large groups.

Fact. More than half of the average DMO's efforts are devoted to meetings of less than 200 people. In fact, larger bureaus often have staff members specifically dedicated to small meetings, group tours, and transient business travel.

Misconception 3. Bureaus own and/or run the convention center.

Fact. Only 5% of DMOs run the convention center in their locations (the Las Vegas Convention and Visitor Authority is one of them). Nevertheless, DMOs work closely with local convention centers and can assist planners in getting what they need from convention center staff.

Misconception 4. Planners have to pay DMOs for their services.

Fact. In truth, the services of a DMO are totally free. Michael Gehrisch, president of the DMAI, points out, "DMOs are a hotel's best friend and a meeting planner's best friend. We don't charge either one. We book business for the hotel without a fee and we provide the same service, for free, to the planner." How is it that a DMO can work for free? Most DMOs are funded through a combination of hotel occupancy taxes and membership fees.

Some may question the need to work through a DMO when planning a meeting, particularly in cases where the bulk of an event takes place at one hotel or at the convention center. The bureau can help a planner work with those entities and can help fill out the convention schedule (including spouse tours and pre- and post-tours) with off-site activities. Since the bureau is an objective resource, it can direct planners to the products and services that will work best to accommodate the needs and budgets of their client.

ADVANTAGES OF USING DMOs TO PLAN A MEETING

There are many things a DMO can do to help an organizer, sponsor, or planner put together a meeting or event. A DMO can assist planners in all areas of meeting preparation and provide planners with detailed reference material. It can also establish room blocks at local hotels and will market the destination to attendees via promotional material, thereby encouraging attendance. A DMO can act as a liaison between the planner and community officials, thus clearing the way for special permits, street closures, etc. The bureau can offer suggestions about ways meeting attendees can maximize free time, along with helping to develop companion programs and pre- and postconvention tours.

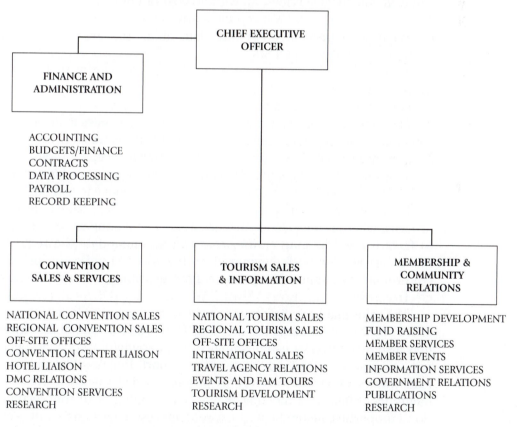

FIGURE 3–1   Organizational chart for a CVB.

A DMO can be an invaluable resource when putting together meetings, expositions, events, and conventions.

ACTIVITIES OF DMOs RELATIVE TO SALES AND MARKETING

Professionals who work in a DMO serve as the sales representative for their destination. DMOs have hotels, restaurants, attractions, convention centers, and many other entities as their members, and they represent them to meeting professionals who need their products and services. There is an entire process that a DMO undertakes with a meeting professional to bring a meeting to its destination.

Site Review and Leads Process   Determining if a site or location can accommodate a meeting's requirements is critical. The CVB is the central information source for advice on site selection, transportation, and available local services, all with no cost or obligation to the meeting or event manager. CVB representatives have the knowledge and information to provide up-to-date data about the area as well as planned future developments.

Regardless of the meeting size, the DMO can serve as the first stop in the site review process. When a meeting manager contacts a DMO, a sales manager will be assigned to assist in securing the necessary information and facts to produce a successful meeting. The sales manager can gather information about preferred dates for the event and find out what facilities are available, whether there are adequate sleeping rooms and meeting rooms, and whether convention facilities are available for the entire time period, including time for exhibitors to move in and out.

In order to represent all their members, most DMOs have a "leads" process, wherein the sales manager circulates meeting specifications to facilities and lodging entities that can accommodate the requirements. Basic information required by the DMO is indicated on the convention lead sheet. Many DMOs now distribute this information electronically.

The sales manager distributes the lead to all member lodging properties capable of handling the meeting. However, the lead distribution may also be limited by establishing certain parameters, such as specifying a location downtown or near the airport. In cases like this, the lead would be forwarded only to properties that meet the requirements identified. If a meeting manager is familiar with the destination's properties, he or she may express interest in certain facilities by name; then only those facilities receive the lead.

Member Awareness Program

The following is a summary of a member awareness program that the Puerto Rico Convention Bureau developed for the small inns community of Puerto Rico.

Bureau

Puerto Rico Convention Bureau

How Was This Program or Material Developed?

By bureau staff

Statement of Objectives

1. To educate representatives from the small inns community of Puerto Rico about group, meeting, and convention business and the potential for them to generate business from this lucrative market.
2. To create awareness of the potential of the group market at an international level and in the United States and Puerto Rico.
3. To present the profile of the local group market.
4. To share data on the Puerto Rico Convention Bureau—what is its role?
5. To offer marketing suggestions for small hotels.

Implementation

Two seminars were offered, one on the West Coast and one in San Juan. Owners of small inns who were members of the Puerto Rico Convention Bureau (PRCB) and the Puerto Rico Hotel & Tourism Association (PRHTA) were invited to participate in the seminars. Participants attended the seminar closer to their properties.

The seminars' content was designed to ensure that all the objectives would be met. During the first segment, the basics of group business, its market segments, and the PRCB's role were explained. For the second segment, a DMC, a meeting planner, and a medium or large hotel were part of a panel discussion. Each of them explained how it could partner with a small inn to join forces and generate additional business.

Evaluation

Representatives from approximately forty small inns attended the seminars. They were able to meet PRCB staff and learn more about group business and the bureau. Some of the small inns represented were not members of the PRCB

(continued)

Member Awareness Program (*continued*)

(they were invited because they were members of the PRHTA), and the PRCB was able to show them firsthand the benefits of being a bureau member.

The event was featured in Puerto Rico's major newspapers, giving the PRCB great exposure in the community.

Source: Entry submitted by Puerto Rico Convention Bureau at the 2002 DMAI Idea Fair.

The DMO sales manager will request that the receiving property send the information directly to the meeting manager, or the sales manager may gather the information, compile it into a package, and send it to the meeting professional. In the United States, federal antitrust laws prohibit DMOs from discussing pricing policies with hotels under consideration. All pricing discussions must take place between the meeting manager and the prospective property. A DMO salesperson may relate to a property that a meeting manager is looking for a specific price range of room rates but cannot negotiate on the meeting manager's behalf.

The DMO sales manager will communicate with the meeting manager and the facilities to ensure that all information is disseminated, received, and understood. Any additional questions will be answered, and the meeting manager will be encouraged to visit the city to personally review the properties being considered. The DMO can be of significant assistance during a personal site review by arranging site inspections. If there are several facilities to review, the DMO sales manager will develop a complete itinerary and schedule appointments with a salesperson at each property. If other facilities must be reviewed during the visit, the DMO will contact the necessary parties and include them in the itinerary. In most cases, the sales manager will accompany the meeting manager on the site reviews and respond to any questions that may arise.

The DMO can also make a meeting manager aware of any local laws and regulations that may impact the meeting. A meeting manager should ask about issues such as unions, taxes, alcohol use laws, and any other peculiarities during the information-gathering process; for example, in Las Vegas and New Orleans, bars can stay open 24/7. A DMO representative can also discuss the condition of the local economy and local

Convention Lead Sheet

The convention lead sheet used by DMOs will usually contain the following information:

- Name of the sales representative or account manager
- Date of the sheet distribution
- File number
- Name of the primary contact for the inquiring group
  - Person's title
- Name of the group or organization
  - Address
  - City
  - State
  - Zip code
- Telephone number, fax number, and cell phone number of the primary contact
- Total number of room nights anticipated
  - Peak room nights and date of peak
- Dates for the event or meeting
- Decision date
- Total anticipated attendance
- Occupancy pattern
  - Day
  - Date
  - Rooms
- Sequential order
- Meeting space requirements
  - Exhibit space
  - Food functions
  - History
  - Competing cities
- Additional information
- Name of person who prepared the sheet and date of preparation

Source: Adapted from *Professional Meeting Management*, 4th Edition. Chicago (IL): Education Foundation, Professional Convention Management Association: 89–90.

economic trends that could have an impact on the meeting. The DMO sales manager should be able to answer most of these questions or find out the answers (see *Professional Meeting Management*, 4th ed., [May 2002]. Chicago (IL), Education Foundation of the Professional Convention Management Association).

DMO Services for Meeting Professionals

The general services that DMOs provide meeting professionals include the following:

- DMOs offer unbiased information about a wide range of destination services and facilities.
- DMOs serve as a vast information database and provide one-stop shopping, thus saving planners time, energy, and money in the development of a meeting.
- DMOs act as a liaison between the planner and the community. For example, DMOs are aware of community events with which a meeting may beneficially coincide (like festivals or sporting events). They can also work with city government to get special permits and to cut through red tape.
- DMOs can help meeting attendees maximize their free time through the creation of pre- and postconference activities, spouse tours, and special evening events.
- DMOs can provide hotel room counts and meeting space statistics as well as a central database of other information on meetings to help planners avoid conflicts and/or space shortages.

The specific services that DMOs can provide for meeting professionals and their meetings are as follows:

- DMOs can help with meeting facility availability—information on the availability of hotels, convention centers, and other meeting facilities.
- DMOs provide a transportation network—shuttle service, ground transportation, and airline information.
- DMOs provide destination information—information on local events, activities, sights and attractions, restaurants, and assistance with tours and event planning.
- DMOs provide housing services—housing reservations for meeting delegates.

- DMOs are a liaison in government and/or community relations— a local resource regarding legislative, regulatory, and municipal issues that may affect a meeting or the meetings industry.
- DMOs can provide access to special venues. Because most DMOs have ties to city departments, personnel have the ear of local government officials. Whether an official letter of welcome from the mayor is needed or the blocking of a road for a street party, a DMO can pave the way.
- DMOs can assist in the creation of collateral material.
- DMOs can assist with on-site logistics and registration.
- DMOs can develop pre- and postconference activities, spouse tours, and special events.
- DMOs can assist with site inspections and familiarization tours as well as site selection.
- DMOs can provide speakers and local educational opportunities.
- DMOs can help secure special venues.
- DMOs can provide help in securing auxiliary services— production companies, catering, security, and so on.

The overall job of a DMO is to sell a destination. A DMO wants clients to be happy, so it is going to do everything it can to match up clients with the perfect setting and services for their meetings.

WHAT INFORMATION DO DMOS HAVE VIS-À-VIS HOTELS?

DMOs keep track of room counts as well as other meetings coming to the area. In this way, they can help planners avoid conflicts with other events. Moreover, as DMOs have firsthand familiarity with the hotels and with meeting space in the area, they can help planners match properties to specific meeting requirements and budgets.

DMAI Services to Member Bureaus and Meeting Professionals

As the world's largest resource for official DMOs, **Destination Marketing Association International** is dedicated to improving the effectiveness of over 1,300 professionals from more than 600 DMOs in more than 25 countries.

DMAI provides members—professionals, industry partners, students, and educators—cutting-edge educational resources, networking opportunities, and marketing benefits available worldwide. Founded in 1914, the association has as its mission to enhance the professionalism, effectiveness, and image of destination management organizations worldwide. In 2005, the association underwent a branding process and changed its name from the International Association of Convention & Visitor Bureaus to the Destination Marketing Association International (DMAI).

As the only association that represents DMOs exclusively, DMAI offers comprehensive year-round education programs, including an annual convention for bureau executives to continue their professional development and to network with peers. The association publishes a weekly electronic newsletter and an online membership directory, and it sponsors DMO-focused research studies through its foundation.

DMAI's DMO members represent all significant travel and tourism–related businesses at the local and regional levels. The association serves as the primary contact point for its destinations for a broad universe of convention, meeting, and tour professionals.

The DMAI actively promotes bureaus worldwide, highlighting the value of using a DMO's services to the media and general public. The DMAI also offers programs and services designed to link DMOs directly with consumers and meeting planners. Direct links to individual DMO Web sites via DMAI's Web site at *http://www.officialtravelguide.com* offers consumers comprehensive, unbiased information on destinations around the world. Meeting planners can access their organization's postconvention history and receive reports via DMAI's **Meeting Information Network (MINT)** database as well as submit RFPs online via the RFP/Bid Proposal Program. The DMAI also sponsors two Destinations Showcase trade shows every year, where bureaus exhibit their destinations to meeting professionals. The DMAI offers research, professional development, and a variety of other member services to DMOs.

In the year 2006, DMAI developed three new membership categories separate from DMO members to include students and educators, state and regional DMO associations, and allied members. Students and educators will find valuable opportunities to learn firsthand how DMOs and tourism boards market their destinations.

Visit *http://www.destinationmarketing.org*, the official Web site of the DMAI. The site contains a listing of DMOs around the world, along with contacts and hyperlinks to more than 600 local CVB Web sites.

Destination Marketing Association International (DMAI) logo.

Destination Marketing Association International (DMAI)

OFFICIALTRAVELGUIDE.COM

OfficialTravelGuide.com is the DMAI's official online travel portal, linking consumers and meeting professionals directly to DMOs and tourist boards. On this site, there is official information for 1,200+ destinations, including information on hotels, conference centers, convention centers, attractions, and activities. Visit http://www. OfficialTravelGuide.com.

MEETING INFORMATION NETWORK (MINT)

The premier convention and meetings database, MINT houses over 34,000 meetings from 17,000 organizations—including associations, corporations, military reunions, sporting events, and government institutions—in a Web-enabled format accessible from any location at any time. It represents a unique collaboration between more than 150 DMOs that voluntarily report detailed meeting history information on the events held in their cities. This online database provides critical marketing and sales direction to thousands of DMOs, hotels, and other convention industry suppliers. Meeting professionals will find that accurate information in MINT regarding their meetings will help in the negotiation process. The meeting information is entered into MINT by participating DMOs—information they received from firsthand sources, including hotels, convention centers, and meeting professionals. This is one reason why it is important for planners to participate in postconvention meetings.

Once meetings are recorded in the MINT database, meeting professionals can encourage suppliers and other interested parties to request a copy of the information in their postconvention reports (PCRs). A PCR serves as an organization's meeting "credit report" to the industry.

Meeting Information Network

Meeting Information Network (MINT) logo.
Destination Marketing Association International (DMAI)

Making sure of the accuracy will reduce the number of unwanted sales calls a meeting planner receives and will make available more qualified information for the next round of negotiations—whether it is with a hotel or a DMO. To get a copy of an organization's history report, e-mail mint@DMAI.org or visit MINT at http://MINT.IACVB.org.

ONLINE RFP

A meeting professional can visit the **DMAI online RFP** at http://www.destinationmarketing.org and select the cities he or she is interested in and either fill out the RFP form provided or attach an already prepared RFP.

With the RFP system of DMAI, meeting professionals can send their meeting specifications to DMOs around the world. Visit http://www.destinationmarketing.org to send a RFP or to seek professional assistance in planning a meeting.

DESTINATIONS SHOWCASE

Destinations Showcase is a fast-paced and productive one-day exhibition and conference, owned by the DMAI, where qualified **meeting professionals** attend valuable **education sessions,** network with industry leaders and peers, and explore a full range of destinations from throughout the world. *It is where meetings business gets done.*

Exhibitors are exclusively from DMOs and their exhibit facilities. Qualified meeting, exposition, event, and convention planning (MEEC) professionals have the opportunity to meet face-to-face with professional staff representing destinations from around the world. A low planner-to-exhibitor ratio facilitates a meeting specifically for the

Destinations Showcase logo.
Destination Marketing Association International (DMAI)

purpose of site review and selection. Planners are required to attend "with RFP in hand" and are encouraged to plan ahead with a pre-event exhibitor list.

Shows are held annually in Washington, DC, and Chicago. Full registration is complimentary, and attendance is restricted to qualified meeting professionals only. Also there are opportunities to earn credit toward the Certified Meeting Planner (CMP) certification at Destinations Showcase! For more information, visit http://www.destinationsshowcase.com.

PROFESSIONAL DEVELOPMENT OFFERINGS

The DMAI provides professional development to DMOs and their employees. It offers the following meeting, convention, training, and certification opportunities to DMO professionals:

- Annual Convention
- Destination Management and Marketing Institute (DMMI)
- CEO Forum
- Global Executive Forum

- COO/CFO Forum
- Sales Academy (Parts I & II and Online)
- Shirtsleeve Sessions

CERTIFIED DESTINATION MANAGEMENT EXECUTIVE (CDME) PROGRAM

The DMAI has a certification program that is the equivalent of the CMP designation in the meetings professional community. Recognized by the DMO industry as its highest educational achievement, the CDME program is delivered under the auspices of the World Tourism Management Centre (WTMC) at the University of Calgary in collaboration with Purdue University and the DMAI. The CDME program is an advanced educational program for veteran and career-minded DMO executives who are looking for senior-level professional development courses. The main goal of the CDME program is to prepare senior executives and managers of destination management organizations for increasing change and competition.

The focus of the program is on vision, leadership, productivity, and implementation of business strategies. Demonstrating the value of a destination team and improving personal performance through effective organizational and industry leadership are the outcomes.

PDM CERTIFICATE PROGRAM

Although the professional destination management PDM certificate is not a designation like the certified destination management executive (CDME), it is recognized throughout the industry as a highly valuable skills package needed for the destination management career journey. DMO professionals who participate in the PDM Certificate Program acquire the knowledge and skills necessary to be more effective and successful destination management professionals.

DESTINATION MARKETING ACCREDITATION PROGRAM (DMAP)

In fall 2006, DMAI launched the Destination Marketing Accreditation Program (DMAP), starting initially with a beta test followed by a full program rollout. Currently utilized by the U.S. Chamber of Commerce, the health care industry, and institutions of higher education, accreditation programs are becoming increasingly popular with organizations that wish to define standards of performance for their member constituents and measure their compliance. DMAI research shows that 93% of DMO executives say their organization would seek accreditation if an acceptable program was developed by the association. DMAP aims to provide a good method to assure staff, volunteer leadership, and external stakeholders that their destination marketing organization is following proper practices and performing at an acceptable level for the industry. "This new accreditation program will provide a platform for official destination marketing organizations to assure their stakeholders that they have achieved the highest accepted standards," remarked DMAI President and CEO Michael D. Gehrisch.

INDUSTRY INFORMATION AND RESEARCH

Under the auspices of the DMAI Foundation, destination management professionals have access to insightful, comprehensive, and industry-specific information that they can use to enhance the effectiveness of their bureau's day-to-day operations and in their business planning. The DMAI offers a wealth of research and resources that provide statistical data and information essential for calculating economic impact, budgeting and strategic planning, marketing and promotion, and education of stakeholders. Below are some of the DMAI Foundation's studies:

> *DMO Compensation and Benefits Survey.* This report, published biannually, provides a baseline for more than 45 job position compensation levels as well as for benefits packages offered to DMO employees in the United States and Canada.

> *DMO Organizational and Financial Profile.* This survey, the most comprehensive of its type for DMOs, provides standards for a variety of operations while also allowing DMOs to compare their operations with their peers. Also published every two years, the report includes information on DMO funding sources, available facilities, tax rates, budgets, staff structure, expense categories, and reserves.

> *Convention Spending Research Program.* Results of this program assist users in estimating the value of meetings, conventions, and trade shows coming to a destination.

DMAI RESOURCE CENTER

As a constantly changing global industry resource, this online center houses valuable information for CVB professionals. With more than 30 categories, the center offers a wealth of resources, such as brand information, sample bureau operations documents, bureau research statistics, helpful links to calendars of industry events, and glossaries

A New Look & Feel

The Greater Minneapolis Conventions & Visitors Association (GMCVA) changed its name to Meet Minneapolis™, Official Convention & Visitors Association and adopted a new logo. "With this name, we strive to create an exciting, differentiating position for the organization that clearly communicates who we are and what we want our customers to do—meet Minneapolis," said Greg Ortale, president and CEO of Meet Minneapolis. The new name and positioning aim to better communicate what the destination does for visitors. "We wanted the name to be inspirational; we didn't want to try to be something we're not," said Ortale. "The name is simple, smart, and to the point. That's Minneapolis."

of industry terms. The Resource Center also strives to serve as a referral source of other industry-related information. Every year other potential surveys are considered as the industry changes and staff, members, committee members, and current events dictate new areas that are worthy of research reports.

DMAI FOUNDATION

The DMAI Foundation was created in 1993 to enhance and complement the DMAI and the destination management profession through research, education, vision, and development of resources and partnerships for those efforts.

The foundation is classified as a charitable organization under Section 501(c)(3) of the Internal Revenue Service Code; therefore, donations to the foundation are tax deductible as charitable contributions. A board of trustees, made up of members of the DMAI and representatives from related industry organizations, runs the foundation.

Summary

DMOs are an integral part of the meetings and convention industry. For over 100 years, DMOs have been working diligently to bring meetings and conventions to their destinations and to service these meetings with a variety of free services. Over the years, DMOs have gone from being destination marketers to destination managers, becoming involved in every aspect of their destinations and therefore enriching the experience for meeting attendees and visitors.

The DMAI is the professional association for DMO employees, and it has been providing a wealth of member services to DMOs since 1914.

Key Words and Terms

For definitions, see the Glossary or go to http://glossary.convention industry.org.

Destination Marketing and
    Management Organization
    (DMMO)

Destination Marketing
    Association International
    (DMAI)

Destination marketing
    organization (DMO)

Destinations Showcase

DMAI online RFP

Education session

Meeting professional

Meetings Information Network
    (MINT)

OfficialTravelGuide.com

Review and Discussion Questions

1. Define the role and function of a destination marketing organization.
2. Name the different ways that DMOs can be funded.
3. Name two things that a DMO does for meetings professionals.
4. Name two things that the DMAI does for meetings professionals.
5. What can the DMAI do for DMOs?

References

Web Sites

http://www.destinationmarketing.org (formerly http://www.iacvb.org)
http://www.officialtravelguide.com
http://mint.iacvb.org

http://www.destinationsshowcase.com

http://www.lvcva.com/index.jsp

http://www.choosechicago.com

http://www.tourismvancouver.com/visitors/

http://www.londontouristboard.com/choose_site/?OriginalURL5/

http://www.hkta.org/eng/worldwide/awar/index.jht*ml*

Organization

Destination Marketing Association International (DMAI)

2025 M Street, NW, Suite 500

Washington, DC 20036

Phone: +1-202-296-7888

Fax: +1-202-296-7889

E-mail: info@dmaiDMAI.org

Web address: http://www.destinationmarketing.org

About the Chapter Contributor

Elaine Rosquist, CMP, is the executive vice president for the DMAI. She is responsible for the day-to-day activities of the association.

DMAI Collateral Material Contributors: Kristen Clemens, Vice President of Marketing and Communications, DMAI; Rhonda Kauffman, Manager of Marketing and Communications, DMAI; and Laura Powell, Laura Powell Productions.

CHAPTER 4

Meeting and Convention Venues

An Examination of the Facilities Used by Meeting Planners, Focusing on How Their Financial Structure Dictates Their Relationships with Planner Clients

Cruise ships are sometimes used for meetings and conventions.
Photo by George G. Fenich, Ph.D.

Chapter Objectives ─────────────────────────────

The chapter provides the reader with an understanding of the following:

- Importance of the physical attributes of a meeting venue in relation to its use for an event
- Ways the venue's financial structure impacts the ability to negotiate for a meeting
- Variations in service levels and service availability in different facilities
- Potential hazards often overlooked by novice planners
- Necessary questions to ask about a facility in order to ensure the success of a meeting

Chapter Outline ─────────────────────────────

Introduction

Hotels

Convention Centers

Conference Centers

Retreat Facilities

Cruise Ships

Specific Use Facilities

Colleges and Universities

Unusual Venues

Common Issues

    Obstacles

    Power

    Rigging

    Floors

    Access

Introduction

Meeting planners work in a variety of facilities. These facilities range in size from hotel suites that hold a handful of people to major convention centers and outdoor festival sites that hold tens of thousands. Anyplace where two or more people gather is a meeting site. Whether it is a multimillion-square-foot convention center or a street corner under a light pole, people will find a place to gather. The meeting planner's job is to match the meeting and the venue. Thus, the planner must determine two things about the group: Who are they, and why are they here? Most events and meetings are appropriate only for a limited range of facilities. A national political convention would not work on a street corner, nor would a board of

A large tent event.
Used by permission of Paradise Light & Sound, Orlando, Florida

directors' meeting work in an outdoor stadium. For an event to succeed, the characteristics of the event must be properly matched to
the facility in which it is held. Whether the venue is the conference
room at the end of a suite of offices or the flight deck of an active
aircraft carrier, the goal of the meeting must fit with the choice of
venue for the meeting to work.

Thus, the planner must be sure to appropriately research the group
and the facilities that may fit the group's needs, understand the needs
and expectations of the group, communicate the benefits offered by a
facility that meets the needs of the group, and verify the arrangements
between the group and the venue. In order to properly exploit the
tremendous range of facilities, a meeting planner must be familiar with
both the physical characteristics of the facility and its financial structure. The combined impact of these two factors determines a meeting
planner's relationship with the facility management and each party's
relative negotiating position. Many other features of a facility are relevant to the success or failure of any meeting, but an understanding of
the significance of the facility's physical form and its financial structure is vital for a meeting planner to effectively use the facility to support the meeting.

The vast majority of meetings take place in conference rooms or
offices on the meeting participants' property. Typically, one room in

a suite of offices is designated as a conference room, and a handful of colleagues gather to address some current issue. Whether scheduled or impromptu, these meetings rarely involve a meeting planner. However, as these meetings become larger and involve more people, the person who has had the position of scheduling these on-property meetings frequently finds himself or herself planning meetings that take place off the property.

Hotels

The second most common place for a meeting is a **hotel.** Hotels and their meeting spaces vary widely in size and quality, but virtually all hotels with any meeting space have at least one small **boardroom.** These boardrooms typically seat fewer than a dozen people, and the more elegant of them have large tables and furniture that would be appropriate in the conference rooms of any major corporation. At the other end of the scale, hotel ballrooms tend to top out at around 60,000 square feet. **Break-out rooms** vary from a little larger than boardrooms up to about half the size of a main ballroom. The whole facility, including break-out rooms, will likely not exceed 100,000 square feet of total meeting space, although a few are larger. In the past few years, there has been a surge in expansion of hotel meeting space. Hotels with more than 100,000 square feet of meeting space are no longer rare; many privately funded hotels are encroaching on the convention venue domain previously dominated by government-funded facilities.

Hotels generally provide a variety of meeting spaces. They typically include a large carpeted ballroom with some sort of themed décor. These ballrooms are generally planned as part of the initial construction of the facility and are typically divisible by the use of movable walls. A common floor plan provides larger divisions flanked by smaller ones accessible from the side corridors. It is not uncommon for the ceiling to be lower in the smaller divisions than in the larger ones. This is not always obvious from printed floor plans. Break-out rooms tend to be decorated and equipped like smaller versions of the ballrooms and serve identical functions for smaller numbers of people.

Some hotels have been so successful at marketing their meeting space that they have found the need to add space. Frequently, they will level out a parking lot to facilitate the regular use of tents. Some space-intensive events can then be moved to the tents. The most common type of event moved to a tent is a meal function or themed party. This space allows the hotel to maintain higher room occupancy levels by reducing the gap in the **shoulders** between meetings. Once the tent ceases to be a viable option, due to either weather or zoning issues, many hotels build spaces specifically designed for exhibits. These **exhibit halls** have a rough, unfinished look to them and tend to be designed more for utility than beauty. These utilitarian facilities are less expensive to maintain, and due to their reduced cost structure, they can be more profitable than the glamorous ballrooms.

In contrast to the stark exhibit facilities, many hotels have beautiful outdoor venues to support social and networking functions. Pools, patios, atriums, and gardens can all be used as meeting locations. When first inspecting a meeting space, a planner should observe all of the physical attributes of the space because the facility's "hardware" has a significant impact on the delegates' comfort and their involvement in the proceedings.

Hotels tend to be owned by major hotel companies or are franchised by a major hotel company to a local owner who manages the facility in accordance with corporate guidelines. Almost all hotels supporting meeting space are part of a larger corporate entity, which is likely to be publicly traded or is a subsidiary of an entity that is publicly traded (the Rosen Hotels in Orlando and the Atlantis in the Bahamas are notable exceptions). Hotels are rarely owned by individuals and almost never owned by local governments, although some are owned by closely held corporations. While a closely held corporation is not likely to have its stock traded on Wall Street, it is just as susceptible to market variations as the publicly traded corporations are. Hotels are intended to be businesses and not charities—their mission in life is to generate profit for the parent company.

Meetings are rarely a hotel's primary business. The primary business of almost all hotels is the sale of sleeping room nights. The meeting space in a hotel business is often a **loss leader,** whose primary purpose is to fill what would otherwise be empty sleeping rooms. This single financial fact of life overshadows all other aspects of any negotiations between a meeting planner and a hotel. There are some hotels that derive significant revenue from their extensive meeting spaces, but these revenues are (significant) ancillary income and are intended to drive their primary business, which remains sleeping room nights. While hotels derive the majority of their revenue from the rooms, many also derive significant income from the restaurants and bars

The Walt Disney World Dolphin Hotel is designed for meetings and conventions.
Used by permission of Paradise Light & Sound, Orlando, Florida

frequented by convention attendees. A smaller percentage of the revenue is derived from the **concessionaires** at the pools, beach, or spa. The dynamic changes somewhat when the hotel is associated with a casino or theme park: Casinos can be moneymaking machines and can have a significant impact on a planner's ability to negotiate; the hotels associated with theme parks have a similar dynamic and are discussed later in this chapter.

Conventional wisdom states that meeting planners do not pay for meeting space in hotels. However, meeting space costs the hotels money—it costs them in the interest they pay on the investment capital they needed to build the hotel, and it costs them in the staff and materials to clean, maintain, and operate the meeting rooms. These costs must be funded from somewhere. The way the costs of the meeting space are covered is to require that a meeting commit to using a minimum number of sleeping rooms for a minimum number of nights. The hotel's goal is to fill the rooms that would not be filled by its regular customers. The closer the hotel gets to 100% occupancy, the happier the stockholders will be.

By linking sleeping room use with meeting space availability, hoteliers found they could induce meeting planners to use their facilities because the meeting space was free, at least to them. Unfortunately, after the system of financially linking sleeping rooms to meeting space became popular, many hotels discovered that some planners were consistently off in their projections, so the hotels were committing large amounts of meeting space to meetings that used far fewer sleeping rooms than the planner had led them to expect. As an incentive for planners to project more accurately and reduce the hotel's losses from inaccurate projections, the hotels introduced **attrition penalties.** These penalties, which can be substantial, become relevant when a meeting uses less than the contracted number of sleeping room nights. (See chapter 12, "Legal Issues in the MEEC Industry," for more discussion of attrition penalties.)

Given the popularity of Internet travel booking sites, many planners are finding that their delegates are getting cheaper rates at the same hotels as they (as planners) are by not booking inside the room block. These rooms often wind up not being counted as related to the meeting, so a planner can wind up paying attrition penalties even if the hotel is sold out due to the number of delegates at that convention. There are clauses that can be added to the contract that address this issue, but they should be discussed with an attorney familiar with these issues. The planner's ultimate goal in this process is to get credit for every room night the hotel sells that it would not have sold if the meeting were held somewhere else. This one issue may be the toughest part of any hotel negotiation.

Other than sleeping rooms, the next most significant source of revenue for most hotels is food and beverage. The hotel's restaurants and bars are generally designed to handle the hotel's regular traffic, which is likely a mix of business travelers and tourists. If the hotel has a nightclub, the probability is that its intended clientele is not the meeting delegates but rather locals or vacationers. The size and staffing levels of these outlets are rarely determined by the needs of the meeting attendees; banquet catering is intended to fill that need. The scope and quality of hotels' banquet departments vary as much as the quality of the sleeping rooms. In a reaction to the reluctance of some meeting planners to agree to elevated sleeping room rates in order to guarantee meeting space, some hotels have linked banquet revenue with meeting space; thus, a meeting planner who meets a

The décor for a fancy dinner.
Used by permission of Paradise Light & Sound, Orlando, Florida

threshold of spending in the catering department gets a break in the meeting room cost.

One linkage that planners should be wary of is the requirement that they use the in-house audiovisual department or pay a fee for the privilege of not using them. This linkage often does not get discussed early enough in the negotiating process that it can be dealt with in a reasonable manner.

Some events do not involve sleeping rooms, and many hotels are reluctant to deal with them; however, the demand for venues to hold the so-called **local event** is great enough that hotels do market to them. In order for the planner of a local social event to get "free" meeting space, he or she would have to guarantee a minimum amount of catering revenue. Since local events do not involve sleeping rooms, they are generally a hotel's last attempt to derive some revenue out of a vacant meeting room. What revenue it derives comes from food service and the commissions paid by other support vendors for the privilege of working in the hotel. These other vendors would include the disc jockey, the florist, the limo service, and the decorator. If lighting or sound beyond the disc jockey's systems were needed, the in-house audiovisual company would pay a commission to the hotel. All of these revenue streams are calculated in the decision to accept a piece of social business once all other higher-revenue opportunities have been exhausted. Since a planner of a local event is just as likely to fall short of his or her projections as a planner of an event involving sleeping rooms, attrition on catering revenue projections is becoming more common for all the same reasons that attrition penalties started becoming attached to sleeping room projections.

Hotels derive revenue from a variety of other non–meeting services as well. The golf courses, spas, equestrian centers, and beaches all provide revenue to the hotel. Hotels often contract with exclusive vendors to provide services within the hotel. Audiovisual companies, destination management companies (DMCs), service contractors, musicians, disc jockeys, florists, and bus companies can all be contracted to the hotel as exclusive vendors of their specialized services, and commissions paid to the hotel can be as high as 40%. Some hotels charge attrition penalties on those services as well. The hotel's theory is that the hotel and the vendor have made an investment in the facility and equipment for the meeting planner's benefit. Should the planner not elect to use these services, the services should be paid for anyway because they were available. It is not always safe to assume that the hotel's exclusive vendor has that honor because it is the most qualified; the negotiated size of the projected commission may be the determining factor.

Hotels do pay some commissions, although the discussion to this point has focused on the commissions paid to the hotels. Travel agents and DMCs as well as site selection companies can be paid commission for the business they bring to the hotel. One of the questions a planner must ask of every travel professional who recommends a facility is what his or her financial connection is to that facility. There is an Internet-based discussion group for meeting planners sponsored by the Meetings Industry Mall Web site (MIMList) currently operated by the company VNU, in which the issue of commissions paid by hotels is frequently a hot topic. A planner would be well advised to ask why a specific site is being recommended.

Hotels attached to theme parks are a special case. It is not uncommon for a theme park–based hotel to include an estimate of how much money the delegates or their families will spend in the attached entertainment facilities when they decide whether or not to take a particular piece of business. Clauses relating the number of theme park passes purchased to the availability of meeting room space can appear in some contracts at these hotels. Meetings planned with sufficient free time to allow the delegates to avail themselves of the golf course or casino may have an easier time contracting their desired meeting space.

If the hotel is attached to a casino, it is possible for the hotel to derive more revenue from the casino than it does from the sleeping rooms. The prices charged for the sleeping rooms are fixed in advance of the guests' arrival, but the potential revenue derived from the casino is limited only by the availability of credit on the guests' accounts. Meetings then can become a means to bring guests to the casino where they potentially spend more money gambling than they will on other activities.

Seasonality and fluctuating occupancy levels can have a significant impact on the cost of using a facility. A hotel with a severe seasonal variation can have an out-of-season price that is as little as half its in-season price. By paying attention to a facility's seasonal occupancy patterns, meeting planners can find some true bargains. A common misconception among meeting delegates is that the incredibly cheap rate they pay to use an exclusive resort is due to their planner's negotiating prowess when it is more likely that the great rate is based on the planner's choice of a venue with extreme seasonal variations.

Planners negotiating with hotels need to consider the entire financial package their business will bring to the facility. The more closely aligned the meeting's financial structure is to the needs of the hotel, the better the deal is that the planner can get for his or her meeting. The entire financial package includes not just the revenue from the meeting itself but also the revenue from the sleeping rooms, the restaurants, the bars, and the exclusive vendors.

When negotiating with any convention facility, planners are not only negotiating on the basis of what they will use but on the basis of what is available whether they use it or not. The availability of specific **amenities** often drives the delegates' expectations of the facility, so it is important that planners match the level of their delegates' expectations with the level of service provided by the hotel at a cost the delegates feel is reasonable. Convention services managers (CSMs) coordinate the activities of various departments in larger hotels to accommodate meetings, conventions, and special events. They meet with representatives of groups or organizations to plan the number of rooms to reserve, the desired configuration of the meeting space, and the banquet services. During the meeting or event, they resolve unexpected problems and monitor activities to ensure that hotel operations conform to the expectations of the group. (For more information, go to www.bls.gov.)

Thus, the meetings, expositions, events, and conventions (MEEC) planner must research, understand, communicate, and verify that the venue meets the needs of the group.

Hotel Web Sites

Gaylord Hotels including Opryland	http://www.gaylordhotels.com
Marriott Hotels	http://marriott.com/property/propertypage/NYCMQ
Mandalay Bay Hotel in Las Vegas	http://www.mandalaybay.com
The Swan and Dolphin hotels at Disneyworld	http://www.swandolphin.com

Convention Centers

Conventional wisdom has it that convention centers are huge. Many are—and the biggest are getting even bigger. **Convention centers** are designed to handle larger events than could be supported in a hotel. Several convention centers feature over a million square feet of meeting space, and their size is both their strength and their weakness. They are meeting facilities with no sleeping rooms. Some are little more than large bare buildings with exposed roof beams; others are mammoth architectural marvels involving magnificent feats of engineering and awe-inspiring vistas.

Compared to hotels, convention centers are more likely to devote the majority of their space to exhibit halls and utilitarian spaces than to plush ballrooms. Hotel lobbies are designed to be comfortable and inviting, but convention center lobbies are designed to facilitate the uninterrupted flow of several thousand delegates who are late for their meetings. This difference in design philosophy is evident in every phase of a convention center's operation. Just as hotels have a variety of space sizes, convention centers also have a variety of spaces. In the typical hotel, the ballrooms are the largest meeting spaces, followed by the exhibit spaces. In a convention center, the exhibit halls tend to be the largest spaces, followed by the carpeted ballrooms. It would not be unusual for the **prefunction spaces** in a

The Las Vegas Convention Center contains over 1 million square feet of space.
Photo by George G. Fenich, Ph.D.

convention center to be larger than the break-out rooms attached to them, unlike a typical hotel where the prefunction spaces tend to be smaller.

Convention centers are more likely to have rooms with built-in stages than hotels are. They are also more likely than hotels to have "congress-style" permanent classrooms, although such rooms would not be as uncommon at conference centers. If we can compare the facilities on the basis of the philosophy of their design, it would appear that hotels are designed by psychologists, while convention centers are designed by industrial engineers. Engineering considerations are relevant in both types of facilities, but the impact of the difference in scale drives much of the difference between how hotels and convention centers operate.

Convention centers are often described as utilitarian and occasionally "cold" when compared to hotels. Convention centers generally do not have spas or swimming pools, exercise rooms, or saunas; they do not have restaurants that stay open when the center is vacant;

and they do not have karaoke bars. Unlike a hotel that is open around the clock, convention centers can (and do) lock the doors at night; the staff goes home when nothing is scheduled. Whereas in a hotel someone is on duty at all times, in a convention center if someone is required to be available at odd hours, that person must be scheduled in advance. This rigidity of structure and scheduling means that the planner who uses a convention center may need to plan in more detail than the planner who holds the same meeting in a hotel.

Unlike the hotel, which is most likely part of a major corporation, most convention centers are owned by government entities. Professional management is frequently contracted to a private company that specializes in managing such facilities (SMG, Volume Services, and Global Spectrum are three such companies). Many convention centers are actively supported by the local convention and visitor bureau (CVB). As with everything that concerns government, the management of this type of facility is ultimately responsible to the taxpayers.

This management structure creates an environment in which the convention center can take a very long view but at the same time must think very short term. Generally, the intent of the government that built the building is that the facility be an economic driver for the whole community; therefore, the facility can take events that benefit the community as a whole, with less concern for driving the demand for sleeping room nights in the surrounding hotels. This is part of the reason why convention centers (unlike hotels) will take events such as local consumer shows that generate no sleeping room nights. While the convention center may be funded in part by some kind of hotel sleeping room tax, it is generally not required to maintain a specific ratio between meeting space and sleeping rooms.

One controversial issue among convention center managers is whether the public-sector or the private-sector companies can do a better job of managing these facilities. There are strongly held opinions on both sides of the issue. Even with all the discussion, one thing is still true: The quality of a planner's event is as dependent on the planner's relationship with the individuals running the facility as it is with how well the event is planned. Especially in a convention center, the more thorough the planning is, the more successful the event.

How does a convention center make money? After all, the taxpayers will not support a big building forever if it makes no money. Convention centers charge for everything they provide on a pay-per-use basis. Every square foot of the building has a price attached to it. Room rental, by the square foot per day, is the center's biggest single

As the old actor said in "The Fantasticks," "See it in lights."
Used by permission of Paradise Light & Sound, Orlando, Florida

revenue source, and every chair, every table, and every service provided by the convention center has a price. The center makes money
on the catering and the concessions. In a hotel, much of the real cost
of holding the meeting is hidden in the sleeping room price; in the convention center, every cost is specifically itemized. This "nickel and
dime" approach is the convention center's way of charging for services
used and not charging for what is not needed.

One overlooked fact that sets convention centers apart from many
other types of facilities concerns the portion of their budget spent on
energy. It is not unusual for a convention center to spend more money
on utilities than it does on its full-time staff. This is not a reflection of
the staffing levels but rather an indication of how expensive it is to
keep a large facility properly climate controlled. Hotels have significant energy bills as well, but unlike a convention center, they are not
trying to control the climate in huge spaces with high ceilings and massive doors that stay open all day.

Like a hotel, a convention center has relationships with vendors
for services it does not provide internally. Such services might include
parking, buses, audiovisual equipment, power, telecommunications,
and florists.

In a convention center, catering is more likely to be contracted to an outside vendor than in a hotel. Each of these vendors pays a commission to the center. This commission may not be in cash but may be in the form of equipment owned by the vendor installed in the building. In many buildings, for example, the facility does not own the soft drink vending equipment; the soft drink company with the exclusive rights in the facility owns and services the equipment in return for a specified level of product sales. Another debate in the convention center industry has to do with whether a facility should have "exclusive" or "preferred" vendors. It is no longer safe to assume that any vendor suggested by a facility is either exclusive or preferred unless the vendor is identified as such. Traditionally, catering was the only exclusive service, but in some facilities power, rigging, audiovisual equipment, security, and telecommunications can be exclusive vendors to the facility. Some of these relationships are the result of governmental regulations, and others are an attempt to avoid liability lawsuits. In contrast, in some convention centers even the catering can be outsourced to vendors other than the ones who have the relationship with the facility. The relationships between the vendors and the facility are fluid and changing, so no planner should ever assume the nature of the relationships without asking specifically.

It is also not safe to assume that an exclusive vendor is somehow more or less competent than an outside vendor. Many convention industry salespeople have tried to paint their competition into a corner with broad-brush statements that may or may not be true. Determining the competence of the facility's preferred or exclusive vendors is one of the toughest jobs a planner must face, and while there are some guidelines, there are no absolutes. Unfortunately, the success or failure of any given meeting often depends on vendors with whom a planner has no experience.

Given the political climate in which most convention centers operate, combined with the size and scope of the events they support, they tend to be bureaucratic and inflexible. Negotiations can take longer than in a hotel, but a convention center is more likely to publish all its rate information either in print or on a Web site than is any other type of meeting facility. It is possible to go through many convention centers' documentation and know before talking to a salesperson what that event is likely to cost. This is difficult (if not impossible) to do in many other types of facilities. With all this information readily available, it becomes the planner's responsibility to assess the information, not the facility's responsibility to guide a novice planner through the process.

Due to convention centers' large size, their bureaucratic nature, the complexity of the decisions associated with them, and their potential impact on the events planned, novice planners should not attempt to bring a large event to a convention center without first working smaller events in other venues. There are better places to start in the meeting planning business. (One of the most planner-friendly types of venues is the conference center, discussed below.)

Thus, the MEEC planner must research, understand, communicate, and verify that the venue meets the needs of the group.

Convention Center Web Sites

Jacob Javits Convention Center in New York City	http://www.javitscenter.com
McCormick Place Convention Center in Chicago	http://www.mccormickplace.com
Moscone Convention Center in San Francisco	http://www.moscone.com/site/do/index
David Lawrence Convention Center in Pittsburgh	http://www.pittsburghcc.com/html/index.htm

Facility Management Company Web Sites

Global Spectrum	http://www.global-spectrum.com
SMG	http://www.smgworld.com

Conference Centers

Much of the thrust of the education for meeting planners has focused on the larger meeting, but many of the most critical meetings determining the future health of an organization involve fewer than twenty-five people. These meetings are often attended by people who understand the importance of the decisions they will make to the careers and livelihoods of the employees of entire corporations. For example, one such meeting might involve the review of pharmaceutical research. The people in the meeting will decide whether to continue to fund development of a potential new drug or abandon it; they will decide which drugs to prepare for regulatory review and which to send back for more tests. The success of these meetings is critical to the survival of the companies that hold them. Hotel boardrooms and conference centers are the ideal venues for such meetings.

For the most part, **conference centers** are small well-appointed facilities specifically designed to enhance classroom-style learning. The Convention Industry Council (CIC) defines a conference center as a facility that provides a dedicated environment for events, especially small events. The International Association of Conference Centers (IACC) has developed a specific set of guidelines as to what constitutes a conference center as opposed to other types of meeting facilities. Adherence to these guidelines essentially guarantees the planner that the facility is well managed and well suited for intense small-group learning situations. Several major corporations, including Aramark, Dolce, Hilton, Marriott, and Sodexho, run conference centers; several smaller companies are also involved and include Conference Center Concepts and the Creative Dining Group.

A planner contemplating using an IACC conference center would be well advised to visit the IACC Web site and ensure that the scope and expectations of the meeting make it appropriate for a conference center in advance of meeting with the facility's salespeople. Conference centers can be either resident or nonresident—the biggest difference between the two is that resident facilities have sleeping rooms and nonresident facilities do not. While it is easy to draw the comparison between hotels and resident conference centers, the comparison would likely be misleading. One of the major differences concerns the conference centers' focus on teaching and learning instead of on elegant parties. This tends to translate into better furniture and a greater tendency toward permanently installed work surfaces as well as permanently installed projection and audio systems.

Many conference centers, whether resident or nonresident, employ a pricing strategy called the **complete meeting package,** which essentially means that whatever the facility owns, the planner may use at no additional charge. This puts the facility's entire inventory of easels, projectors, microphones, and sound systems at the planner's immediate disposal. For the planner, this is a flexible way to work in that he or she is freed from the task of getting scheduled audiovisual companies to provide their equipment requirements in advance.

Some conference centers are in remote locations. Some of the nonresident centers are part of large corporate office complexes and are offered to the public only when the parent company is not using the facility. The IACC guidelines have a distinctly "corporate" feel to them. The guidelines strictly control the inside of the meeting rooms. The impact in variations of location would be felt less inside the classroom than it would in the supplemental activities the delegates would partake of when not in meetings. Suburban and rural conference centers routinely feature high-quality golf courses, while the more urban centers would link to cultural and sporting activities located in the city centers. Some of the more rural facilities offer horseback riding or outdoor activities such as hiking or skiing in season.

When choosing a conference center, a planner should review not only the facilities offered by the center but the expectations of the delegates attending the event. A nonresident facility might be better if all the delegates are local, and a rural facility might be better if the delegates have a tendency to slip away at midday when they should be in classes. A review of the event's history is important in determining if a conference center will work for the event.

Like hotels, conference centers are generally owned by corporations, although some are closely held family businesses. They are not government entities; therefore, they operate more like hotels than convention centers, except that their meeting spaces are focused almost exclusively on classroom-style education. Conference centers can also have seasonal patterns (much like hotels). For example, a conference center located in the midst of several ski slopes will be much less expensive in the summer than it will be in the winter, and a conference center located in an urban area may be the same price year-round. If the event dates are flexible, moving a date a week or a month could yield significant savings.

Conference centers using the complete meeting package tend to be entirely self-contained. If outside vendors are used, they will likely be transparent to the planner. By using the complete meeting package concept, the facility ties all its revenue into a single bundle of services, so the only variable is the number of delegates who actually show up as opposed to those who register.

Attrition penalties take on a new meaning in a conference center. It is not unusual for a conference center to charge a planner a fixed price for up to a certain number of delegates. If some of the delegates do not come to the event, the planner is still responsible for the full amount of the contract. This fee is not based on the ability of the facility to resell the rooms but on 100% of the negotiated facility fee regardless how much of the facility is used. Although the planner's tasks on site are less intense than would be the case in a convention center, the planner's ability to predict room night use is very critical.

Planners deciding whether to use the complete meeting package or buy their own equipment need to look beyond the simple cost of the projector or microphone and evaluate the proper use of their time. Is their time well spent hauling a large plastic case through airport security, or is it better spent making sure the coffee is refreshed and lunch is ready on time? Many planners see their jobs in terms of cost containment. While that is surely part of the job, it would seem that helping guarantee the success of the meeting is the more appropriate goal. Sometimes a penny saved is not a penny earned—sometimes it is a pound lost in a missed opportunity. The planner's job is to know the difference.

Thus, the MEEC planner must research, understand, communicate, and verify that the venue meets the needs of the group.

Conference Center Company Web Sites

Aramark	http://www.aramarkharrisonlodging.com
Hilton	http://www.hiltondirect.com
Marriot	http://marriott.com/meeting/default.mi
Dolce	http://www.dolce.com

Retreat Facilities

Retreat facilities can be viewed as a special group, much like rural conference centers. They are more likely to be owned by a family or closely held corporation than the other facilities and to focus on a smaller portion of the conference center market. Not-for-profit entities, charitable organizations, and religious groups own many of the retreat facilities. Several evangelical organizations run retreat facilities as part of their internal training programs, and other groups can use these facilities when the parent organizations are not using them. In addition to the classroom learning typical of a conference center, retreat facilities specialize in some unique extracurricular learning opportunities: Some retreat facilities are at dude ranches, some are clusters of cabins in the woods where nature is part of the lesson plan, and others are attached to religious facilities where a spiritual message is incorporated into the program. Many planners, out of fear that their delegates may not appreciate the opportunities presented by the unique environment, can unjustly overlook retreat facilities.

These unique meeting environments can be used as a stimulus to energize a moribund group of delegates. The challenge of using these facilities derives from one of their greatest strengths—their relative isolation. Transportation and logistical issues become magnified due to the distance from airports and highways. These impediments can be overcome, and the result can be well worth the effort.

Thus, the MEEC planner must research, understand, communicate, and verify that the venue meets the needs of the group.

The following are Web sites containing information on multiple retreat facilities and sharing a common site.

http://www.allaboutretreats.com

http://www.retreatfinder.com

Cruise Ships

In a sense, cruise ships are floating hybrids of hotels, conference centers, and full-service resorts. To leave it there, however, would be to do them a disservice. Cruise ships seem underrated as meeting venues, but with proper planning, they can provide a satisfying meeting experience.

The quality of the planning for a cruise event has a greater impact on the success of the meeting than it does with any other type of venue. A ship moves by its own schedule, which could have more to do with the tides than it does the ability of a group of guests to be at the dock on time. Failure to properly accommodate the ship's schedule into the transportation plan can have disastrous results. Unlike a building, once the ship leaves port, latecomers are left behind.

Cruise ships have long been considered ideal venues for incentive trips. There are few options available to a planner that can provide as romantic an ambiance as a cruise ship; however, romantically inclined couples often have children attached. Many of the cruise lines have well-developed children's programs—in fact, the children's programs on many of the ships are better developed than in many major resorts. As for the singles, the larger ships have options for them as well.

The size and availability of meeting rooms vary widely among the different ships. Meeting planners should not look only at the spaces on the ship identified as "meeting facilities" to the exclusion of other spaces. Many of the larger ships have extensive theaters and lounge facilities that, depending on the size of the group, can be reserved for the group's exclusive use. These spaces can provide the facilities needed for the business and educational parts of a meeting.

Cruise ship meeting rooms are indistinguishable from those found in a hotel.
Photo by George G. Fenich, Ph.D.

Many cruise lines offer complete meeting packages in the same way as conference centers do. These complete packages routinely include everything except the bar tab and taxes. By carefully working with the ship's technical staff, it is possible that the entire meeting's technical needs can be accommodated with the onboard equipment. In many ways, this is no different from working with a conference center.

Cruise lines market "special interest" cruises. Some of the riverboats offer fall foliage cruises; whale watch cruises and special music cruises are also available. One cruise that may present an opportunity for an unusual incentive is the "migration" cruise. Cruise ships migrate like the birds, and as the ship changes its base of operations, the cruise could become a unique experience.

The relative isolation of many conference and retreat centers is one of their greatest strengths as meeting facilities, but a ship at sea can be even more isolated. A meeting held while the ship is under way will have a different attendance pattern than the same meeting held when the ship is in port. Schedule planning coordinated with the ship's schedule can have a significant impact on a meeting's attendance. One issue many meeting planners face is keeping the delegates in the meetings. Hotels adjacent to casinos and theme parks are notorious for having low delegate attendance at the sessions. On a ship at sea, out of range of cell phones and pagers, a meeting that requires perfect attendance could have a greater opportunity for success than in many competing facilities.

Many planners overlook ships as meeting facilities except for incentive trips, but that shortchanges the potential of these mobile meeting venues. The MEEC planner must research, understand, communicate, and verify that the venue meets the needs of the group.

Cruise Ship Web Sites

Carnival Cruise Lines	http://www.carnival.com/cms/carnivalmeetings/default.aspx
Story about meetings on cruise ships	http://www.uniquevenues.com/cruise-ship-meetings.html

Specific Use Facilities

Theaters, **amphitheaters, arenas, stadiums,** and sports facilities tend to be underused as meeting facilities, but depending on the needs of the meeting, they can support a variety of events. Spectacular and impressive events can be planned for any facility designed for public assembly.

Most of these facilities are focused on events for the general (ticket-buying) public, and a closed event for an invited audience can be a welcome change for their staff. Even though the front office staff might welcome the meeting planner, the planner needs to carefully determine that sufficient house and technical staff will be available to support the event. Entertainment events generally occur on evenings and weekends, and it is not unusual for the usher staff to be people for whom this is a second job or (in the case of those who are available during the day) retirees. The availability and demographics of the staff may or may not be an issue for any given event, but it should be discussed with the facility management prior to contracting the event.

Like convention centers, these facilities are almost always owned by government agencies or are public–private partnerships. Nonprofit

An unusual venue for a hospitality event.
Used by permission of Paradise Light & Sound, Orlando, Florida

foundations own some, but corporations own a few. They are like convention centers in the amount of planning required but are unlike convention centers in that while dealing with large numbers of people is their greatest skill, meetings are not their primary business. Depending on the facility's public event schedule, long rehearsal and setup times may not be available. If a facility has a resident sports team that might go into postseason play, the management might be reluctant to confirm space availability more than a few weeks in advance.

Finances in a special use facility can be a hybrid between the practices of the convention center and the practices of the conference center. There is generally a fixed fee for the use of the facility and a specific subset of its equipment and services. "Normal" cleanup, comparable to a public event, would likely be included in the facility rental fee; the facility would probably require a minimum level of staff for which there would be an hourly charge based on a minimum number of hours. All other labor, equipment, and services would be exactly like those of a convention center, on a bill-per-item system.

Among the specific use facilities, **theaters** can be ideal meeting facilities. They come equipped with comfortable chairs arranged in sweeping curved rows for maximum comfort; they have lighting positions and sound systems built in; and they have staffs that know how to use them. If the delegates are local, they probably know where the theater is and do not need directions. The stages are designed for acoustics and the seats arrayed to enhance visibility. One of the ironies of this industry relates to the amount of time and energy expended converting hotel ballrooms into theaters and how few meetings are done in theaters.

On the surface, it would seem that the better technically equipped a theater is, the more of the theater's equipment the meeting's support team would use and the less it would need to bring in. This, however, is not usually the case. In many theaters, any equipment that is moved must be restored to its "found" location. The economics of that policy works if the equipment's found location is in a storeroom somewhere out of the way. Where the policy does not work is when the equipment's found location is in an "in-use" position. The cost of putting the equipment back to its in-use location can be greater than merely removing the rental equipment and packing it in a truck for the run back to the warehouse (this is especially true of lighting and projection but is less true of audio). If the theater has custom draperies for the stage, those will be used because finding replacement drapes of the correct size can be difficult.

Another issue with using the in-house equipment has to do with reliability. Many theaters, particularly educational and community theaters, are not funded to the point where their equipment can be considered properly maintained or reliable. A lighting designer, unsure of the condition of the installed equipment, would likely import his or her own rather than take a risk.

Catering in a specific use facility may require more planning than in some other venues. Given that the venue's primary revenue sources are based on ticketed events, they would probably have a well-developed concessions operation, but they may or may not have well-developed catering capabilities. Menu selection could be an issue, depending on the scope of the meeting, and the kitchen equipment, which is intended for a concessions environment, may or may not be capable of supporting the menu needs of a meeting.

Entertainment venues range in size from huge outdoor stadiums to hole-in-the-wall nightclubs. Planners who wish to use these venues can be successful if they are careful to remember that entertainment (not meetings) is the venue's primary business and that services considered standard in a hotel or convention center may not exist in an entertainment venue. Thus, the MEEC planner must research, understand, communicate, and verify that the venue meets the needs of the group.

Colleges and Universities

It would seem that since colleges and universities devote all their energies to education and research, they should be ideal meeting facilities. Some are, but it is important for a planner to remember that while meetings bring often badly needed cash to an educational institution, most colleges are not set up for major meetings, and their staffs may not be as adept at responding to immediate meeting needs as those in a full-time meeting facility might be. The planner using an academic facility needs to investigate and coordinate deep into the institution's organizational structure. For example, it is not sufficient to discuss with the person in alumni relations who booked the use of the faculty center after hours to ensure that the lawn sprinklers have, in fact, been turned off for the evening; the planner must verify such details directly with the department responsible.

The impact of seasonality on hotels and other meeting facilities is moderate compared to the impact of seasonality on most academic facilities. During summer vacation, most college campuses turn into ghost towns, and a vacant college campus could provide an effective meeting site. The planner who wishes to use a college campus for a large meeting may have to make some extra logistical arrangements. College classrooms are generally open and airy with plenty of light, but they are not known for comfortable furniture. A student chair with a writing arm may be acceptable for a twenty-something student but may not be acceptable for a forty-something conference attendee. College dorms have beds and the rooms are generally arranged along hallways like hotels, but that is where the similarities end. College dorm rooms have single beds instead of doubles or queens, and most of those are a longer length, so standard linen does not fit. It would probably be a good idea to contract with the college's linen service to provide bed linen and towels.

While many dorm rooms are singles, the majority are doubles. The process of arranging and processing roommate assignments can be a full-time job. If the meeting is large, it might be a good idea to hire an intern for this task. Another issue sometimes overlooked is that dorms generally have bathrooms shared among several rooms. While that might be appropriate for groups of high school and college athletes, it would likely not be acceptable for a meeting of professionals such as doctors or stockbrokers. Newer or recently renovated dorms have elevators, but many older dorms still do not have handicapped accessibility to upper floors. Considerable savings can be realized using college campuses, particularly if a college's athletic facilities are part of the meeting plan; however, not all meetings will work in this environment.

Many meeting planners have less than fond memories of college food. With the advent of professional food service management companies operating many college food service operations, the food quality on many campuses has improved considerably; planners should be aware, however, that a college dining hall would never be elegant. Equally important is that the quality of the food served is a direct result of the budget available. The quality of the college food that the planner may wish to forget is more likely a function of a small budget than a function of inadequate kitchen capabilities. With an adequate budget, the planner can provide high-quality meals in an academic environment.

College art museums and student centers can provide interesting and exciting locations for meetings. The art museums provide especially interesting opportunities for conversations that can enhance a networking event. All of the delegates to the event probably will have opinions on the art that surrounds them, and this art can be the link that motivates strangers to converse. One common mistake planners make when using art centers is the tendency to redecorate them. Without spending a lot of money, it is unlikely that the planner can provide more impressive décor than what the museum's galleries already offer. If the planner feels the need to engage in a massive redecorating project, it might well be that the art museum is not the correct venue for the event.

The art centers and theaters at colleges and universities have a unique attribute that many planners and most of the general public frequently overlook. Unlike the staff in the majority of meeting and special event venues, for the people who run these facilities daily and who take great pride in and care deeply about the condition of the building and its contents, this type of venue is not just a job—it is a passion. This is not to say that people in other venues do not care. They do, but not with the intensity (even obsession) that the academic theater and art people demonstrate. Any planner who intends to use one of these facilities must understand the sensitivities involved. Equally important, planners must convey this message to their own staff. The traveling staff (mere "transients" in the eyes of the permanent staff) must be sensitive to the fact that in spite of the large amount of money they will be spending on this event, they are visitors (and not necessarily even welcome). It is entirely likely that the budget for this one event is greater than the resident staff's monthly or even annual budget, and some jealousies may arise.

Thus, the MEEC planner must research, understand, communicate, and verify that the venue meets the needs of the group.

College and University Web Sites

University of Minnesota Continuing Education and Conference Center	http://www.cce.umn.edu/ conferencecenter
San Diego State University, Extended Studies Center	http://www.ces.sdsu.edu/facilities

Unusual Venues

Meeting planners continually insist on having meetings in places that were never designed for meetings. Flight aprons, airplane hangars, remote islands, nature preserves, city parks, open meadows, and athletic fields are all unusual venues that are often used for meetings. Perhaps the most common of these unusual venues is a large tent in a parking lot. All of these venues have more in common with each other than they have differences.

None of these venues has support equipment, so virtually everything needed for the event must be brought in. These venues also have little or no staff. In addition to all the normal concerns a planner needs to deal with for an event, the planner using these facilities will need to provide all the support services normally considered the purview of the facility. Such services could include portable restrooms, parking, and trash removal. Weather is an issue in any outdoor venue, but that is no different than would be the case with a pool party at a hotel.

One challenge that frequently catches planners by surprise is obtaining permits. Many local governments require permits to use parks or even private property for special events. Failure to procure the proper permits can lead to an event being shut down at the last moment. Not only must the police and fire department be notified, but in many places the building code office must be notified as well. Tents must usually be inspected by the fire department. In some areas,

A fashion show in an airplane hangar.
Used by permission of Paradise Light & Sound, Orlando, Florida

generators are under the purview of the fire department; in others, there is a special office that deals with electrical issues. This office may be part of the Building and Zoning Department or may be part of a designated special events office.

Airport facilities have the additional issue of heightened security. More stringent security measures have been implemented there than ever before. Failure to conform to these security procedures can be detrimental to the event. For those planners who need an aeronautical theme, an airplane museum would likely be a better choice than a working airport. Political rallies are sometimes held at airports just as they used to be held at railroad stations in previous elections. The constant noise of the aircraft in the background does give the impression of excitement, but it can also obscure important parts of a candidate's speech. The quality of the sound system, too often the last item considered, is vitally important to success of this type of event.

Tents routinely show up as meeting venues. Tents fall into three categories: pole, frame, and clear span. An open-sided **pole tent** or **frame tent** set up on the grass is one of the simplest of all meeting venues. It requires little advance planning beyond making sure the tent rental people can get set up in time. Permits are required in many jurisdictions. Weather is a factor, but adding tent sides and air conditioning can reduce the impact of weather. The tent may require a floor so that rain drainage flows under the floor and not over the feet of the people in the tent. Lighting or decorating a tent can also be a challenge. To hang lighting in a pole tent requires special brackets to attach the lights to the poles if the poles are sturdy enough to support them; therefore, for a pole tent, supporting the lighting from the floor on boom stands or truss towers may be a better plan.

A **clear span tent** has a strong roof structure, and it is possible to hang lighting from its beams by using special clamps. Since the purpose of the tent is to create a meeting space where none previously existed, other support services such as power, water, and restrooms may also not exist and will have to be brought in. If lighting is to be hung in a clear span tent, the lighting should be hung before the floor is put in, since many of the tent floors will not support the scissor lifts used by the lighting and décor people during setup.

All unusual venues share a general lack of support and equipment. All of them have heightened challenges with security and logistics, but some venues have additional unique challenges.

Access to the meeting site is an issue in some remote locations. One perfectly delightful special event venue in Park City, Utah, is only accessible via horse-drawn sleigh and then only in the winter. Another venue is in a park not far from Orlando, where the only access to the island where events are held is via a wooden bridge that is not strong enough to support a vehicle, while its slatted wooden deck makes it impossible to roll catering carts. When Disney's Discovery Island was still being used as a special event venue, the only way to bring material to the island was on a float barge because the water was too shallow for anything larger to dock, and there are many stories about the "amp rack that almost got away" on the trip to the island. In fact, there are unconfirmed rumors that one amp rack *did* get away and still rests on the bottom of Bay Lake.

Access can also be an issue even if there are roads directly to the area. Some roads flood in the rainy season, while others are impassable in the winter. Even if the road is substantial enough to support the delivery trucks, is there a dock where they can be unloaded, or will a forklift be needed? If a forklift is needed, who supplies the driver?

One would think that outdoor sports arenas with their large array of seats or bleachers would be easy venues in which to work, and while they are easier to deal with than many other outdoor venues in that they come with restrooms, they also present their own challenges.

Osceola Art Festival, 2001.
Used by permission of Paradise Light & Sound, Orlando, Florida

The irrigation systems for the landscaping at professional or competition fields are fragile enough that driving heavy loads over them can break the piping beneath the surface. Some venues prohibit anything heavier than a golf cart. Forget building a stage on a soccer field unless it is properly padded with plywood sheeting—pushing that cart of riser tops across the grass is not likely to pass muster with the facility's head of grounds.

While the technicians have one set of challenges dealing with outdoor sports venues, caterers have another. It is not uncommon for caterers to dump the leftover ice out on the ground, which will kill the patch of grass underneath. Ice should be dumped in a storm drain, on the pavement, or in a mulched area. Also, portable bars for serving liquor are heavy and can damage the ground underneath, so they need to be placed on pavement or have a sheet of plywood underneath. That plywood should only be in place a few hours, or the grass underneath will die. There are plastic flooring pieces that will distribute the weight and still allow the grass to breathe and are preferable to plywood if they are available. Portable bars also leak. If the water was clean, that would not be a problem; however, while most of the runoff from the bars is melted ice, some of it is excess from the soft drink dispensers.

This excess contains sugar, which attracts ants. The ants then dig up the grass in search of more sugar, and soon there is an anthill behind third base. The partially melted ice from the shrimp buffet must also be disposed of properly, or the smell from the shrimp will last long after the event is over.

Public parks can be beautiful venues except that they are open to the public. If the event is a public event such as an art show, a public park with its regular traffic can be an ideal location. If the event is more private, especially if it involves alcohol, a public park may not be such a good idea.

When planning an outdoor convention function, an indoor backup plan is vital to the success of the event. For an arts festival like the one in Osceola, Florida, an indoor plan is simply not feasible. A professional planner should always recognize the potential for weather to have an impact on the event.

Common Issues

Regardless of where an event is held, there are some issues that all events have in common. Many of these issues are logistical, such as transporting the delegates from the airport. The following issues are common to most (if not all) meeting venues and for most (if not all) meetings.

OBSTACLES

Perhaps a planner's greatest challenge is to overcome the obstacles in the way of the delegates' ability to be successful as a result of the meeting. The facility can present many obstacles that a planner will need to overcome. An example of such an obstacle would be an understaffed or undersized registration desk, another would be inadequate parking space for the delegates who drive, and yet another would be a noise ordinance that prohibits loading between the hours of 10:00 P.M. and 6:00 A.M. Physical obstacles are not limited to disability considerations. There are also questions of how the delegates will get from their rooms to the gala dinner in their formal gowns if it is raining and whether the buses transporting the guests to the off-site venue can get to the actual door of the venue.

POWER

Most outdoor special events and many events in smaller indoor venues have power requirements that exceed the power available. A generator usually provides this power, but generators are expensive. Properly anticipating the power needs is even more important in this type of event than one in a traditional meeting venue. With a generator, the planner will pay not only the daily cost to rent the generator but a fuel charge as well. The fuel consumption is determined by two factors: how long the generator runs and how much power is actually drawn from it. The fuel cost will be a multiple of the cost per gallon of fuel, the amount of use time, and the power consumption. The planner has control over only two of the three elements in this equation.

For any meeting or special event using video or name entertainment or more than a few trade show booths or large scenic units will have special power requirements. Power is expensive; for example, the power to run the sound system can be more expensive than the rental of the equipment. Many convention centers offer a discount if the power is requested early. The technical vendors can calculate power requirements fairly easily. If the discount for requesting power early is 30%, which is a fairly common discount, it would make sense to order 10%–15% more power than estimated. In this way, ample power is available for less than it would have cost to place the power order after all the detailed requirements had been calculated.

Power charges are not based on consumption but on the maximum amount of power deliverable at any one time. To meter the actual power consumption and charge accordingly is illegal in many states. This would make the facility a utility company and subject to rate regulations. It would appear that generator use is charged based on power consumption, but it is actually based on fuel consumption. A generator that is idling uses fuel even if it is supplying no power. Turning a generator off when it is not needed will save money.

RIGGING

Plaster ceilings are a production rigger's worst nightmare, and precast concrete roofs with no steel underneath run a close second. Any event involving more than a few hundred people or video image magnification (IMAG) should involve lighting suspended from the ceiling. Unless the facility is unusually well equipped for lighting from ceiling positions, lighting must be accomplished by hanging trusses, and hanging trusses involves rigging. Theaters (but not necessarily hotels) are generally adequately equipped for lighting without hanging trusses.

The hotel's contracted rigging company will require access to all floor plans not less than two weeks in advance of the event. While it would seem that two weeks' lead time on a floor plan should be simple

A lighting grid in a sports arena.
Used by permission of Paradise Light & Sound, Orlando, Florida

for an event contracted a year in advance, generating an accurate floor plan turns out to be a challenge many planners cannot accommodate. In some jurisdictions, the fire marshal, building code inspector, or safety officer can refuse to allow a show to be hung without a detailed hanging plan. Having to cancel a show at the last minute due to failure to submit paperwork can be a career-ending mistake.

Most facilities contract rigging to an outside company for liability protection. This is in addition to the normal reasons one would out-source any task that the facility management may not have enough experience to properly supervise. Given that riggers' normal job description involves hanging "live loads" over the heads of the general public, they take their work seriously. Their sometimes "obstructionist" attitude is intended to keep people safe and is not meant to impede the event. Adequate advance notification of schedules and requirements can help ensure that the event venue is hung properly and on schedule.

FLOORS

It is not safe to assume that just because the building has a ground-level loading door big enough to drive a tractor-trailer through that once it fits through the door, the floor will support it. Even though the floor may be made of four inches of steel-reinforced concrete on the ground, the utility boxes in the floor may not be so well designed. One Orlando-area facility dug up and repoured the concrete around several floor pockets because the constant forklift traffic drove them into the ground. It is also not safe to assume that a certain size of scissor lift can be brought into the ballroom. For events where these issues are relevant, the planner must ask about the floor load (amount of weight the floor can support without failing) because the information is rarely readily available as part of the site inspection.

Ballrooms are carpeted, and many hotels insist that plastic sheeting be placed over the ballroom carpet during the move-in and move-out process. If the facility has such a requirement, it is important that the exposition services contractor (ESC) and all technical vendors know about it in advance. The requirement to cover the floor with Polytack or one of several similar products is becoming more common. Failure to submit a proper floor plan to the people who apply the floor covering or failure to properly schedule the installation can result in expensive delays.

Many academic theaters have polished wood floors on the stages. Nailing or screwing into them is not recommended and is generally a fast way to be refused the use of the venue in the future. These floors are not designed for heavy loads such as scissor lifts or forklifts, so staffing and equipment requirements may need to be adjusted to compensate.

ACCESS

Not only must the delegates be able to find the venue and its entrance, but the technical support and catering people need to gain access as well. The design of the loading access can have a significant impact on an event's finances. For example, there is a facility in southern Florida where the only way to gain loading access to the ballroom is to back a truck along a sea wall for 100 yards, and a 21-foot truck will not make the corner but a 17-foot truck will. The closest a tractor-trailer can park is a quarter mile away. An event here whose technical support equipment is shipped on a tractor-trailer would need to be unloaded off site and the equipment trucked in to the loading dock using a smaller truck—at considerable additional expense. There is another facility on Florida's west coast where the loading access to the ballrooms is via an open-sided elevator with no top attached at the outside

A load-out for a large trade show.
Used by permission of Paradise Light & Sound, Orlando, Florida

of the building. In this part of Florida, it rains almost every afternoon in the summer. A load scheduled for 4:00 P.M. in July stands an excellent likelihood of having a problem.

The presence of truck-height docks is not enough to guarantee smooth loading. Some facilities, including those of the Gaylord Palms and the Walt Disney World Dolphin, have elevators from the docks to the ballroom. Access to the theater at the Orange County Convention Center involves two elevators and a push down the hall between them. The number and location of the docks are significant. The only Orlando-area major convention hotels with adequate dock space are the Gaylord Palms (in spite of the elevator) and Marriott's Orlando World Center. One would think that the Orange County Convention Center, with half a mile of continuous dock space, would have adequate loading capabilities, but even that fills up for some events, as incredible as it seems. On the other hand, the Morial Convention Center in New Orleans is all on one level, with loading docks lining one entire side of the building.

Summary

Obtaining accurate information is essential to planning successful meetings. Detailed and thorough research is the first step in the process. This first step is much easier now than it was in the past and promises to become even easier, as the Internet and World Wide Web provide planners powerful resources with which to plan their events. Many of the best meeting facilities have extensive Web sites with volumes of available information. Some venues have 360-degree visual imaging that allows a planner to remotely view the facility. This technology is becoming more and more affordable and common. Before calling a sales representative, a planner should visit the facility's Web site and print out everything that might be of interest. Once having studied the material and determined that the facility may be appropriate for the event, then and only then should the planner call the facility's salespeople to open the dialogue.

The most important component of dealing with any facility is the development of an open, honest, and trusting relationship with all parties involved. Unfortunately, there are facilities that will take advantage of that relationship, just as there are planners who do not deal honestly with their suppliers. In spite of the risks involved, the attempt must be made because the success of every event depends on the interaction between the planner and all the other parties. This relationship begins with understanding what each of the participants brings to the relationship and what each one needs.

Communication begins with a set of requirements. The more accurate the requirements are, the better. It is important to note, however, that the words "accurate" and "detailed" are not the same thing. On contact, the hotel needs to know how many people are coming, but they do not need the names until relatively close to the event. Accurate and timely listings of requirements are the first step in developing a successful relationship; verification of the documentation returned by the venue is the other half of this communication. Not only should the planner provide requirements, but the venue should also reply and acknowledge that it understands the requirements and how it will fulfill each requirement as appropriate.

The key to working with any venue is fourfold: research, understand, communicate, verify. Research, understand, communicate, verify. Repeat until done! This chapter provides information that can be used by meeting planners in the first two steps of the process. The rest is what separates the best planners from the rest.

Key Words and Terms

For definitions, see the Glossary or go to http://glossary.conventionindustry.org.

Amenity	Exhibit hall
Amphitheater	Frame tent
Arena	Hotel
Attrition penalty	Local event
Boardroom	Loss leader
Break-out room	Pole tent
Clear span tent	Prefunction space
Complete meeting package	Seasonality
Concessionaire	Shoulder
Conference Centers	Stadium
Convention Center	Theater

Review and Discussion Questions

1. What is the single most important thing a planner can provide a venue to ensure the effective and cost-efficient execution of a meeting?

2. What is an attrition penalty, and why should a planner care?

3. What is the single most significant difference between a hotel's meeting space and a convention center's meeting space?

4. What is the single most important activity that facility personnel depend on the meeting planner to provide?

5. How is the financial structure of a hotel different from that of other facilities? What is a hotel's biggest source of revenue?

6. Why is seasonality important to a planner?

7. Why is ceiling height significant?

8. Why should a meeting planner care about zoning laws?

9. What should be a planner's greatest concern for an outdoor event? What should a planner do about it?

About the Chapter Contributor

Bob Cherny has spent almost his entire career on the facility side of the meetings industry. As an undergraduate in theater at Brandeis, he served as a student assistant supporting facility activities. During graduate school at the University of South Carolina, he was scene shop foreman and was responsible for the proper operation of the theater. Bob spent twenty years at the Tupperware Convention Center, Orlando's first full-time convention center, starting as technical director and ending as general manager. The Tupperware Convention Center was a pioneer in the meetings industry.

After leaving Tupperware, Bob went to Disney Event Productions, where he provided technical and facility support for clients in several of Disney's Orlando-area hotels. He then went to Paradise Light & Sound, supporting meeting planners in their use of meeting facilities. Bob returned to managing a facility and moved to the Osceola Heritage Park and Silver Spurs Arena in Kissimmee. In his tenure there, he supported a variety of equestrian and entertainment events, which included concerts, rodeos, and county fairs. Seeking to focus more on the convention industry than on the mix of events found in the arena, Bob returned to Paradise, where he serves as sales manager.

CHAPTER **5**

Exhibitions

Trade shows are used throughout the world to promote products and companies. This one takes place in Chang Rai, Thailand.

Photo by George G. Fenich, Ph.D.

Chapter Objectives

The chapter provides the reader with an understanding of the following:

- Definitions of different types of exhibitions
- Exhibition models
- Types of exhibition facilities
- Types of exhibition programs
- Ways exhibition management companies operate
- Role of exhibitors
- Fundamentals of exhibition planning
- Exhibit design principles
- Methods to maximize exhibition return on investment
- Ways exhibitors work with exhibition management and service companies

Chapter Outline

Introduction
History
Definitions
Organization of the Exhibition
   Exhibition Model
   Facilities
   Programs
Exhibition Service Contractors
Exhibition Planning
   Location
   Shipping and Storage
   Marketing and Promotion

Technology
Housing and Transportation
Risk Management and Crisis
   Management
Exhibitors' Perspective
   Why Exhibit?
Exhibit Design Principles
Planning for Success
   Exhibitors
   Exhibit Staff
   Exhibition Management and Service
      Contractors

Introduction

With over 13,000 **trade shows** and exhibitions annually in North America alone, the long history of exhibitions has turned into a

The Consumer Electronics Show (CES)

Every January, over 2,700 exhibiting companies and over 140,000 visitors converge on Las Vegas, Nevada, for the annual global technology trade show called CES. In the two weeks prior to the show, over 3 million gross square feet of empty **exhibition** space are converted into a high-tech showplace, complete with high-speed Internet access for thousands of computers and multilevel exhibits that look like they are permanent fixtures.

When CES opens to great fanfare, visitors flood the aisles and engage exhibitors with a myriad of questions about their products, services, pricing, and events. The hotels, restaurants, and casinos of Las Vegas are full of visitors and their families from around the world. Late into the night, companies sponsor events and hospitality suites to keep the conversations going with their potential customers, while breakfasts and lunches are heavily attended because industry leaders give keynote addresses.

Behind the scenes, the organizing company is solving hundreds of problems as they arise. Hotels are hosting private events by organizations and companies that are lavishing perks on their best customers. Exhibit managers for companies are frantically searching for lost deliveries of packages and keeping track of hundreds of leads, not to mention ensuring the exhibit staff is in the right place at the right time. Service contractors are responding to the demands of exhibitors and the organizer. Media personnel are searching out the new products that will make resounding profits in the coming year.

Then when the show ends, there are immediate scrambles. The carpet begins to come up; exhibitors frantically pack up all their belongings as service contractors dismantle the exhibits. Cabs are at a premium as thousands try to get to the airport at the same time. Within a few days, CES is a memory, and the exhibit space is empty once again. Hopefully, however, exhibitors will continue their follow-ups to turn leads into sales. The organizing company will immerse itself in what it can do better next year, and attendees are back at work with more knowledge of the industry than they had a few weeks before.

thriving, ever-changing industry. This chapter provides an overview of the industry and looks at it from the perspective of organizers, attendees, and exhibitors.

History

Trade fairs began in Europe in the Middle Ages, if not before. They began when craftsmen and farmers started bringing their products to the center of the town or city to meet their potential customers. These were the beginnings of the "public" trade fair, and this type of interaction between producers and buyers continues today in the crafts and food industries.

Eventually, the business-to-business industries realized the value of meeting, sharing information, and providing previews of their products to potential customers. This buyer–seller format was termed an "exhibition" and typically took place in a large city at a facility built specifically for the exhibition. This part of the industry blossomed in the late 1800s, with many facilities being built strictly for world-class exhibitions. For example, the Crystal Palace in London was opened for the "Great Industrial Exhibition of All Nations"; in the United States, facilities were opened in Chicago and Philadelphia to commemorate "world's fairs" that, in reality, were trade shows highlighting the industrial advances of participating countries.

The interior of Amsterdam RAI in Holland with a trade fair in progress.
Dorling Kindersley Media Library

By the mid-twentieth century, trade associations had grown and saw the potential of trade shows being held in conjunction with their annual meetings as a way to stimulate communication in the industry and expand their revenues gained from the annual meeting. As the trade shows grew, it became imperative that trade associations outsource the management of their trade show business to outside companies—thus the growth of trade show management companies and service providers.

Definitions

A trade show is typically a business-to-business event. The exhibitor is usually a manufacturer or distributor of products or services specific or complementary to those industries. Often, attendance is restricted to buyers from the industry, and business credentials are required for registration. Educational programs may or may not be a part of the trade show program, although in recent years educational programs have expanded as a method of attracting attendees. Sponsorship or management of the trade show either is under the auspices of a trade association or has evolved under the sponsorship of a management company. Some trade shows are the result of initiatives by companies and are fully intended to be profit-making ventures. Usually, trade shows are annual events, although some occur more frequently and others less frequently. Major organizations may also have regional trade shows that are smaller than their regular national or international event. (See chapter 14, on international issues, for more information on global trade shows.) Examples of U.S.-based trade shows include the following:

ABA. Held annually, it is the annual trade show for the American Booksellers Association.

CES. The Consumer Electronics Show is held annually and is sponsored by the Consumer Electronics Association.

International Hotel/Motel & Restaurant Show. The International Hotel/Motel & Restaurant Show is the premier trade event for the hospitality industry. The show is a must-visit for caterers, restaurant owners, and hoteliers. The venue is the Jacob K. Javits Convention Center in New York City.

NRA. The National Restaurant Association trade show, held each year in Chicago, features over 1,700 exhibitors and 60,000 visitors. The NRA also holds a number of regional trade shows each year.

Exhibition Forecast

The trade show and exhibition market continued its recovery in 2004 and is showing signs of expansion. Across-the-board spending by exhibitors and attendees resulted in a 5.8% increase in overall spending to $9.15 billion in 2004—a rate not seen since 2000. That follows a 1.5% spending growth rate in 2003 and a decline of 1.2% in 2002. During the first half of 2005, many corporations reported increasing funding for business-related travel, which is expected to drive trade show expenditures up 6.1% to $9.71 billion by the end of the year. Spending on exhibitions and trade shows is expected to rise 5.8% on a compounded annual basis from 2004 to 2009, driven by a 6.8% gain in total exhibit space spending. Overall, spending on trade shows and exhibitions will reach $12.1 billion by 2009.

Source: http://www.expoweb.com/Benchmarks_Research/2005Oc1032005120018PM.htm

PITTCON. The Pittsburgh Conference, which is held annually in various cities, is a large trade show directed toward the chemical industry.

The definition of a trade fair has become close enough to that of a trade show that the terms are used interchangeably. The term "trade fair" is more often used outside the United States than is the term "trade show." Trade fairs are discussed in more detail in chapter 14, "International Issues in MEEC." Although the historical definition of the term "exhibition" is quite different from what it means today, this term has also evolved to mean a trade show or trade fair. In this chapter, we refer to trade shows and exhibitions interchangeably.

Consumer or **public shows** are expositions that are open to the public. This type of show is used by a consumer-based industry to bring their goods directly to their market's end user. Show management may or may not charge an admission fee, and attendance is usually not restricted. Following are some types of consumer shows:

- Automobile shows
- Computer-related shows
- Garden and home maintenance shows
- Recreation shows

An automobile show.
PhotoEdit Inc.

- Sporting goods shows
- Travel destination shows

Consumer shows are often regional in nature, with exhibitors traveling from city to city with their displays and products. They also provide excellent opportunities for companies to brand or test-market new products.

The term **exposition** has also evolved to be similar in meaning to a trade show. An association meeting may include an exposition (or expo). This is the trade show segment of the association's annual gathering.

Organization of the Exhibition

EXHIBITION MODEL

We now discuss a general exhibition model (see Figure 5–1) that provides an overview of how all the components of a trade show or exhibition come together to meet the objectives of each stakeholder. As can be seen in the figure, the exhibition management company (organizer)

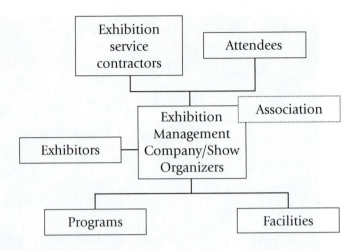

FIGURE 5–1   The exhibition model.

is the center of the exhibition model. Although the organizing company may be a trade association or a company subcontracted to a trade association, it may also be a separate company organizing the trade show as a profit-making venture. The organizing company is responsible for all aspects of the trade show. Think of it as the "systems integrator" responsible for implementing the show, marketing it to buyers and sellers, and gathering together all the resources needed for success.

Buyers and sellers are also key parts of the exhibition model. Typically, buyers are the attendees; sellers are the exhibitors. For success, the correct buyers must attend the trade show and bring sufficient business to the exhibitors (sellers) so that they will continue to exhibit at subsequent trade shows.

Service contractors are the element that makes the trade show work. They supply personnel, materials, and services to the organizer, buyers, and sellers. Obviously, facilities are also needed to conduct the trade show. Facilities range from small hotels with conference centers to megaconvention centers, such as those in Las Vegas, Chicago, and Orlando. Facilities also include adjacent lodging and entertainment facilities that are used by the exhibitors and visitors.

To be profitable, the show organizer must find the right mix of buyers, sellers, service contractors, and facilities.

FACILITIES

Meeting and convention facilities have kept pace with the growth of the industry. From small regional facilities to megaconvention centers

TABLE 5–1	Examples of Convention Center Size

Center	Square Feet of Exhibit Space	Number of Booths	Meeting Rooms
McCormick Place (Chicago)	2.2 million	27,500	114
Orange County Convention Center (Orlando)	2.1 million	5,942	94
Las Vegas Convention Center	1.3 million	4,600	103
Morial Convention Center (New Orleans)	1.1 million	5,400	140
Sands Convention Center (Las Vegas)	1.04 million	8,000	23

Source: "The Most Comprehensive Guide to North American Meeting Facilities." (April, 2005), *Meetings & Conventions*, 40 (5).

located in major cities, regions have understood the benefits of attracting trade shows and conventions to their area. Table 5–1 shows some of the largest convention centers and their plans for expansion.

The trade show organizer must take into account a number of factors in selecting the correct facility. These include:

- Facility size
- Facility amenities (including telecommunications and dining, setup and teardown times)
- Availability of service contractors
- Preferences of exhibitors
- Preferences of attendees
- Logistical considerations (including airline service and local transportation)
- Cost
- Lodging and entertainment resources

Hotels are also investing in larger exhibit areas and expanding their conference centers. They must be considered as alternatives to convention centers for smaller trade shows.

PROGRAMS

The trade show management company must also consider the types of programs offered in addition to the trade show itself. Trade show programs have evolved to encompass additional programs that serve to boost attendance. Programs to consider include the following:

- Educational programs
- Entertainment programs
- Exhibitor programs
- Special sections (on the trade show floor) for emerging companies, new exhibitors, or new technologies
- Celebrity or industry-leading speakers
- Meal programs
- Continuing education units (CEUs) or certifications for educational programs
- Spouse and children programs
- Internet access and e-mail centers

Exhibition Service Contractor (ESC)

As mentioned, an **exhibition service contractor (ESC)** provides products and services to the **exhibition management company** and exhibitors. Their services are often key to the success of a trade show. Typically, the trade show organizer will provide exhibitors with a list of authorized service contractors to select from and enable the two parties to deal directly with each other. (See chapter 6, "Service Contractors," for more information.)

Here are some types of services that exhibition service contractors provide:

- Freight handling
- Sound and audiovisual needs
- Marketing services
- Special lighting installations
- Arrangements for exhibit furniture, carpet, and amenities
- Telecommunications needs
- Computer needs
- Access to electrical, gas, and water resources

Some freight being unloaded in a convention center.
Used with permission of Paradise Sound & Light, Orlando, Florida

- Floor plan layout
- Storage and warehousing of materials
- Installation, maintenance, and dismantling of exhibits
- Provision of models, entertainers, and additional exhibit staff

Arranging and managing these services for a large show can be quite complex for the exhibition management company and exhibitors. Convention centers, management companies, and even exhibitors have become accustomed to working with various arrangements and companies. Because the service contractors operate in a very competitive environment, they have learned that customer service, fair pricing, and responsiveness to customer needs are important. This provides organizers and exhibitors a level of comfort in relying on service contractors to take care of the problems that arise with organizing a successful trade show.

Service contractors, in conjunction with the exhibition management company, usually develop an exhibitor service manual that shows all the details that an exhibitor needs to plan and implement an exhibit program for the trade show. It also includes the forms needed to order services from the service contractors and the rules and regulations of the exhibition management company, convention center or hotel, and local government.

Despite the controls and organization put in place by the exhibition management company and service contractors, disputes arise. When this occurs, it is important to get all concerned parties involved in achieving a successful resolution. The show manager is responsible for the compliance of exhibitors, attendees, and service contractors to the show rules.

Exhibition Planning

LOCATION

Exhibition planners consider a number of variables when deciding on the location of the trade show or exhibition. Everyone will agree, however, that location has a major effect on attendance. Thus, a balance must be attained between location cost and the ideal attendance level.

Many organizations that conduct annual meetings and trade shows stay in the same city year after year. They have found that by doing so, they can negotiate the best agreements with the local convention center and hotels and still retain the optimum attendance levels. Typically, these are association meetings that have strong educational programs and are held at an attractive site.

However, other organizations or exhibition management companies prefer to move their trade shows from city to city each year, and this strategy also helps attract visitors. Not only is a different local attendance base able to attend inexpensively, but out-of-town visitors may be attracted by different local tourist offerings as well.

Organizations and exhibition management companies often survey their membership or potential attendees to assess their preferences on location. The success of convention centers in cities such as Las Vegas, Orlando, and San Francisco is indicative of organizations paying attention to the needs and desires of their members and potential audience. Expansion of the convention facilities in each of these cities indicates that the cities value the revenue generated by large trade shows.

SHIPPING AND STORAGE

Once the location is chosen, the booths and other trade show materials need to be transported to the site. While air freight may sometimes be used, over-the-road freight by truck is the most common. Charges are typically per hundred pounds and are based on the distance the freight must travel.

Since an exhibitor cannot afford for the freight shipment to arrive late for a trade show, extra time is allowed for transit. Thus, the exhibitor must arrange for temporary storage of the materials at the destination prior to the move-in date for the trade show or exhibition as well as possible storage of the freight containers while the show or exhibition is open. When the show closes, the whole process is reversed. Some exposition service contractors such as GES of Freeman have separate divisions of their company that deal with shipping and storage. For more information, see Chapter 6 on service contractors.

MARKETING AND PROMOTION

Without exhibitors, the trade show or exhibition will not be successful; without attendees, exhibitors will not return. Exhibition planners must pay serious attention to marketing and promotion programs that will fill their exhibition hall with both exhibitors and attendees. Regardless of the type of show, attendance is the key to success.

The most common form of marketing to potential exhibitors is advertising in trade publications. Until recently, well-established trade shows and exhibitions had little trouble marketing to potential exhibitors—the exhibit halls were full, and waiting lists of exhibitors were commonplace. However, the past few years have seen many companies downsizing their exhibit space or opting to exhibit at fewer trade shows, so management companies have now placed a renewed focus on marketing to potential exhibitors. Trade shows are now in competition for exhibitors, and exhibition management companies are working hard to retain existing exhibitors and attract new ones.

Exhibitors want to invest in a trade show or exhibition because their potential customers are in attendance. It is primarily the responsibility of the exhibition management company to target and market to the right audience. This is typically done through direct mail and advertising in trade publications. Management companies (for business-to-business trade shows) must provide programs beyond the exhibit hall that help attract visitors. Often, educational programs are provided as an incentive, or prominent industry leaders are hired to give keynote addresses that attract visitors. Contests, gifts, discount programs, and other tools to attract visitors have been commonplace.

Exhibitors are also involved in helping boost attendance at trade shows. Usually, they are given a number of free passes to the show

Free samples are a way for exhibitors to entice attendees to sample their products.
Photo by George G. Fenich, Ph.D.

that can be distributed to their best customers. Exhibitors are also encouraged to sponsor or conduct special events and to promote them to their customer base.

Public exhibitions also require promotion to be successful. Typically, public shows are marketed through advertisements in trade publications or local public media. Advertisements may offer discounts for purchasing early tickets or may promote special events or speakers who will attract the largest number of attendees. Promoting public exhibitions is a daunting task because the potential attending audience is so large that it requires a significant expense to reach them through print, radio, and television advertising. Producers must be confident that their investment in promotion will result in reaching the attendance objectives and must also be attentive to other events that may be occurring during the exhibition time period that can affect attendance.

Another factor is weather. Unlike business-to-business trade shows that have many people coming from outside the city, the public show usually is dependent on the local population for attendance. One episode of bad weather can drastically affect the bottom line of a show producer (for example, locals will not venture out to a public show in the midst of a serious snowstorm). The National Western Stock Show, held in Denver each January, is a good example of this. Years with extreme cold and snow greatly reduce attendance, but during years of unseasonably mild weather, attendance skyrockets. The solution for the National Western Stock Show has been to extend the show to a sixteen-day period, ensuring there will be "good days" and "bad days." This has led to a more consistent overall attendance figure from year to year.

TECHNOLOGY

Advances in technology have made trade show and exhibition management, as well as the exhibition itself, easier and more productive (for more information, see chapter 13, on technology). Let us look behind the scenes and see how technology has been introduced into the industry:

- The Internet has had a great impact on how trade shows and exhibitions are marketed to potential visitors. Most shows have Web sites that allow visitors to register online. Visitors can view exhibitor lists, review educational programs, and even make their travel arrangements online. They can also view interactive floor plans to efficiently plan their time.

- Lead retrieval systems are a great benefit to exhibitors. Systems are in place that enable the exhibit staff to "swipe" a visitor's card and get all of that person's contact information in a format that is usable on the company computer system, saving many hours of entering business card data. Most recently, radio frequency identification (RFID) has been added to attendee badges to track and record their movements.

- Technology is also used in promoting a company's products. Many companies now give visitors inexpensive CD-ROMs instead of bulky brochures. The CD-ROMs can contain much more information and more elaborate presentations that the potential customer can view at his or her leisure.

HOUSING AND TRANSPORTATION

Housing and transportation are essential elements to the success of any trade show. A large part of any organizer's time is spent negotiating room blocks in the host city and airline and car rental discounts for

Bus transportation along many routes is necessary for a large convention.
Photo by George G. Fenich, Ph.D.

attendees and exhibitors. Recently, the trend has moved toward out-sourcing housing and transportation arrangements to local convention and visitor bureaus or third-party housing vendors. Regardless of how housing and transportation issues are handled, the expectation is that they will be "transparent" to the attendee or exhibitor.

Hotel facilities are also a factor to be considered when determining the location of the trade show or exhibition. Are the local facilities adequate for the projected attendance? Are the negotiated room rates within the budget of the typical attendee or exhibitor? What is the proximity to the trade show site, and will local transportation need to be provided? What are the weather conditions of the host city during this period? Will weather affect attendance or even cause cancellation of the show? What are the safety issues that must be considered for attendees? What is the potential for labor problems to arise in the host city or at host hotels? Do the convention center and local hotels comply with ADA accessibility requirements?

Additionally, the largest trade shows often require dedicated local ground transportation to assist visitors and exhibitors in getting from their hotels to the trade show site. When determining whether dedicated ground transportation is required, consider that safety is often the key decision point. Even if hotels are within walking distance from the convention center, the conditions of the city between the hotels and the center may dictate that it is in the best interests of the organizer to provide transportation. For example, in New Orleans there are many hotels within walking distance of the convention center, but in the summer when temperature and humidity are both in the 90s, the meeting organizer is better off to provide transportation. When choosing ground transportation providers, be sure to take into account experience, availability, special services, insurance, condition of vehicles, labor contracts, and cost.

Risk Management and Crisis Management

Organizing a trade show or exhibition is a risky business, and so is exhibiting at a trade show. If things are not done right, the trade show can become a colossal failure. Both trade show organizers and exhibitors need to consider having a risk management program. A risk management plan does the following:

- Provides the procedures for identifying potential risks
- Quantifies each risk to determine the effect it would have if it occurs
- Assesses each risk to determine which risks to ignore, which to avoid, and which to mitigate
- Provides risk avoidance steps to prevent the risk from occurring
- Provides risk mitigation steps to minimize potential costs if the risk occurs

Always keep in mind that a trade show or exhibition is a business venture that should be given every chance to succeed, so knowing how to set up a risk management plan and apply risk management principles will help ensure success.

Crisis management has also become critical to trade show organizers. A crisis is different from a risk in that it poses a critical situation that may cause danger to visitors or exhibitors. Examples of recent crises include the 9/11 attacks in New York City, the riots during World

Trade Organization meetings, and the Hurricane Katrina disaster. Trade shows that were under way on 9/11 were either canceled or curtailed midway through the schedule. Organizing companies suffered deep losses for these events.

Every trade show organizer should have a crisis management plan that addresses the prevention, control, and reporting of emergency situations. The plan should address the more likely types of emergencies, such as fire, food-borne illnesses, demonstrations, bomb threats, terrorism, and natural disasters, and should contain all the procedures to be followed in the event of an emergency situation.

Consider having a crisis management team who is well versed in assessing the potential for a crisis, taking actions to prevent emergencies, and taking control should a situation occur. The crisis management team should be represented in the site selection process.

Exhibitors' Perspective

If exhibitors were not successful from a business perspective, trade shows and exhibitions would not exist. Exhibiting at trade shows or exhibitions is often a key part of a company's marketing strategy. Companies invest a significant portion of their marketing budget in trade show appearances and must see a positive return on their investment. This section of the chapter looks at the issues that face the exhibiting companies.

WHY EXHIBIT?

It is important for a company to know why it is exhibiting, and analysis of the potential reasons is a major part of planning for the trade show. Some of the reasons that companies participate in a trade show or exhibition include the following:

- Branding of their name in the industry
- Annual presentation of products to industry analysts
- New product rollout
- Opportunities to meet with potential and existing customers
- Chances to learn about customer needs
- Occasions to meet with trade media
- Opportunities to learn about changes in industry trends and competitor products

It is important that companies exhibit at the right trade shows. Far too often a company analyzes its **return on investment (ROI)** and cannot understand why a particular trade show was not a success. Perhaps it exhibited at the show for years and recently their return has dropped. This may possibly be due to not noticing a change in the trade show's theme and audience; it may no longer be an appropriate venue for the company.

Therefore, it is important that an exhibitor continually evaluate its trade show program and ensure that it is exhibiting at the right shows in order to meet its potential customers.

Determining trade show ROI is more critical than ever in determining whether a company is attending the right shows and using the right strategy and planning techniques. Often, however, determining ROI is ignored, citing "We can't tell whether a sale was derived from a trade show lead or not" or "We don't have the data to be accurate." Avoid these excuses by determining actual expenses and revenue generated by the trade show exhibit leads.

The trade show floor at the G2E convention.
Photo by George G. Fenich, Ph.D.

Why Companies Exhibit

It is interesting to ask companies why they exhibit. There are many different answers to this question, but too often the answer is, "Because our competitors are there," or "Because we have to." Obviously, these companies do not put a lot of thought or effort into their trade show programs. For example, at one trade show, one company's staff did not even show up for the first day of the show. Their competitors were busy, and the show had a maximum capacity of attendees, but their exhibit was dark and empty. What message did this send to potential customers? When asked about the situation, the company gave the answers cited above. Fortunately, when the president of the company was made aware of the situation, he initiated a complete review of their trade show program, resulting in significant improvements at future shows.

When calculating ROI, establish all the expenses that are a part of the trade show. Typical expenses include:

- Space rental
- Service contractor services (electrical, computer, etc.)
- Personnel travel (including hotel and meals)
- Customer entertainment
- Preshow mailings
- Freight charges
- Photography
- Brochure printing and shipment
- Promotional items
- Training
- Postshow mailings

One method to determine revenue from the trade show is to set a time limit on business that was the result of leads from the trade show. It is easy to maintain the lead list and determine which ones resulted in actual business; after a period of time, however, the business may very well be the result of other activities and not the trade show. Thus, the formula for trade show ROI is "ROI = revenues minus expenses," where revenues include revenue from the trade show leads and expenses include those listed in the bulleted list above.

Exhibit Design Principles

Although exhibit design may be limited by the rules established by the exhibit management company, the constraints of the facility, or the business culture of the host country, there are some general principles we can discuss. These principles include selecting the right size for your company's budget and purposes, choosing the right layout of the exhibit to meet your purposes, and using proper signage, lighting, and personnel. Exhibits and the space they occupy are a significant corporate investment, and thought must be given to these factors.

Exhibit size is a major consideration, if only because of cost. The more space an exhibit occupies, the more it costs in space rental, materials, labor for setup, additional staff, and maintenance. So, be sure to balance the costs with the benefits of having a larger exhibit. A larger exhibit typically means being noticed by visitors, and it creates a better impression if it is done well. It gives the impression that the company is in a solid financial situation and is a leader in the industry. However, the space must be used well and convey the messages that the company desires to impart to potential customers.

Companies that participate in a large number of trade shows or exhibitions will have exhibits that range in size from very small (for less important or more specialized trade shows) to very large (for their most important trade shows). For example, Xerox, which exhibits at over thirty trade shows per year, has very large exhibits for information technology shows but also smaller peninsular or in-line exhibits for specialized trade shows or smaller regional shows. Some companies even have two or three exhibits at the same trade show: a large one promoting the main theme and message they want to communicate and smaller exhibits in other halls to promote specialized products or services.

Space assignments are often given by the exhibition management company based on a number of factors, including desired space size, seniority of participation, and points garnered by participation in other marketing programs. From the organizer's perspective, this type of arrangement helps retain exhibitors and favors their highest-paying exhibitors.

When selecting space, the company trade show manager should consider the following:

- Traffic patterns in the exhibit hall
- Location of entrances
- Food facilities and restrooms

A standard trade show booth.
Photo by George G. Fenich, Ph.D.

- Location of industry leaders
- Location of competitors

It is the responsibility of the company trade show manager to notify the exhibit management company if the company is holding any special events in the exhibition, hosting any celebrities who would draw an unusually large crowd, or giving a loud presentation from a stage.

Exhibit layout is also linked to the objectives a company establishes for the trade show or exhibition. If a company's main objective is to meet as many people as possible and establish its brand in the industry, a large open exhibit is appropriate. This type of layout encourages people to enter the exhibit, and it facilitates a large amount of traffic flow. There will be a few parts of the exhibit that require visitors to stay for a period of time, such as product demonstrations.

Another type of layout may even purposely discourage people from entering, and parts of the exhibit may be by "invitation only." Why would a company do this? If the purpose at the trade show is to meet with serious buyers or existing customers, it is important to limit visitors to only those falling in these categories. The average visitor to the trade show may not be wanted by the staff; therefore, this exhibit layout is set up to minimize traffic through the exhibit.

Most trade show floor plans in the United States are based on a 10-foot × 10-foot grid, with the smallest allowable exhibit being this size. This is known as the **standard booth**. Typically, standard booths are set up side-by-side and back-to-back, with an aisle running in front of the booths; standard booths may also be used to line the inside walls of the exhibit area. Companies may combine standard booths to create an **in-line exhibit,** using multiple standard booths to give greater length to the exhibit.

Island booths are created by grouping standard booths together into blocks of four, nine, or larger configurations. Island booths have aisles on four sides and can be an excellent format for medium-sized companies. **Peninsular booths** are made up of four or more standard booths back-to-back, with aisles on three sides.

Multilevel exhibits are often used by large companies to expand their exhibit space without taking up more floor space. The upper floor may be used for special purposes, such as meeting areas, private demonstration areas, or hospitality stations. Exhibitors using multi-level exhibits must be aware of the unique regulations of the exhibition facility when considering this type of exhibit.

As mentioned, exhibitors must be aware of the location of food facilities, restrooms, entrances, and other special event areas. Each of these affects the traffic flow in the aisles and can either hinder or help an exhibit. Although many companies strive to be directly in front of an entrance, it may create more problems than expected because of the large amount of traffic. The exhibit staff may have difficulty discerning between serious visitors to the exhibit and those just trying to get in or out of the exhibit hall. Food service areas may create unexpected lines at lunchtime that spill into an exhibit area, essentially making the area useless for that time.

Small exhibitors face a different set of problems. If they have an in-line exhibit, their options are limited in how the exhibit is organized. If they want to maximize interactions with visitors, they may "open" the exhibit by ensuring that there are no tables or other obstructions between the aisle and their staff. If, on the other hand, they want to focus interaction on serious potential customers, their approach may be to block off the inside of the exhibit as much as possible and have meeting areas within the exhibit.

Lighting can enhance booth appearance and attractiveness.
Photo by George G. Fenich, Ph.D.

Many people who pass by or through an exhibit only read the signs that the company is displaying, so signage is important in planning the exhibit. Signs must communicate clearly and quickly the messages that the company wants to convey to visitors. Detailed itemizations of equipment specifications on signs are almost always ignored. Signs should instead focus on selling points and benefits to the user.

Lighting technology has come a long way in the past twenty years. Today, many companies use pinpoint lighting to focus visitors' attention on their products and signage, and color lighting is often used to accentuate certain parts of an exhibit to communicate a mood for the visitor. Lighting is also important for areas that will be used for discussions or meetings with potential customers.

Exhibit staff must also be used wisely. All areas of the exhibit must be covered, and the right people must be in the right places. For large exhibits, greeters should be used to staff the outside of the exhibit and should direct visitors to the areas of their interest after initially greeting them. Technical staff may be stationed with the products displayed, being able to provide answers to the more detailed questions that a visitor may ask. Corporate executives may roam the exhibit or cluster near meeting areas to enable staff to find them when needed. Often, serious customers want to be introduced to senior executives, and those executives need to be available.

Small exhibits have a special set of staff problems. Usually, the main problem they face is having enough staff to cover the busy times of the trade show or having too much staff for the exhibit size. Again, it is important that the right people are used to staff the exhibit and that staff assignments are planned according to the show's busiest times.

Planning for Success

There are three phases of planning to ensure that the trade show exhibit is a success. Prior to the trade show, significant planning must take place to ensure that everything, including the staff, exhibit, brochures, and products, arrives at the exhibition on time. Just as important, planning prior to the show must include establishing the objectives the company wants to accomplish because the objectives set the stage for how the exhibit is presented, the messages the signage conveys, and the approach the staff take with exhibit visitors. Establishing objectives helps the company to give thought as to how the exhibit will operate as well as what messages it needs to give to visitors.

Planning for the exhibit operation is also key to success. Everything must work, and everyone must know his or her role. The person in charge of the exhibit must coordinate staff schedules, product demonstrations, and a myriad of other details that result in the visitor seeing a flawless exhibit. Many aspects of exhibiting must also be coordinated with the exhibition management company or service companies during the time of the trade show.

A post trade show plan is essential for success. Three components of the post trade show period must be planned:

1. Follow up all serious leads obtained during the trade show.
2. Monitor to ensure that all commitments made during the show are fulfilled. Often staff promise a visitor that they will send information or have someone call the visitor.
3. Evaluate the results. This includes determining the ROI and post trade show feedback from staff to determine lessons learned for future performance improvement.

The Accepted Practices Exchange (APEX) Initiative has adopted the following definitions that relate to this area.

Exhibit Booth. Individual display area constructed to exhibit products or convey a message.

Exhibitor. (1) Person or firm that displays its products or services at the show and (2) those who attend an event to staff an exhibit.

Exhibit Manager. (1) Person in charge of individual exhibit booth and (2) show management staff member in charge of entire exhibit area.

EXHIBITORS

A company must consider the demographics and psychographics of people attending a trade show when deciding where to exhibit and in which shows to participate. Exhibitors and booth personnel are prime examples of face-to-face marketing and are looking for a return on their investment when participating. For example, companies such as Coca Cola or Pepsi exhibit at the National Restaurant Association Show in Chicago because the attendees represent businesses that purchase these products. A company that manufactures machines for folding bed sheets will not participate in this show but can be found at the American Hotel and Lodging Association (AH&LA) show in New York. Large companies (for example, Microsoft or IBM) will have full-time employees who do nothing but coordinate the company exhibits and the shows in which they participate; smaller companies will have people who work on trade shows as part of a larger job, such as marketing manager or director of communications. A company has to be sure to determine that those attending a particular trade show are decision makers rather than "tire kickers"—they want to interface with buyers who will undertake the transaction rather than attendees who have to get approval from a higher authority.

EXHIBIT STAFF

The most important part of any exhibit is the staff. A company may have a superb exhibit—attractive, open, inviting, and informative—but if the staff are untrained, communicate poorly, and do not dress professionally, the exhibit will communicate the wrong message to a visitor about the company and its products or services. Therefore, it is important that, whether for a large or small exhibit, the staffers are the best they can be.

Models are used to "meet and greet" potential clients at the booth.
Photo by George G. Fenich, Ph.D.

Staff must be trained to "meet and greet." It is important that visitors are greeted warmly and made to feel welcome at the exhibit. Staff must also "qualify" visitors to determine if they are potential customers or not. By asking the right questions and listening to visitors, they can easily determine whether to spend more time with them, pass them to another staff member, or politely move them through the exhibit. Time is important, especially during the busy times at a trade show, so qualifying visitors is an important step in focusing your staff's time.

Many companies provide product demonstrations or even elaborate productions about their products or services. This aspect must be well managed and focus the visitors' attention on the main messages the company wants to communicate.

EXHIBITION MANAGEMENT AND SERVICE CONTRACTORS

Before, during, and after the trade show, a company will be working with the exhibition management company and service contractors. As previously described, these companies play a critical role in the show coming together and providing all the needed services to the exhibiting companies.

From the exhibitor's perspective, these companies are critical for success. They provide the space, lighting, décor, carpeting, setup, teardown, lead retrieval systems, and all the other services for the trade show program. The person tasked by the company to coordinate all these activities must develop a relationship with the management company and service companies. The person must have a clear understanding of all contract requirements, deadlines, and exhibitor responsibilities. During the trade show or exhibition, representatives from these companies are on site to assist exhibitors with problems and last-minute needs.

The exhibition management company and service companies also offer additional marketing opportunities for exhibitors to consider. Based on their objectives for the trade show, exhibitors can choose to invest in any of these types of programs:

- *General Sponsorships.* These programs usually involve the company's name being included on printed materials for the trade show or being posted in a prominent place in the exhibit hall.
- *Special Event Sponsorship.* Special events are often conducted during the trade show schedule and include receptions, press conferences, or entertainment. Companies that sponsor these events have their names mentioned prominently in promotional materials and at the event.
- *Advertising in the Show Daily.* Large trade shows usually have a daily newspaper available to all exhibitors and attendees each morning. It reviews the previous day's activities and previews upcoming events. Exhibitors have the opportunity to advertise in the show daily.
- *Advertising in the Show Directory.* Almost all trade shows provide attendees with a show directory, packed with information about the show and exhibitors. Advertising opportunities also exist for this show directory.
- *Promotional Items Sponsorship.* Management companies may also offer sponsorship opportunities to companies for badge holders, tote bags, and other promotional items given to registered attendees.

In S. L. Morrow's book *The Art of the Show* (Dallas, IAEM Foundation, 2002), Sam Lippman presents an excellent set of tips for

A sign indicating where to find the office of the service contractor at a trade show.
Photo by George G. Fenich, Ph.D.

exhibitors on how to maximize their relationship with exhibition management, dividing his tips into three levels. Level one tasks are those
that are essential to exhibiting—meeting all the requirements set by
the organizing company to ensure that exhibitors take advantage of
the many offerings provided to them for marketing their company's
exhibit.

Level two tasks require a more proactive approach. These
involve tasks such as organizing press conferences, advertising in
the show daily, and sending special offers to attendees before the
trade show.

True trade show professionals operate at level three and help ensure the show is a success. At this level, the company trade show managers work in close collaboration with the show organizers to promote the show and do not hesitate to provide special expertise to help the show succeed. Companies operating at this level provide speakers and special events that attract attendees; they also provide volunteers to help the show organizers, and they use their internal resources to assist show management at every level (not just financial).

Summary

Whether large or small, trade shows and exhibitions are business ventures that must be thoroughly planned for success. All components of the exhibition model must be blended together to create a positive experience for the attendees, the exhibitors, and the organizing company or association.

For an exhibiting company, a trade show is a significant investment from the marketing budget. Therefore, it is critical that planning take place that considers activities before, during, and after the trade show to maximize the ROI. Organizing companies must address the needs of attendees and, just as important, the needs of the exhibitors. Exhibitors are the lifeblood of the trade show, providing the excitement and resources that ensure a show's success.

Key Words and Terms

For definitions, see the Glossary or go to http://glossary.convention industry.org.

Exhibition	Multilevel exhibit
Exhibition management company	Peninsular booth
	Public show
Exhibition service contractor (ESC)	Return on investment (ROI)
	Standard booth
Exposition	Trade fair
In-line exhibit	Trade show
Island booth	

Review and Discussion Questions

1. What is the difference between a typical trade show and a public show?
2. Give some examples of services that exhibition service contractors provide to exhibitors.
3. What attributes of an exhibit layout would a company want if its major objective is branding?
4. Describe the layout of a peninsular exhibit.
5. What kinds of additional marketing opportunities do management companies typically offer?
6. Why is risk management important to an exhibition management company? To an exhibitor?
7. What factors are considered by an exhibition management company when determining the location of a trade show or exhibition?
8. What are the three phases of planning that a company trade show manager must address?

References

Trade Publications

Convene, PCMA, 2301 S. Lakeshore Drive, Suite 1001, Chicago, IL 60616

Exhibit Builder, P.O. Box 4144, Woodland Hills, CA 91365

Exhibitor Magazine, 206 S. Broadway, Suite 475, Rochester, MN 55903

EXPO, 11600 College Boulevard, Overland Park, KS 66210

Facility Manager, IAAM, 635 Fritz Drive, Coppell, TX 75019

IdEAs, 5501 Backlick Road, Suite 105, Springfield, VA 22151

Meetings & Conventions Magazine, Reed Travel Group, 500 Plaza Drive, Secaucus, NJ 07094

Tradeshow Week, 12233 W. Olympic Blvd., Suite 236, Los Angeles, CA 90064

Books

Chapman, Edward. 1995. *Exhibit marketing.* New York: McGraw-Hill.

Miller, Steve. 1996. *How to get the most out of trade shows.* Lincoln-wood, IL: NTC Business Books.

Morrow, S. L. 2002. *The art of the show.* Dallas: IAEM Foundation.

Weisgal, Margit. 1997. *Show and sell.* New York: American Management Association.

Web Sites

Center for Exhibition Industry Research	http://www.ceir.org
EventWeb	http://www.eventweb.com
ExhibitorNet	http://www.exhibitornet.com
International Association of Exhibition Managers	http://www.iaem.org
Professional Convention Management Association	http://www.pcma.org
Trade Show Central	http://www.tscentral.com
Trade Show News Network	http://www.tsnn.com

About the Chapter Contributor

Ben McDonald is the vice president of BenchMark Learning, Inc. Founded in 1995, BenchMark Learning assists businesses with training and development solutions primarily in the sales and business development areas. They have since expanded their services and partnerships to include the full spectrum of sales solutions, business development, benchmarking, and competitor analysis in order to provide their clients with a total solution for increasing revenue.

CHAPTER 6

Service Contractors

One of the services provided by exhibition service contractors is booth design and construction.

Photo provided by GES

Chapter Objectives

This chapter provides the reader with an understanding of the following:

- Service contractors and their role in MEEC
- Roles of general service contractors and specialty contractors
- Exhibitor-appointed contractors
- Associations in service contracting

Chapter Outline

Introduction

Service Contractor Responsibilities

    General Service Contractors (GSC)

    Trade Unions

Evolution of Service Contractors

Organization of a Service Contracting

    Company

Specialty Service Contractors

Exhibitor-Appointed Contractor

Relationship between Contractors and

    Show Organizers

Associations in the Service Contractor

    Industry

So How Does It All Work?

Introduction

An event producer or show manager (or organizer) may have all the tools at his or her fingertips to promote, sell, and execute a show or conference, but there are many pieces of equipment that he or she does not have. For example, while you might be a great cook, you do not make the frying pan or the spatula—you turn to experts for that. For exhibitions and events to be produced smoothly and efficiently, the producers and managers must rely on professional service contractors to give them—and the exhibitors—the tools necessary to be successful. These people are called service contractors, and this chapter discusses their various roles in the process, their relationship with the organizer, and their relationship with each other.

Service Contractor Responsibilities

A **service contractor** is anyone who provides a product or service for the exhibitor or show management during the actual show or conference. Service contractors can be the florist, the electrical company, the registration company, the models and hostesses, and just about every service provider you can think of. Some service contractors are hired by the show organizers to assist with their needs, and others are hired directly by the exhibitor.

Meetings, expositions, events, and conventions (MEEC) service contractors and their roles have evolved over time. Historically, they were referred to as decorators, based on their earliest primary function as service contractors, which was to "decorate" the empty space of a convention center or hotel ballroom. This decorating function included pipe and drape, carpets, backdrops, booths, and furnishings.

Over the years, service contractors have expanded the scope of their activities to match the growing sophistication of MEEC. Today, service contractors can be, and likely are, involved in every aspect of the event from move in, to the show itself, to teardown, and to move out. As a result, the service contractor provides an important interface between the event organizer and other MEEC suppliers such as the convention center itself, hotel convention services, exhibitors, local labor, and unions. Many service contractors will work with the organizer to lay out trade show floors, in part because they have spent the time to take careful measurements of every MEEC venue in the host community (see D. G. Rutherford, *Introduction to the Conventions, Expositions, and Meetings Industry*, New York, Van Nostrand Reinhold, 1990). Service contractors are also involved before the setup of the show when they send out exhibitor kits and other information.

GENERAL SERVICE CONTRACTOR (GSC)

The **general service contractor (GSC)** (also called the official show contractor or exposition services contractor) is hired by the show manager to handle the general duties necessary to produce the show on site. The Convention Industry Council (CIC) definition of a general service contractor is "an organization that provides event management and exhibitors with a wide range of services, sometimes including, but not limited to, installing and dismantling, creating and hanging signage and banners, laying carpet, and providing booth/stand furniture." Sometimes the show will have an official contractor (appointed by show management), whose CIC definition is "an organization appointed by show management to provide services such as setup and teardown of exhibit booths and to oversee labor, drayage, and loading dock procedures."

GSCs are responsible for assisting the show organizer with graphic treatments for the entrance and all signage, putting up the pipe and

Trucks and equipment from the Freeman companies transport and handle freight.

Photo by George G. Fenich, Ph.D.

drape or hard wall exhibits, placing aisle carpet, and creating all the official booths, such as association centers, registration area, lounges, and special areas. More important, general service contractors offer the show organizer a valuable service by hiring and managing the labor for a particular show because they have standing contracts with unions and tradespeople, and they know how to hire enough labor to move a show in and out based on the requirements of the show. It is their responsibility to move the freight in and out of the facility, manage the flow of trucks coming in and out of the facility, and oversee the storage of crates and boxes during the show, all of which is called **drayage** or **material handling**.

"Drayage" is a somewhat confusing term that may be traced back to medieval times. According to *Webster's New Universal Unabridged Dictionary*, drayage is the sum charge paid for the use of a dray (a dray is a low, strong cart with detachable sides used for drawing heavy loads); today, drayage refers to the price paid for having trucks transport products. The transport vehicle can be a truck or a plane, and the fee includes many aspects of the transportation service. Service contractors may charge for services such as crating an exhibit in a box, using a forklift to get the box onto a small truck that takes the crate to a local warehouse or storage facility, and then putting it onto an 18-wheeler for over-the-road transport. The reverse happens at the other end and ultimately leads to unloading at the convention center or event site. There the service contractor will also supervise the unloading of the crate and delivery of it to the proper booth. After the crate is unpacked, the service contractor will arrange for storage of the empty crate until the show is over; then the whole process is reversed. The price for drayage is based on the weight (not the size) of the materials or crate. The fee is based on each 100 pounds of weight and thus is called hundredweight. A bill of lading is completed by the shipper and delineates what the package contains, who owns it, where it is going, and whether there are any special instructions. This is the official shipping document, and authorities at checkpoints such as state borders and especially national borders may insist on examining it.

Many GSCs have expanded into specialty areas. Thus, general service contractors today may provide audiovisual equipment, security, cleaning, and more. This is done for a number of reasons. GSCs, relying on the concept of relationship marketing, are building on the relationships they have established with show organizers over years of interaction. Provision of a wide range of services also gives the show organizer the advantage of one-stop shopping. By using a GSC that provides general and specialty services, the show organizer does not have to deal with a multitude of companies to produce the show. Providing an array of services also allows the GSC to increase revenues and, it is hoped, profitability.

A GSC not only serves the show organizer but is the official service contractor for exhibitors. Exhibitors can rent everything they need for their exhibit—from a simple chair to a complete exhibit—from the GSC. Some general service contractors will build a booth for exhibitors, store it, and ship it to other shows on behalf of the exhibitor.

The GSC adds value to his or her services by creating the **exhibitor service manual** (exhibitor services kit) along with the show organizer. This manual is a compilation of all the show information, such as dates, times, rules, and regulations, for both the show manager and the city. Also included are all the forms necessary for an exhibitor to have a successful show. These forms typically include orders for carpet,

Signage is an important service.

Photo by George G. Fenich, Ph.D.

furniture, utilities, setup and dismantling, and drayage. Some show organizers also include promotional opportunities to help exhibitors do preshow and on-site promotion. The service manuals can be printed and mailed; service manuals now exist as CD-ROMs or on the Internet as well, allowing exhibitors to order services and products online.

On site, the GSC works with both the show organizer and exhibitor to ensure a smooth move in and move out. He or she is often the conduit to a facility to make sure that the rules and regulations are observed. Many times, the GSC solves problems for the exhibitors by finding lost freight, repairing damaged booths or crates, and cleaning the carpets and booths in the evenings.

The services provided by a GSC can include the following:

Show Services
- Account management
- On-site coordination of the event
- Pipe and drape
- Entry areas
- Offices
- Registration areas
- Setup and dismantling of booths
- Planning, layout, and design
- Carpet
- Furniture
- Signs
- Graphics
- Backdrops
- Interface with labor and unions
- Cleaning
- Transportation services
- Material handling
- Customer service

Exhibitor Services
- Exhibit design and construction
- Booth setup and dismantling
- Carpet
- Furniture and accessories
- Signs/signage
- Interface with labor and unions

This simple example of rigging was used to attract attention to a booth selling chairs.
Photo by George G. Fenich, Ph.D.

- Rigging
- Material handling
- Exhibitor kit

TRADE UNIONS

Exhibition service contractors as well as show organizers will make use of tradespeople in the community to help set up and tear down the show. Many of these tradespeople will be members of a trade union. Everyone involved in a show should be aware of the local laws and policies regarding use of unionized personnel. The primary issue is whether the community is located in a "right-to-work" state; in this type of state, an individual working in a specific trade is *not* required to join the trade union representing that skill, so show organizers and participants are free to hire whom they please, regardless of whether they are union members. However, if the community is not in a right-to-work state, then people working in the trades (such as electricians, plumbers, riggers, porters) must belong to the union. In these communities there can be significant repercussions if the proper union

The Case of Exhibiting in a Unionized City

Service contractors can play a pivotal role in dealing with unionized labor. This is especially problematic because (1) the unions and rules vary throughout the United States, and (2) local labor is essential for putting together an event or trade show. The following portrays one exhibitor's interaction with unionized labor in a city in the northeastern United States. The exhibit, in its crate, was transported to the convention center in a tractor-trailer, and according to local rules, the trailer had to be driven by a member of the Teamsters Union. On arrival at the convention center, the driver opened the back of the trailer but could do no more to facilitate removal of the crate. That required a forklift, and the forklift is considered a piece of heavy equipment (not a truck) and thus had to be operated by a member of the Heavy Equipment Operators Union. So they waited for the forklift operator, who then moved the crate to the exhibit booth and placed it on the ground. At that point, the exhibitor was eager to get set up but could do nothing until a member of the Carpenters Union arrived to take the nails out of the crate—wood and nails are a job for a union carpenter. The crate was opened, but the exhibitor was restricted from doing anything himself that a union member should do. Thus, he waited for a member of the Porters Union to come to take the exhibit contents out of the crate. That was followed by a string of different union members who each did a separate but distinct job and would not infringe on the responsibilities or activities of a different union. So the exhibit frame that was made from pipes had to be assembled by someone from the Plumbers Union because only plumbers handle pipes. The products and cloth were assembled and laid out by a member of the Stage Hands Union— after all, an exhibit is part of a "show." The sign over the booth required someone from the Heavy Equipment Operators Union to drive a bucket lift, while a member of the Riggers Union occupied the bucket to "rig" the sign. The exhibitor could not even plug his VCR into the electrical outlet provided by show management—that had to be done by a member of the Electricians Union. The telephone had to be plugged into a jack provided by a member of the Communications Workers Union, and the flowers had to be "arranged" by a member of the Agricultural Union. Of course, the cleaning people, security, and other service personnel had to be members of the appropriate union. In addition, part of a supervisor's pay in each of these unions had to be paid by the exhibitor in proportion to the amount of time that union spent at his booth. Further complicating matters is that unless special fees are paid, there can be significant time lapses between when one union member finishes a particular job and when the next arrives. And—oh yes—if any union rule is violated or the exhibitor tries to do something himself, all the unions will boycott that booth

(continued)

and refuse to work. Obviously, a service contractor who is knowledgeable about local union rules and has established an ongoing relationship with local labor can be worth his or her weight in gold to an exhibitor or show organizer.

members are not used. For example, in some locales, exhibitors cannot even carry their own materials from their automobile to the trade show booth; they must use a member of the porters union.

However, unions do serve a number of laudable purposes. They represent a class of workers (such as electricians) when negotiating with management over pay scales and working conditions and carry more clout than any single worker could possibly have. Unions also set very specific guidelines regarding termination of an employee and will provide a union member with legal council if necessary. In addition, they help to ensure that working conditions are safe and comfortable. Lastly, they work with government agencies to help establish guidelines for the construction trades.

Evolution of Service Contractors

Today, service contractors are evolving and changing to meet the needs of the client and the environment. One of the major changes has been increasing the scope of their work to center on meeting the needs of exhibitors. As is the case with the organizers of events, service contractors have come to the conclusion that it is the exhibitors who are the driving force of the trade show segment of MEEC. Further, they have come to understand that exhibitors have more trade shows and vendors than ever to choose from, along with increased numbers of marketing channels through which to promote and distribute their products. Thus, both service contractors and show organizers are directing their attention to the needs of the exhibitor. Exhibitors are reacting to this effort by getting much more specific about their wants and needs, and also becoming much more discreet and selective when choosing a service contractor. Exhibitors spend huge amounts of money to participate in a trade show and want the best return on investment (ROI) they can get. In today's economic environment, exhibiting companies have to justify the expense of a trade show and are looking to service contractors to help with that justification and to show the value added by participating in the show.

In the long run, service contractors must deliver quality service and products to the user, whether it is the organizer or the exhibitor. Otherwise, both constituents will seek other marketing avenues and strategies, with organizers left out in the cold. The status quo does not hold true any longer, and some companies have decided to forgo trade shows in which they have participated for years. The well-known COMDEX trade show appears to be facing exactly this type of problem, as is that of the National Association of Television Production Executives (NATPE). In lieu of exhibiting at an alternative trade show, some companies are developing their own private trade shows targeted to specific markets or customers.

Still another change for service contractors is that many facilities are now offering to do in-house what used to be the exclusive domain of service contractors. For example, many convention centers are now offering to install utilities, such as electricity, water, steam, and gas, and may no longer allow service contractors to do this. Venues are also providing services, including cleaning, security, audiovisuals, and room setups. This approach is cutting into the business and revenues of service contractors.

The advent of **exhibitor-appointed contractors (EACs),** which are discussed later in this chapter, has cannibalized the business of the service contractor. This trend began in the mid-1980s when the courts ruled that service contractors could not have exclusive right to control and negotiate with organized labor. Thus, an EAC from out of the area had the legal right to compete with service contractors and set up a booth for an exhibitor. EACs are a subset of service contractors that, rather than work from one city or location, work for the exhibiting company and travel throughout the country setting up and dismantling their booths. Their success is based on the long-term relationship they have built with the client company, that is, relationship marketing. Because exhibitor-appointed contractors work for the same company over many trade shows and events, they are more knowledgeable about the client company's needs and can provide more efficient service than the broader service contractor.

This competition between service contractors and EACs has encouraged the service contractors to provide more specialized, streamlined, and efficient service to exhibiting companies. For example, one service contractor now provides exhibiting companies with the same service representative before the trade show opens, during the show, and after the show for reconciliation and billing. This lets the customer deal with one source for ordering of all services and products, creates a one-stop service desk, and provides a single master bill representing every product and service used. This is analogous to an individual who gets a different credit card receipt for each transaction but a single cumulative bill at the end of the month. A service contractor named TEG has a program called the "Gold Advantage" for its best customers that provides a special customer service representative who is available twenty-four hours a day, seven days a week, and a private service center that has a lounge, fax, phone, copy services, and so forth. The large service contractor GES Exposition Services has brought the traditional service desk to the customer by equipping its sales representatives with personal digital assistants (PDAs) so that they can go to a booth and provide on-the-spot service. Freeman Decorating has a program called "ExhibiTouch," where touch-screen computer kiosks are located throughout the exhibit floor; a client can go to the kiosk and transact most business requests, ascertain freight status, and print forms (order forms, invoice summaries, and shipping labels).

Service contractors are also expanding into the area of event marketing. This too is based on the desire by clients to do most of their business with someone or some company they know and trust—relationship marketing. The show organizer or association host may sponsor some events, but corporations put on most events. As a result, many exhibitors are now responsible for corporate events outside the traditional trade show floor. The service contractors, having developed a long-term relationship with the exhibitor, are now developing corporate events programs, multievent exhibit programs, private trade shows, new product introductions, hospitality events for clients, multicity touring exhibitions, and more nontraditional promotional campaigns.

Technology is also changing the way service contractors do business. As with many businesses, the computer is eliminating many activities traditionally done with pen and paper, including updating floor plans, tracking freight, and monitoring small package deliveries. For example, as little as ten years ago, floor plans had to be drawn by hand using drafting instruments. A simple booth change, because it affects the entire show layout, could take a week or more to redraft; now, thanks to computer technology, changes are almost instantaneous. Freeman Decorating, for example, has a program called "Design Vault" on its in-house network. Design Vault includes floor plans and artists' drawings for every major convention facility in the country. Thus, clients can take a virtual tour through the venue and make floor plan changes immediately.

Service contractors are also using technology to help them with drayage. Again, pen and paper are being replaced with computer

A welcome kiosk outside a convention center, such as this one, is a product supplied by a service contractor.

Photo provided by GES

technology that allows tracking of all sizes of shipments faster and more accurately. Everything is online, so when a truck enters or leaves a facility, it is in the computer system and freight managers can go to the central computer to check the status of not only the vehicle but its contents as well. The Global Positioning System (GPS) on many trucks allows satellite tracking of its location. This technological monitoring happens on the trade show floor, too. An exhibitor can contact the service contractor and know which crates are still on the truck and which have been delivered to the booth. Small packages, such as brochures, can be tracked in the same fashion.

Still another use of technology embraced by service contractors is Web site development. They produce Web sites for show organizers that include interactive floor plans, exhibitor show information, booth reservation services, and even personal itineraries for show attendees (see Martha Collins, "The Evolution of the General Services Contractors," *Expo Magazine*, February 1999, pp. 1–5).

Organization of a Service Contracting Company

Service contractors are businesses and, like most businesses, are organized into functional areas. This means that there are different departments grouped by a common activity or function that support the mission of the company. The department that controls and directs the company can be called "administration" and may include the general manager (GM) or chief executive officer (CEO), marketing personnel, assistants, receptionists, and the like. Some of the other departments or divisions are as follows:

- *Sales.* This group is typically divided or broken up into national sales and local sales or special events. Some companies also have a separate exhibitor sales department that takes over from national sales in dealing with exhibitors. Exhibitor sales will provide each exhibitor with an inventory of the supplies available and the cost of each item. Exhibitor sales also work to encourage exhibitors to upgrade from standard to superior-quality products at a higher price. Exhibitor sales typically will have an office and a full-time presence at the trade show to facilitate interaction between production and exhibitors, and will sell additional products and services on the trade show floor.
- *Logistics.* This department handles planning, scheduling, shipping, labor relations, site selection, and preparation. It also determines the flow and delivery of booth materials—with booths in the center of the hall being delivered before booths by the doors so that access is not blocked. This department may also work with the exhibit facility and lay out all the different-sized booths, aisles, food service areas, registration, and so on. Today, this is done using computer technology known as CAD/CAM.
- *Drayage and Warehousing.* This section oversees the transportation of materials, booths, exhibits, etc., along with their temporary storage in the host city. Drayage may include air transport, tractor-trailers, and local transportation.
- *Event Technology.* This department oversees technology, special effects, and reports and does the planning and subsequent installation of the output of the production department.
- *Event Services.* This group has responsibility for on-site coordination, registration, and exhibitor kits. The exhibitor kit tells exhibitors everything they need to know about the facility, capacities, rules, regulations, labor, and move-in and move-out

The primary communications link between show organizers and/or exhibitors and the ESC is the service center on the trade show floor.
Photo provided by GES

times, along with the array of services provided by the service contractor.

- *Production.* Woodworking, props, backdrops, signs, electrical needs, lighting, metal work, and so on are provided by the production department. At Freeman Decorating in New Orleans, clients regularly request backdrops that look like the French Quarter or a swamp. These are produced on large boards like those used in theater productions; however, they are painted by two men who have worked there for years, with the backdrops laying flat on the floor and the men standing up, using paintbrushes like those used for oil painting—except that these paintbrushes are five feet long!

- *Accounting and Finance.* This group oversees accounts receivable, accounts payable, payroll, and financial analysis.

Two of the largest GSCs are Freeman Decorating (http://www. freemanco.com) and GES Exposition Services (http://www.gesexpo. com). The Freeman companies have three divisions: Expositions, Events and Environments, and Exhibits. Their headquarters is in Dallas, Texas, and they have offices in twenty-three cities throughout North America.

Begun in 1927, they are a full-service contractor for expositions, conventions, special events, and corporate meetings. The company is privately held and owned by the Freeman family and company employees.

GES Exposition Services is headquartered in Las Vegas but has offices in all the major cities across North America. GES is a wholly owned subsidiary of Phoenix-based Viad Corp., a $1.7 billion publicly held corporation traded on the New York Stock Exchange under the symbol VVI.

Specialty Service Contractors

Specialty service contractors deal with a specific area of show production, whereas the GSC tends to be broad and generic. Specialty service contractors can be either official contractors (appointed by show management) or exhibitor-appointed contractors (see below). They handle all the services needed to complete the exhibit:

- *Audiovisuals.* Services and supplies to enhance the exhibits through audiovisual methods.
- *Business Services.* Copying, printing, faxing, and other business services.
- *Catering.* Food and beverages for show organizers and for individual exhibitors.
- *Cleaning Services.* Cleaning of public areas, especially carpet, along with booths, offices, and nonpublic areas.
- *Communications.* PDAs, cell phones, and wired and wireless services.
- *Computers.* Rental of computers and monitors.
- *Consulting.* Pre-event planning, coordination, facilitation, layout and design, and booth design.
- *Drayage.* Over-the-road transportation of materials for the show, transfers, and delivery of materials from a local warehouse or depot to the show site, airfreight, and returns.
- *Electrical Services.* Electrical power for the exhibits.
- *Floral Services.* Rental of plants, flowers, and props.
- *Freight.* Shipping of exhibit materials from the company to the show and back using various kinds of shippers (common carriers, van lines, and airfreight).

GES Exposition Services

SALLIE SARGEANT

Senior Director of Corporate Communications, GES Exposition Services

GES Exposition Services is a premier provider of exhibition and event services in the trade show industry, staging some of the most recognizable trade shows in the world. Headquartered in Las Vegas and with offices in every major convention market, GES designs and produces world-class trade shows across North America for show organizers and their exhibitors. True to its Las Vegas roots, style, and reputation, GES never fails to light up their clients' stage.

HISTORY

GES dates back to 1939, with a Kansas City company called Manncraft that specialized in signs, window trimmings, and small displays. In 1969, the Greyhound Corporation purchased Manncraft, and growth through acquisitions began. In the early 1970s, offices were opened in Los Angeles, San Francisco, Chicago, and San Diego through acquisition as well as organic growth. In 1973, Greyhound acquired Las Vegas Convention Services Company, and the stronghold in Las Vegas began. In 1979, Manncraft changed its name to Greyhound Exposition Services—GES was born.

GES expanded into the Pacific Northwest in 1991 through acquisitions in Seattle and Portland. By the end of 1992, GES was headquartered in Las Vegas, with offices in most major West Coast cities. At this point, the company had 500 full-time employees. Recognizing the projected growth of the trade show industry, GES decided to establish nationwide service. In May 1993, GES made the largest acquisition in its history by purchasing United Exposition Service Company, whose city operations included virtually every major convention market east of the Mississippi.

With the United acquisition, Greyhound Exposition Services changed its name to GES Exposition Services to reflect "The New GES." In October 1993, GES acquired Andrews, Bartlett & Associates, a major regional contractor based in Hudson, Ohio; in November of the same year, it acquired Gelco Convention Services, based in Miami, enhancing the Orlando operation.

During early 1995, GES expanded into Canada through the acquisition of Panex Show Services and Stampede Display and Convention Services, gaining

(continued)

GES Exposition Services (*continued*)

offices in Toronto, Calgary, and Edmonton. By June of that year, Concept Convention Service had joined the GES family, with offices in Phoenix, Tucson, and Albuquerque.

GES acquired ESR Exposition Services, one of New York City's leading trade show and event contractors, in May 1998. In June that same year, GES also acquired Puliz of Utah, Inc., a noted trade show and corporate events company with locations in Reno and Salt Lake City.

In October 1998, Panex, Canada's largest trades and event-marketing company, changed its name to GES CANADA Exposition Services Limited.

SERVICES

During the early days of conventions, the primary role of GES was to provide carpet, pipe, and drape for booths. In today's high-tech world, trade shows involve sophisticated designs and tireless technical support.

GES provides a comprehensive one-stop shop for events and trade shows that includes the following services: show planning, logistics, material handling, floor plans, exhibits and design, signs and graphics, carpet and furnishings, installation and dismantling, and extensive exhibitor support.

Exhibitor Support

Before the show, GES assists exhibitors through the GES National Servicenter, located in Las Vegas. The Servicenter is open nationwide during business hours and processes more than 25,000 exhibitor orders and answers more than 10,000 phone calls every month.

Technology

At the show, GES representatives use the GES Wireless Ambassador. This handheld computer allows GES staff members to research and place orders, check freight information, and access up-to-the-minute data right from the exhibitor's booth, ensuring the highest level of customer service. GES has also developed the Automated Freight & Package Receiving system that uses bar coding to ensure packages and deliveries are received efficiently and reliably at the show.

STATISTICS

Each year, GES Exposition Services lays 56 million square feet of aisle carpet, produces more than 3,000 trade shows and events, delivers 650 million pounds of freight, prints 700,000 booth identification signs, produces approximately 7 million square feet of graphics, and rents enough extension cords to reach from coast to coast through its Trade Show Electrical division.

As GES has grown to provide a one-stop shop for increasingly sophisticated expositions, many of unprecedented size and complexity, it has tackled several challenges involved in the design and management of these "mega" trade shows. For example, during the world's largest gathering for the construction and construction materials industry, which is called the CONEXPO–CON/AGG trade show and is held every three years, cement batch plants of colossal proportions are erected. Onlookers are often awestruck by these monoliths—large-scale machinery so immense that it must be showcased in the convention center parking lot.

High-value customer service and innovative custom design bridge yesterday's Greyhound Exposition Services, once focused on small and simple conventions, and today's behemoth, GES. GES is a modern and efficient company that capitalizes on cutting-edge technology to orchestrate large and sophisticated events. GES now produces 80% of the largest trade shows in Las Vegas, relishing in the orchestration of large volumes of people, freight, and union workers in an efficient and customer-conscientious way. There is no doubt that the GES trade show niche—specializing in the biggest of the big shows—accurately reflects its modern hometown image.

As for what lies in the future, GES sees still brighter horizons ahead. GES has begun to create the groundwork for future innovation in the industry, harnessed by its ability to design and build exhibits in ways that allow exhibitors to effortlessly market their products. In this vein, GES has led the industry with its innovative technology development, which will continue to set industry standards in trade show logistics in the years to come.

Finally, GES will continue to respond to the demands of its customers, among them the companies and organizations that put on the largest and most recognizable shows in the industry. In this sense, GES demonstrates continuity with the past—the company has always specialized in offering high-value services to exhibitors and show organizers and continues this tradition of excellence.

- *Furniture.* Rental of furniture (often fancier than that in your home) for exhibits.
- *Internet Access and Telephones.* Rental of equipment and lines on the show floor.
- *Labor Planning and Supervision.* Expertise on local rules and regulations regarding which tradespeople to work with, union requirements, and supervision of workers on site.
- *Lighting.* Design and rental of lighting.
- *Models and Hostesses.* Hiring of temporary exhibit or demonstration personnel.
- *Photography.* Publicity for show organizers and for individual exhibitors.
- *Postal and Package Services.* Postal services for both organizers and exhibitors.
- *Security.* Security for booths during closed hours and for entrances during show hours.
- *Translators.* Simultaneous translation of speeches and presentations for show organizers and communication services between sales representatives and foreign attendees for exhibitors.
- *Utilities.* Plumbing, air, gas, steam, and water for technical exhibits.

Besides the standard needs listed earlier, each show has its own needs. For example, a show in the food and beverage industry will have a contractor who supplies ice and cold storage, while a show in the automotive industry might have a contractor who cleans cars.

Exhibitor-Appointed Contractor (EAC)

As companies do more and more shows, their exhibits become more involved, and they often want one service supplier working with them throughout the year, or they have a favorite vendor whom they have worked with in a city where they do many shows. This is particularly true with regard to the installation and dismantling of the exhibit. Most times, show organizers will allow this, assuming that a company meets the qualifications for insurance and licensing. This company is called an exhibitor-appointed contractor (EAC). As EACs, they perform the same duties as a specialty contractor but only for that exhibitor, not the show manager. The CIC definition is "any company other than the designated 'official' contractor providing a service to an exhibitor . . .

The Translator Who Knew too Much

A small American company decided that it wanted to exhibit at a trade show in Europe. One of the things it determined was that none of the sales managers who were going to staff their booth spoke any language except English, so it was decided that a translator fluent in Spanish, Italian, and German would be hired. The translator worked so well that she was hired to provide services at another trade show a year later. At this second show, attendees asked many of the same questions asked at the first trade show. Since the questions were repetitive, the translator had learned the answers and would simply answer the attendees without translating or asking the sales managers. Response at this show was low, in spite of high attendance, and reactions to the products being displayed at the booth were poor. When the company manager did a postshow assessment, he uncovered the reason—the attendees got the impression that since a mere translator knew about the products, they must be very simplistic and not cutting edge. So at all future trade shows, the translator was told to always translate, to always ask the sales managers, and to never answer on her own!

and can refer to an install & dismantle company (I&D house), photographer, florist, or any other type of contractor."

Some services may be provided only by the official service contractor and are called **exclusive services.** This decision is left up to the show manager, who makes that decision based on meeting the needs of the show and the rules and regulations of the facility or ensuring the smooth move in and teardown of the show. Can you imagine what would happen if every freight company and installation company tried to move their exhibitors' freight in all at once? It would be chaos! So material handling (drayage) is often handled as an exclusive service. Many facilities have very specific guidelines regarding the use of exhibitor-appointed contractors; for example, in some cases, the exhibitor must make application to the facility to use one.

Relationship between Contractors and Show Organizers

One of the first actions that show organizers take when developing an event is to hire the GSC. This partnership develops as the show develops. General service contractors will often recommend cities

Representatives from the ESC work with show organizers and exhibitors to create a successful event.

Photo provided by GES

where a show should be held, the times of the year that would be best, and the facilities that fit the event. It is important to hire this company early on.

The process for hiring service contractors is through a **request for proposal (RFP).** The show organizer creates a list of questions and specifications for each show. Other areas of concern include knowledge of the industry, knowledge of the facility, other shows being handled in the same industry, size of the organization, and budget. A sample RFP can be found at http://www.esca.org.

As the show is developed, a GSC watches closely to suggest how marketing themes and association logos can be used in entrance treatments and signage so that when a show comes alive, it looks and feels the way the show organizer wants it to. Color schemes, visual treatments, and types of materials all come from the mind of the GSC.

Specialty service contractors work with show organizers to help exhibitors save time and money. Reviewing the past history of a show can tell a service contractor what types of furniture, floral, and electrical needs the exhibitors have used. This permits the specialty contractors

Exhibition Services and Contractors Association (ESCA)

According to the Exhibition Services & Contractors Association Web site, ESCA is:

The association for firms engaged in providing services and materials for the hospitality industry: Trade shows and exhibitions, conventions and meetings, and sales meetings

- The voice of the exhibition service industry
- A clearinghouse for the exchange of information between members and all other entities of the vast trade show and convention industry
- A source for leading general service contractors, specialty contractors, independent contractors, and their suppliers
- A source for discounts and assistance in the current business climate

MISSION STATEMENT

ESCA is dedicated to the advancement of the exhibition, meeting, and special events industries. Through the education, information exchange, and level of professionalism shared by members and their customers, ESCA promotes cooperation among all areas of the exhibition industry.

ETHICS STATEMENT

Members of ESCA recognize the need for standards of professionalism in the relationship between contractor and customer and within the industry as a whole. They recognize that their customers come from every aspect of the exhibition, meeting, and special events industry, ranging from the organizer to the attendee. All ESCA members pledge themselves to conduct their business activities with integrity. ESCA members understand that they are responsible for the professional conduct of persons in their employ. Consequently, they undertake, through exemplary conduct at all times, to secure observance by their employees of this code of ethics.

ESCA members pledge themselves to act in accordance with the following principles of the ESCA code of ethics. Responsibilities of all members include the following:

1. *Accuracy.* ESCA members will provide factual and accurate information about their services and the services of any firm they represent. They will not use deceptive practices.

(continued)

Exhibition Services and Contractors Association (ESCA) *(continued)*

2. *Disclosure.* ESCA members will provide complete details about terms and conditions of any services, including cancellation and service fee policies, before accepting deposits.

3. *Delivery.* ESCA members will provide all services as stated in their agreement or written confirmation or provide alternate services of equal or greater value, or appropriate compensation.

4. *Cooperation.* ESCA members will serve in a spirit of partnership with show management, other contractors, facilities management, and exhibitors.

5. *Responsiveness.* ESCA members will offer prompt, reliable, and courteous service at all times.

6. *Compliance.* ESCA members shall abide by all federal, state, and local laws and regulations.

7. *Regulations.* ESCA members will comply with all codes and standards regarding safety, performance, show rules, and regulations.

8. *Confidentiality.* ESCA members will treat every customer transaction confidentially and not disclose any information without permission of the customer, unless required by law.

9. *Conflict of Interest.* ESCA members will not allow any preferred relationships with suppliers and subcontractors to interfere with the interests of their clients.

10. *Disputes.* ESCA members will work with their customers to resolve disputes quickly and fairly, and if necessary, through mediation or then through arbitration.

Note: Contact information for ESCA: ESCA, 2260 Corporate Circle, Suite 400, Henderson, NV 89074-7701; e-mail: Info@ESCA.org.

to offer money and time-saving tips to the show organizer and pass those savings on to exhibitors. All of this creates a feeling of goodwill among exhibitors, who will then continue to exhibit at the show.

After a time, the service contractor knows the show as well as the show organizer. This can provide added value to the show organizer because as staff changes occur, the service contractor becomes a living historian of the show and its particular nuances.

A Case Study of the Relationship between Service Contractors and Show Organizers

On September 11, 2001, many exhibitions and events were in progress all over the world. Service contractors worked hand in hand with organizers to get shows moved out, and they held shipments for exhibitors while the airlines were not allowed to fly and trucks were being used to transport emergency equipment.

But for the trade show industry, the most important factor post-9/11 was how to handle the cancellation of many of the events. Many people were afraid to fly. There were conventions and exhibitions scheduled for the Jacob Javits Convention Center in New York and the Washington, D.C.-area facilities that were being used by emergency crews. These shows were asked to move their dates or to cancel. These decisions affected not only the show organizers but also the bottom line for the service contracting industry itself. Many had already spent money on both creating show entrances and graphics and preparing staff to work the shows.

The partnership between show organizers and service contractors allowed a compromise. Service contractors billed show organizers only for materials purchased to date and then agreed not to receive payment until the show had been rescheduled; exhibitors were not billed for services they had not used but were asked to agree to use the same services at a later date. Everyone worked together to provide creative solutions.

Because of the partnership between service contractors and show organizers, the effect of September 11 on trade shows was somewhat minimized. Although the combination of the resulting economic slump and fear of travel hurt the technology shows, manufacturing shows showed only a 3%–10% decline. Many of the shows that were to have been held immediately after September 11 and were canceled had successful 2002 shows, indicating that the future would be strong.

Associations in the Service Contractor Industry

There are several associations for individuals and companies in the service contractor industry, including the following:

Canadian Association of Exposition Management (CAEM). Canadian association of show organizers and the people who work for service contractors. Their Web site is http://www.CAEM.ca.

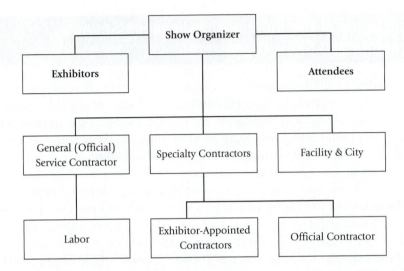

FIGURE 6–1   Relationship between show organizer and service contractors.

Exhibit Designers & Producers Association (EDPA). Organization serving companies engaged in the design, manufacture, transport, installation, and service of displays and exhibits primarily for the trade show industry. Their Web site is http://www.EDPA.com.

Exhibition Services & Contractors Association (ESCA). Organization serving general and specialty contractors. Their Web site is http://www.ESCA.org.

Exhibitor-Appointed Contractors Association (EACA). Association representing exhibitor-appointed contractors and other individual show floor professionals that provides exhibit services on the trade show floor. Their Web site is http://www.EACA.com.

International Association for Exhibition Management (IAEM). Association of show organizers and the people who work for service contractors. Their Web site is http://www.IAEM.org.

National Association of Consumer Shows (NACS). Association of public (consumer) show organizers and the suppliers who support them. Their Web site is http://www.PUBLICSHOWS.com.

So How Does It All Work?

Take a look at the organizational chart in Figure 6–1 and see how the GSC interacts with the show organizer, the facility, the exhibitors, and the other contractors. Remember that exhibitions are like small cities and that the show organizer must provide everything a city does—from safety (security and registration) to a place to work (think of the exhibits as offices), electricity and water, and transportation (shuttle buses). But it has to be done in a very short period of time (sometimes less than a week). Communication among the parties always must be functioning properly, and often it is the GSC who provides that conduit. The coordination of all the contractors likely is the responsibility of the general service contractor, who is acting as the right hand of the show organizer.

Summary

Service contractors are the backbone of the exhibition industry—their support structure allows the show organizers and exhibitors to create an atmosphere that is smooth and efficient. Understanding the responsibilities of each contractor will allow a show organizer to offer the exhibitors the best possible service as well as create a successful environment for buyers and sellers to do business in the exhibition format.

Key Words and Terms

For definitions, see the Glossary or go to http://glossary.convention industry.org.

Drayage

Exclusive service

Exhibitor-appointed contractor (EAC)

Exhibitor service manual

General service contractor (GSC)

Material handling

Request for proposal (RFP)

Service contractor

Specialty service contractor

Review and Discussion Questions

1. What types of services do specialty contractors provide?
2. What are some of the questions that should be asked in an RFP?
3. Describe the difference between a general (official service contractor) and an exhibitor-appointed contractor.
4. How can the GSC assist the show organizer as they both prepare for the show?

About the Chapter Contributor

Susan L. Schwartz, CEM, has been involved in every aspect of exhibition management, including registration, exhibit sales, floor management, marketing, promotion, and educational programming. Susan currently teaches trade show management courses at the University of Nevada–Las Vegas. She is the executive director of the Exhibition Services & Contractors Association.

CHAPTER 7

Destination Management Companies

Destination management companies arrange ground transportation. In Thailand, that includes elephant transport.
Photo by George G. Fenich, Ph.D.

Chapter Objectives

This chapter provides the reader with an understanding of the following:

- What needs the destination management industry meet
- How destination management companies (DMCs) interact with meeting planners, local hotels, event participants, and various suppliers at a destination
- How DMC business is conducted
- What competitive factors are at work in the business process
- What projects DMCs pursue
- How DMCs deliver their contracted services

Chapter Outline

Introduction

Services Offered by DMCs

DMC Clients and Customers

Structure of a DMC

DMC Resources

DMC Business Process

   Comparison between Advertising Firms and DMCs

   Basic Business Requirements

   Sales Process

Identification of New Business Opportunities

Proposal Stage

Site Inspections

Contracts of Services

Program Preparation

Program Operations and Production

Billing and Follow-Up

Destination Management Fictional Case Study

Introduction

One of the many career disciplines that exist in the meetings, expositions, events, and conventions (MEEC) industry is destination management. Careers such as meeting management, hotels, convention centers, convention bureaus, airlines, catering, and restaurant management are the more commonly known outside of the meetings and events industry. However, within the industry, destination management plays a key role in the successful planning and delivery of meetings, conventions, and events.

The Convention Industry Council (CIC)/Accepted Practices Exchange (APEX) glossary defines a destination management company as follows:

> A professional services company possesses extensive local knowledge, expertise and resources, specializing in the design and implementation of events, activities, tours, transportation and program logistics. Depending on the company and the staff specialists in the company, they offer, but are not limited to, the following: creative proposals for special events within the meeting; guest tours; VIP amenities and transportation; shuttle services; staffing within convention centers and hotels; team building, golf outings and other activities; entertainment, including sound and lighting; décor and theme development; ancillary meetings and management professionals; and advance meetings and onsite registration services and housing.

Destination management companies (DMCs) offer a critical layer of management and are hired by meeting planners to provide local knowledge, experience, and resources to corporate and association gatherings. DMCs work cooperatively with airlines, hotels and resorts, convention centers, and other service suppliers in the delivery and implementation of MEEC. Successful MEEC events require comprehensive local knowledge of destination infrastructure, local laws and statutes, and applicable regulations, plus qualified information about supplier availability, capabilities, and capacities. Each destination is unique, and only an extensive and ongoing experience in that particular destination, gained through actual project work, can ensure a successful event. While incentive travel is not a specific part of the MEEC industry, DMCs are a key element in that industry as well.

In discussing DMCs and their services, the client project—be it a meeting, exhibition, event, or convention—is typically referred to within the DMC industry as a **program.** A program includes all activities and services provided by a DMC to a customer group while visiting a destination over a finite time frame.

Services Offered by DMCs

DMCs are engaged by meeting and event planners to suggest what combination of destination resources might best fit and satisfy the goals for a particular gathering. After these services are determined, the DMC plans, sets up, and delivers those services. The following is a list of typical services offered by DMCs:

- Hotel selection
- Event venue selection

- Creative itineraries
- Special event concepts
- Creative theme design
- Event production
- Sightseeing options
- Team-building activities
- Meeting support services
- Transportation planning and delivery
- Dining programs
- Entertainers
- Speakers
- VIP services
- Staffing services
- Budgeting and resource management
- Incentive travel

DMC services often include parties and special events designed for companies and organizations to facilitate networking among attendees, to celebrate accomplishments, or to introduce new ideas and/or products. Planners rely on DMCs to provide unique and creative event concepts that will accomplish specific goals within the client's budget and other organizational limitations. In addition to typical meeting management support services such as transportation and group leisure activities, all aspects of event production, such as staging, sound, and lights, are offered by DMCs. DMCs are a reliable resource for entertainment options, from a small trio for background music at an intimate cocktail party to headline entertainment for large **special events**. Familiarity with local musicians and access to the best entertainers are vital for a good DMC. Additionally, DMCs are often expected to suggest and supply décor elements to enhance event spaces and venues. These elements include but are not limited to props, floral designs, lighting effects, table linens and decorations, and sometimes outdoor tenting.

Transportation logistics are a key element of DMCs. Airport "meet and greet" services, along with hotel transfers and baggage management, are offered by all DMCs. Multihotel convention shuttle service is often designed and managed by DMCs. Moving groups of participants—large or small—is an important component of most events that requires precise timing and execution, local expertise, and management responsibility best provided by a professional DMC.

Every element of an event must come together if success is to be achieved.
Used by permission of Paradise Light & Sound, Orlando, Florida

DMCs also provide sightseeing tours, often customized to optimize the attendees' travel experience. DMCs offer recreational activities, including golf and tennis tournaments, hiking, fishing, horseback riding, and team-building activities.

Because of the creative element associated with meetings and events and the variety of each group's needs and expectations, the list of DMC services is almost limitless. One customer may require many

Destination Management Companies and Incentive Travel

The CIC glossary offers the following definitions related to incentive travel:

Incentive Travel. A travel reward given by companies to employees to stimulate productivity.

Incentive Travel Company. A company that designs and handles some or all elements of incentive travel programs.

In 1999, the Incentive Federation conducted a study that was designed to determine users' objectives, practices, costs, and results across all levels of American business. The survey revealed that using merchandise and travel to motivate can be highly effective and cost-efficient. The first phase of that study, conducted in 1997, reported that $22.8 billion was spent by U.S. businesses on incentive travel and merchandise in 1996 to motivate consumers, employees, dealers, and salespeople as a means of improving performance. Incentive travel primarily is used in programs to increase sales, purchases, or (in the case of employees) productivity or quality. The official Society of Incentive & Travel Executives (SITE) definition of incentive travel says that it rewards people for specific results in formal incentive programs, but many companies that offer travel use it in more loosely structured programs in which employees or customers are singled out to attend a motivational meeting. One study, "Does Incentive Travel Improve Sales Productivity?" conducted in 1997 for SITE at the University of Luton in the United Kingdom, examined employee attitudes at a leading insurance company and found a direct link between the incentive travel program and improved performance.

What distinguishes incentive or motivational travel from traditional travel is the focus on creating an extraordinary experience for the winner, one that builds morale, communicates the corporate message, or fosters improved communications between employees and/or the company and its customers. Businesses use incentive travel to motivate employees to work toward a common goal, recognize employees for performance, get people to make a purchase they might not otherwise make, reinforce a marketing message. Noncash awards such as travel are used to avoid the pricing or compensation issues raised by the use of cash.

The use of individual incentive travel has grown increasingly popular at companies that want to let their winners travel independently. They have developed individual award programs that sometimes add some bells and whistles not available to the usual traveler; most, however, are simply certificate programs that individual winners can redeem at will.

Destination management companies are an often-overlooked but critical resource for companies with incentive groups too small for incentive travel companies to service. DMCs can arrange everything from rooms and ground transportation to elaborate events, special meals, and unique experiences most travelers can't obtain on their own.

Source: Adapted from an online article by the Incentive Travel Federation that can be found on www.info-now.com/article55#crit#crit#.

services from a DMC, while another may choose to contract a DMC to provide only one or two components of the overall event.

DMCs prepare detailed proposals for services, which are based on the planner's specifications and budget. A professional meeting planner will provide the DMC with as much information about the participants as possible so that the DMC's proposed itinerary of activities and services can be designed to best suit the group's purpose, demographics, and expectations. Initial proposals often include more than one suggested itinerary, thus providing the client with several options, with costs and full details about each included service.

DMC Clients and Customers

DMC clients and customers are those who plan meetings, exhibitions, events, conventions, and incentive travel programs. In this chapter, the terms "customer," "client," and "planner" are used to describe the person, organization, or company for which the DMC is providing services. The client is the representative of the customer company or organization who makes the decision to purchase DMC services. The planner, representing the customer company or organization, is the person whom the DMC works directly with on programs and events. The customer, client, and planner could be three separate entities or one in the same.

It is important to note that those who participate in the services and activities provided by a DMC are almost always associated with the same company or group, such as a corporate sales force or people who all belong to the same professional organization. Rarely do DMCs service the leisure traveler or tour groups that include "random" participants who have no common connection with others in the group. However, the value of DMC services is recognized by large tour operators and is increasingly employed to assist with transportation and/or tours for these large groups; for example, a cruise ship company might employ DMCs to manage land tours, transportation, and excursions. A DMC may contract directly with the company or organization whose employees or members will be participating in the program, or it may contract with a professional meeting planner who is offering his or her meeting services to the participating company or organization (see Figure 7–1).

Most planners consider the DMC as a local extension of their own office in the destination. They expect the DMC to be their "eyes and ears" in the destination, always acting on their behalf to offer unbiased experience-based suggestions on matters concerning logistics, venues, event concepts, and social program content. Planners depend on DMCs to help them design event programs that meet their specific

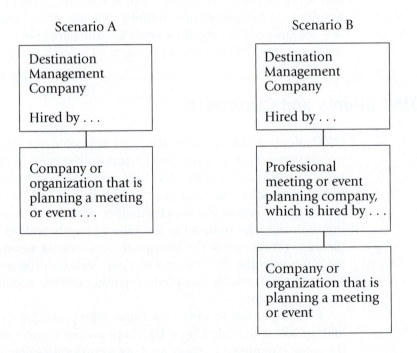

FIGURE 7–1   Sample flow chart.

needs, which can vary in size, budget, length, and purpose. Sample event programs are as follows:

Corporate Meetings

- National sales meetings
- Training meetings
- Product introductions
- Dealer and/or customer meetings

Conventions and Conferences

- Industry trade shows (food, construction, aircraft, etc.)
- Professional trade shows and conferences (for architects, doctors, teachers, etc.)
- Fraternal organizations (VFW, Lions, etc.)
- Educational conferences (medical symposia, other professional groups)
- Political conventions

Incentive Programs

- Sales incentives
- Dealer incentives
- Service manager incentives

Special Events

- Super Bowl
- Final Four basketball tournament
- PGA golf tournaments
- Olympics
- Important corporate occasions

DMCs offer their services to the planners, organizers, and decision makers who are responsible for these events. A DMC is both a consultant and a contractor. Customers contract with a DMC to add a layer of local professional management at the destination level; by hiring an expert in the destination, the planner adds a critically important element to the team: local knowledge. While the meeting planner may be quite experienced at the planning and implementation of meeting programs and events, he or she is not likely to be highly experienced in the particular destination.

The DMC becomes the voice of experience on the team when it comes to questions of logistics, choice of local suppliers, and viability of program components.

Structure of a DMC

Unlike hotels, resorts, convention centers, and restaurants, a DMC does not require an extensive capital investment to start up and operate its business. The DMC office is usually located in office space somewhere near the area where most meetings and events take place at its destination. Proximity to major airports is also an advantage, since so many program services involve group arrivals and departures.

Primary responsibilities and job titles for a DMC can vary from company to company. Many DMCs are small stand-alone single-office companies that are locally owned and operated where the owner usually runs the company and plays a major role in sales, operations, and administration. Other larger companies may have offices in multiple destinations, with local staff fulfilling management responsibilities on all levels (see Table 7–1 and Figure 7–2).

DMCs must find business opportunities, propose appropriate services, contract the business, set up and prepare for the group's

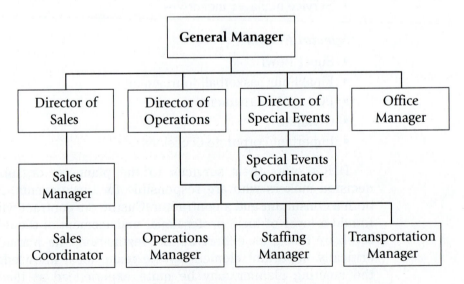

FIGURE 7–2 Sample DMC organizational chart.

TABLE 7–1	Categories of DMC Job Responsibilities, with Sample Job Titles

Management and Administration
- General Manager
- Office Manager
- Accounting Manager
- Executive Assistant
- Administrative Assistant
- Receptionist
- Research Assistant

Sales and Marketing
- Director of Sales
- Director of Marketing
- Director of Special Events
- Sales Manager
- Sales Coordinator
- Proposal Writer
- Research Analyst

Operations and Production
- Director of Operations
- Director of Special Events
- Operations Manager
- Production Manager
- Transportation Manager
- Staffing Manager

Field Staff
- Meet and Greet Staff
- Tour Guide
- Transportation Manager
- Event Supervisor
- Field Supervisor
- Equipment Manager

arrival, deliver the contracted services to the customers, and follow up with billing and program reconciliation. Supplier companies must be contracted, **field staff** must be hired, and program staff must be assigned. Field staff, which include tour guides, hospitality desk staff, and airport "meet and greet" staff, are usually temporary employees who are hired by a DMC only for the term of the program, and it is common for field staff in a destination to work for more than one DMC as the needs arise for their services.

The job titles listed above are examples and can vary from company to company. The fact remains that there are sales and promotion responsibilities, operations and production responsibilities, and management and administrative responsibilities. As in most companies, the levels of authority and reporting lines can and do vary, usually based on the size of the company and the qualifications of its staff. In Table 7–1, the Director of Special Events title appears under Sales and Marketing as well as **Operations and Production** because this position can be either or both, depending on the company and the individual executive's area of expertise.

DMCs do not normally own transportation equipment (vehicles), props, décor, or other supplies that they package and sell to the customers; they buy or rent from selected suppliers and manage those products and services in the context of the larger event program. As such, the DMC becomes a "conduit" for the services of a myriad of local supplier companies, which—combined with DMC staff and management—produce the overall desired program components.

A critical characteristic for a successful DMC is its complete objectivity in recommending and selecting suppliers and services for the client's program. Meeting planners depend on their DMC to select the absolute best provider for the services that fit their clients' budget and program specifications. When the DMC disassociates itself financially from the products and services offered to meeting planners, they can be assured that their purchasing dollar is optimized and that there is no financial conflict of interest by the DMC as it contracts with suppliers. Meeting planners and clients should feel comfortable that the DMC is earning its money for its management services and not from some financial "arrangement" with the supplier companies.

DMC Resources

As local experts who are positioned to assist planners with their projects in a destination, DMCs are expected to provide vital resources for those planners:

- *Products.* The products that a DMC offers are presented in a portfolio of services. Besides logistical services, which consist primarily of transportation and related support staffing, these services may include creative elements that the DMC has custom designed, such as theme parties, customized tours, and creative team-building activities. Some items are exclusively offered, while others are stock items usually offered by other DMCs in the same destination. New ideas are necessary to revamp offerings and create new ones, so the biggest single challenge facing DMCs is the need to constantly innovate and be creative. A new idea is a valuable commodity, and DMCs have experienced difficulties with this sort of intellectual property. It is considered unethical to "borrow" a DMC's creative ideas without employing the DMC.

- *Reputation.* The key asset for any DMC is a track record of customer satisfaction. As service is the DMC's primary product, client satisfaction is the best indicator of a DMC's reputation at the destination. Since a DMC is hired as a valued consultant and is a layer of management for the planner, it makes sense that the DMC's reputation would be a major factor in winning business. It is said that a DMC is only as good as the last program or event that has been completed. Equally important as customer satisfaction is the DMC's reputation among local suppliers—it is critical for the DMC to have established good relationships with key suppliers in the destination and for the DMC to have earned a reputation as a quality professional company with which to do business.

- *Experience.* Possibly the most valuable advantage a planner finds in a DMC is experience in the industry. Given the almost infinite number of challenges a DMC can face in the course of doing business, experience is the best teacher. Having a company that has been through the trial-and-error process is most important. Considering the relative ease of entry into the DMC business (primarily due to low start-up costs), experience is the critical element that distinguishes newcomers from established professional DMCs.

- *Relationships.* One of the key resources that a DMC is expected to bring to the table is relationships. In addition to established relationships with quality suppliers, also important are relationships with airports, hotels, law enforcement, regulatory agencies, city hall, and other people who can get things done for the planner's group while visiting the destination. The term "destination savvy" is often used when describing a DMC who has the right connections and knows how to use them.

- *Suppliers and Vendors.* Other than local knowledge, virtually everything that a DMC sells to a planner must be purchased from supplier companies—packaged, managed, and delivered. The DMC is expected to have an inventory of competent, high-quality suppliers who become partners in delivering the final program content. It is easy to determine that a caterer is needed for an off-property event; however, a DMC is expected to know the best of the available caterers in the area that can satisfy the specific needs and demographics of a group. This knowledge and experience are required in all supplier categories, including

DMCs may make arrangements for models, this one in costume.

Photo by George G. Fenich, Ph.D.

transportation equipment, props, floral supplies, lighting, sound equipment, event venues, and entertainers. The DMC is expected to know the appropriate combinations of suppliers that can make an event a success and (equally important) who to stay away from. Reliable vendors and suppliers are critical for a successful program.

- *Credit and Buying Power*. The DMC should have ongoing relationships in its community. It should develop good credit ratings through business volume and professional business dealings with hotels, supplier companies, and the independent staff who work for the DMC year-round. Unexpected things can—and do—happen during programs that require changes and additional services to be added on site, so the DMC must have the clout and buying power to make things happen quickly and without incident.

DMC Business Process

The DMC business process has been compared to other enterprises, particularly advertising firms. Although very different industries, there are many similarities between advertising firms and DMCs that help to illustrate the business process of DMCs. Each is expected to be creative and innovative. Immense pressures ride on the outcome and success of the contracted services in terms of a customer company's image and reputation. The DMC, like an advertising firm, is also expected to protect and enhance the image and reputation of its customers.

COMPARISON BETWEEN ADVERTISING FIRMS AND DMCS

Typically, an advertising firm identifies a target account and contacts the account's decision maker, hoping to demonstrate the advertising firm's capabilities to the potential client. This is done through direct and electronic communications and through presentations that illustrate the capability of the advertising company, usually with examples of their other successful jobs.

Similarly, a DMC seeks out new accounts to request an opportunity to present its capabilities that will meet the customer's requirements. DMCs also present this information through direct and electronic communications and presentations, and these presentations almost always exhibit their competence by using examples of their other successful programs.

Many different advertising firms are apt to make presentations to the same prospective customer. Typically, the customer will choose two or more advertising firms to compete for the account; at that point, the customer will give the competing firms specific guidelines outlining what is required and expected. The advertising firms will then develop more elaborate and creative advertising campaigns and services that they believe will attract the customer's favor and win the business. In most cases, these sample ad campaigns are presented to the customer without cost for the customer to use in evaluating the various advertising firms.

Similarly, the potential DMC customer will usually choose two or more DMCs to bid on its program, based on a set of specifications. Each DMC then provides detailed creative **proposals** for service that it believes will best satisfy the client's specifications. These proposals are almost always delivered free of charge, intended to gain the customer's favor and to win the account.

Just as the advertising firms spend valuable time and resources pursuing potential business opportunities, so do DMCs. That time and expense are justified by winning advertising firms and DMCs because they hope to add an account on which to build future revenues and profit. Losing advertising firms and DMCs have spent valuable time and resources for no immediate return and must make up the lost expense on future successful accounts.

A major issue in the DMC industry is the practice of providing detailed proposals at no cost to customers. Because of the often-considerable cost and time required to formulate a customized proposal, DMCs must choose wisely when determining what potential business to pursue. The fictional case study at the end of the chapter illustrates one potential scenario for obtaining new business projects. Business is secured by DMCs in other ways, as discussed later in this chapter.

BASIC BUSINESS REQUIREMENTS

Some prerequisites are essential to the destination management business process. The following items are some basic requirements to operate a DMC:

- Staff
- Temporary field staff
- Office
- Technology
- Licenses and insurance
- Community contacts
- Customer contacts
- History
- Destination resources

A strategically located office with competent, experienced staff and employees is a basic necessity to successfully operating a business in any destination. Convenient proximity to major hotels, convention facilities, tourist attractions, and event venues is a must, and every top DMC must have access to the best possible technology available. DMC clients are usually larger companies and often major corporations that use highly sophisticated technology and expect compatible electronic communications capabilities with their chosen

DMC. Communications equipment, office computer capabilities (including database management), imaging software, and high-speed Internet are all expected to be standard for today's DMC. The quick processing of information and the ability to make on-the-spot changes and produce professional documents and graphics are also industry necessities.

Without a doubt, a DMC must be legally insured for business liability as well as having other standard coverage, such as workers' compensation and automobile insurance. Each destination also has some unique laws and local licenses required to perform DMC services. Customers and planners must be confident that their chosen business partners are adequately insured and knowledgeable about local laws and ordinances that could affect the successful operation and production of their programs and events.

As with many businesses in the service sector, destination management is a relationship-driven industry. Customers and planners literally put their reputations and jobs on the line when selecting a DMC. DMCs must have extensive community contacts among hotels, attractions, convention bureaus, airports, and law enforcement as well as the supplier community. It is only with cooperation from these valuable relationships—gained through repeated work experiences—that a DMC can properly service its clients.

Relationships outside of the destination community (that is, in the customer community) are also important to the success of a DMC. The most valuable asset a DMC has is its **history** of success. A DMC's reputation and track record are the best proof that a planner can rely on when choosing a DMC partner.

Finally, the destination community must have the necessary resources to execute a well-run program or event. It is not enough for the community to have a caterer; it must have competitive caterers with reputations for high standards, skills, and quality. This is true for all contracted supplier services, such as transportation providers, entertainers, and attractions.

SALES PROCESS

For DMCs to be successful, new business projects must be continually found and secured for the company. Business opportunities present themselves in a variety of ways. Not all DMCs service all business sectors: Some DMCs specialize in association convention business, some in **corporate meetings** and events, and others in international travel groups; some DMCs work with individual travelers, while others focus heavily on the domestic incentive market. Most DMCs operate in multiple markets, which are usually determined by the nature of their destination.

The infrastructure and appeal of the destination dictate which of the mentioned market segments DMCs will find suitable to do business with. Different infrastructures, such as convention centers, convention hotels, resorts, and airport facilities, all play into the equation. Destination appeals such as natural and man-made attractions play heavily into whether or not corporations will plan important meetings and/or incentive travel rewards in a location. Beaches, mountains, forests, weather, quality golf availability, fishing, theater, arts, culture, gambling, and theme parks all can exhibit destination appeal.

As in most businesses, DMCs have annual business plans, which include budgets for revenue and expenses. To create the business plan, a sales and marketing plan is developed and implemented. Portions of this plan include items such as the following:

- Industry trade show attendance
- Sales calls on new and existing customers
- Membership and participation in various industry associations
- Community sales efforts and networking at industry events
- Utilization of representation firms
- Brochures and other collateral materials
- Company newsletters
- Partnerships and memberships in DMC industry groups

IDENTIFICATION OF NEW BUSINESS OPPORTUNITIES

The first stage of the sales process is to discover new business opportunities and pursue those customers. Almost all new business opportunities involve going where the customers are or where the customers do business, for example, going to industry trade shows that potential customers are known to attend. Some examples of these trade shows are the American Society of Association Executives (ASAE), Center for Association Leadership, Meeting World, Incentive Travel & Meetings Exposition (IT&ME), and Meetings West. Sales executives representing DMCs must carefully research these trade shows to maximize their sales and marketing dollars. Knowing in advance which potential customers will attend and knowing what business opportunities they represent better ensure the DMC's prospects for creating new client relationships.

Some customers, particularly corporate customers, incentive companies, and meeting management companies, will sometimes designate a "preferred" DMC in selected destinations. For DMCs, this is known as a "house account"; these accounts are very important and require careful maintenance. Whenever planners from a house account require services, the chosen DMC is in a position to help without going through the often-rigorous competitive bid process with other DMCs. There is great competition for such accounts, and competitor DMCs are always eager in their attempts to take over these accounts. Periodic visits to these customers and open lines of communication are vital in maintaining these relationships. In addition to continued good service, part of the successful maintenance of these relationships may include membership in the same industry organizations as the planners because attending these organizations' conferences and meetings allows DMC representatives to visit and network among planners.

Memberships in industry organizations such as the Professional Convention Management Association (PCMA), Meeting Professionals International (MPI), Health Care Exhibitors Association (HCEA), International Special Event Society (ISES), and Society of Incentive & Travel Executives (SITE) are typically part of a DMC's business plan. Using these memberships to learn about managing meetings, conventions, events, and conferences while working alongside potential and current customers has obvious advantages.

Sales efforts on the local destination level are considered by most companies to be an important part of any sales plan. Creating relationships with local industry representatives who do business with the same customers and planners as the DMC is an efficient way to identify new business opportunities. Networking at local hospitality industry functions, such as local Hospitality Sales and Management Association International (HSMAI) monthly meetings or convention bureau "mixers," is a common practice among successful DMCs. Staying abreast of industry news, networking with people who work in the industry, and knowing changes in services and staffing within the local industry make for a well-informed DMC.

Because a local "one-destination DMC" does not enjoy the economy of scale of a national DMC, such as USA Hosts, consortiums have been formed; for example, the group called the Network Companies was formed in order to pool resources from individual one-city DMCs for sales and marketing purposes. Other such DMC groups exist primarily for the sharing of mutual sales and marketing efforts and expenses.

In some cases, particularly with DMC groups, it makes sense to employ professional **representation firms** to call on particular market segments in which they specialize. Usually, this representation is contracted for a particular geographic location; New York, Chicago, and London are good examples of places where a representation firm might be contracted. These companies typically call on existing (as well as new or potential) customers in the geographic area on behalf of a DMC. They will seek to familiarize planners about the DMC while trying to uncover leads for future business. When appropriate, these representation firms will sometimes also serve as a local liaison between the customer and the DMC.

Collateral materials are essential to a comprehensive sales and marketing plan. Collateral materials include brochures, letterheads, business cards, proposal shells, and fact sheets for the various activities and services offered by the DMC, and a DMC will often produce a company newsletter to enhance the company's image and recognition in the industry. Brand names are difficult to establish in the DMC industry, as most DMCs are one-city companies that tend to be smaller than DMCs that operate in multiple destinations. Multicity DMCs, such as PRI, have an easier time establishing brand identity due to more national exposure among clientele.

USA Hosts is one of the largest DMCs in the United States.
Provided courtesy of Terry Epton, Executive Vice President, USA Hosts

PROPOSAL STAGE

Once a DMC has secured the sales lead, contacted the customer, and convinced that customer to consider the DMC as a possible supplier and partner in an upcoming program, the DMC will be asked to provide a proposal of services. The following items must be considered and addressed in this proposal stage:

- Project specifications
- Research and development
- Creativity and innovation
- Budget
- Response time
- Competition

As a DMC begins to determine exactly what to offer a customer in a proposal of services, the client's project specifications become a valuable tool. A great deal of detailed information is usually included in these specifications:

- Group size
- Choice of hotel or resort type
- Meeting space allotments
- Dates of service
- Types of services required
- Demographic information about the attendees
- Management's goals for the meeting or event
- Approximate budget available for the meeting or event
- History regarding the group's past successes and challenges
- Various other "include" and/or "do not include" items
- Deadlines for completion and proposal submission

Armed with these specifications and other information gained through ongoing customer contact, previous experience with the customer, and other research, the DMC will determine what items to offer in the proposal of services. The first step is usually a series of creative meetings among DMC staff to discuss what might best satisfy the client specifications to win the business. After these meetings, the research and development of proposal components should begin. Availability of suppliers, venues, transportation, and entertainers and bids for services such as catering, transportation equipment, and venue costs are all reviewed and incorporated into the proposal. Costs for all items must be identified for budgeting and pricing decisions.

A winning proposal not only satisfies the client specifications but also satisfies the client's desire to exceed the expectations of the participants of the particular program. Creativity and innovation are usually prized as high-value items in proposals. Selected programs become a reflection of the customer company; therefore, creative and innovative components, along with a thorough well-designed program, tend to win the business. Response time is a critical factor when producing proposals. Creativity takes time, and if a proposal is rushed, less creative, more standard items might be offered, but a proposal that does not meet its deadline will seldom win the business.

A final and critical step in the proposal process is pricing. Several factors must be considered when pricing the items included in the proposal:

- Total estimated costs to deliver the proposed services
- Staff time and involvement necessary to carry out the proposed services (before, during, and after the program)
- Amount of DMC resources necessary to operate the program
- Unknown costs (factored into the planning stages)
- Factors surrounding supplier choice and availability
- Time of the year and local business activity during a particular season
- Costs of taking staff and company capacity off the market for this customer
- Factors regarding competitive bids on the project

Depending on the competitive factors at hand, decisions must be made about how to approach a given business opportunity. DMC resources are finite and must be allocated as efficiently as possible. If a planner is entertaining bids on a project, the DMC may well be pitted against two, three, or more competitors. Deciding how much time and company effort are appropriate to dedicate to a particular bid involves an educated management decision (the DMC in some cases may choose not to bid at all). The following types of questions should be answered by a DMC prior to making a final decision on how much effort to dedicate to a given opportunity:

- What is the revenue potential of this business opportunity?
- What is the value of a future relationship with this customer?
- How much proposal work will be involved in this bid?
- What is the bid deadline?
- How many companies are bidding?
- Which competitors are bidding?
- What success rate does our company have on similar projects?
- What success rate do our competitors have?
- What time of year will the program be operating?
- What are the approximate odds of winning this program?
- How profitable will this program be?

DMCs do not give estimates but rather design a program with suggested components and offer it at prices that are assured should their proposal be accepted. Each proposal will be different in various ways. If a selection of tours and activities is requested in the bid specifications, each DMC will offer a selection that it feels will best fit the demographics of the group, budget, and factors such as time constraints and season. For example, if a theme party is specified, the competitors will hope to prevail with a creative mix of décor, entertainment, and food and beverage, and these proposals often vary greatly in style, concept, and price.

Given the variety among proposal elements offered by the competing DMCs, a customer is not in a position to choose a winning bidder based solely on price. Some other important factors must be considered, such as the following:

- Is the proposal feasible?
- What is the perceived value of services offered?
- Will the participants appreciate the suggested program?
- Will the quality be sufficient to make the program or event a success?
- Is the DMC capable of producing the program or event in an acceptable manner?

Planners tend to be measured on the outcome of the meetings and events they plan. Choosing a DMC can be a decision not entirely based on price because some things are too important to simply award to the lowest bidder. Every planner's choice must be balanced and well thought out—planners can literally find themselves placing their job temporarily in the hands of the chosen DMC if the program is an important one. One can see the value of developing a good relationship before, during, and after the bidding process. A DMC that delivers a successful, well-run program for a planner may well become that planner's preferred supplier for years to come.

SITE INSPECTIONS

While not always required, an often-expensive component of the sales process in terms of DMC time and resources is the **site inspection,** which is a physical review of proposed venues, services, tours, and/or activities prior to the actual program. A site inspection may be required at any point in the sales process. The site inspection visit by the planner could occur prior to the proposal as a part of the information gathering, after the proposal and prior to the customer decision, or after the choice of a DMC as a first step in the finalization of a program or event. Site inspections can vary in time and detail but always require special attention by busy DMC sales and/or operations executives.

These inspection trips must be carefully planned and orchestrated to show a customer the places and inclusions of the proposed program and also to demonstrate the DMC's operational skills, organization, and community contacts and relationships. The site inspection can often be the most critical step in winning a customer's business, as this is the time when the DMC has an opportunity to develop a relationship with the customer and gain the customer's confidence. Many programs have been won or lost over a seemingly simple lunch conversation during a site inspection.

CONTRACTS OF SERVICES

Contracts are necessary in all aspects of the meetings and events industry. Hotels, convention centers, cruise ships, airlines, and DMCs all produce contracts, which spell out exactly what is being purchased and the details of the purchase (see chapter 12, on legal issues, for more information). DMC contracts can vary in size depending on the amount of services required.

PROGRAM PREPARATION

After a program is contracted, a transition begins, moving from active selling to operations and production. At this time, all suppliers that will be employed by the DMC in the course of satisfying the contract

Meeting rooms and their layouts should be checked during site inspections.
Pearson Education/PH College

are notified that the program is definite, and their services are confirmed. Operations staff, which are usually different from the sales staff in larger DMCs, meet with the sales representatives to review the customer's needs, program goals, and any details that will be factors in the successful delivery of the program.

During this phase of the business process, participant numbers can fluctuate, requiring the DMC to reevaluate costs and other operational details. With active involvement by the client, other activities and services may be added or removed from the program during this planning time; it is most important that the DMC be available and responsive to these changes. As a contracted member of the customer's team, the DMC is responsible for the destination management portion of the larger over-all customer event—the DMC must be fully cooperative and flexible.

The program's project manager, either an operations or events man-ager, assumes primary responsibility for the entire program or event. During the setup period, each activity and service for the program is reviewed and confirmed in detail. Full-time and part-time professional program managers, supervisors, tour guides, and escorts are scheduled well in advance. Other managers may be assigned to various portions of the program, such as transportation, food and beverage, tours and activities, entertainment, and/or hospitality desk management.

PROGRAM OPERATIONS AND PRODUCTION

DMCs exist to produce programs and events, coordinating numerous staff and suppliers into one cohesive program of products and services. The DMC utilizes its vast experience and collective talent to provide a layer of consulting and hands-on management of a variety of assets, resources, suppliers, and staff to produce an outwardly seamless program of events. Some of the categories that are important in the on-site management of programs and events are as follows:

- Transportation management
- Event production
- Tour and activity management
- Support staff supervision
- Supplier and vendor management
- Meeting support
- Customer relations
- On-site changes, challenges, and contingencies
- Troubleshooting
- Community liaison
- Information sources

After finding the opportunity, creating proposals, conquering the competition, earning the planner's confidence, contracting the program, and making careful preparations, it is up to the operations and production staff to successfully deliver the program. At this point, everything is on the line—the image of the sponsoring organization, the reputation of the planner, future prospects for the DMC with the planner, the DMC's reputation in the destination—and (depending on the program) large sums of money are all at risk.

If the program is for a major association's convention, the association's members' perception of the organization is at stake. The American Medical Association, the American Bar Association, the National Automobile Dealers Association, the National Association of Television Program Executives, and the National Association of Secondary School Principals are all examples of associations that would employ a DMC to propose and deliver selected components for their conventions. Meeting and event planners for these prestigious associations and others are orchestrating major events with thousands of participants. The participant's perception of the convention can easily be affected by the quality of shuttle transportation to and from the convention hall, networking events, cocktail parties, and meal service as well as activities such as the annual golf tournament and optional sightseeing tours. All of these items are potentially the DMC's responsibility—the shuttle has to operate efficiently, the events must live up to participants' expectations, the activities and tours must be entertaining and well run, providing value for price. The participants are the association planner's customers. Membership renewals and future convention attendance are affected by the quality of the program delivery.

DMCs may arrange outdoor performances.
Used by permission of Paradise Light & Sound, Orlando, Florida

Similar dynamics are in effect with corporate programs. The annual new model dealer shows for automobile manufacturers have millions of dollars riding on their outcome. Insurance companies reward top sales producers with **incentive programs** that effectively show the best of their workforce how the company values their service. Computer companies and software companies produce new product introduction events either as stand-alone events or in conjunction with industry conventions. The success of these ventures has the future of the sponsoring companies at stake.

Through these examples, one can clearly see the tremendous pressure of running a logistically sound and high-quality program of events. This pressure is riding on the shoulders of the meeting and event planners and the DMCs chosen to support them. The DMC's operations and production staff have one chance to deliver the program: An event cannot be rescheduled for the next day if the venue is not ready; if the bus and limousine suppliers do not provide equipment as ordered, the departure time cannot be changed. When the curtain goes up, the show must go on. Reliability and responsibility are the most important issues; price runs a distant second to reliability. However, all DMCs are not equal, and choosing the best fit for a particular program is essential. A close working relationship that fosters confidence, easy communication, and a mutual understanding of goals and priorities requires that the planner's DMC contact be instantly available, and the planner must be immediately available to the DMC's operation manager throughout the course of the program.

Transportation management is a major part of a DMC's business. It encompasses routing, equipment (vehicle) use, staff requirements, special venue considerations, equipment staging areas, driver briefings, staff scheduling and briefings, maps, signage, and preparations for driver breaks, as well as reconfirmation of all these services. Transportation scenarios and requirements are usually scattered throughout the program itinerary.

Corporate programs often begin with airport transfers. Airport transportation services customarily include "meet and greet" service and luggage management. Meet and greet service consists of DMC staff holding welcome signs and greeting arriving guests from the sponsoring company. Management of the arrival manifest (a detailed list of each guest's name, arrival flight, and time) by the airport transportation manager is a key component of the service. The manager schedules both staff and equipment with the arrival manifest as a guide. People change flights, miss flights, and fail to accurately supply flight information, and flights can be delayed or canceled. Because of the inaccuracies common to arrival manifests, the transportation manager must not only expect surprises but plan for them. Constant communication is necessary between the DMC and the airlines, the DMC and the transportation equipment suppliers, and the DMC and the airport meet and greet staff. Equally important is the need to keep open communication with the hotel(s) to which the participants are being transferred and with the meeting planner, who is probably receiving information about individual participants' changes in travel plans.

When airport transfers are run properly, the participants receive a friendly welcome by someone who knows their name, after which they are directed to the proper baggage belt to identify their luggage. From there they are brought, along with their luggage, to the waiting vehicle ready to transport them to their hotel. Motorcoaches, minibuses,

Meet and greet services are not limited to the United States. Ugandan dancers and others welcome the Malaysian prime minister.
AP Wide World Photos

vans, sedans, and limousines could all be used at the direction of the planner, depending on the service purchased. A DMC must proactively manage the changes and challenges of airport transportation. The first impression made on a participant is the arrival transfers, and the last impression is the departure transfers.

Transportation requirements often include shuttle services between the shuttle focus (perhaps an event venue) and the participating hotel(s). Shuttle supervisors, dispatchers, and directional staff, sometimes referred to as "human arrows," manage this personalized service. Point-to-point transfers are often required to move groups of participants during a program. Whatever the transportation requirement, the DMC is expected to plan, prepare, and deliver the service in a timely and efficient manner.

Event production is also a major part of destination management. Events can be large or small, on a hotel property or in a remote location. Events can be extensive, lavish, and expensive; events can be fun, casual, and unpretentious. Some examples follow:

- Cocktail receptions and networking events
- Breakfasts, luncheons, and dinners
- Dining events at unique venues
- Gala dinner events
- Extravagant theme parties
- Outdoor and indoor team-building events

These events all have a purpose and a budget. DMC production staff must deliver the contracted event in a fashion that satisfies the purpose of the event. There are several types of events:

- Events that promote corporate staff and top executives to meet and mingle with their company's middle management
- Events that provide an opportunity for the company's salespeople to interact with their largest customers and dealers of the company's products
- Events that culminate at the final night of an incentive program with the intent to "knock the socks off" the attendees and fire them up about the next sales campaign
- Events that simply provide a casual atmosphere for company employees to network and renew acquaintances since their last meeting

A very large "extravaganza" event must be produced as contracted. The production staff must manage the event venue, security, suppliers of sound and light equipment, staging, entertainers, décor, floral designs, table linens, food and beverage, environmental concerns, staff, and countless other details. Experience is essential. Strong working relationships are necessary with all key suppliers; choosing appropriate staff and producing a production schedule are essential to a successful event. Holding preliminary meetings that bring together the key suppliers to discuss and provide input on the production schedule is a fundamental step in the planning process. Realistic setup/move-in schedules and cooperative suppliers ensure a smooth-running event.

Operations staff must be familiar with all the necessary municipal regulations regarding insurance, fire safety codes, crowd control, and police requirements. Considering all these issues, there is no substitute for experience, and working with a DMC that has a known track record of success is a necessity.

Whether planning and operating sightseeing tours, setting up a scavenger hunt, putting on a golf tournament, or running a hospitality desk, strong organizational skills, sound preparation, and a sense of commitment and responsibility are essential traits for a professional DMC operations manager. Everything is riding on his or her performance. Planners tend to bond with the managers and become dependent on them to be their on-site consultants in the community. On-site questions and requests for **VIP services** with little advance notice are not unusual. Here are some sample questions:

> "Where can I send my VP of marketing and her husband for a romantic dinner? She just realized that today's their wedding anniversary!"

> "My company president is arriving early in the corporate jet. Can we get a limo to the executive airport in forty-five minutes?"

> "The boss just decided he wants a rose for all of the ladies at tonight's party."

> "Can we get Aretha Franklin to sing 'Happy Birthday' to one of our dealers during her set at the party tonight?"

A wise person said, "It is often the little things, the details, that separate great events from ordinary ones." Knowing someone's favorite wine, song, or dessert can turn an ordinary event into one that will be remembered forever. Things that are not in the contract but become available to add special touches to an event are great opportunities for a production person with a passion for success. A production manager who has solid relationships with his or her suppliers can often see those suppliers being swept up in the process and wanting to suggest additions or program improvements. Suppliers do this because they want the event that they are associated with to be the best it can be as well as to establish an ongoing relationship with the DMC for possible future events. Planners are typically pleased to be presented with options. Confetti cannons for the dance floor area, additional accent lighting, and separate martini bars are good examples of on-site event upgrades.

DMC operations and production managers must be knowledgeable about every facet of the programs and events that they manage. They must be knowledgeable about the customer, the destination, the group's participants, the event venues, the suppliers, the staff, and many other factors. On-site challenges and changes are a fact of doing business. As a result, operations and production managers must constantly be troubleshooters, looking for what might be an issue later in the program and keeping the planner aware of every important detail that changes or may need to be changed.

Much of an operations or production manager's day is spent confirming and reconfirming services. Constant communication with vendors and suppliers who are participating in a program is critical to ensure that final participant counts and timing are accurate as well as reconfirming all service details. Another form of reconfirmation is "advancing" a venue—the DMC staff arrive well ahead of a group to make sure that the service staff and the event location are prepared and properly set up prior to the participants' arrival. Details such as number of seats, room temperature, serving instructions, menu inclusions, and beverage service are all examples of items that should be verified while advancing a dinner event.

Operations and production managers are a trusted source of information for the planners, serving as community liaisons for the DMC's customers. DMC representatives are typically asked to recommend restaurants, golf courses, beauty salons, doctors, dance clubs, antique shops, and other service providers. DMC representatives are expected to be experts in all facets of their community.

Throughout each program and event, operations and production managers must carefully monitor the original contracted services and all changes that occur after the original itinerary and contract are signed and approved. Every addition to the program, such as changes in participant counts, times of service, and additional services, must be documented. Accurate, up-to-the-minute data on the actual services delivered must be kept for billing purposes. To avoid billing disputes, it is also important to identify who authorized each change or addition; ideally, these authorizations are in writing and approved in advance by the client.

BILLING AND FOLLOW-UP

The final invoice for a program or event should mirror the contract of services agreed on prior to the operation of the program. Actual services delivered should be outlined along with the number of participants that each line item is based on. In most cases, items are billed on "lot" costs or on a per-person basis. Lot costs are fixed and independent of the number of participants and include bus hours, the price of an entertainer, or a décor package for a ballroom. Per-person pricing is based on the actual number of participants, such as food and beverage at a luncheon that is usually billed at a fixed price per person, plus tax and gratuities.

All additions or deletions to the originally contracted services should appear on the invoice. The grand total for the program should be reflected along with all deposits and payments received prior to the final billing. Whenever possible, final billing details should be reviewed and approved by the planner or representative on site at the completion of the program while details about the program's operation, additions, and changes are still fresh in everyone's mind. The more time that elapses between the time the program is completed and the receipt of the final invoice creates opportunities for disputes about program details (for example, participant counts, times, and items that were approved to be added to the program).

While not a standard with all DMCs, the practice of sending follow-up program evaluations is extremely valuable in obtaining customer feedback about the quality of a DMC's services. Using this critical feedback to improve services is key to staying in the best possible form for future programs and events. The responses and comments received by the DMC can also be a valuable tool in the training and evaluation of employees and management, since senior

Destination Management Fictional Case Study

It was Thursday afternoon, and American Hosts Sales Manager Andrew Christensen received the call just before five o'clock as he was adding final touches to handouts and his PowerPoint presentation for a Monday morning meeting at the local convention and visitor bureau.

With the Genesis Automotive planners in town for a site inspection through the weekend, Andrew was not expecting any new assignments. In an hour, he was meeting the two Genesis planners at their hotel and later briefing them at dinner about the venues he had scheduled for visits on Saturday. Andrew had a town car reserved with a local livery company's best driver.

A special location was necessary for the introduction of the new Genesis SUV. Andrew had both the Sports Arena and the Water Front Amphitheater on tentative hold, and their representatives were briefed on the client's needs and the special circumstances surrounding the event. Four other venues were also on hold, but Andrew was confident that one of his top two recommendations would meet the client's expectations.

Since the phone was already ringing, Andrew took a deep breath and cleared his head of other issues, and as he greeted the unknown caller, he heard, "Andrew, I'm glad I caught you! This is Kathy Hashimoto at Randford Research. I have a project and may need your help." Andrew did not know it, but he was about to embark on his biggest sale in three years—because he was on the job, because he was prepared, and because he was open to the possibilities that this unexpected caller provided.

Andrew recognized Kathy Hashimoto's name, and everybody knew Randford Research, one of the largest defense contractors in the world, but he needed some instant background on this client. As Kathy began to introduce herself and the reason for her call, Andrew clicked into the customer profiles on his computer and reviewed the notes he had entered ten months ago after the MPI conference. Without hesitation he said, "Hello, Kathy. This is a nice surprise! Of course I remember. We met in the Florentine's lobby after the final night reception at MPI. I helped carry your cartons to the taxi during that awful downpour."

"Mister, you're quick! I remember I hardly had time to give you my card as I dashed for the taxi. But I know your company and I believed you were someone I could trust. I liked the fact that you volunteered to lend a hand when I needed one, and you didn't know if I was a customer or not. I got your note and just took a peek at your Web site."

Kathy paused a long second and began, "Hey, Andrew, I just got handed an event at the National Aircraft convention and it's only six months out. It's a crucial event for Randford and it's in your city. My regular planner is on a maternity leave and it looks like you and I are going to have to pick up the pieces."

Andrew winced as he looked at the time, but he said, "I'll be glad to help. Do you want to give me your specifications now, or would you prefer to e-mail me your requirements?"

Kathy immediately said, "Here's the basics now, and I'll send the details in an e-mail tomorrow. First, on the night of September 20 we need a special venue for 750 people, all VIPs. Senator Germain is our keynote speaker. It has to be unique and elegant, with separate space for cocktails and passed hors d'oeuvres before a sit-down dinner. It's black tie, private sedans, and visible security on site." Andrew made notes and began to ask for more details, but Kathy continued, "That's it for now. Do some homework while I locate and send the specs. Then call me in the morning."

As Kathy ended the conversation, Andrew quickly entered the relevant program information into his computer profile. He then sent multiple voice mail messages, advising key coworkers in both sales and operations that they needed to brainstorm with him first thing tomorrow. Finally, he sent an e-mail to Kathy Hashimoto, briefly summarizing the assignment and thanking her for the opportunity and the trust she was placing in him and American Hosts. He confirmed that he would call her at 9 A.M. the next morning after a short planning session with other staff in his office. With only ten minutes before his scheduled meeting with the Genesis clients, Andrew turned off his computer, picked up the printed site inspection schedules, and headed out the door.

The next morning, after meeting briefly with key sales and operations staff in his office, Andrew made the 9 A.M. call, which served to gather additional program information and to demonstrate to Kathy that he could be depended on to follow through on his commitments. From the call and the subsequent e-mail, he received the following specifications:

- September 20
- Reception 6 P.M.
- Dinner 7 P.M.
- 750 people
- Black tie
- Visible security in dress regalia
- Elegant, quiet, sophisticated atmosphere

(continued)

- Red carpet, white-gloved service
- No press and very strict guest list
- No cameras or recording equipment
- Security clearances probable
- Seating in sixes and eights (tables of six preferred)
- Head table of approximately ten people
- Avoid pork, veal, and game entrées
- Understated and refined entertainment through dinner, followed by dance orchestra (swing band or similar—no heavy rock-and-roll)
- Transportation by limousines and sedans (dark colors)
- Budget commensurate with venue and final event scenario

Armed with these details, Andrew and his planning team would first create general recommendations and tentatively reserve several event venues to be presented to Kathy Hashimoto, along with very specific follow-up questions to identify and secure the final "best choice." Just six months away from the actual event, time was precious and the venue had to be confirmed. To move the client toward a good, prompt decision, Andrew needed to narrow down a list of sites that fit the general criteria and were definitely available on September 20. From experience, Andrew knew that suggesting a great venue that was not available for the event could be a career-limiting mistake.

To create their initial wish list, the planning group exchanged information in a brainstorming session, concentrating entirely on the best possible venues. Other components such as theme, caterer, table decoration, floral arrangements, sound and light, room décor, transportation, and security would be strongly influenced by the site selected. As they discussed potential sites—not restricting their creativity but being realistic about space requirements—they considered indoor as well as tented outdoor options. They carefully evaluated and ranked the resulting venues according to "best choices" and their reasons. As the team broke to check messages, sales coordinator Melissa Unger called each of the "first choice" venues to determine availability and buyout price.

When they resumed, Melissa verified that three venues were available but that deposits would be required to hold beyond ten days—and if another client requested the space within ten days, then American Hosts would have to deposit immediately.

The group then discussed ground transportation. Sedans were specified, and for VIPS a certain number of luxury cars and limousines might also be required. At the same time, the National Aircraft convention had already created tremendous demand for the best transportation equipment. Melissa would call their two most dependable transportation companies and noted that quality vehicles may need to be imported from nearby cities—at an extra cost—if they were not available locally.

Before discussing remaining issues, the planning group created a list of questions to be presented to Kathy Hashimoto on Monday. Her answers to these ten questions would be pivotal to creating theme, décor, menu, entertainment, and other items that would distinguish this event:

1. Has this group gathered previously at a similar event?
2. If so, when and where?
3. What place did they like best? Why?
4. What place did they like least? Why?
5. What theme did you think was the most successful? What entertainment? What speaker? Why?
6. What is your vision for this year's event?
7. Are there any restrictions or additional special requests for food and beverage, seating, and so on?
8. What about wine preferences and bar service?
9. What are the demographics of the group in terms of age and gender?
10. What hotel(s) will house your participants?

Andrew and Melissa reviewed their files for similar programs that had been created over the past few years. Kathy might want to know more about their experience with these kinds of VIP events. She would certainly want to know specific advantages and disadvantages of each site.

During the Monday call, Kathy was relieved to learn that good venues still were available, and she was pleasantly surprised to be presented with specific questions instead of an "off-the-shelf" program. "I get suspicious," Kathy had said, "when my DMC gives me its idea of a fabulous program this early in our planning process. It makes me think it wasn't custom designed to fit my needs." During the conversation, Kathy said two other things that made

(continued)

Destination Management Fictional Case Study (*continued*)

Andrew take special note. She pointed out that the senator's arrival path would not be known until four hours before the event, and two years ago, Kathy's boss objected to using stretch limousines "because they were too 'glitzy' for this conservative crowd." Andrew knew that two or three alternate plans would be needed for the senator, allowing maximum flexibility to meet the tight restrictions of government security staff; he also knew that sedans (preferably dark ones) were essential and that creative use of something other than limousine vehicles might be considered.

Within days of their earliest conversation, Andrew had created a detailed event proposal, beginning with a summary of the basic assignment to ensure that he and Kathy were communicating effectively and fully understanding one another. In addition to the basic program information in chronological order, Andrew provided a detailed description of every aspect of the event, from participant pickups at the hotels, to transportation to the event itself, to return transfers to the hotels. This description helped Kathy and her staff members visualize the event as it would unfold and supplied all the details so that only minor adjustments would have to be made.

A separate security plan was also included. It was created with the help of the local police department, along with supervisors from the hotel security department, the transportation supplier, and the chosen event venue—the historic Opera House. A military color guard was secured from a nearby naval air station, which provided visible security and a military presence during an opening flag ceremony. Plainclothes personnel from the local police department who were fully knowledgeable about their city, the transportation routes, and the Opera House provided close and professional security.

Two weeks after receiving the proposal, Kathy Hashimoto visited the city on a site inspection to walk through the entire event. Andrew and his team accompanied her to the Opera House, which offered a breathtaking welcome for the all-important first impression. The venue offered spacious public areas filled with original artwork and meticulously restored design elements. However, the kitchen and pantry area offered tremendous challenges. "Our caterer is a wonder," Andrew assured Kathy. "Through the use of specially fitted trucks, portable cleanup facilities, and hidden parking lot tenting, they have successfully served some of our city's most famous events."

Following the site visit, adjustments were made based on the additional details that Kathy provided. A revised document provided new specifications.

All prices were included and minimum number of participants stipulated in order to calculate accurate pricing. If numbers were to vary significantly, a new price quotation would be required. Following a few minor adjustments that Kathy requested, a final document in the form of an official contract was sent for her signature.

The American Hosts operations and production staff were offered many challenges with the Opera House. Among other "firsts" on this event, American Hosts had a local construction company create a temporary floor above the ground-level seating area of the concert hall. This was accomplished by an elaborate use of scaffolding, plywood, and carpeting. This new floor above the seats put the dinner portion of the event in the main concert hall, which made a perfect location for classical dinner music and vignettes from the local opera company. The existing lighting and décor in the main concert hall of the Opera House provided an awe-inspiring setting for such an important occasion. Most important, the theme was set and décor embellishments were kept to a minimum, leaving the bulk of the budget for quality food and entertainment.

Six months passed, and it was the night of the big Randford event. Everything was in place. During this period, Andrew and the entire American Hosts staff had been actively involved with the Randford program. The operations and production managers for American Hosts, Dale Young and Kellie Doolan, worked long hours to make the vision a reality. This event was a first of its kind, and many details presented issues that were not previously considered by Andrew or Kathy. For example, the acoustics in the Opera House were fabulous, if not legendary; however, dinner service noise was not part of the normal Opera House equation. Felt liners in the serving trays, table padding, and some creative use of hanging acoustical baffles above the dinner area minimized the noise. Thankfully, Kellie, the production manager, was present for the sound check in the afternoon.

Important troubleshooting is an ongoing part of the preparations for any special event. There is no substitute for experience, and in this case, a minor slip could have changed the evening's outcome. Dale Young, the operations manager, had planned three possible transportation scenarios that delivered the senator and the guests to the venue in comfort, safety, and elegance. Dale, too, had to scramble when word of an antiglobalization demonstration came to light a little over twenty-four hours prior to the event. Because Dale and Kellie had fine-tuned their production schedule and handpicked the staff assigned to the various component parts of the event, they had the time to find and fix these two potential problems.

(continued)

Destination Management Fictional Case Study (*continued*)

From the time Andrew entered the initial information into the computer database, the Randford event's computer files and program templates were created for each member of the team to follow. This formed the single centralized database for creation of the event proposal, adjustments, additions, changes, and further adjustments, as well as a template for final billing.

The cocktail reception prior to dinner took place in the grand foyer of the Opera House, which concluded with the U.S. Marine Color Guard, obtained from a nearby military base, marching the guests into a thrilling "reveal" of the elegant dinner layout.

After dinner, Senator Germain began his presentation by stating, "I'm speechless! Mere words cannot describe how honored I am to stand here and address this group in such impressive surroundings. Never have I been so overwhelmed by an event."

The following letter accompanied the closing payment after Kathy received the final invoice.

Dear Andrew,

What a night! You, Dale, Kellie . . . your entire team created an awesome event. Our president is still raving about it. The food was spectacular, the setting magnificent, and the little special touches—menu design, flowers, and individual gifts—were perfect! You guys are great to work with. You were truly our partners throughout the process. Can you help me in Dallas next October?

Sincerely,

Kathy Hashimoto

This case, though fictional, shares a slice of life for DMC executives. Business opportunities do not always present themselves when it is convenient. As Louis Pasteur once said, "Chance favors the prepared mind." Clearly, our DMC sales executive, Andrew Christensen, was prepared and not overly stressed by demands on his time and attention. Successful DMC executives bring a wealth of knowledge and hands-on experience to a client's project, which includes remaining calm, cool, and collected throughout the process. These DMC executives have and know how to use the technology available to them, and they draw not only on their own experience but also on the experiences of the professional staff around them. Finally, in this relationship-oriented industry, it is vital that DMC executives earn and keep the confidence of their customers because a customer often entrusts the DMC with his or her reputation.

This fictional scenario was admittedly a glamorous one. Much of a DMC's work is less exciting. Research and development of program components are a part of the job, but so is creative writing, job costing, negotiating, purchasing, and managing within the supplier community, the hospitality community, and even the staff of the DMC.

management cannot always be on site to evaluate their operations managers at work.

Summary

The DMC niche in the MEEC industry is a secure and growing one. It is secure because the customer companies and organizations that sponsor meetings will always need local expertise. The depth of local destination knowledge, local contacts and connections, community standing, buying power, and hands-on experience (with the implementation of programs and events) is not readily available to organizations outside of the destination. DMCs have evolved in some interesting ways. The very first ones grew from the ranks of wholesale tour operators and ground operators, which specialized in providing tours and transportation for visiting travel groups. In the late 1950s, the specialization in association programs and higher-end corporate programs demanded a wider range of services, including dining programs, expanded activities, and special events. While that may seem like a long time to some of our readers, the hotel and meetings industries are ancient in comparison. Today, national multidestination DMC companies exist, there are DMCs on at least six continents, and consortiums of local one-destination DMCs exist; as in other industries, consolidation appears to be under way. However, just as individual one-of-a-kind hotels still prosper along with the giant hotel chains, so do some unique and skilled one-destination DMCs.

Destination management is still establishing itself as a key component in the meetings and events industry. Founded in 1995, the Association of Destination Management Executives (ADME) is committed to the initiative that professional destination management is a critical and necessary component to every successful meeting or event. As a primary goal, ADME continuously seeks to identify and promote the value of destination management as a necessary resource for planners of meetings, events, and incentive travel programs. ADME goals also include becoming the definitive source of information, education, and issues-based discussion of destination management for the meetings, events, incentive, and hospitality industries.

The professional designation "DMCP" (Destination Management Certified Professional) was introduced by ADME in January 2000. This professional certification is only available to individuals who have qualified for an extensive exam administered by ADME. Applicants are screened through a detailed questionnaire, which chronicles the applicant's experience and industry education. For more information about ADME, visit their Web site at http://www.adme.org.

As the industry goes, so goes the DMC business. The economy, in general, and the meetings industry in particular are good barometers for the health and vitality of the DMC industry. History has taught those participating in the meetings industry that the level of growth and the maintenance of revenues are very vulnerable. The recession of the 1980s, followed by the Iraqi invasion of Kuwait and the subsequent war in the Middle East, has taught us that travel can be interrupted and curtailed due to factors beyond the control of the corporations that are active in the industry; airlines, hotel companies, and DMCs have learned these lessons. However, the long-term outlook for the industry is bright. DMCs that are strong and financially sound stand to gain market share and greater brand recognition when temporary threats and business slowdowns are overcome.

In addition to ADME, Web sites of the following organizations are recommended for those interested in the meetings and events industry (each of these organizations has strong DMC membership):

Meeting Professionals International (MPI)	http://www.mpiweb.org
Professional Convention Management Association (PCMA)	http://www.pcma.org
Society of Incentive & Travel Executives (SITE)	http://www.site-intl.org

Key Words and Terms

For definitions, see the Glossary or go to http://glossary.
conventionindustry.org.

ADME

Corporate meeting

Destination management
    company (DMC)

Field staff

History

Incentive program

Operations and production

Program

Proposal

Representation firms

Site inspection

Special event

VIP services

Review and Discussion Questions

1. What is a DMC?
2. Name a DMC.
3. What services are offered by DMCs?
4. Produce an organizational chart for a DMC.
5. What is the process by which a DMC gets business?
6. What resources does a DMC provide to a meeting planner or sponsor?
7. What are the basic business requirements for a DMC?
8. What are some of the professional organizations that a DMC might be a member of?
9. What is ADME?

About the Chapter Contributor

Terrence J. Epton, CITE, DMCP, is a thirty-year veteran of the DMC industry and chief executive officer of the first and largest DMC in the

United States, USA Hosts, Ltd. Terry holds both the CITE (Certified Incentive Travel Executive) and the DMCP (Destination Management Certified Professional) designations. He served six years on the International Board of Directors for SITE as a director and officer, and he has twice been president of ADME.

CHAPTER 8

Special Events Management

Fireworks make an event even more special. This is a special event staged on a battleship in Mobile, Alabama.

Photo by Kenneth E. Manis, courtesy of Classic Fireworks by Events, Inc., Mandeville, Louisiana.

Chapter Objectives

This chapter provides the reader with an understanding of the following:

- Working definition of a special event
- Importance of a workable plan for staging a special event
- Planning tools used in special events management
- Importance of city and community infrastructure when hosting a special event
- Merchandising and promoting of a special event
- Sponsorships for special events
- Target markets for procuring attendance at a special event
- Basic operations for preparing for a special event
- Components of a special events budget
- Breakdown of components of a special event

Chapter Outline

Introduction

Planning Tools for a Special Event
- Understanding of Community Infrastructure
- Merchandising and Promotion of Special Events
- Distinctive Roles of the Promotional Mix Model
- Sponsorships for Special Events
- Media Coverage for Special Events

Target Market for a Special Event

Preparation for a Special Event

Budget for a Special Event
- Rental Costs
- Security Costs
- Production Costs
- Labor Costs
- Marketing Costs
- Talent Costs

Breakdown of a Special Event

Introduction

The words "special event" are used as an umbrella term that encompasses all functions that bring people together for a unique purpose. Most events require some sort of planning on the part of the organizer. A special event, such as a city **festival** or **fair,** can mean working with

community infrastructure, merchandising, promoting, and (in some cases) dealing with the media. The event can be as small as the local community Kiwanis picnic or as large as a global film festival. Special events are imbedded in **meetings** and **conventions** and at amusement parks, parades, festivals, fairs, and exhibits.

The Convention Industry Council (CIC) glossary (located on its Web site at http://www.conventionindustry.org/glossary) includes the following definitions related to special events:

> *Special Event.* A one-time event that is staged for the purpose of celebration; a unique activity.
>
> *Special Event Tour.* A tour that is designed around a particular event (for example, the Kentucky Derby, Mardi Gras, or the Rose Bowl Parade).
>
> *Special Events Company.* A company that presents special effects and theatrical acts. This type of company may contract to put on an entire event or only parts of one. It sometimes hires speakers as part of its contract.

A special event can bring organizations together for the purpose of fund-raising; establishing a city or community as a local, regional, or national destination; or stimulating the local economy. The event can also be an opportunity for an association or a corporation to favorably position itself with a community or with consumers. Sponsoring a specific type of event can provide a marketing edge and another avenue for reaching customers. For example, Buick Automobiles sponsors numerous PGA golf tournaments, in part because the demographics of the audience match their target clientele; Volvo does the same thing with the U.S. Open tennis tournament. Busch Beer sponsors NASCAR races, Nokia sponsors the Sugar Bowl football game, and Macy's sponsors the Thanksgiving Day parade. The list goes on and on.

Orchestrating a special event takes more than an idea. It takes planning, understanding the target market, having basic operational knowledge, using effective communications, working with volunteers or volunteer organizations, working within a budget, promoting the event, and even creating the logistics for breaking down an event. Simply stated, the event planner needs to understand the who, what, when, where, and why of the special event.

There are a variety of special events that take place to promote a destination or an occasion. One example is Groundhog Day

Groundhog Day History

EUROPEAN ROOTS

Groundhog Day, February 2, is a popular tradition in the United States. It is also a legend that traverses centuries, its origins clouded in the mists of time, with ethnic cultures and animals awakening on specific dates. Myths such as this tie our present to the distant past when nature did indeed influence our lives. It is the day that the groundhog comes out of his hole after a long winter sleep to look for his shadow. If he sees it, he regards it as an omen of six more weeks of bad weather and returns to his hole. If the day is cloudy and hence there is no shadow, he takes it as a sign of spring and stays above-ground.

The groundhog tradition stems from similar beliefs associated with Candlemas Day and the days of early Christians in Europe, when for centuries the custom was to have the clergy bless candles and distribute them to the people. Even then, it marked a milestone in the winter, and the weather that day was important.

The Roman legions, during the conquest of the northern country, supposedly brought this tradition to the Teutons, or Germans, who picked it up and concluded that if the sun made an appearance on Candlemas Day, an animal (the hedgehog) would cast a shadow, thus predicting six more weeks of bad weather, which they interpolated as the length of the "Second Winter."

U.S. ROOTS

Pennsylvania's earliest settlers were Germans, who found groundhogs in profusion in many parts of the state. They determined that the groundhog, resembling the European hedgehog, was a most intelligent and sensible animal and therefore decided that if the sun did appear on February 2, so wise an animal as the groundhog would see its shadow and hurry back into its underground home for another six weeks of winter.

The Germans recited:

For as the sun shines on Candlemas Day, So far will the snow swirl until the May.

This passage may be the one most closely represented by the first Punxsutawney Groundhog Day observances because there were references to the length of shadows in early Groundhog Day predictions.

Another February 2 belief, used by American nineteenth-century farmers, was "Groundhog Day—Half your hay." New England farmers knew that we were not close to the end of winter, no matter how cloudy February 2 was; indeed, February 2 is often the heart of winter. If the farmer didn't have half his hay remaining, there may have been lean times for the cows before spring when fresh grass arrived.

The ancient Candlemas legend and similar beliefs continue to be recognized annually on February 2 due to the efforts of the Punxsutawney Groundhog Club.

Source: Adapted from "Groundhog Day: 1886 to 1992" by Bill Anderson. Available at http://www.groundhog.org/faq/history.shtml.

celebrated in Punxsutawney, Pennsylvania. Once a small town event, millions of television viewers now awake to the early-morning cheers and chants for Punxsutawney Phil, the beloved groundhog who will let us know if we are in for another six weeks of winter should he see his shadow.

Another successful small city event that draws over 100,000 visitors to central Pennsylvania is the summer Central Pennsylvania Arts Festival. It will bring over 125,000 people to downtown State College and the University Park campus of Penn State to celebrate the arts with its nationally recognized Sidewalk Sale and Exhibition, a gallery exhibition, and music, dance, and theatrical performances in a variety of traditional and nontraditional venues. (For more information, go to http://www.arts-festival.com.)

A film festival can be a dream come true for moviegoers as they seek out famous actors who might be walking right next to them, as on the streets of Park City, Utah, during the Sundance Film Festival. Founded in 1981, the festival has garnered international recognition, attracting tens of thousands of visitors each year to this quaint little town to view over 3,000 film submissions.

These special events came from a historical tradition that ultimately grew to attract thousands of visitors to some very remote areas. Continuing to attract visitors requires planning and information, such as an understanding of the community infrastructure, merchandising and promoting the event, developing sponsorships, and working with the media. This is the art and science of special events management.

Using Festivals in the Off-Season: "Rockin' Mountains"

The typical image of the Rocky Mountains and Colorado is one of snow-covered peaks in winter dotted with skiers. But what happens when summer rolls around and people cannot ski? What do the ski resorts do, shut down? The answer is a resounding "No!" They put on music festivals using the same facilities occupied by skiers in the winter. The setting is idyllic, with music carrying through the clean air against the awesome backdrop of mountain peaks.

This use of Colorado mountain ski facilities to host off-season musical events started in 1949 when concerts were held in the town of Aspen. At the time it was called the Goethe Bicentennial Celebration. Some of the events included the Minneapolis Symphony Orchestra playing in a tent that held 2,000 people. This special event has continued and grown into the Aspen Music Festival and School; during the summer of 2006, the event included over 800 international musicians. During these periods, students, faculty, and visiting musicians perform almost 250 classical pieces, ranging from symphonies to children's programs. There are three major **venues,** the largest of which is a tent that holds over 2,000 people and is made from the same fabric as the Denver airport terminal.

Another ski resort that has turned to musical events to attract visitors in the off-season is Telluride, Colorado. Nearly every summer weekend, the town hosts a musical event. The biggest special event is the Telluride Bluegrass Festival, which has taken place for over thirty years. It runs for four days in June and attracts 10,000 people per day. Telluride also hosts a Jazz Festival, a Chamber Music Festival, and a Blues and Brews Festival.

In Winter Park just west of Denver, three weekends are occupied with music festivals. Concertgoers sit on the slopes and watch bands perform against the backdrop of the Continental Divide. A Rockfest features an eclectic lineup of post-Pop artists ranging from the latest break-out bands to "old-school" favorites. In July, Winter Park holds the "Hawgfest," a Harley-Davidson-inspired blowout targeted to baby boomers. They also hold a Jazzfest, with music that runs the gamut from the best in smooth jazz to progressive jazz.

The towns of Aspen, Breckenridge, and Telluride have banded together to form the Colorado Music Alliance, which has hosted and marketed events in these three locations plus a number of small, somewhat isolated communities, including Silverthorne, Crested Butte, Estes Park, Durango, Steamboat Springs, and Nederland. This proves that festivals are a good way of drawing tourists who would not otherwise travel to an area during the off-season. The festivals bring economic activity when there would be none, and the attendees may like the location enough to come back during the busy season.

Special Events: History and Background

Festivals and special events have been part of human history since time immemorial. Humankind has celebrated births, weddings, and deaths throughout history and held special gatherings such as the Olympics and gladiatorial contests. However, most historians credit the use of the term "special event" in modern history to a Disney imagineer named Robert Janni. The problem Disney faced was that the families who frequented the theme park were worn out after a day of adventure and most left by 5 P.M. each day, even though the park stayed open hours longer. In order to keep attendees at the park, he proposed producing a nightly parade called the "Main Street Electric Parade" with numerous floats decked out with lights. It was a success in keeping people in the park in the evening. When asked by a reporter what he called this parade, he replied "A Special Event." The use of special events to attract or maintain crowds is used to this day.

A special event is a celebration of something—that is what makes it special. Goldblatt defines a special event "as a unique moment in time celebrated with ceremony and ritual to satisfy specific needs."

Special events can include:

- Civic Events
  - Centennials
  - Founders Day
- Mega-Events
  - Olympics
  - America's Cup
  - Hands across America
  - World's Fairs
- Festivals and Fairs
  - Marketplaces (in ancient days)
  - Community events
  - Fairs (not-for-profit)
  - Festivals (for profit)
- Expositions
  - Meeting place for suppliers and buyers
- Education
- Entertainment
- Sporting Events
  - Super Bowl
  - World Series
  - Masters Golf Tournament
  - Belmont Stakes
- Social life cycle events
  - Weddings
  - Anniversaries
  - Birthdays
  - Reunions
  - Bar mitzvahs/bat mitzvahs
- Meetings and Conventions
  - Political national conventions

(continued)

Special Events: History and Background (*continued*)

- National Restaurant Association conventions in Chicago
- PCMA annual conferences
- Retail Events
  - Long-range promotional events
  - Store openings

- New product rollouts
  - Xbox
  - Microsoft
- Religious Events
  - Papal inaugurations
  - Hajj (Mecca)
  - Easter
  - Quanza

Source: Adapted from Joe Goldblatt, *Special Events: Event Leadership for a New World,* 4th ed. Hoboken, New Jersey: John Wiley and Sons, 2005.

Planning Tools for a Special Event

Special events management, like any other form of managing, requires planning tools. The first of these tools is a vision statement of your event. This vision statement should clearly identify the who, what, when, where, and why of the event. As the event begins to unfold, it is important to keep those involved focused on the vision. This can be accomplished by continually monitoring, evaluating, and (where possible) measuring the progress toward the outlined goals of the event (see chapter 9, "Planning MEEC Gatherings").

The "who" of planning an event are those people or organizations that would like to host and organize it. In the case of the St. Patrick's Day Parade in Chicago, Illinois, it is the city that hosts and coordinates the marchers, the floats, and the bands. The "what" is a parade demonstrating Irish pride and local tradition. The "where" of the parade is downtown Chicago, with the floats and bands marching down Michigan Avenue. The big question of "why" is one of tradition, pride, fun, and tourism. This, in turn, promotes the city and brings revenues to local businesses. When the city decided to serve as the host of this event, it needed to incorporate the tools of special events management.

Some management tools used in staging events:

- Flow charts and graphs are needed for scheduling. Look at any program for a meeting; there are start and end times, times for coffee breaks, a time for lunch, and a time for the meeting to resume and to end. The flow chart can be as romantic as a wedding ceremony **agenda.** The chart can also be the order of floats for a parade, the program for a talent show, or the sequence for a weeklong international conference. A flow chart scheduling an event's activities helps guide attendees and guests and makes the execution of the event flow smoothly.
- There should be clearly defined setup and breakdown **schedules.** These provide the event manager with an opportunity to determine tasks that may have been overlooked in the initial planning process.
- Policy statements need to be developed to guide in the decision-making process. Policy statements provide a clear understanding of commitments and what is expected to fulfill them. Some of the commitments to be considered are human resources, sponsors, security, ticketing, volunteers, and paid personnel.

UNDERSTANDING OF COMMUNITY INFRASTRUCTURE

Another key ingredient for planning a successful event is an understanding of the infrastructure in the community where the event is to take place. This infrastructure might include the CEO of the company, politicians, prominent business leaders of the community, civic and community groups, the media, and other community leaders. Without a buy-in from the city leadership, a community is less inclined to be supportive. The role of business leaders in the infrastructure could be to provide sponsorships, donations, staff, or a possible workplace for the coordination of the event. Many times community groups serve as volunteer workers for the event and are also an extension of the advertising for it.

Early on, it must be recognized whether or not a community or a company is truly committed to hosting any type of special event that will call on their support by not only the financial commitment but also the physical and emotional commitment it will take to manage an event from start to finish. For a promoter or special events management company to maintain a positive reputation, there needs to be a solid infrastructure in place.

Jane Byrne at the Chicago St. Patrick's Day parade.
Mayor's Press Office, City of Chicago

MERCHANDISING AND PROMOTION OF SPECIAL EVENTS

Merchandising and promoting a special event are other planning tools for attracting attendance and increasing the overall profitability for the event. Just because a community decides to host a craft fair or street festival does not mean that there will be the attendance necessary to meet vendors' and visitors' needs. Profit for the vendor and a memorable experience for the attendee are two main objectives for a special event. The special event requires all the promotional venues that an event management company or civic group is able to afford.

Understanding and utilizing the **promotional mix model** (see Figure 8–1) is pivotal in order to meet the goals of the event marketing plan. The role of promotion in special events management is the coordination of all the sellers' efforts to set up channels of information and persuasion to sell or promote the event. Traditionally, the

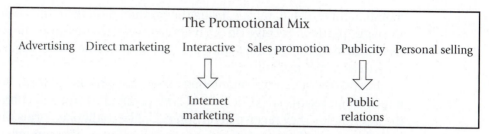

FIGURE 8–1 Elements of the promotional mix for successful special event management.

promotional mix has included four elements: advertising, sales promotion, publicity and/or public relations, and personal selling. However, this author views direct marketing and interactive media as additional elements of the promotional mix. Modern-day event marketers use many means to communicate with their target markets, and each element of the promotional mix is viewed as an integrated marketing communications tool. Each of these elements of the model has a distinctive role in attracting an attendee to the special event, each takes on a variety of forms, and each has certain advantages.

DISTINCTIVE ROLES OF THE PROMOTIONAL MIX MODEL

Advertising   Advertising is defined as any paid form of nonpersonal communication about the event. The term "nonpersonal" means advertising that involves mass media (e.g., TV, radio, magazines, and newspapers). Advertising is the best-known and most widely discussed form of promotion because it is the most persuasive, especially if the event (for example, a home and garden show) targets mass consumers. It can be used to create brand images or symbolic appeals for the brand and can generate immediate responses from prospective attendees.

Direct marketing is a form of advertising that communicates directly with the target customer with the intent of generating a response. It is much more than direct mail or catalogs—it involves a variety of activities including database management, direct selling, telemarketing, direct-response ads, the Internet, and various broadcast and print media. An example of direct marketing is a company such as Mary Kay Cosmetics or Tupperware. Rather than distribution channels, they rely on independent contractors to sell their products directly to consumers. These contractors directly communicate with the customer, maintain their own database, bring the product directly to the customer through "parties," receive direct response, and finally (after the sale is made) deliver the product directly. The Internet has also fueled the growth of direct marketing.

Interactive or Internet marketing allows for a back-and-forth flow of information: Users can participate in and modify the form and content of the information they receive in real time. Unlike traditional forms of marketing such as advertising, which are one-way forms of communication, this type of media allows users to perform a variety of functions: It enables users to receive and alter information and images, make inquiries, respond to questions, and make purchases. Many event attendees will go to a Web site to garner information about a special event such as a concert and then purchase their tickets directly online. For a special event such as the Aspen Music Festival, attendees can go to the festival's official Web site, view the schedule, learn about the event and the surrounding area, purchase tickets, and request additional information—all forms of direct marketing. In addition to the Internet, other forms of interactive media include CD-ROMs, kiosks, and interactive television.

Sales Promotion   Sales promotion is generally defined as those marketing activities that provide extra value or incentives to the sales force, distributors, or ultimate consumers with the intention of stimulating sales. A popular form of sales promotion is the coupon. Many events will use a two-for-one attendance coupon to stimulate attendance on slower days.

Publicity and Public Relations   Publicity and public relations are two separate components. Publicity is the component that is not directly paid for, nor does it have an identified sponsor. When an event planner gets the media to cover or run a favorable story on a special event, it affects an attendee's awareness, knowledge, and opinions. Publicity is considered a credible form of promotion, but it is not always under the control of the organization or host of the event. In the case of Punxsutawney Phil, the groundhog used in the city's quest to determine if spring is six weeks away, all of the national broadcasting television stations send a camera crew and reporter to publicize this unique event. If those reporting the event have a positive experience, it will favorably affect the public's perception of the event; unfortunately, the reverse is also true. The planners have little control over the end result.

The purpose of public relations is to systematically plan and distribute information in an attempt to control or manage the image and/or

How Atlantic City Uses Special Events

Atlantic City is located in New Jersey on the Atlantic Coast. During its heyday as a seashore destination in the 1920s and '30s, it attracted hundreds of thousands of tourists from New York and Philadelphia during the summer season. However, tourist numbers dropped dramatically after Labor Day, the end of the summer season when young people returned to school. The city fathers hit on the idea of staging a special event in mid to late September, a time when the weather was still quite pleasant at the shore. They decided to produce a beauty contest that would feature young women showing off their talents, including—you guessed it—a bathing suit contest. That special event came to be known as the Miss America Pageant and helped to put Atlantic City on the map during the off-season for decades. It was a very special event. (The pageant has now moved to a different venue.)

Atlantic City attempted another special event with decidedly different results. The heyday mentioned above gave out in the 1960s and '70s as inexpensive jet travel enabled tourists to seek more distant travel destinations. Atlantic City saw its fortunes dwindle, and a disastrous cycle started: decreasing numbers of tourists, followed by the closing of stores, hotels, and restaurants, followed by still fewer tourists. It got so bad that at the end of one summer season, the mayor was quoted as saying, "Will the last person to leave Atlantic City please turn out the lights." Again, the city fathers came up with an idea for a special event that would bring fame to the city once more. They were successful in bidding to host a presidential national convention in the early 1970s. They thought the press would cover the convention and make numerous mentions of the location, thus getting national publicity, but it did not work out as they had planned. The convention was boring because the presidential nominee became known well in advance of the convention. The media, with little to focus on inside the convention, looked for stories around the city. What they found was poverty, slums, dirty streets, etc.—and that is what they reported. The negative publicity was just the opposite of what the city fathers had planned.

publicity of an event. It has a broader objective than publicity because its purpose is to establish a positive image of the special event. Public relations can be the reason for hosting the special event altogether! Tobacco companies have used special events such as a NASCAR race (Winston Cup) or tennis tournament to create a more positive image with consumers.

Personal Selling   Personal selling is the final element of the promotional mix model, and it is a form of person-to-person communication in which a seller attempts to assist and/or persuade prospective event attendees. Typically, group tour sales are the best prospects for personal selling of a special event. There are several touring companies that purchase large groups of tickets for special events. Unlike advertising, personal selling involves direct contact between the buyer and seller of the event, usually through face-to-face sales. Therefore, personal selling is more appropriate and feasible by meeting face-to-face with a group of representatives, whereas meeting face-to-face with each individual prospective attendee is not. Some examples of events that group tours may attend include the Indianapolis 500, the Kentucky Derby, and the Jazz Fest in New Orleans. Group tour organizers will meet face-to-face with event planners or talk via telephone to purchase tickets for an event.

SPONSORSHIPS FOR SPECIAL EVENTS

Sponsorships help to ensure profitable success for an event. They are an innovative way for event organizers to help underwrite and defray costs. Sponsorships should be considered more than just a charitable endeavor for a company—they can be a strong marketing tool.

Event sponsors provide funds or "in-kind" contributions and receive consideration in the form of logo usage and identity with the event. Recent trends of sponsorships show rapid growth. **Sporting events** have long been the leader in securing sponsorships for teams and athletes; however, their market share has dropped as companies began to distribute sponsorship dollars to other events, such as city festivals and the arts.

There are five compelling reasons why company sponsorships are growing and diversifying:

1. Economic changes
2. Ability to target market segments
3. Ability to measure results
4. Fragmentation of the media
5. Growth of diverse population segments

This shift in sponsorships from sports events to that of festivals and the arts over the past decade has emerged because companies are cognizant of the effective tool that a sponsorship can be for overall company marketing plans.

The Great Garlic Cook-Off

The Annual Garlic Festival is held in the "Garlic Capital of the World," Gilroy, California, at Christmas Hill Park during the last full weekend of July. This festival's origin lies in the pride of one man, Rudy Melone. Melone felt that Gilroy, California, should celebrate its superior production of the "stinking rose," otherwise known as garlic. He then began what is referred to as "the preeminent food festival in America."

In December of each year, the Gilroy Garlic Festival begins its request for original garlic recipes. Citizens of Canada and the United States are asked to participate. Recipes are then submitted by amateur chefs, and eight are chosen to participate in the festival cook-off. Winners are awarded monetary prizes for their well-done work.

Another tradition practiced by the Garlic Festival is the nomination of a "Queen of Garlic." To date, only twenty-four women can claim this title. Contestants are judged on a personal interview, talent, a garlic speech, and an evening gown competition. The queen represents Gilroy at various festivities before and during the festival.

Over the last twenty-eight years, the Garlic Festival has attracted over 3 million attendees and raised money for local nonprofit organizations. More than 4,000 volunteers are recruited to work the event and participate in activities such as picking up trash, parking cars, and serving lemonade. The Gilroy Garlic Festival is known not only for its garlic pride and knowledge but for its ability to bring the community of Gilroy together. Their Web site states, "Where else can one feast on food laced with over two tons of fresh garlic, enjoy three stages of musical entertainment, shop in arts and crafts, view the great garlic cook-off and other celebrity cooking demonstrations, spend time in the children's area, visit interactive displays set up by many of our sponsors, soak up some glorious sunshine, and mingle with a fun bunch of garlic-loving people?"

Source: http://www.gilroygarlicfestival.com

When looking for sponsorships for a special event, organizers must determine if the event fits the company. Planners must always examine the company's goals and be sure to research the competition. Special events organizers should aid the sponsors with promotional ideas that will help them to meet their goals. Promoters of an event need to ensure that sponsors get their money's worth.

Remember that sponsors have internal and external audiences to whom they are appealing. The internal audience of a corporation is its

New York City Marathon

SPONSORSHIP

The New York City Marathon boasts 30,000 runners with more than 2 million spectators—the largest live sporting event in the world, broadcast to over 330 million viewers in more than 154 territories. Television coverage includes a live five-hour telecast on WNBC in New York, a one-hour national telecast on NBC, and various live and highlight shows internationally.

New York Road Runners and the New York City Marathon are fortunate to have the support and commitment of our fine sponsors and strategic partners. Their continued support makes the New York City Marathon a world-class event year after year.

Sponsors

Adecco	Gatorade	Poland Spring
Aestiva	Georgia Pacific	Pontiac
Aleve	ILX Systems	PowerBar
Amtrak	Lamisil AT	Ronzoni
Andersen	Mirror Image	Saranac
Best Buy	Moishe's	Tiffany & Co.
Breathe Right	Motorola	Time Warner Cable
Chock Full O' Nuts	New York Apple	UPS
Dannon	Association	Walrus Internet
Dole	Nextel	

Source: http://www.nyrrc.org/nyrrc/mar01/about/sponsors.html

employees, who must be sold on the sponsorship of the event. A company needs to provide opportunities for employee involvement. If the special event is a charitable marathon, employees may be asked to actually participate in the marathon or raise funds for the charitable cause. Those employees who participate may be featured in promotional material or press releases.

Selling to the external audience of the corporation (the consumer) is done in a variety of ways. First, the company might feature its logo on the event's products. The company can promote its affiliation with the special event by providing its logo for outdoor banners and for specialty advertising items, such as T-shirts, caps, or sunglasses.

The types of specialty products are limitless and are excellent venues for advertising. The sponsoring company may wish to appoint an employee spokesperson to handle radio or television interviews.

MEDIA COVERAGE FOR SPECIAL EVENTS

Generating media coverage for special events is one of the most effective methods for attracting attendance. Ideally, an event organizer wants to garner free television, radio, and print coverage. In order to attract the media, a promoter must understand what makes for good TV, radio, or print coverage and what does not.

When a camera crew is sent to film an event by assignment editors at a TV station, they will look for a story that can be easily illustrated with visuals captured by a camera; they also look for a vignette that can entertain viewers in thirty seconds or less. If an event organizer wants television or radio stations to cover the event, he or she needs to call it to their attention with a press release or press conference. There are no guarantees that the station or the newspaper will air the footage or print the story; however, the chances are better if a camera crew shoots footage or a reporter does an interview. When this happens, the event has free advertising. Remember, special events provide ideal fodder for the evening news, whether it be an interview with a celebrity who will be attending the event or an advance look at an art exhibit.

Within the promotional mix model, the biggest way to attract attention to the event is with television, radio, and print media through publicity. This "free" type of promotion offers something that advertising cannot match—credibility. These media sources are an excellent way to reach all types of consumers.

Event organizers try to present the unusual to the press. At the opening of a steak restaurant in a hotel in Tulsa, Oklahoma, a special event was staged where the management hosted a "Moo-Off." Community leaders were invited to a dinner featuring the restaurant's signature food and beverage items. They were then asked to "Moo" in the voice of their favorite celebrity. The audience bellowed their Mae West Moos, Jack Nicholson Moos—even an Elvis Presley Moo. Moo-ers were gonged by specially selected judges (city leaders), and the winner of the event donated the cash prize to a community charity. The event caught the attention of the media and was featured on the evening news. The event organizers used well-timed radio segments to enhance the credibility of the Moo-Off. The restaurant manager was featured on local radio stations during morning and afternoon drive times, which peaked TV interest on the day of the event. Although it initially appears

A Very Special Wedding

A couple from Texas wanted to be sure their wedding was special, so they decided to have it in New Orleans. They were enamored with the charm of the city: moss-draped oak trees, antebellum homes, and horse-drawn carriages. They decided to invite 100 people and contacted a local destination management company (DMC) to make the arrangements. Their specification was that the DMC arrange a rehearsal dinner for 12 people and a reception for 100. Such costs as transportation to New Orleans, hotel accommodations, and the church were not part of the bid. Their stated budget for this wedding reception and dinner was $250,000. That's right—a quarter of a million dollars ($2,500 per guest)! When the planner heard this, her reaction was twofold: (1) How could she possibly put together this event and spend that much money? (2) If that was their proposed budget, how could she try to up-sell them?

The rehearsal dinner was held in a private dining room at the famous Arnaud's restaurant in the French Quarter. The real money was spent on the reception. They rented the art deco Saenger Theater for the evening, but there was a problem. Like most theaters, the floor sloped toward the stage, so they removed all the seats and built a new floor that was level, not sloped. The interior of the theater was so beautiful that it needed little decoration. The New Orleans Police Department was contracted to close the street between the church and theater to cars so that the period ambiance would not be disturbed for the couple and their guests while being transported in their horse-drawn carriages. When the couple and their guests entered for the evening, they were greeted by models in period costume and served mint juleps while a gospel group sang. A blues band followed and the night was topped off by not one but two sets by Gladys Knight and the Pips. The affair was catered by Emeril Legasse and only included heavy hors d'oeuvres (not even a sit-down dinner). The ultimate cost for this event was almost $300,000, and the couple was delighted.

Note: The planner was Nanci Easterling of Food Art, Inc.

that the promoters of the Moo-Off did not have to work too hard to obtain media coverage, their professional expertise in advance promotion of this event is what guaranteed its success. Once the media found out about the Moo-Off, the event sold itself; the organizers' main work was to ensure that the media found out about it.

Promoters of special events have long recognized what TV and radio coverage can do for an event. Here are some helpful hints for attracting television and radio coverage:

1. Early in the day is considered the best time to attract cameras and reporters. Remember, a crew must come out, film, get back to the studio, edit the film, and have the segment ready for the 5 P.M. or 6 P.M. newscast that night.

2. The best day of the week to attract news crews is Friday because it is usually a quiet news day. Saturday and Sunday have even fewer distractions, but most stations do not have enough news crews working the weekend who can cover an event.

3. Giving advance notice for a special event is very helpful to assignment editors. Usually about three days' notice, with an explanation of the event via a press release and telephone follow-up, is very helpful in securing media coverage. If an interview is involved, a seven-day notice is a good time allotment for coverage.

Target Market for a Special Event

Bringing special events to a community has not changed much over the years; however, consumers have changed. They are much more selective and sophisticated about the events they will attend. Since the cost of attending events has risen, consumers are much more discerning about how they spend their entertainment dollars, which creates a demand for quality for any special event.

The most valuable outcome a special event can generate for a community is positive word of mouth. In order to create this positive awareness, an organizer recognizes that the event cannot appeal to all markets. A promoter will determine the target market for the community's event.

Target marketing is defined as clearly identifying who wants to attend a certain type of event. For example, a Brittany Spears concert has been determined to appeal to a female audience from generation Y. To stage a profitable concert, promoters will direct their advertising dollars to that particular targeted audience, and all promotional items will also be geared toward that age group.

Most communities know that a special event will have a positive economic impact on the community and the region. This has created competition to attract events. A city will commonly use inducements to lure the special event to the community. These inducements may

Britney Spears enter-
tains at a concert.
AP Wide World Photos

include free entertainment space, security, parking—even the "key to the city" for the celebrity providing the entertainment.

A successful event has two vital components: The community is supportive of bringing the event to the city, and the event meets the consumers' need. For example, every year on Labor Day weekend, New Orleans is host to a special event called "Southern Decadence." This three-day event is targeted to gay and lesbian people, and they "strut" around the city freely. New Orleans is probably one of the few communities in the United States that would be supportive of bringing such an event to its city.

Preparation for a Special Event

Basic operations for staging an event need to be established and include the following steps:

1. Secure a venue.
2. Obtain **permits.**
   a. Parade permits
   b. Liquor permits
   c. Sanitation permits
   d. Sales permits or licenses
   e. Fire safety permits
3. Involve necessary **government agencies** (e.g., if using city recreation facilities, work with the department of parks and recreation).
4. Involve the health department (if there will be food and beverage at the event).
5. Meet all relevant parties in person so that any misconceptions are cleared up early.
6. Recognize the complexities of dealing with the public sector. (Sometimes public agencies have a difficult time making decisions!)
7. Recognize the logistics that a community must contend with for certain types of special events, (e.g., street closures for a marathon).
8. Set up a security plan, which may include the security supplied by the venue and professional law enforcement. (Pay attention as to which security organization takes precedence.)
9. Secure liability insurance (the most vulnerable area is the liability attached to liquor and liquor laws).
10. Determine ticket prices if the special event involves ticketing.
11. Determine ticket sale distribution if the special event involves ticketing.
12. Cover other basic business support functions:
    a. Accounting systems (general ledger, financial reporting, accounts payable, accounts receivable, and payroll)
    b. Human resources systems (recruiting, personnel records, and job classifications and descriptions)
    c. Accommodations (talent, media, officials, support staff, and spectators)
    d. Registration

e. Ticketing (mail order, seat inventories, seat assignments, and gate sales)

f. Scoring and results (scoreboards and displays)

The type of special event being held will determine the degree of preparedness needed. The larger the event, the more involved the checklist is. Preparedness should produce a profitable and well-managed event.

Budget for a Special Event

For any event to be considered a success, it must also be considered profitable. Profitability requires understanding the key elements involved in the cost of an event. The six basic areas that make up the costs for a special event include rental, security, production, labor, marketing, and talent.

RENTAL COSTS

Depending on the type of event, renting a facility such as a convention center or ground space to put up a tent requires payment of a daily rental charge. Convention centers usually sell the space based on a certain dollar amount per square footage used. Most facilities charge for space even on the move-in and move-out days, but multiday events can usually negotiate a discount.

SECURITY COSTS

Most convention centers, rental halls, and hotels provide limited security. This could mean that a guard is stationed at the front and rear entrances of the venue. Depending on the type of event, such as a rock concert performed by a band that has raucous fans, more security may be required. European football (i.e., soccer) matches require even more security. Actual costs will depend on the city and the amount of security needed.

PRODUCTION COSTS

Production costs are those associated with staging a special event and vary depending on the type of event. For example, if the special event is a large home and garden show, there are costs associated with the setup of the trade show booths. As with many home and garden

In a Land Far, Far Away

Gansbaai, South Africa–based Grootbos Private Nature Reserve overlooks Walker Bay and provides guests a unique opportunity to view flora, fauna, and marine life. Its lodges are a two-hour drive from Cape Town, accessed by tar road or helicopter, and it's the destination of choice for people planning weddings, incentives, birthday parties, and product launches. Popular event spots at Grootbos include the wine cellar, the main lodges, and the pool area. For a taste of local events, marketing and reservations manager Florentina Heger says nothing beats a "South African braai at our boma nestled in the Milkwood Forest"— in other words, a South African barbecue in an open outdoor event space. Picnics in the Milkwood Forest are also popular, with lunch accompanied by violinists and cello players providing music or published authors reading their works. Dinner could consist of a six-course gala event or dishes served in small portions to encourage guests to circulate and mingle as they eat. Weddings here are typically beach affairs, with whales seen in the distance and sushi, champagne, and salmon- and trout-wrapped mussels served after the ceremony.

Source: Adapted from an article in *Special Events* magazine by Christine Landry. Available at http://specialevents.com/venues/events_destination_known_20011110.

shows, exhibitors bring in elaborate garden landscapes that are very time consuming and labor intensive to set up and break down. Labor costs for decorators need to be calculated to estimate the production costs based on the type and size of trade show booth. There are also electrical and water fees needed for a home and garden show, and these costs must be included in the production costs. Other production costs include signage or banners for each booth and pipe and drape fees.

LABOR COSTS

The city where the special event is being held will affect the labor costs involved in the setup and breakdown of the event. Some cities are unionized, and this can add higher costs to an event because of the higher wages. Holding an event in very strict union cities means that the organizer of the event must leave more of the handling to the union crew. In some cities, the union allows the exhibitor to wheel his or her own cart with brochures and merchandise; in others, exhibitors cannot carry anything other than their own briefcases.

It is hard to believe that this is the inside of a tent used for a special event.
Used by permission of Paradise Light & Sound, Orlando, Florida.

When selecting a city for an event, the role of unions has been an important influence. Most special events organizers will pass the higher costs on to the exhibitor or will increase ticket prices.

MARKETING COSTS

The costs associated with attracting attendees can make up a large portion of the budget (see Table 8–1). Here, the event organizer examines the best means of reaching the target market. Trying to reach a mass audience may mean running a series of television commercials, which can be very expensive. Most event organizers use a combination of promotions—elements of advertising, direct marketing, publicity and public relations, sales promotions, interactive or Internet marketing, and personal selling—to attract the attendee. All of these need to be budgeted.

TALENT COSTS

Virtually all special events use some type of talent or performer: a keynote speaker, a band or orchestra, a sports team, a vocalist, an

TABLE 8–1	The ABC Special Event

Statement of Revenues and Expenses (In Dollars)

Revenues	Budget	Actual
Admission	5,000	6,000
Exhibit booth sales	10,000	11,000
Food and beverage sales	2,000	4,000
Total	17,000	21,000

Expenditures		
Rental	1,000	1,000
Labor (Security)	500	500
Production	2,000	3,000
Marketing costs	3,000	4,000
Talent	—	500
Total	6,500	9,000
Surplus	10,500	12,000

animal, etc. While the organizer may have grandiose thoughts about the quality of the talent used, price has to be considered and matched to the special events budget—the high school class reunion probably cannot afford to have Madonna perform.

Before an event, it is essential that a planner do a projection of all costs and revenue. These projections are essential to whether a community will host another event. Repeat events are much easier to promote, especially when the organizers have made a profit.

Breakdown of a Special Event

Special events have one thing in common: They all come to an end! Breaking down the event usually involves a number of steps. Once the attendees have gone, there are a variety of closing tasks that an organizer must complete.

Weddings are a very special event and can be big business. This is especially true for Disney where thousands of couples are married each year.

Ting-Li Wang, the *New York Times*

First, the parking staff should expedite the flow of traffic away from the event. In some cases, community police are able to assist in traffic control.

A debriefing of staff should take place to determine what did or did not happen at the event, and there may be issues pending that will need documentation. It is always best to have written reports to refer to for next year's event. Consider having the following sources add information to the report:

1. *Participants.* Interview some of the participants from the event. A customer's perceptions and expectations provide invaluable insight.

2. *Media and the Press.* Ask why it was or was not a press-worthy gathering.

3. *Staff and Management.* Get a variety of staff and other management involved in the event to give feedback.

4. *Vendors.* Ask vendors how the event could be improved because they have a unique perspective.

The following steps should also be taken in a final assessment of the event:

1. Finalize the income and expense statement. Did the event break even, make a profit, or experience a loss?

2. Finalize all contracts from the event. Fortunately, most everything involved with putting together the event will have written documentation. Compare final billing with actual agreements.

3. Send the media a final press release on the overall success of the event. Interviews with the press could be arranged. This could be especially newsworthy if the event generated significant revenues for the community.

4. Provide a written thank-you for those volunteers who were involved with the event in any way. A celebration of some sort with the volunteers may be in order, especially if the event was financially and socially successful.

Once the elements of breakdown have taken place, the organizers can examine the important lessons of staging the event. What would they do or not do next year?

Summary

Creating a memorable event requires that an organizer meet and exceed an attendee's expectations. Recognizing that the special event could be a meeting or convention, a parade, a festival, a fair, or an exhibit and understanding the objectives of the event are necessary for each planner. Having the planning tools in place is the keystone for success in managing the gathering. Special events management works with and understands the community infrastructures to help support the event.

It can be costly if a planner does not decide in advance which part of the promotional mix model of the event is used. The promotional mix model includes advertising, direct marketing, interactive or Internet marketing, sales promotion, publicity and public relations, and personal selling. Helping to defray costs by seeking sponsorships for a special event is another way to successfully market an event, and it is also an important marketing tool for the corporation sponsor. Working with the local and/or national media is the most effective way of attracting attendance. An organizer also needs to understand what makes for good media coverage, whether print or broadcast. The target

International Special Events Society (ISES)

INTRODUCTION TO ISES

The International Special Events Society (ISES) is comprised of over 4,000 professionals and 41 chapters all over the world representing special events producers (from festivals to trade shows), caterers, decorators, florists, destination management companies, rental companies, special effects experts, tent suppliers, audiovisual technicians, party and convention coordinators, balloon artists, educators, journalists, hotel sales managers, specialty entertainers, convention center managers, and many more.

ISES HISTORY

ISES was founded in 1987 to foster professionalism through education while promoting ethical conduct. ISES works to bring professionals together to focus on the event as a whole rather than its individual parts. Membership brings together professionals from a variety of special events disciplines including caterers, meeting planners, decorators, event planners, audiovisual technicians, party and convention coordinators, educators, journalists, hotel sales managers, and those from many other professional disciplines. The solid peer network ISES provides helps special events professionals produce outstanding results for clients while establishing positive working relationships with colleagues.

ISES MISSION

The mission of ISES is to educate, advance, and promote the special events industry, its network of professionals, and its related industries. To that end, it strives to:

- Uphold the integrity of the special events profession to the general public through its "Principles of Professional Conduct and Ethics"
- Acquire and disseminate useful business information
- Foster a spirit of cooperation among its members and other special events professionals
- Cultivate high standards of business practices

WHAT DOES ISES MEAN?

- Professional Development and Certification
  - Affiliation with local chapters provides education and exchanges of ideas.

- ISES keeps members on top of industry trends through educational programs such as the annual Conference for Professional Development (CPD) and accreditation programs such as the Certified Special Events Professional (CSEP).

- Recognition

  - ISES honors industry excellence through its prestigious awards program, the ISES Esprit Awards. The Esprit Awards fuel a spirit of competition within designated categories. The categories recognize the best and most creative professionals within the special events industry. Esprit Awards gain global visibility and recognition for ISES members.

- Strategic Alliance

  - ISES and *Special Events* magazine currently have a strategic alliance that provides benefits to ISES members. ISES recognizes *Special Events* magazine's link to www.specialevents.com as "the official and premier magazine of the special events industry in North America" and The Special Event as "the official and premier trade show for this industry in North America."

- Networking

  - Involvement means building relationships with other professionals from your region and beyond. The exchange that takes place increases business contacts, as well as potential client bases, and/or provides employment opportunities. By committing time through their memberships, members invest in themselves and the industry while gaining a competitive edge.

Source: Adapted from the ISES Web site. If you would like additional information about ISES, please contact ISES Headquarters, 401 N. Michigan Ave., Chicago, IL 60611-4267, USA; phone: 800-688-ISES (4737) or 312-321-6853; e-mail: info@ises.com.

There is also a magazine focusing on this area called *Special Events*; its Web site is http://specialevents.com. A trade show specifically targeted to special events has a Web site at http://thespecialeventshow.com/07intro.

market for the special event must always be considered in the objectives, the promotions, and the continuation of the event.

The basic operations and/or logistics for the event follow the planning and promoting. A checklist of the items that need to be handled or looked into is a must for all planners; planners should also create checklists that will help develop the overall special events budget, which requires regular reviews of the statement of revenues and expenditures. The breakdown is the final step and includes another checklist for the closure of the event. Always remember your volunteers—without them, the event would not take place!

Key Words and Terms

For definitions, see the Glossary or go to http://glossary.convention industry.org.

Agenda	Meeting
Community infrastructure	Promotional mix model
Convention	Schedule
Fair	Sporting event
Festival	Venue
Government agency	

Review and Discussion Questions

1. Discuss the types of events that a city might host.
2. What does the vision statement of an event provide for an organizer?
3. Discuss the types of planning tools that aid in successful event management.
4. What are the distinctive roles of the promotional mix model?
5. What are the benefits for sponsorships at a special event?
6. What are some tips for working with broadcast media?
7. What are some basic operations for staging an event?
8. Discuss costs associated with the event budget.
9. Outline the elements of breakdown for a special event.
10. Consider special events opportunities for your community. How would you offer advice as an event planner to encourage attendance?

About the Chapter Contributor

Cynthia Vannucci holds a Ph.D. in man/environmental relations, plus an M.B.A., and a B.S. in hotel administration. She has also earned several industry certifications in marketing, sales, meeting planning, and education. She is an associate professor at Metropolitan State College in Denver, where she serves as the director of meetings and conventions.

Planning MEEC Gatherings

Planning and organizing of national political conventions are functions of the MEEC industry.

Pearson Education/PH College

Chapter Objectives

This chapter provides the reader with an understanding of the following:

- Differences in association and corporate meeting planning
- Motivations influencing meeting objectives
- Clear and concise meeting objectives using the SMART technique
- Purpose of a needs analysis
- Process of site selection
- Information needed on an RFP
- Establishment of budgetary goals
- Effective evaluation instruments

Chapter Outline

Introduction

Setting of Objectives

Importance of Education

   Professional Certifications

Needs Analysis

Development of SMART Objectives

Site Selection

Request for Proposal

Budgetary Concerns

   Step 1: Establish Goals

   Step 2: Categorize Expenses

   Step 3: Identify Revenue Sources

Cost Control

Control in MEEC

   Evaluation Design

Introduction

A meeting planner or organizer may be familiar with all of the elements of the meetings, expositions, events, and conventions (MEEC) industry. However, it takes good planning, organizing, directing, and control to put these diverse elements together and make it work. In order to accomplish this, the organizer needs to understand the group, its wants and its needs: Who are they? Why are they here? Then objectives can be set that will guide the program delivery to meet these wants and needs while staying within budget constraints. It should be noted that this chapter on planning might be considered the first step in putting together a good meeting or event. The approach follows commonly held theories on the functions of management regarding planning, organizing, influencing, and controlling. The other aspect of putting on a good event is the implementation of the plan, which is covered in the next chapter.

Setting of Objectives

Two questions are necessary for a planner to ask: Who is the group? Why are they here? When planning programming for a meeting, these are followed by asking, "What is the objective of this meeting?" This simple question is the basis of much of the planning process. *Webster's Dictionary* defines "objective" as "something aimed at or strived for" along with "being the aim or goal" (*Webster's Unabridged Dictionary,* (1983) 2nd ed. New York (NY: Simon & Shuster). All meetings and events should begin with clear, concise, and measurable objectives. Meeting objectives is the basis for virtually all components of the planning process, whether it is for corporate meetings, association meetings, special events, trade shows, or virtual meetings held via the Internet. The objectives of the meeting will impact **site selection,** food and beverage requirements, transportation issues, and especially program content.

Most people attend meetings for three reasons: education, networking, and to conduct business. Some people participate in association **annual meetings** for the networking and educational offerings; others may attend primarily to develop business relationships and to make sales. If the planner does not design the program content and scheduling to accommodate these objectives, then the attendees may become dissatisfied.

Another key point is that program planning, especially for association meetings, begins months or years before the actual event. The average meeting attendee does not understand how much effort goes into planning even simple events, let alone something as complex as an association's annual meeting and trade show. As with much of the hospitality industry, the real work goes on behind the scenes, and unless something goes wrong, the attendees are blissfully unaware of the planning process and the coordination and cooperation necessary to produce an event. The meeting planner and the support staff should be invisible to the attendee.

Good meeting objectives should focus on the attendees. What will make the attendees want to attend the meeting? What will be their **return on investment (ROI)** or **return on objectives (ROO)?**

What makes your event more desirable than your competitor's event? Some of the key planning components that are directly affected by the meeting objectives are discussed in the following text.

Importance of Education

A key component of MEEC is to provide an environment conducive to education. Sponsors of meetings are increasingly cost-conscious with the planning and implementation of their events and have high expectations for the ROI achieved by employees or association members. Poor planning in logistics or in program content can spell disaster for the meeting planner. Gone are the days when conventions were viewed as primarily recreational events and expense accounts were plentiful. If the actual benefits of attending the meeting cannot be justified, then funding for attendance at a meeting or membership fees for an association may be withheld. In cases where the attendee is paying out of his or her own pocket to attend, good program content becomes a much more critical issue—people are usually much more careful with their own money than with someone else's. It is a fact that attendee expectations are seldom lowered. If you provide child care and all meals one year, then the same (or better) services will be expected the subsequent year. It is a constant challenge for the meeting planner to continuously improve the content and execution of meetings and conventions while keeping the price of attendance affordable.

Technological advances made in the last decade have provided additional challenges and opportunities for meeting planners. Web and videoconferencing technologies are becoming more sophisticated and affordable. Why spend the money to hold a physical meeting if a virtual meeting will achieve the same objectives? On the other hand, using technology has the potential to bring in additional revenues by webcasting workshops, providing Internet-based distance learning, and creating virtual trade shows. In addition, CD-ROMs or DVDs of speakers and sessions can be created with video, handouts, and other resources to be offered for sale at the convention or anytime in the future. Thus, people who could not attend the meeting can still participate and benefit from the experience.

PROFESSIONAL CERTIFICATIONS

Increasingly, people within a particular industry seek to differentiate themselves by becoming "certified" or "licensed" in a specific skill or

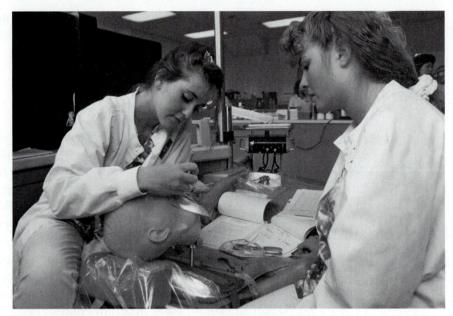

Medical education is an important part of MEEC.
Robert Harbison

by being recognized for achieving a certain level of competence in a career field. Most people cannot afford the luxury of quitting their job to go back to school for academic instruction. Instead, they rely on their professional associations to provide current information and continuing education in their particular field. Programs may be offered at the annual convention, at regional seminars, or through distance education over the Internet. Individuals receive **continuing education units (CEUs)** for each workshop they attend, and these CEUs will be a part of the qualifications to become certified or licensed. Physicians are a good example: To retain their medical license, doctors are required to take a certain amount of **continuing medical education (CME)** courses to keep current with innovations in health care.

In the meetings and convention industry, one of the most recognized designations is the **Certified Meeting Professional (CMP),** which is administered by the **Convention Industry Council (CIC).** To date, there are some 10,000 meeting professionals who have earned this designation, primarily those working in meeting management, convention services, and sales. One of the benefits of receiving a certification is that it demonstrates some level of competency in the profession. If the meeting planner has his or her CMP, the hotel salesperson knows that the planner has some expertise in the field. Certifications are often noted on business cards and used in correspondence to indicate what certifications have been earned. For example, John Smith, CMP, CAE, means that John Smith has earned the Certified Meeting Professional and Certified Association Executive designations. Certification programs are also a good source of revenue for associations, as application and testing fees, study materials and manuals, and periodic recertification can cost hundreds to thousands of dollars.

Needs Analysis

As part of setting objectives for a meeting, a **needs analysis**—a method of determining the expectations for a particular meeting—must be undertaken. A needs analysis can be as simple as asking senior management what they want to accomplish at a meeting and then designing the event around those expectations. It should be remembered that the needs of corporate and association meeting attendees are very different (see chapter 2). For example, if the CEO wants to hold the meeting at the exclusive Ritz Carlton Buckhead in Atlanta, provide deluxe suites for all attendees, have all meals catered, and states that expense is no object, then the meeting planner's job is much easier. However, in the real world, it takes more work to develop a needs analysis. The first step is to know your attendees by asking the question "Who are they?" A planner must collect demographic information of both past and prospective attendees. This is much easier for an annual event, such as an association meeting or corporate management meeting. The planner keeps a detailed **history** of who attended the meeting, their likes and dislikes, and all pertinent information that can be used to improve future meetings. Questions to consider include the following:

- What is the age and gender of past attendees?
- What is their level of expertise—beginner, intermediate, advanced?
- What is their position within the organization's hierarchy—new employee, junior management, senior management?
- What hotel amenities are preferred—indoor pools, spas, tennis courts, exercise rooms, wireless Internet access?

- Are there specific medical needs or dietary restrictions for attendees—kosher, Muslim, vegetarian, diabetic?
- Who is paying the expenses?
- Will meeting attendees bring guests or children to the event?
- Are networking opportunities important?
- How far are attendees willing to travel to attend the meeting?
- Will international guests attend who require interpreters?
- Are special accommodations needed for people with disabilities?
- What are the educational outcomes expected at the meeting?

Some of this information can be answered by questions on the meeting registration form, and other information can be obtained through association membership or company records. Most planners do some type of evaluation after an event to provide feedback that can be used to improve the next meeting. This is covered later in the chapter.

Development of SMART Objectives

Once the planner has determined the needs of the attendees and sponsoring organization, objectives must be written in a clear and concise format so that all parties involved in the planning process understand and are focused on the same goals. A common method of writing effective meeting objectives is to use the **SMART** approach. Each letter of the SMART approach reminds the planner of critical components of a well-written objective:

*S*pecific. Only one major concept is covered per objective.

*M*easurable. There must be a way to quantify or measure whether the objective has been achieved.

*A*chievable. It must be possible to accomplish the objective.

*R*elevant. The objective should be important to the overall goals of the organization.

*T*ime. The objective should include the time frame for when it must be completed.

It is also good to begin meeting objectives with an action verb (e.g., achieve, promote, understand, design) and to include cost factors if applicable. List—by name—the person or department responsible for achieving the objectives.

TABLE 9–1	Tests for Evaluating Objectives

1. Is the objective written using SMART?
2. Can the ultimate outcome be measured?
3. Can the objective be clearly understood by those responsible for accomplishing it?
4. Is the objective realistic and attainable while still presenting a challenge?
5. Is the ultimate outcome of the objective justified by the time, effort, and expense utilized in achieving it?
6. Is the objective consistent with company and organizational goals?
7. Can accountability for outcomes be clearly established from the objective?

Source: Adapted from MacLaurin, D. J. and Wykes, T. (1997). *Meetings and Conventions: A Planning Guide.* Meeting Professionals International, Dallas, TX.

Sample Meeting Objectives

*   The Meetings Department of the International Association of Real Estate Agents will "generate attendance of 7,500 people at the 2009 annual meeting to be held in Orlando, FL."
*   The Education Committee of the National Association of Catering Executives (NACE) will "create a NACE professional certification program by the 2010 annual meeting."
*   The Brettco Pharmaceutical Corporation will "hold a two-day conference, October 2 and 3 in Chicago, IL, for the 12 regional sales managers to launch 5 new product introductions for 2008. Total meeting costs not to exceed $15,000."
*   Jill Miller will "complete the graphic design for the convention program by May 3, 2008."

Designing well-written meeting objectives can be a very positive activity for the meeting planner. Objectives serve as signals to keep the planning process focused and on track. At the end of the meeting, the planner can communicate to management what goals were achieved or exceeded, or what was not achieved and why. If objectives are met, it helps demonstrate the ROI that the meeting planner

TABLE 9–2	Site Selection Process

1. Identify the meeting objectives.
2. Gather historical data.
3. Determine the physical requirements.
4. Consider attendee expectations.
5. Select general area and type of facility.
6. Prepare an RFP.
7. Review and evaluate choices.
8. Select site.

Source: Connell et al., *4th Edition Professional Meeting Management*, 2002, Professional Convention Management Association, Chicago, IL: p. 42.

provides to the organization. If objectives are not met, then management can focus resources on finding out the causes of failure and correcting them for the next meeting.

Site Selection

The site selection process can begin after meeting objectives are developed. The objectives will guide the planner in deciding the physical location for the event, type of facility to use, transportation options, and many other meeting components. Depending on the type of meeting, site selection may take place days, weeks, months, or years before the actual event. For major conventions, a city is usually selected three to five years in advance. Some large associations, such as the American Library Association, have determined meeting sites (cities) decades into the future. However, small corporate meetings usually have a much shorter lead time. Results of a study by *Successful Meetings* (2003) indicates that approximately 75% of management meetings, 64% of training and education meetings, and 80% of sales meetings are planned six months or less in advance. Table 9–2 lists eight steps to the site selection process.

Contrary to popular belief, the association meeting planner is usually not the final decision maker when it comes to which city will be selected to host a convention. Typically, determining the actual site is a group decision made by a volunteer committee, with much input from the board of directors and the association staff. The meeting planner will review numerous reference materials, talk with other planners, and possibly make recommendations but usually does not personally make the final decision. The corporate planner may have more influence over site selection, especially for smaller meetings. But for larger corporate meetings, the CEO or chairman of the board may make the decision. Sometimes locations are chosen because of the availability of recreational activities (for example, golf), not because the meeting facilities are outstanding. It differs with each organization.

Meeting planners are regularly bombarded with site selection information. There are several trade publications, such as *Successful Meetings, Meetings & Conventions Magazine, Convene, Corporate Meetings and Incentive Travel*, and *EXPO*, that meeting planners may subscribe to for little to no cost. These magazines are either independently owned or affiliated with one of the major meetings-related professional associations, such as the Professional Convention Management Association (PCMA) and Meeting Professionals International (MPI). The magazines are funded through advertising sales from hotel chains, transportation companies, convention facilities, and many other service providers to the meetings industry. Other key advertisers are the actual locations competing for the convention dollar. Special advertising inserts or destination guides are common and promote regions ("Meetings on the Gulf Coast"), individual cities ("San Antonio Meeting Planners Guide"), states ("Conventions in California"), and countries ("The Korean Connection: Asia's Convention Destination"). These special advertising segments can showcase local culture, attractions, and facilities; provide testimonials of past events; and serve to entice the planner to consider their location. Other special supplements are designed to showcase other characteristics such as "Second-Tier Cities," "Unique Venues," "Meetings on College Campuses," "Cruise Ship Conventions," "Affordable Meetings," or "Golf Destinations."

Other factors to consider in site selection are the rotation of locations and the location of the majority of the attendees. In the United States, the planner may want to hold a major convention in the East (Boston) one year, the South (New Orleans) the next, the Midwest (Chicago) the third year, and the West (San Francisco) the fourth year. This allows attendees to enjoy a wide variety of meeting locations, and attendees who live on one side of the country are not always traveling many hours and through several time zones to attend the meeting. But

The Links at Spanish Bay, part of the famous Pebble Beach Golf Resort, is often chosen as a site for small meetings and incentive trips.
Photo by George G. Fenich, Ph.D.

if most of the attendees live on the East Coast, it may be preferable to hold the meeting in a city conveniently located there. However, some association meetings, such as the National Association of Broadcasters or the Consumer Electronics Show, are so large that they are extremely limited in their choice of cities. In 2006, approximately 152,200 people attended the Consumer Electronics Show (CES), one of the largest trade shows in the United States. According to its Web site, CES used 1.69 million square feet of exhibit space and most of the 139,000 sleeping rooms available in Las Vegas. Few cities can compete with Las Vegas as far as total amount of exhibit space and sleeping rooms that are concentrated in a relatively small area.

Cost is another consideration. In addition to the costs incurred by the meeting planner for meeting space and other essentials, the cost to the attendee should be considered. Some cities, mostly **first-tier cities,** are notoriously expensive for people to visit. For example,

Smith Travel Research shows that of the cities in the United States, the average cost (not highest) of a hotel room is the most expensive in New York ($198), followed by New Orleans ($161), Boston ($128), San Francisco ($126), and Washington, DC ($123)—and that does not include taxes. At the other end of the spectrum are Macon (GA) at $49 per night, followed by Montgomery (AL) at $52, Bismarck (ND) at $52, and El Paso (TX) at $53. It all depends on what is important to attendees—cost or location. Another option is to hold a meeting in a first-tier city at a first-class property in the off-season or during slow periods, such as around major holidays. Most hotels discount prices when business is slow.

The mode of travel is another factor in site selection. How will the attendees get to the location? Air? Road? Rail? In the post-9/11 business climate—and more recently the scare over liquid explosives—airline carriers have been struggling to survive. Many people are still cautious about flying, and checking in at airports has become such an ordeal that many people prefer to drive to meetings rather than fly. For example, a fifty-minute flight from Las Vegas to Los Angeles can take five hours or more with all the security precautions and delays. You can usually drive that distance in less time. Some cities, such as Baltimore, Maryland, are actively promoting their convention facilities to this drive-in market, especially from the Washington, DC, area. On the other hand, the availability of flights (air lift) can be an important consideration in site selection. Those cities with the greatest number of flights per day include Chicago (1,405), Atlanta (1,183), Dallas (995), and Washington, DC (833). There are some cities that are convention destinations (have a convention center) and have no air lift; these include Anchorage (AL), Davenport (IA), Huntington (WV), and Wheeling (WV).

The type of hotel or meeting facility is also a major consideration. There are a variety of choices, including metropolitan hotels, suburban hotels, airport hotels, resort hotels, and casino hotels. In addition, there are facilities called conference centers especially designed to hold meetings. The **International Association of Conference Centers (IACC)** is an association in which the member facilities must meet a list of over thirty criteria to be considered an approved conference center (visit http://www.iacconline.com/ for more information). Other options are full-service convention centers, cruise ships, and university campuses. These facilities are discussed at length in chapter 4, "Meeting and Convention Venues."

Meeting space requirements are also critical in the site selection process. How many meeting or banquet rooms will be needed? How much space will staff offices, registration, and prefunction areas require? Floor plans with room dimensions are readily available in the facilities' sales brochures or on their Web sites. Good diagrams will also provide ceiling heights, seating capacities, entrances and exits, and location of columns and other obstructions. Most major hotel chain Web sites (for example, http://www.hyatt.com, http://www.marriott.com, http://www.hilton.com) will provide direct links to their hotels and their specifications information.

Request for Proposal

Once the meeting objectives are clearly defined and the basic location and logistics are drafted, the meeting manager creates a request for proposal (RFP). The RFP is a written description of all the major needs for the meeting. The CIC, a federation of over thirty MEEC industry associations, has created a standardized format that may be used. It is copyright free and may be downloaded at http://www. conventionindustry.org.

The RFP will contain basic information:

- Meeting name
- Meeting start and end dates
- Key contact information
- Expected attendance
- Number and type of sleeping rooms required
- Number and size of meeting and exhibition space required
- Food and beverage requirements
- Acceptable rates for rooms, meeting space, and food and beverage
- Expectations of "comps" or free services
- Cutoff date for the submission of RFPs

Once the RFP is completed, it is disseminated to hotel properties and convention facilities that may be interested in submitting a bid for that meeting. Typically, the meeting planner can submit the RFP via the Internet directly to preferred hotels and the **convention and visitor bureaus (CVBs)** of desirable cities for distribution to all properties or to the Destination Marketing Association International (DMAI)

REQUEST FOR PROPOSAL

Meeting Name: _____

Contact Information:

Prefix: ❑   Mr. ❑   Ms. ❑   Other: _____ **Proposal due date:** _____

Last Name: _____

First Name: _____

Address: _____   City: _____

State/Province: _____   Postal Code: _____

Country: _____

Phone: _____   Fax: _____

E-mail: _____   Web: _____

Meeting Information

Sponsor of Meeting: ❑ association   ❑ corporate   ❑ other: _____

Type of meeting:

❑ Board   ❑ Committee   ❑ Incentive

❑ Education   ❑ Convention   ❑ Management

❑ Retreat   ❑ Trade show   ❑ Other: _____

Decision made by:

❑ Primary contact   ❑ Board   ❑ Committee

❑ Chief staff officer ❑ Management company ❑ Other

Meeting Dates (mm/dd/yy) Start: _____ End: _____

Alternate Dates (mm/dd/yy) Start: _____ End: _____

Expected Meeting Attendance: _____

Largest Meeting Setup:

❑ Theater   ❑ Herringbone   ❑ Hollow square

❑ Schoolroom   ❑ Rounds of 8   ❑ Board

❑ U-shape   ❑ Rounds of 10   ❑ Other: _____

FIGURE 9–1   Sample request for proposal.

Functions Required:

❏ Breakfast   ❏ Dinner   ❏ Morning break

❏ Lunch   ❏ Reception   ❏ Afternoon break

LARGEST meal period:

❏ Breakfast   ❏ Dinner   Largest function attendance: _____
❏ Lunch   ❏ Reception

Preferred Arrival Dates (mm/dd/yy):

    Arrive: _____   Depart: _____

Alternate Arrival Dates (mm/dd/yy):

    Arrive: _____   Depart: _____

Preferred Location/Facilities:

❏ Airport   ❏ Conference center   ❏ Convention hotel

❏ Golf resort   ❏ Ocean resort   ❏ Citywide

❏ Downtown   ❏ Rounds of 10   ❏ Mountain resort

❏ Gaming   ❏ Suburban   ❏ Other: _____

Rates:

❏ Under $100   ❏ $126–$140   ❏ $156–$170   ❏ Over $200

❏ $101–$125   ❏ $141–$155   ❏ $171–$200

Special Requirements (check items for which you would like additional information sent to you):

❏ Audiovisual services   ❏ Shopping

❏ Beach   ❏ Shuttle/ground transportation

❏ Child care   ❏ Special assistance/disabilities

❏ Diabetic menu   ❏ Spouse/guest/youth programs

❏ Fitness facilities   ❏ Teleconferencing

❏ Golf   ❏ Tennis

❏ Hired entertainment speakers   ❏ Theme parties/special events

❏ Kosher food   ❏ Tours/sightseeing

❏ Off-premises catering/banquet facilities   ❏ Vegetarian menu

FIGURE 9–1   Sample request for proposal *(continued)*.

❏ Official airline

❏ Official car rental company

❏ Official travel agency

❏ Water sports

❏ Other: _____

Past Start Date(s)	Past End Date(s)	City	State/ Province	Hotel/Facility Name	Total Number of People	Exhibit Facility Type	Total Room Pickup

Group History

Exhibit Information

Type of Show: ❏ Consumer show (public)   ❏ Trade show (private)

Exhibit Booth Size: _____ 8 × 10 _____ 10 × 10

_____ tabletop

Gross Exhibit Area (sq. feet): _____

Exhibit Move In: ❏ Sun ❏ Mon ❏ Tues ❏ Wed ❏ Thurs ❏ Fri ❏ Sat

Exhibit Move Out: ❏ Sun ❏ Mon ❏ Tues ❏ Wed ❏ Thurs ❏ Fri ❏ Sat

Show First Day: ❏ Sun ❏ Mon ❏ Tues ❏ Wed ❏ Thurs ❏ Fri ❏ Sat

Show Last Day: ❏ Sun ❏ Mon ❏ Tues ❏ Wed ❏ Thurs ❏ Fri ❏ Sat

Preferred Location *(list all that apply)*

State: _____   City: _____

Region: _____   Country: _____

FIGURE 9–1   Sample request for proposal *(continued)*.

Web site at http://www.destinationmarketing.org. Some hotel chains, such as Hyatt, guarantee a response to an RFP within twenty-four hours of receipt. The RFP also serves to allow hotels to examine the potential economic impact of the meeting and decide whether or not to create a bid for it. If the group has limited resources and can only afford an $89 room rate, then major luxury hotels may not be interested in the business; however, smaller properties or hotels in **second-tier cities** may be very interested in hosting the event. If a meeting facility decides to submit a proposal, then the sales department will review the meeting specifications and create a response.

Fam trips (familiarization trips) are another method of promoting a destination or particular facility to a meeting planner. Fam trips are a low- or no-cost trip for the planner to personally review sites for their suitability for a meeting. These trips may be arranged by the local CVB or by the hotel directly. During the fam trip, the hotel or convention facility tries to impress the planner by showcasing its property, amenities, services, and overall quality. Throughout the visit, the planner should visit all food and beverage outlets, look at recreational areas, see a variety of sleeping rooms, check all meeting space, monitor the efficiency of the front desk and other personnel, note the cleanliness and overall appearance of the facility, and (if possible) meet with key hotel personnel. A seasoned meeting planner always has a long list of questions to ask. A lot depends on the selection of a hotel—make a mistake and the whole meeting could be in jeopardy.

Once the planner has reviewed the RFPs and conducted any necessary site visits, then the negotiations between the planner and the sales department at a facility can begin. This process can be quite complex, and careful records of all communications, concessions, and financial expectations should be well documented.

Budgetary Concerns

Following the objectives, budgetary issues are usually the next major consideration in planning a meeting or event. How much will it cost to produce the event? Who will pay? How much (if anything) will attendees be charged for registration? What types of food and beverage events are planned, and what will be served? Will meals be provided free or at an additional cost to the attendee? What additional revenue streams are available to produce and promote the meeting? If the event is being held for the first time, the planner will have to do a lot of estimating of expenses and potential revenues. An event that is repeated benefits by having some historical data to help the planner compare and project costs. The basis for a meeting budget can be developed by establishing goals, identifying expenses, and identifying revenue sources.

STEP 1: ESTABLISH GOALS

Financial goals are important and should incorporate the SMART approach. They may be set by the meeting planner, by association management, or by corporate mandate. Basically, what are the financial expectations of the event? Not every meeting or event is planned for profit. For example, an awards ceremony held by a company to honor top achievers represents a cost to the company, and no profit is expected; similarly, a corporate sales meeting may not have a profit motive. The ultimate goal of the meeting may be to determine how to increase business and thus "profit," but the meeting itself is not a profit generator but is an expense for the company. Most association meetings, on the other hand, rely heavily on conventions to produce operating revenue for the association. For most associations, the annual meeting (and often an accompanying trade show) is the second highest revenue producer after membership dues. The financial goal for an annual meeting may be based on increases or decreases in membership, general economic trends, political climate, competing events, location of the event, and many other influences. For any event, there are three possible financial outcomes:

1. *Break-Even.* Revenue collected from all activities covers the expenses, and no profit is expected.
2. *Profit.* Revenues collected exceed expenses.
3. *Deficit.* Expenses exceed revenues.

STEP 2: CATEGORIZE EXPENSES

The CIC manual (2000) suggests categorizing expenses by their different functions:

- *Indirect Costs.* **Indirect costs** are listed as overhead or administrative line items in a program budget and are organizational expenses not directly related to the meeting, such as staff salaries, overhead, or equipment repair.
- *Fixed Costs.* **Fixed costs** are expenses incurred regardless of the number of attendees, such as the cost of meeting room rental or audiovisual equipment. A specific dollar amount of profit can even be set as a fixed cost.
- *Variable Costs.* These are expenses that can vary based on the number of attendees, such as food and beverage.

Exercise for Types of Expenses

Below is a list of possible expense items. Can you determine which costs are direct, indirect, and variable?

- Administrative overhead
- Registration materials
- Speaker travel, expenses, and honoraria
- Signs, posters, and banners
- Gratuities and gifts
- Printing and photocopying
- Room rental
- Decorations and flowers
- Car rental
- Shipping and freight charges
- Complimentary registrations
- Translators and interpreters
- Temporary staff
- Web site design and administration
- Child care
- Food and beverage functions
- Promotion
- Multimedia equipment
- Staff travel and expenses
- Taxes
- Office furniture and equipment
- Insurance
- Supplies
- Labor charges
- Session taping
- Shuttle service
- ADA compliance
- Telecommunications
- Security guards
- Postage and overnight delivery costs

Source: MacLaurin, D. J. and Wykes, T. (1997). *Meetings and Conventions: A Planning Guide.* Meeting Professionals International, Dallas, TX.

Expenses will vary according to the overall objectives of the meeting and will be impacted by location, season, type of facility, services selected, and other factors. For example, a gallon of Starbucks coffee in San Francisco at a luxury hotel may cost you $80 or more; a gallon of coffee at a moderate-priced hotel in Oklahoma City may only cost $25 or less.

STEP 3: IDENTIFY REVENUE SOURCES

There are many ways to fund meetings and events. Corporations include meeting costs in their operating budgets, and the corporate planner must work within the constraints of what is budgeted.

Associations usually have to be a bit more creative in finding capital to plan and implement an event because associations have to justify the cost of the meeting with the expected ROI of the attendee. It can be quite expensive to attend some association meetings. Consider a hypothetical example of one person attending an association annual meeting: transportation ($300), accommodations for three nights ($450), food and beverage ($200), registration fee ($500), and miscellaneous ($100), for a total of $1,550. Depending on the city and association, this amount could easily double. It is a complex process to create an exceptional yet affordable event. If the registration fee is too high, people will not attend; if it is too low, the organization may not achieve revenue expectations. But there are more possible sources of funding available other than registration fees, including the following:

- Corporate or association funding
- Private funding from individuals
- Exhibitor fees (if trade show)
- Sponsorships
- Logo merchandise
- Advertising fees (such as banners or ads in the convention program)
- Local, state, or national government assistance
- Sales of banner ads or links on the official Web site
- Renting of membership address lists for marketing purposes
- "Official partnerships" with other companies to promote their products for a fee or a percentage of their revenues
- Contributions in cash or in-kind (services or products)

Estimating expenses and revenues can be accomplished by first calculating a **break-even** analysis, in other words, the revenue that must be collected to cover expenses.

Cost Control

To stay within budget and reach the financial objectives, it is important to exercise cost control measures. Cost control measures are tools for monitoring the budget. A large event for thousands of people may be managed by only a few meeting planning staff, and the opportunities for costly mistakes are rampant. The most important factor is to make sure the facility understands which person from the sponsoring organization has the authority to make additions or changes to what has been ordered. Typically, the CEO and the meeting planning staff are the only ones who have this "signing authority." For example, a board member may have an expensive dinner in the hotel restaurant and say, "Put it on the association's bill," but the restaurant cannot do so without the approval of a person who has **signing authority.** This helps keep unexpected expenses to a minimum.

Another cost control measure is to accurately estimate the number of meals that will be served. The **guarantee** is the amount of food that the planner has instructed the facility to prepare and will be paid for. If the planner estimates 500 people will attend a dinner and only 300 show up, the planner is responsible for the 200 uneaten dinners—an expensive waste of money. This is covered in depth in chapter 11, "Food and Beverage."

Outsourcing part or the entire meeting planning process can also keep costs down. Many companies prefer to hire independent meeting planners to organize and implement their events rather than keep a meeting planner on staff; then the company does not have to provide salaries and benefits and can hire planners as needed. In addition, there are many ancillary activities that go into the planning and managing of a meeting, such as housing, registration, transportation, exhibits, marketing, educational programming, child care, and technology, that can be outsourced to other professionals. By hiring companies that specialize in particular activities, the planner is better able to remain focused on managing the entire process.

Control in MEEC

Creating and implementing most meetings is a team effort. Many meeting planners will conduct an evaluation after each meeting to obtain feedback from the attendees, exhibitors, facility staff, outsourced contractors, and anyone else involved in the event. Individual sessions may be evaluated to determine if the speakers did a good job and if the education was appropriate. Overall, evaluations may collect data on such things as comfort of the hotel, ease of transportation to the location, desirability of the location, quality of the food and beverage, special events and networking opportunities, and number and quality of exhibitors at a trade show convention. This information may be collected by a written questionnaire after the event as well as by telephone, fax, or Web-based collection methods. One of the fastest and least expensive methods is to broadcast an e-mail with a link to the questionnaire. Many software packages are available that will design, distribute, collect data, and tabulate results for you. No special knowledge of statistics is required. There are Web sites for programs that involve little or no cost (http://www.freeonlinesurveys.com, http://www.surveymonkey.com and http://www.zoomerang.com) or cost several hundred dollars (http://www.surveypro.com). The data concerning speakers and logistics will assist the meeting planner and program planning committee to improve the programming for subsequent years (see chapter 10 on producing MEEC meetings).

Just as in setting good objectives, the meeting planner's first step in doing an evaluation is to determine what is to be evaluated: What information is needed? Who will utilize it? How will the results be communicated to those who participate in the evaluation? Evaluations can be time-consuming and expensive to design and implement. It may cost thousands of dollars to print, disseminate, collect, and analyze evaluations. Unfortunately, some of the data collected by planners is often filed away and not used appropriately—especially if the results are negative regarding the event. No board of directors or CEO wants to hear that the site selected to hold a meeting did not meet attendees' expectations. However, negative comments may ultimately turn into a favorable marketing tool. If the attendees indicate they did not like the location of the meeting (Chicago in February), then by selecting a warmer climate (Palm Springs) for the next meeting, the planner can promote how much the attendees' opinions matter and that the organization will consider the directives of the attendees.

EVALUATION DESIGN

A good evaluation form is simple and concise and can be completed in a minimal amount of time. An evaluation for a meeting can be a single sentence: "Was this meeting a good use of your time?" Response options can be "Yes" or "No." This would be good for short departmental meetings or training sessions. For larger events with multiple sessions and activities, a more in-depth evaluation is called for, and a good source for questions can be your event goals and objectives. If the meeting is an annual event, it is important to ask similar questions each year so that data may be collected and analyzed over time.

Self-administered surveys are the most common evaluation tool. The evaluation instrument should collect both **quantitative data** and

qualitative data. Quantitative or "hard" data is represented numerically so that data can be compared by assigning ranks or scores and calculating averages and frequencies of responses. This data can be statistically manipulated using advanced mathematical formulas and designs; however, most planners like to keep things simple, and averages and frequencies of responses are the most common outcomes of interest. If, on a scale from 1 to 10, the attendees rated the hotel an average of 9.5, then the planner can demonstrate that the hotel selection was appropriate; on the other hand, if the attendees rated the quality of the food at the opening reception as a 3, then the planner needs to address what went wrong and why.

Asking open-ended questions represents qualitative or "soft" data. It is a descriptive record of what is observed and then written in the attendee's own words. For example, the questionnaire might ask "What did you enjoy most about the conference?" Then adequate space would be left for the person to write his or her response. Qualitative data can be time-consuming to analyze and report, so this type of question should be kept to a minimum. Too many open-ended questions can result in pages of unrelated responses that will quickly be scanned and probably ignored by management. Whereas quantitative data provides hard numbers that can be statistically manipulated, qualitative data provides the "why." Quantitatively, the attendees might rate the hotel a 9.5 on a 10-point scale, but what exactly did they like? The qualitative question "What did you like most about the hotel?" can provide the details. To allow for speedy completion of evaluation forms, many planners use checklists such as the one shown in Figure 9–2.

Designing a questionnaire from scratch can be daunting. Building on what others have developed is a good start. The CIC has the following suggestions when designing and implementing a survey:

- Keep it simple and easy to complete—one page if possible.
- Ask specific questions, addressing only one concept per question.
- Avoid using professional jargon, abbreviations, and acronyms.
- Start the evaluation with easy questions, and save difficult or more personal questions for the end of the survey. People are more likely to complete a survey once they have invested time in starting to fill it out.
- Ask personal or proprietary questions in ranges:
  - What is your age? 18 to 25? 26 to 35? 36 to 45? Over 45?

"What activities did you attend?"

❑ Opening reception   ❑ Breakfast   ❑ Lunch   ❑ Dinner

Another simple option is to word questions so that a minimal amount of responses are offered:

Did you utilize the e-mail stations provided in the registration area?

❑ Yes   ❑ No

Alternately, the attendee can select from a list of predetermined responses to communicate his or her opinion:

How would you rate the opening session speaker?

❑ Excellent   ❑ Good   ❑ Fair   ❑ Poor

Using a ranking scale is also popular:

Please rank the following items 1–5 in their importance to you in registering for this conference, with 1 being the most important and 5 being the least important:

Registration fee   Quality of program   Cost of transportation

Hotel expense   Recreational activities

FIGURE 9–2   Sample checklist.

- How much does your company spend on training each year? Less than $1,000? $1,000 to $5,000? $5,000 to $10,000? Over $10,000?
- Keep evaluations anonymous. People are much more honest if they cannot be linked to their responses. Providing a name should be optional.
- Include contact information on the form so it can be mailed or faxed if not collected on site.
- Number all questions to make coding easier and to avoid mistakes.
- Forms should be readable. Design, fonts, graphics, and colors should be kept visually simple.
- If evaluating a session with multiple speakers, be sure to identify the speakers by name on the evaluation form.
- If possible, have an attendant stationed in each session room or in the hall between meeting rooms to collect evaluation forms; alternately, have clearly marked evaluation collection boxes available.

Timing is also an issue with administering evaluations. If you collect data on site immediately after an event, you may increase your response rate. You can remind attendees to complete and return evaluations before moving on to the next session. Other planners prefer to wait a few days to ask for feedback because this gives the attendee time to digest what actually occurred at the meeting and to form an objective opinion not clouded by the excitement of the event. In fact, evaluation scores tend to decrease when attendees are surveyed a few weeks after an event, especially concerning speaker evaluations. A particularly humorous speaker may entertain the attendees and receive high marks when evaluated just after a session, but if he or she is evaluated a week later, attendees may feel that the speaker was entertaining but did not actually teach them anything of value and may rate the speaker less positively. See Figure 9–3 for a sample evaluation form.

The process of evaluating a meeting should begin in the early stages of meeting planning and tie in with the meeting objectives. Costs for development, printing, postage, analysis, and reporting should be included in the meeting budget. Evaluation is a valuable component of a meeting's history by recording what worked or did not work for a particular event and should be a cyclical process whereby the evaluation results feed directly into next year's meeting objectives. Committees plan most large meetings; evaluation results are the means by which information is passed from one committee to the next.

Summary

Planning a meeting or event is a long process that often requires input from a lot of people or committees. Setting clearly defined objectives is the first essential step in creating effective program content and managing logistics. The planner must begin with a clear understanding of the purpose and expectations of the meeting. The objectives will impact site or city selection, type of facility used, and services required. The planner must also understand the motivations of the attendees: Why should they attend? Is attendance voluntary or mandated by management? Planning a corporate event and an association event can be very different processes. Education has replaced recreation as the driving force for most meetings; however, people like to be entertained as well as educated, so the planner must attend to all the needs of the attendees and provide both.

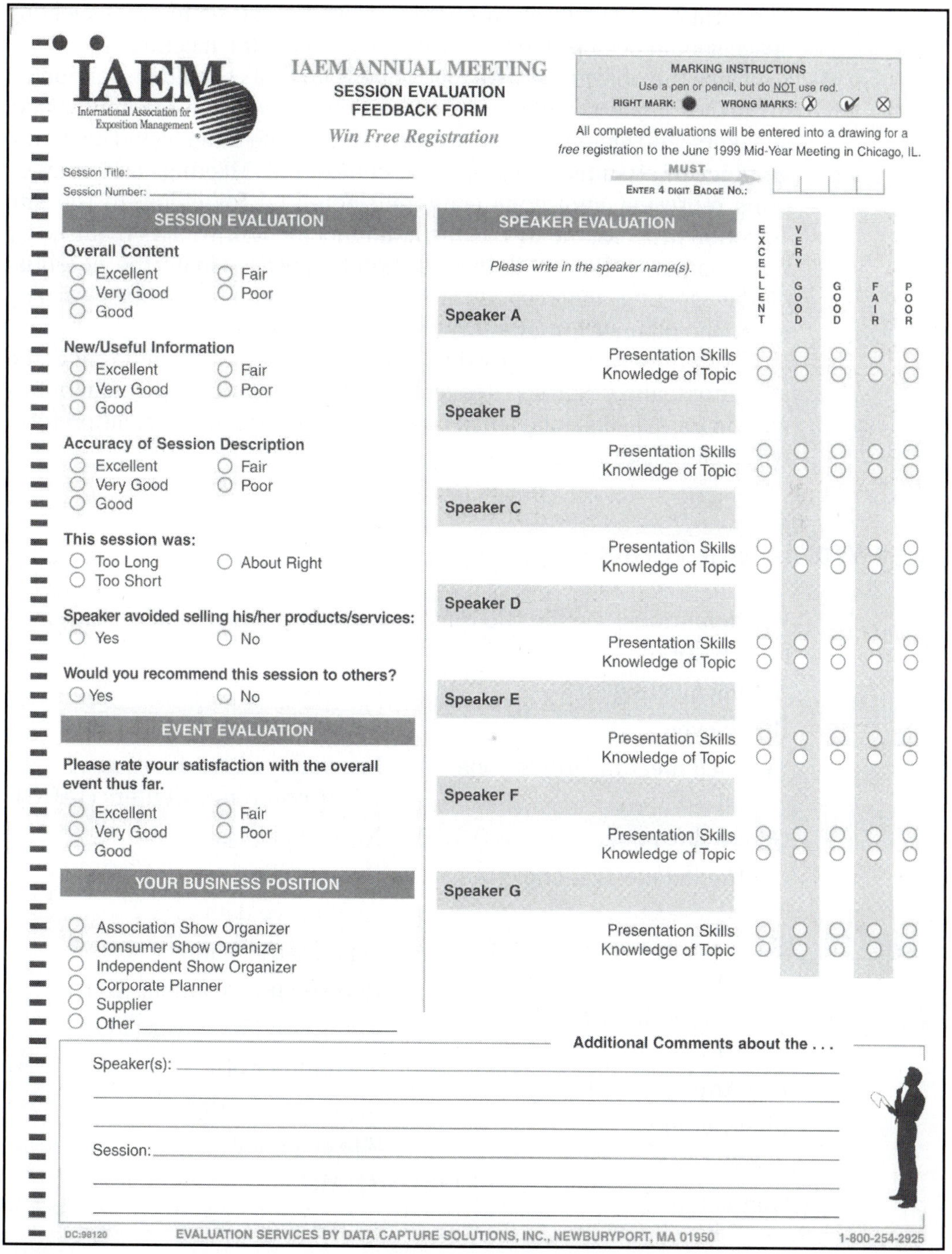

IAEM
International Association for Exposition Management

IAEM ANNUAL MEETING
SESSION EVALUATION FEEDBACK FORM
Win Free Registration

MARKING INSTRUCTIONS
Use a pen or pencil, but do NOT use red.
RIGHT MARK: ● WRONG MARKS: ⊗ ✓ ⊗

All completed evaluations will be entered into a drawing for a *free* registration to the June 1999 Mid-Year Meeting in Chicago, IL.

Session Title: ____________

Session Number: ____________

MUST → ENTER 4 DIGIT BADGE NO.: ☐☐☐☐

SESSION EVALUATION

Overall Content
○ Excellent ○ Fair
○ Very Good ○ Poor
○ Good

New/Useful Information
○ Excellent ○ Fair
○ Very Good ○ Poor
○ Good

Accuracy of Session Description
○ Excellent ○ Fair
○ Very Good ○ Poor
○ Good

This session was:
○ Too Long ○ About Right
○ Too Short

Speaker avoided selling his/her products/services:
○ Yes ○ No

Would you recommend this session to others?
○ Yes ○ No

EVENT EVALUATION

Please rate your satisfaction with the overall event thus far.
○ Excellent ○ Fair
○ Very Good ○ Poor
○ Good

YOUR BUSINESS POSITION

○ Association Show Organizer
○ Consumer Show Organizer
○ Independent Show Organizer
○ Corporate Planner
○ Supplier
○ Other ____________

SPEAKER EVALUATION

Please write in the speaker name(s).

	EXCELLENT	VERY GOOD	GOOD	FAIR	POOR
Speaker A					
Presentation Skills	○	○	○	○	○
Knowledge of Topic	○	○	○	○	○
Speaker B					
Presentation Skills	○	○	○	○	○
Knowledge of Topic	○	○	○	○	○
Speaker C					
Presentation Skills	○	○	○	○	○
Knowledge of Topic	○	○	○	○	○
Speaker D					
Presentation Skills	○	○	○	○	○
Knowledge of Topic	○	○	○	○	○
Speaker E					
Presentation Skills	○	○	○	○	○
Knowledge of Topic	○	○	○	○	○
Speaker F					
Presentation Skills	○	○	○	○	○
Knowledge of Topic	○	○	○	○	○
Speaker G					
Presentation Skills	○	○	○	○	○
Knowledge of Topic	○	○	○	○	○

Additional Comments about the . . .

Speaker(s): ____________

Session: ____________

DC:98120 EVALUATION SERVICES BY DATA CAPTURE SOLUTIONS, INC., NEWBURYPORT, MA 01950 1-800-254-2925

FIGURE 9–3 Session evaluation feedback form.

The format of the education sessions as well as the setup of the meeting space should be appropriate to the objectives of the meeting.

Once the objectives are clear, a needs analysis should be conducted to further guide the planner in selecting appropriate meeting space, speakers, and amenities that are expected by the attendees. The demographics of attendees must also be considered. Meetings and conventions represent enormous economic potential for cities. In the site selection process, the RFP is the announcement of what is required by the planner. CVBs and individual hotels must evaluate the potential of the meeting and respond accordingly. Interested properties may invite the planner for a fam trip to visit the property.

Evaluations of the individual sessions, the overall conference, the exhibitors, and other key items should be conducted to provide information for subsequent events. Creating a user-friendly evaluation form will ensure a good response.

Key Words and Terms

For definitions, see the Glossary or go to http://glossary.convention industry.org.

Annual meeting

Break-even

Certified meeting professional (CMP)

Continuing education unit (CEU)

Continuing medical education (CME)

Convention and visitor bureau (CVB)

Convention Industry Council (CIC)

Fam trip

First-tier city

Fixed costs

Guarantee

History

Indirect costs

International Association of Conference Centers (IACC)

Needs analysis

Outsourcing

Qualitative data

Quantitative data

Return on investment (ROI)

Return on objectives (ROO)

Second-tier city

Signing authority

Site selection

SMART

Review and Discussion Questions

1. What are the three principal reasons people attend meetings and conventions?
2. What are the key differences in planning an association annual meeting and planning a corporate event?
3. What are some considerations that should be addressed in the site selection process?
4. Write a meeting objective for an association annual meeting and a corporate meeting.
5. What are some ethical considerations of taking fam trips?
6. How does a meeting planner find information about a city, hotel, meeting facility, or service provider?
7. Why might a meeting planner select a second-tier city in which to hold a meeting?
8. How does a meeting planner use attendee demographics in designing and implementing an event?
9. Identify and discuss four sources of revenue for a convention.
10. How do planners control meeting costs?
11. What is the major difference between attendance at an association annual meeting and a corporate meeting?
12. Why do planners go through the effort and expense of evaluating meetings?

References

Connell et al. 2002. *Professional meeting management*, 4th ed. Chicago: Professional Convention Management Association.

Consumer Electronics Show. 2006. http://www.answers.com/topic/consumer-electronics-show (accessed October 24, 2006).

Convention Industry Council. 2000. *The convention industry council manual*, 7th ed. McLean, VA: Convention Industry Council.

Green, R., and J. Withiam. 2003. Preliminary report of the APEX Resumes & Work Orders Panel. Conference presentation, International Association for Exhibition Management Annual Convention, Orlando, FL, December 11.

Las Vegas Convention and Visitors Authority. 2006. Las Vegas visitor statistics. http://www.Ivcva.com/press/statistics-facts/index.jsp. (accessed October 27, 2006).

MacLaurin, D., and T. Wykes. 1997. *Meetings and conventions: A planning guide.* Toronto, Ontario: Meetings Professional International Canadian Council.

Ramsborg, G. et al. 2006. *Professional Meeting Management, 5th Ed.* Kendall/ Hunt Publishing, Dubuque, Iowa.

State of the industry report. 2003. *Successful meetings*, VNU Business, New York, NY. January.

About the Chapter Contributor

Curtis Love, Ph.D., is an associate professor and graduate coordinator in the Tourism and Convention Administration Department at the William F. Harrah College of Hotel Administration at the University of Nevada–Las Vegas (UNLV). His teaching and research concentrations are in the area of meetings, conventions, and exhibitions. Prior to joining UNLV, he was the vice president of education for the Professional Convention Management Association.

CHAPTER 10

Producing MEEC Gatherings

The entire conference program is displayed on this bigger-than-life-size wall graphic.

Photo by George G. Fenich, Ph.D.

Chapter Objectives _____

This chapter provides the reader with an understanding of the following:

- Process of registration for a meeting or event
- Housing arrangements for a meeting or event
- Elements of a meeting and event specification guide
- Importance of pre- and postconvention meetings

Chapter Outline _____

Introduction

It should be noted that this chapter flows from, and goes hand in hand with, the previous chapter on planning. One has to plan a meeting or event and then implement that plan. Further, this chapter begins with a discussion of programming that takes place months or even years in advance of the event. This is followed by a discussion of registration, housing, and evaluation and the order in which the planner would develop each.

Program Implementation

Once the basic objectives of the meeting have been identified, the site selected, and the budget set, the meeting program can be developed in detail. Some major concerns are addressed in this process: Is the programming to be designed in a way that facilitates communication between departments within a corporation? Is the programming geared toward training new employees in the use of a particular computer system? Is the programming geared to educate the members of a professional association and lead toward a certification? To address these concerns, the planner must consider several factors:

- Program type
- Program content (including track and level)
- Session scheduling
- Refreshment breaks and meal functions
- Speaker arrangements
- Audiovisual equipment
- Management of on-site speakers
- Ancillary events

PROGRAM TYPE

Each type of program or session is designed for a specific purpose, which may range from provision of information to all attendees, to discussion of current events in small groups, to hands-on training, to panel discussions. The following are typical descriptions of the major program types and formats.

General or Plenary Session   A general session or plenary session is primarily used as a venue to communicate with all conference attendees at one time in one location. Typically, the general session kicks off the meeting with welcoming remarks from management or association leadership, outlines the purpose or objectives of the meeting, introduces prominent officials, recognizes major sponsors or others who helped plan the event, mentions ceremonial duties, and lists other important matters of general interest. General sessions last between one and one and a half hours. Often, an important industry leader or a recognizable personality will give a **keynote address** that will help set the tone for the rest of the meeting. For a corporate meeting, this may be the CEO or the chairman of the board, whereas an association may elect to hire a professional speaker in a particular subject area, such as business forecasting, political analysis, leadership and change, or application of technology, or use a motivational speaker to address the audience. Many planners use highly recognizable political, sports, and

A general session at a convention.
PhotoEdit Inc.

entertainment personalities. These individuals are hired not for their personal knowledge of the association and the various professions it represents but as a "hook" to interest people in coming to the meeting. If the National Association of Plumbing Professionals hires Paris Hilton to be its keynote speaker, you can bet she was not hired for her extensive knowledge of the plumbing industry; however, her presence at the meeting is sure to drive up attendance in the heavily male-dominated plumbing industry. As a note, it is not uncommon to spend $75,000 to $100,000 or more (plus travel expenses) to hire a well-known sports or entertainment figure to speak at a general session. General sessions may also be held at the end of a convention to provide closure and summarize what was accomplished during the meeting or as a venue to present awards and recognize sponsors. Attendance at closing general sessions is typically smaller than at opening sessions as people make travel plans to return home early.

Concurrent Session A concurrent session is a professional development or career enhancement session presented by a credentialed speaker who provides education on a specific topic in a conference-style format. Alternately, several speakers may form a panel to provide viewpoints on the topic at hand. Group discussions at individual tables may also be incorporated. Concurrent sessions typically serve groups of 150 attendees, and several sessions may be offered simultaneously at a specific time. They typically last between one and one and a half hours.

Workshop or Break-Out Session   Workshops or break-out sessions are more intimate sessions that offer a more interactive learning experience in smaller groups where participants may learn about the latest trends, challenges, and technologies of a specific field. These sessions are often presented by experienced members or peers of the association and may involve lectures, role playing, simulation, problem solving, or group work. Workshop sessions usually serve groups of 150 or fewer attendees. These are the mainstay of any convention, and dozens (or even hundreds) of workshops may be offered throughout the course of the event, depending on the size of the meeting. A large association, such as the American Library Association, has over 1,000 workshop sessions at its annual convention! Workshops typically last between fifty minutes and one hour.

Roundtable Session   Roundtable sessions are small interactive discussion groups designed to cover specific topics of interest. Basically, eight to twelve attendees convene around a large round table, and a facilitator guides discussion about the topic at hand. Typically, several roundtable discussions will take place in one location, such as a large meeting room or ballroom; attendees are free to join or leave a particular discussion group as desired. Roundtables can also be useful for continued and more intimate conversation with workshop speakers. The role of the facilitator is to keep the discussion on track and not allow any one attendee to monopolize the conversation.

Poster Session   A poster session is another more intimate presentation method often used with academic or medical conferences. Rather than utilizing a variety of meeting rooms to accommodate speakers, panels or display boards are provided for presenters to display charts, photographs, a synopsis of their research, etc., for viewing. The presenter is scheduled to be at his or her display board at an appointed time so that interested attendees may visit informally and discuss the presentation. For example, a person who is conducting preliminary research may participate in a poster session to encourage other researchers to review and provide feedback about his or her project. Poster sessions help presenters gain exposure and increase

Session Description

Workshop 14: Effective E-Mail Marketing

Corbin Ball, CMP, Corbin Ball & Associates

3:30 P.M. to 4:45 P.M. (1530–1645)

Room 314

Over 35 billion e-mail messages are sent daily—more than the combined total number of phone calls, faxes, and paper mail messages sent. This is expected to grow to 50 billion messages in 2010. How can your company effectively develop e-mail as a primary marketing vehicle? What are the most effective options?
  Attend this session to:

- Discover the top ten steps in developing an effective e-mail marketing campaign.
- See recent e-mail surveys about customer expectations.
  - Understand delivery options for bulk e-mailing.
- Enhance your own e-mail effectiveness.

Track: Marketing

Level: Intermediate

Source: Adapted from the IAEM annual meeting program 2002.

the variety of educational opportunities at a convention without using a lot of meeting rooms. A poster session at one meeting may develop into a workshop at a subsequent meeting.

PROGRAM CONTENT

The average attendee will only be able to sit through three to six sessions on any given day. It is critical that the attendee be as well informed as possible about the content of each session and the appropriateness of the session to his or her objectives for attending the meeting. For association meetings, programming objectives are developed months in advance and used extensively in marketing the convention to potential attendees. Program content is not a "one size fits all" proposition—the content must be specifically designed to match the needs of the audience. For example, a presentation on Basic Accounting 101 might be good for a junior manager but is totally inappropriate for the chief financial officer. A good way to communicate to attendees how to select which programs to attend is to create tracks and levels. **Track** refers to separating programming into specific genres, such as computer skills, professional development, marketing, personal growth, legal issues, certification courses, or financial issues. A variety of workshops can be developed that concentrate on these specific areas. **Level** refers to the skill level the program is designed for: beginning, intermediate, or advanced. Thus, the speaker who is assigned a session can develop content specifically tailored for a particular audience, and attendees can determine if a session is targeted to their level of expertise.

SESSION SCHEDULING

Timing is critical in program development. The planner has to orchestrate every minute of every day to ensure that the meeting runs smoothly and punctually. Each day's agenda should be an exciting variety of activities that will stimulate attendees and make them want to attend the next meeting. One of the biggest mistakes planners make is double-booking events over the same time period. If a planner schedules workshops from 8:00 A.M. to 1:00 P.M. and the tee time for the celebrity golf match is at 12:30 P.M., then he or she stands to lose any of the attendees who want to attend the golfing event. Trade shows are another challenge. If workshops are scheduled at the same time that the trade show floor is open, attendees must choose between the two options. If attendees choose to attend the education sessions, the exhibitors will not get the traffic they expect; conversely, if attendees go to the trade show rather than attend the sessions, there may be empty meeting rooms and frustrated speakers.

Another major issue is allowing enough time for people to do what comes naturally—do not expect to move 5,000 people from a general session into break-out sessions on the other side of the convention center in ten minutes. Plan thoughtfully. Allow sufficient time for people to use the restroom, check their e-mail or voice mail, say "hello" to an old friend, and comfortably walk to their next workshop. If these delays are not planned for in advance, then there may be attendees disrupting workshop sessions by coming in late— or worse, by skipping sessions.

Typical Association Meeting Schedule

While no two conventions are the same, the following time line provides a good idea of a typical meeting's flow.

DAY ONE

8:00 A.M. Staff office and pressroom area setup

   Exhibitions are set up

   Facility staff hold preconvention meeting

   Registration is set up

DAY TWO

8:00 A.M. Association board meeting

   Registration opens

   Staff office opens

   Exhibition setup continues

   Preconvention workshops are set up

1:00–4:00 P.M. Preconvention workshops (with break)

   Various committees meet

   Program planning committee finalizes duties for meeting

5:00 P.M. Private reception for board members and VIPs

7:00–9:30 P.M. Opening reception

DAY THREE

6:30 A.M. Staff meeting

8:00 A.M. Registration open

   Coffee service begins

9:00 A.M. General session

10:30 A.M. Break

10:45 A.M. Concurrent workshops

Noon–1:30 P.M. Lunch

1:30–5:00 P.M. Exhibitions open

5:00 P.M. Registration closed

DAY FOUR

6:30 A.M. Staff meeting

8:00 A.M. Registration open

Coffee service begins

9:00 A.M.–4:00 P.M. Exhibitions open

Noon–1:30 P.M. Lunch provided on show floor

1:30–2:30 P.M. Workshops

2:45–3:45 P.M. Workshops

4:00–5:00 P.M. Workshops

Teardown of trade show starts

5:00 P.M. Registration closed

7:00 P.M. Cocktail reception

8:00–10:00 P.M. Banquet and awards ceremony

DAY FIVE

7:00 A.M. Staff meeting

8:00 A.M. Registration open

Trade show teardown continues

9:00–10:30 A.M. Closing session

Staff office is packed up
Pressroom is closed

10:45 A.M.–Noon Program planning committee meeting

Noon Registration closed

3:00 P.M. Postconvention meeting with facility staff

REFRESHMENT BREAKS AND MEAL FUNCTIONS

As with scheduling workshops, it is important to schedule time for attendees to eat and refresh themselves throughout the day. Food and beverage functions can be quite expensive, but (depending on the objectives of the event) it may be more productive to feed attendees than have them wandering around a convention center or leaving the property to find a bite to eat. Refreshment breaks provide the opportunity to catch up with old friends, make business contacts, network, and grab a quick bite or reenergize with a cup of coffee. Breaks and meals are excellent opportunities for sponsorship; companies can gain attendee recognition by providing food and beverage. Attendees get fed, and the planner does not have to pay for it. Everybody wins!

Unfortunately, most food and beverage events are high in carbohydrates and sugar: bagels, muffins, and pastries for breakfast; cookies for breaks; rice, potatoes, and pasta for lunch or dinner. These foods are inexpensive and easy to prepare and serve, but they tend to make attendees drowsy. Adding some protein with nuts and cheese or adding raw vegetables and fruits to the offerings is healthier and will keep attendees more focused.

Cocktail receptions and dinners provide their own set of challenges. Overindulgence in alcohol not only can be detrimental to the health of attendees but has the potential to cause liability issues for the meeting planner. If alcoholic beverages are provided, staff should be trained as to when to stop serving individuals who have consumed too much. Provide lots of healthy snacks, and limit salty foods. There are a variety of ways the planner can limit alcohol consumption; for example, drink tickets or a cash bar will greatly reduce drinking. Remember, hungover attendees are not very focused!

SPEAKER ARRANGEMENTS

For large conventions, it is almost impossible for the meeting planner to independently arrange for all the different sessions and speakers. The meeting department often works together with the education department to develop the educational content of the meeting; in addition, a program committee comprising industry leaders and those with special interests in education will volunteer to assist the meeting planner. These volunteers will work diligently to decide which topics are appropriate for the sessions and who the likely speakers might be. It is the job of the committee to be the gatekeeper of educational content. Subcommittees may be created to focus on finding a general session speaker, workshops, concurrent sessions, student member events, and so on. As you can read in "The Life of a Session Topic" on page 299, the committee has to work quickly.

Volunteer Speakers   Most associations cannot afford to pay all of the speakers at a large convention. A moderate-sized convention of 2,500 people may have 100 or more sessions offered at a three-day event. Remuneration for speakers may range from providing no assistance at all to paying a speaker fee and all expenses (as is the case with a paid general session speaker).

The Planning Committee Process: The Life of a Session Topic

No two organizations conduct program planning in the exact same way. In some organizations, the company makes all the decisions about topics, formats, and presenters. Other groups prefer to have programming driven by member needs. Evaluations of each session help determine good topics and speakers that may be used for subsequent meetings. A "call for topics" can alert the programming committee to perceived topics of interest to the membership. On average, it takes about a year to finalize programming for a major event. However, most of the planning for next year's meeting happens in the few months directly following the current event. It is the job of the planning committee to determine topic needs, find appropriate speakers, plan logistics, and communicate the information to the graphics and Web designers to create the physical program and virtual counterpart. The following is a month-to-month overview of the planning process for the typical nonprofit association.

January 7

- Current year's annual meeting in progress
- Call for topics included in registration bags and on organization Web site
- Standing committees (finance, communications, diversity, international, education, sponsorship, ethics, legal) meet and suggest topics to programming committee
- First meeting of program planning committee held on the last day of current year's meeting
- Opening comments from program planning chair, self-introductions, team-building exercise, establishment of tentative theme and objectives for next year's meeting
- Session evaluations collected and sent to evaluation vendor

January 17

- Data from evaluations returned to home office from vendor
- Written comments typed and grouped into topic areas
- Broadcast, fax, and e-mail call for topics to membership
- Post information about current show on Web site. Include photos and memorable events.

(continued)

The Planning Committee Process (*continued*)

January 30
- Collect call for topics and evaluation results, and distribute with program planning books to committee for review

February 15
- Two-and-a-half-day program planning session at headquarters hotel for next meeting
- Divide into subcommittees and elect subcommittee chairs
- Workshop committee
- Concurrent committee
- General sessions committee
- Student program committee
- Preconvention workshops
- Finalize theme for meeting
- Review high-scoring speakers, and consider a repeat session
- Review call for topics, and decide which are appropriate for program
- Decide session type, track, and level. Assign to subcommittee.
- Type: general session, concurrent, and workshop
- Track: professional development, technology, and management issues
- Level: advanced, intermediate, and beginning
- Subcommittee reviews and assigns a member to coordinate each session

March 1
- Begin artwork design for graphics for convention program and physical layout
- Design logo and color scheme

June 15
- Preliminary program copy due to staff. Includes:
  - Session title
  - Session objectives
  - Speaker information
  - Session type, track, and level

- Copy editing by staff
- Preliminary layout with graphics department, print and Web design

July 10

- Final program committee meeting and host hotel
  - Adjust speakers and/or topics
  - Assign room numbers and seating requirements
  - Finalize general session speaker
  - Staff approves all changes
  - Graphics department finalizes program
  - Web design is finalized

August

- Send speaker kits and contracts
- Planning committee members for next year's meeting are identified
- Chair and subcommittee chairs are selected

September

- Preliminary program sent to prospective attendees
- Preliminary program uploaded to Web site

October

- Early bird registration begins, and speaker contracts returned and confirmed
- Rooms and transportation arrangements made for speakers if required
- Daily monitoring of room block and registration
- Some speakers may contact early registrants and start discussing topics in Web-based chat rooms and bulletin boards
- Possible second mailing (time to react if registrations are off)

November

- Make adjustments to program
- Send final program to printer
- Copies of speaker handout due

(continued)

The Planning Committee Process *(continued)*

- Prepare signage for rooms and speaker nameplates
- Arrange for a person to introduce speaker (committee member)
- Prepare session evaluation sheets

December
- Send registrant lists to speakers

January 3
- Final programs drop-shipped (delivered directly to the facility)
- Handouts printed locally and delivered to meeting site
- Programs and registration materials inserted in registration bags

January 7
- Convention begins
- Confirm speaker is present
- Appoint staff to monitor session room
- Conduct head counts at beginning and end of session
- Collect session evaluations
- The entire process repeats for the next year

Benefits of Using Volunteer Speakers
- It reduces expenses (the person may already have budgeted to attend the meeting, so no housing or transportation costs are required).
- The speaker is knowledgeable about what industry topics are important.
- A popular industry leader may increase attendance at the sessions.
- Relationships between the speaker and the event sponsors are built.

Challenges of Using Volunteer Speakers
- The speaker may not adequately prepare for his or her presentation.
- The speaker may not be a good presenter even if he or she is knowledgeable about the topic.
- There may be a personal agenda (the speaker may use the sessions to promote himself or herself or to publicize a company).

Paid Speakers   A more expensive but often more reliable source of speakers is to contact one of the many speaker bureaus that represent thousands of potential speakers for your event. A **speaker bureau** is a professional talent broker who can help find the perfect speaker to match your event objectives as well as your budget. Typically, a speaker bureau has a stable of qualified professionals who can talk on whatever topic you desire; fees and other amenities range from the affordable to the outrageous. If you are a small Midwestern association of county clerks, you are not going to be able to afford Michael Jordan as your keynote speaker at your **annual meeting,** but you might be able to afford a gold medal Olympian from the 1980s who can talk about teamwork and determination for a bargain price of $4,000.

Providing high-priced, popular paid speakers will most likely increase attendance at your meeting. The smart way to provide such talent is to have the costs of the speaker sponsored by a key exhibitor or leader in the industry. The general session is a high-profile event, and it may be cost-effective for a company to fund the keynote speaker to promote itself to a maximum number of attendees. For example, a $30,000 speaker for a group of 5,000 attendees is only $6 per attendee—that may be less expensive than designing and distributing a traditional mailing!

Another source for speakers is local dignitaries, industry leaders, and university professors. As they are local, you will not incur transportation and lodging costs; in addition, their services are often free or very affordable. The local convention and visitor bureau (CVB) or university can assist you in finding people who are willing to help. A small gift or honorarium is customary to thank these individuals for their time and effort.

Speaker Guidelines   Speaker guidelines or speaker kits should be developed to inform the speakers (paid and nonpaid) of the logistics required to speak at an event as well as to clearly define the expectations of the organization. Speaker guidelines vary from one group to the next, but most should include the following:

- Background information about the association
- Date and location of the meeting
- Special events or activities available to the speaker
- Date, time, and location of speaker's room for presentation
- Presentation topic and duration

Michael Jordan not only plays basketball but is a speaker as well.

AP Wide World Photos

- Demographics and estimated number of attendees for the session
- Room set and audiovisual equipment requests and availability
- Request for short biography
- Names of other speakers (if applicable)
- Remuneration policy
- Dress code
- Location of **speaker ready room** (where he or she can practice or relax prior to speaking)
- Instructions for preparing abstracts or submitting final papers (typically for academic conferences)
- Instructions for prepared handouts
- Transportation and lodging information
- Maps and diagrams of hotel or facility

Online Speaker Bureaus

Sources for well-known or affordable speakers can be found at a variety of Web sites. Speakers are separated into several categories based on subject matter and price. Streaming video is often available for you to view actual presentations online; otherwise, the speaker bureau should be able to supply you with a videotape or DVD of any person it represents. The best way to determine if a speaker is right for your audience is to attend an actual session and decide for yourself if he or she is worth the expense. Web sites to visit include:

National Speakers Bureau	http://www.nsaspeaker.org
Speakers.com	http://www.Speakers.com
Leading Authorities	http://www.LeadingAuthorities.com
Premiere Speakers	http://www.Premierespeakers.com
National Speakers Bureau	http://www.nsb.com

- Deadlines for all materials to be returned
- Guidelines for speaking to the group (e.g., attendees are very informal; attendees like time for questions and answers at the end of a session)

It is not uncommon to include a variety of contractual agreements that must be signed by the speaker:

Presenter Contract A presenter contract is a written agreement between the presenter and the sponsor to provide a presentation on a specific topic at a specific time. A contract should be used regardless of whether the speaker will be paid or not. The contract will verify in writing expenses that will be covered, relationship between the two parties, promotional material needed to advertise the session, deadlines for audiovisual and handout materials, disclosure statements pertaining to any potential conflict of interest, sales or promotion of products or services, penalties for failure to perform the presentation, and allowable conditions for termination of the contract.

Tape, CD-ROM, and Internet Authorization and Waiver If the session will be recorded in any way or if content will be made available on a CD-ROM or on a Web site via print or streaming video, the speaker must be informed and must agree. Some speakers do not want their presentation materials to be accessed on the Internet, where the materials may be easily copied and used by others. Selling audiocassettes, CDs, DVDs, or videos of programs is an additional revenue stream for associations. Since attendees are limited in the number of sessions they can attend each day, by purchasing recordings of missed sessions, they can have the information from the sessions they missed.

AUDIOVISUAL EQUIPMENT

Most hotels and meeting facilities do not allow meeting planners to provide their own audiovisual equipment, such as LCD projectors, televisions, and VCR/DVD players. Rental and servicing of this equipment are a huge revenue stream for facilities. Audiovisual equipment is extremely expensive to rent. In many instances, it costs as much to buy the equipment as it does to rent it. A 27-inch television, which may be purchased at a discount store for $250, may cost the planner that amount in rental fees *each day!* In addition, in locations that are under union jurisdiction, the planner may have to hire a union technician just to plug in an overhead projector.

Thus, controlling audiovisual costs is very important. Speakers are asked months in advance what their needs will be to ensure the availability of the equipment for the group; realistically, however, most presenters do not start working on their presentation until shortly before the event. Unfortunately, there tends to be a discrepancy between what the presenter thinks will be necessary and what will actually be used for a presentation. A speaker may request a TV/DVD system, high-intensity LCD projector, and CD player in June, but by the time the meeting takes place in October, only a standard overhead projector is needed—a serious waste of resources for the planner.

Another good idea is to provide speakers with a template to use in preparing overheads and handouts. You can request that all slides and handouts be developed with a certain font, such as Arial or Times New Roman, and dictate the text and background colors that should be used. Also provide a crisp logo for the organization or event, which will provide some uniformity in the "look" of the meeting.

Attendees often expect traditional paper handouts at educational sessions. In an effort to reduce expenses and conserve resources, some groups have opted to put all handouts on a CD-ROM and make it available free or for a nominal charge. Likewise, some groups will post all the handouts on their company Web site rather than distribute them at the meeting. If handouts will be used, remember to request a master copy well in advance of the meeting. You can e-mail the masters to a convenient copy shop at your destination and have everything printed and delivered to your meeting facility. Unfortunately, the fate of most handouts is to be thrown away at the hotel (too heavy to pack) or never referred to again.

MANAGEMENT OF ON-SITE SPEAKERS

For a large meeting with multiple speakers, keeping track of who is where and what is going on is a monumental task. Recruiting volunteers or hiring temporary staff to assist you will make a big difference. The worst thing that can happen is to have a speaker not show up for your meeting and you not realize it. Likewise, most speakers expect some sort of recognition for their time and effort; they want to feel special. This checklist will help.

Speaker Checklist

- Send a welcome letter. A polite letter of welcome and appreciation should be waiting for speakers at check-in. It should contain all important contact numbers, a current schedule, a map to session rooms, a confirmation of audiovisual requirements, and a personal thank-you for attending. Any special amenities such as health club or VIP lounge privileges that have been arranged should also be included.
- Ask speakers to leave you or a designated person a voice mail on their arrival.
- Assign a staff member or a volunteer to contact the speaker prior to the session for last-minute changes, emergency copying needs, and answers to any questions.
- Provide a speaker ready room, a quiet place for speakers to test equipment, have a snack, rest, and otherwise mentally prepare for the presentation.
- Assign a staff member or a volunteer to introduce the speaker to the audience.
- Collect evaluations of the speaker from attendees.
- Provide a complimentary copy of audio- or videotaping (if done).

Keynote speaker at a political convention using high-tech equipment.
Pearson Education/PH College

- Present a small gift in appreciation. Be considerate—gift certificates, engraved pens, and other light items are appreciated. Your speaker may be heading to the airport after the presentation and does not want to be burdened with large unwieldy items.
- Send a thank-you letter and evaluation scores as soon as possible after the event.
- Ask speakers to evaluate their experience at your meeting: Were the travel and lodging accommodations acceptable? Were there any problems with audiovisual or room setup?

A new trend is to develop **preconvention sessions** so that attendees come better prepared to the education session. Chat rooms or blogs may be created months in advance for people to begin discussions on a topic. The speaker may facilitate discussion and then design the actual presentation based on what has transpired online. Similarly, some speakers will do a preassessment of the attendees to determine the level of knowledge of the group; after the session, attendees can be reassessed so that the amount of learning that occurred may be measured.

ANCILLARY ACTIVITIES

There are a variety of activities that may be incorporated before, during, and after the actual scheduled program. In today's hectic business environment, many people try to squeeze a short vacation into their meeting schedule. More and more we are seeing husbands, wives, significant others, and children attending meetings as guests. Some meeting attendees tack on a few extra days at the beginning or end of the scheduled meeting to spend some quality time with their family and friends. While the meeting attendee is attending workshops and trade shows, the guests want something to keep them occupied, and tours, shopping excursions, cultural events, sport events, dinners, museums, festivals, and theatrical shows are all popular diversions. Every city, no matter how small, has something of interest to explore. The key is not to let these **ancillary activities** interfere with your overall program objectives—ancillary activities should not be more attractive than the program! Ancillary activities must be provided, and it is important that they are appropriate to the age, gender, and interests of the guests.

If possible, limit participation in planning ancillary activities for two reasons: additional effort and liability issues. As a planner, you need to concentrate on what is going on in the meeting facility, not whether the bus to the mall is on time. If possible, outsource the management of ancillary activities to a local **destination management company (DMC),** a company that specializes in arranging activities and is an expert on the local area (see chapter 7 on DMCs for more information). Likewise, if something should happen and people are injured at an event that you arranged, you do not want to worry about liability issues. For example, if child care is offered by the sponsoring organization, additional insurance may be needed to protect the organization from any liability issues. Child care is definitely a service that must be outsourced to a professional child care service because special licensing is needed to ensure the safety and security of children.

The safest route is to provide a list of local activities and the Web site address of the convention and the CVB; then let the attendees plan their own activities. Be warned: When holding meetings in popular

Example of a Company Specializing in Programs for Children

ACCENT on Children's Arrangements is a company that specializes in children's programs at meetings and conventions. The following is from the Accent on Children's Arrangements Web site.

What makes ACCENT on Children's Arrangements different from other providers?

Age-Appropriate Adaptation—From infants to teens, ACCENT on Children's Arrangements' professional programming is geared toward the needs of each age group and offers children the opportunity to meet new friends, learn new skills, and play fun games.

Customized Service and Planning—ACCENT on Children's Arrangements creates customized programs to meet each client's needs and budget. The same thing doesn't work for every group, environment, time of year or setting, and ACCENT takes all of this into consideration when planning a program.

Edu-tainment—ACCENT on Children's Arrangements combines education with entertainment to produce a unique concoction of Edu-tainment.

High Level of Supervision—Without dampening the fun or hampering the activities, all children are carefully supervised by responsible CPR-trained adults who have been specially trained to meet ACCENT on Children's Arrangements' high standards. All caregivers have to meet ACCENT's stringent screening, selection, and training process as well as necessary legalities. ACCENT thoroughly performs criminal checks and background references on all caregivers.

Safety and Security—ACCENT on Children's Arrangements' photo security procedure, "SecurChild®", is a positive identification system for check-in and check-out (ACCENT photographs and documents the parent or guardian who drops off the child and ensures that only that person picks up the child). Camera-monitored children's centers are optional. Additionally, ACCENT prepares in-depth fire and emergency safety plans specific to each meeting location.

STAFF AND MANAGEMENT TEAM

ACCENT on Children's Arrangements' Management Team has years of experience in the education and hospitality field and understands the special requirements of children's programs. Key members of the management team are

ACCENT's Program Managers who work with a group from the beginning and are responsible for developing a curriculum that fits the group, the meeting location, and the needs of the children. ACCENT's Program Managers are on site for the entire program and are responsible for the successful implementation.

Flexibility—ACCENT on Children's Arrangements works its magic in any major destination site from early morning to late in the evening. Headquartered in New Orleans, Louisiana, the company is set up to take all children's programs on the road and travel with clients, offering consistency and reliability no matter where the client event is planned.

Registration—Starting with group publicity and inclusion in all meeting communications, ACCENT on Children's Arrangements is a partner in the registration process, providing customized pre-event registration online or by phone, mail, or fax. In addition, ACCENT creates parental consent and waiver forms and sets up on-site registration for larger programs.

Experience—ACCENT on Children's Arrangements' founder, Diane B. Lyons, is a recognized leader in the meeting industry; she has a master's degree in education and professional experience as a teacher. She created ACCENT to meet the emerging needs of professional parents, and for more than fourteen years, ACCENT has been the leading provider of children's programs throughout the country, cultivating and constantly revising programs to ensure they meet the needs of meeting planners, parents, and children nationwide.

A Promise—Diane B. Lyons founded ACCENT on Children's Arrangements in 1991 with one employee, one office, and one promise: To provide children's services at corporate, society, association, and other group meetings and events that exceed the most stringent safety and security needs while captivating the attention of children and easing the concerns of parents.

For more than fourteen years, ACCENT has been exceeding that promise and has grown into a 12-person headquarters office with 10 part-time staff throughout the U.S. and more than 200 contract employees due to the company's dedication to its clients and its commitment to exceeding client expectations.

Source: ACCENT on Children's Arrangements, Inc. Headquarters, 615 Baronne Street, Suite 303 New Orleans, LA 70113, phone: 504-524-1227 fax: 504-524-1229 e-mail: info@accentoca.com

resort locations such as Orlando, Florida, or Las Vegas, Nevada, the available attractions can quickly become distractions for your attendees. It is not uncommon to lose a few attendees in Las Vegas when the call of the slot machines is louder than an hour-long workshop on a dry topic.

Registration

To attend most conventions or trade shows, some type of registration is typically required. Registration is the process of gathering all pertinent information and fees necessary for an individual to attend the meeting. But it is much more than merely collecting money because registration data is a valuable asset to any association or organization that is sponsoring an event. Registration begins several weeks prior to the event and usually lasts right up to the final day, although discounts are often provided to attendees who register in advance. For example, they might be offered an **early bird rate** as an incentive to send their money in six weeks early; the association can then use that money to pay deposits or bills coming due. When attendees register early, the planner can determine if registration numbers are at anticipated levels. If not, the planner can increase marketing or negotiate with the hotel or meeting facilities about lowering expectations and financial commitments that may have been promised.

Data collected on the registration form may include name, title, occupation, address, e-mail address, phone and fax numbers, membership category, desired workshop sessions, social functions, optional events, method of payment, special medical or dietary needs, and liability waiver. A recent addition has been to ask attendees where they are staying (and how long) so that the economic impact of the meeting can be determined. Some organizations inquire about the size of the company, number of employees, or financial responsibility of the attendee (whether he or she makes or recommends purchase decisions). This registration data can be used before, during, and after the meeting.

Prior to the meeting, the data can be given or sold to exhibitors or advertisers so they can promote their company, products, and services before the actual meeting. It may also be used to market to potential attendees who have not committed to attend. Advertising stating "We have 7,500 qualified buyers attending this year's convention" may entice more companies to register or exhibit. Preregistration data can also help the planner monitor interest in special events or particular workshops

REGISTRATION FORM

NAME OF ASSOCIATION

DATES OF MEETING   CITY, STATE

Name: _____

Address: _____

City: _____ State: _____ Zip: _____

Name as it should appear on badge: _____

Title: _____ Company: _____

Spouse or companion name: _____

Please check the appropriate box (see brochure for rates)

Accommodations

Single   _____ nights @ $_____ per night

Double   _____ nights @ $_____ per night

Triple   _____ nights @ $_____ per night

Suite   _____ nights @ $_____ per night

                                        Subtotal $_____

Registration (see brochure for fees)

_____ Members   @ $_____

_____ Nonmembers   @ $_____

_____ Students   @ $_____

                                        Subtotal $_____

Special Events (see brochure for fees)

_____ Tickets for opening reception   @ $_____

_____ Tickets for dine around   @ $_____

_____ Tickets for closing banquet   @ $_____

_____ Tickets for golf tournament   @ $_____

_____ Tickets for preconference tour   @ $_____

_____ Tickets for postconference tour   @ $_____

_____ Tickets for children's program   @ $_____

                                        Subtotal $_____
                                        Total $_____

Please indicate any special needs:

Accommodations _____

Food and Beverage _____

FIGURE 10–1   Registration form.

that may be popular. If a particular workshop is getting a lot of interest, then the planner can move it to a larger room or increase seating.

During the meeting, registration data can be used as a promotional tool for the press to gain media attention for the organization, sponsors, and exhibitors. It can also help the local CVB in justifying the costs of marketing and soliciting groups to come to their city. Hard facts, such as using 3,000 rooms and 200,000 square feet of meeting space, are music to the ears of hospitality companies. For the attendees, technology now allows them to automatically access, via computer, who is at a particular meeting and beam the entire attendee list into a personal data assistant (PDA) for future use.

After the meeting, registration data can be used to update association membership records, solicit new members, or be sold to interested parties. Most important, it can be used to help the planner with logistics and to promote the next meeting. By examining registration data over time, it gives the organization a better view of who is attending its meeting and if there are any trends apparent, such as changes in gender, age, education, or title of attendees.

REGISTRATION FEES

There may be several different pricing structures for a single meeting. For association meetings, members typically receive a discount on the cost of registration, which helps encourage people to become members of the association, but not all members will pay the same price. For example, in 2007 the Professional Convention Management Association (PCMA) charged professional members (meeting planners) $640, suppliers (hotel salespeople, CVBs) $740, university faculty $430, and student members $220. These are the early bird preregistration prices available until about six weeks prior to the convention. After the **cutoff date** for preregistration, all prices increased by $50 to $100. All attendees, regardless of how much they pay, receive the same opportunities for education and networking and are invited to the scheduled meals, breaks, and receptions; however, additional activities, such as golf, tours, or special entertainment functions, may incur a separate cost.

For some events such as the Exhibitor Show, an annual trade show for people in the exhibition industry, registration fees are based on what the attendee wants to attend: Entrance to the trade show is free, but education sessions may cost up to $150 per workshop; additional events, such as dinners and receptions, may be purchased separately. All-inclusive registrations are also an option, with full registration and attendance to all education programs costing well over $1,000.

Associations usually offer substantial registration discounts to their members. The nonmember rate to attend may well exceed the difference between the cost of membership and the member rate, making it desirable to join the association. This is a clever way for associations to increase their membership base, and it provides an opportunity to promote other products and services to the new members. Registration fees are often waived for VIPs, members of the press, speakers, and local dignitaries. Complimentary registrations must be monitored closely because there may be costs involved if the meeting has food and beverage or if other events are available.

PREREGISTRATION

Preregistration is the process of registering attendees weeks or months in advance of an event. This benefits the planner in several ways: It provides information about the attendees of a meeting or event, it assists the meeting planner regarding room capacities for educational sessions, and it helps the session speaker with an estimation of the number of attendees for a session. Typically, advanced payment is also required to preregister. The early bird discount rate is a major incentive to preregister. Logistically, as people are arriving for the event, preregistration can reduce congestion in the registration area as well as reduce long lines and waiting time. A quick check-in to collect a name badge and other meeting materials and to confirm the person's arrival is all that is necessary.

Whether it is paper-based or electronic, a registration form must be completed by the prospective attendee. The simpler and easier to complete, the better the form is; for example, a one-sided registration form is easier to fax than a form with printing on both sides. Common information to include on a preregistration form follows:

- Name, date, and location of meeting
- Name and title of person
- Company name and address
- Phone, fax, and e-mail address
- Fee category (member, nonmember, student) and cost
- Additional guest registration
- Early bird deadline
- Policies regarding payment method (check, money order, credit card, electronic payment) and accepted currency

Registration desk at the G2E convention.
Photo by George G. Fenich, Ph.D.

- Cancellation and refund policies
- Housing information
- Official airline information
- Request for Americans with Disabilities Act (ADA) accommodations
- Request for special dietary accommodations
- Reservations for particular sessions
- Participation in ancillary activities requiring additional fees

ON-SITE REGISTRATION

Like the front desk of a hotel, the registration area is the first experience an attendee has with a meeting, convention, or trade show. A slow or inefficient registration process can set the tone for the entire meeting. The registration area should be heavily staffed the first day and should remain open throughout the event. If international guests are expected, registration materials may need to be translated, and interpreters may be necessary to facilitate a smooth check-in. For particularly large groups, the check-in process can be expedited by mailing each attendee a name badge (without the plastic holder), identification card, and other material along with a confirmation letter prior to the event. The attendee has only to go to a registration counter and show identification and registration confirmation; then the registration attendant will give the attendee a badge holder, conference program, and any other materials. If a trade show is involved, having a separate area for exhibitor registration is a good idea.

Registration is one of the areas often outsourced by the meeting planner, especially for large events. It is a complex process that requires much training on the part of the registration attendants. Some hotels or convention centers have arrangements with temporary agencies that provide staff that do registration on a regular basis; some registration management companies even handle housing as well.

Housing

Not all meetings require housing arrangements. If housing is needed, there are basically four methods of handling housing for attendees:

1. Attendees arrange for their own room. Lists of hotels may be provided, but the meeting sponsor makes no prior arrangements regarding price negotiations or availability.

2. A group rate is negotiated by the planner at one or more properties, and attendees respond directly to the reservations department of their choice.

3. The meeting sponsor handles all housing, and attendees book rooms through the sponsor. Then the sponsor provides the hotel with a rooming list of confirmed guests.

4. A third-party **housing bureau** (outsourced company) handles all arrangements and either receives a fee from the sponsor or is paid by the CVB (in some cases the CVB functions as the housing bureau).

Having attendees make their own hotel reservations is the easiest method because it totally removes that responsibility from the planner. But remember, the facility is going to base its pricing to host the event on the total revenues it anticipates from the group. Sleeping rooms represent the largest amount of potential revenue for the hotel, so if you do not block rooms, you will most assuredly pay a premium for renting meeting space and other services. The room block is a key negotiation tool for the planner.

The last three options require that the meeting planner establish a rate for the attendees. The room rate will reflect prior negotiations with the sales department in which the total value of the meeting to the facility is considered. A certain number of rooms, called a "block," will be reserved, and rooms are subtracted from this inventory as attendees request them. This can be a gamble for the meeting planner. As with food and beverage events, the planner must estimate how many people will be attending. If the planner blocks 100 rooms and only 75 attendees show up, he or she may be held responsible for part (or all) of the cost of those rooms. The difference between rooms blocked and rooms "picked up" (actually used) is called attrition (this is discussed in more detail in chapter 12 on legal issues). A serious challenge to planners these days is attendees booking rooms outside the block; that is, they bypass the hotels for which the planner negotiated special pricing and find other accommodations. If the host hotel charges $199 per day and a smaller, less luxurious hotel down the street is charging $99, a certain percentage of the attendees will opt for the lower price. Sometimes, by calling the hotel directly or by using a discount hotel broker on the Internet, attendees can get better prices in the same hotel for less than what the planner negotiated. If large numbers of attendees do this, then the meeting planner is going to get stuck paying for a lot of unused rooms. One method of reducing this potentially expensive problem is to establish review dates in the hotel contract whereby the planner can reduce (or increase) the **room block** by a certain percentage at a certain time. The closer to the actual meeting dates, the less likely the hotel will allow a reduction in room block because the hotel must have time to try and sell any unused rooms and recoup any losses. A hotel room is a perishable commodity—if it is not sold each day; the potential revenue is lost forever.

Having attendees call or reserve rooms online directly with the hotel is a good option. The attendees should benefit by the negotiated room rate, and the hotel handles the reservation processing directly; the meeting planner will need minimal involvement. For larger meetings where multiple properties are used, it is advisable to provide a range of hotel prices to accommodate the budgets of all the attendees.

Handling attendee reservations in-house is possible but is easiest with small groups. If the event is a small high-profile event, the planner can have attendees reserve rooms with the organization, and a **room list**—which includes type of room, ADA requests, smoking or non-smoking status, arrival and departure dates, names of additional guests in the room, and special requests—will be created to give to the hotel. Handling reservations in-house can be quite time-consuming and may require additional staffing.

Alternatively, a housing bureau can be of great assistance. Outsourcing the housing process to a third-party vendor or CVB is most prevalent with medium and large meetings. Some groups, such as the National Association of Broadcasters or Consumer Electronics Show, are so large they require most of the hotel rooms in the host city. Housing for a so-called citywide meeting is best left to professionals who have the most current technology and are well equipped to handle thousands of housing requests. Making reservations through a housing service can be done by mail, phone, or fax and on the Internet. The housing bureau may charge a fee per transaction; this cost may be paid by the sponsoring organization, or in some cases the local CVB will absorb some or all of the cost. Indeed, many CVBs and even hotels operate their own housing bureaus as a service to meeting planners.

REGISTRATION AND HOUSING COMPANIES

Several companies have developed over the last few years that specialize in handling both conference registration and housing. Visit their Web sites at the following addresses:

Allmeetings	http://Allmeetings.com
MPbid	http://MPBID.com
Passkey	http://Passkey.com
StarCite	http://StarCite.com

Specification Guide

One of the challenges in the meeting and events profession is that there are few standardized policies, procedures, and terminology. To begin a codification of definitions and standardized practices, an industrywide task force called **Accepted Practices Exchange (APEX)** was created. As mentioned in chapter 1, one of APEX's first initiatives was the development of accepted practices regarding terminology. Another APEX initiative was the standardization of resumes and work orders, which are the primary record of communication and logistics between the meeting planner and the facility. The APEX Resumes and Work Orders Panel was established in January 2002 to review common practices and to develop standards. The committee found that many terms were used interchangeably to describe the document used by a planner to communicate specific requirements for a function; these included catering event order, meeting resume, event specifications guide, staging guide operations manual, production schedule, room specs, schedule of services, working agenda, specifications sheet, and group resume. After a considerable amount of effort and input from all types of meeting planners, hotel convention service managers, destination management companies, exhibit managers, and CVBs, the panel created a format that, if adopted, will greatly facilitate the communication between planners and the entities that service their meetings.

The panel proposed that the term "specification guide" be adopted industrywide to describe this document. It is defined as follows:

Specifications Guide (Spec Guide). The industry-preferred term for a comprehensive document that outlines the complete requirements and instructions for an event. This document is typically authored by the event planner and is shared with all appropriate vendors as a vehicle to communicate the expectations of services for a project. It sometimes is called a STAGING GUIDE, RESUME, or BIBLE.

The specification guide is a three-part document:

1. Narrative. General overview of the meeting or event.

2. Function Schedules. Timetable outlining all functions that compose the overall meeting or event.

3. Function Setup Orders. Specifications for each separate function that is part of the overall meeting or event (this is used by the facility to inform setup crews, technicians, catering and banquet staff, and all other staff regarding what is required for each event).

The APEX panel also recommended a standardized timetable for communication between the planner and the facility and service providers. Recognizing that these guidelines may differ depending on the size, timing, and complexity of the individual event, they do provide a useful general format, seen in Table 10–1.

The specification guide contains quite a bit of detailed information. The meeting planner along with catering and convention services staff will need access to a copy. If any changes are made, they should be recorded in all copies. Fortunately, as software is created and disseminated in the industry, this document will be easier to maintain

TABLE 10–1	Timetable for Communications	
Size of Event	Submit Resume in Advance	Receive Return from Facility and Vendors
1–500	4 weeks	2 weeks
501–1,000	6 weeks	4 weeks
1,000+	8 weeks	6 weeks

and update. Some planners and **convention services managers (CSMs)** now download this information onto their PDA, so a five-pound three-ring binder is reduced to a few portable ounces. Changes to the spec guide can be made easily and beamed to the appropriate people.

Pre- and Postconvention Meetings

What is certain for all meetings is that changes to the spec guide are unavoidable. In fact, one of the chief responsibilities of a good meeting planner is to react to and manage change—often unexpected change.

PRECONVENTION MEETING

A day or two prior to the actual beginning of a meeting, the planner should partake in a preconvention (pre-con) meeting. This is a gathering of all critical people representing all departments within the facility who will impact the group. In addition to the CSM, who is the primary contact for the planner, the following representatives may be requested to attend the meeting: catering or banquet manager or food and beverage director, audiovisual representative, sales manager, accounting manager, front desk manager, bell staff or concierge, housekeeping manager, security manager, engineering manager, switchboard manager, recreation manager, and all outside service providers, such as transportation, special events, and decorators. Often the general manager of the facility will stop by, be introduced, and welcome the planner. The pre-con meeting allows the planner to meet and visually connect with all the various people servicing the event. In most cases, this will be the first time the planner meets many

A preconvention meeting often includes the meeting planner, CSM, and catering manager.

Dorling Kindersley, Media Library

of these people. Each representative is introduced, and any changes or additions of duties in their respective departments are reviewed. After each individual department has been discussed, the planner should release the person to return to his or her duties. The specification guide is reviewed page by page with the CSM; all changes are made, guarantees are confirmed, and last-minute instructions are conveyed. The pre-con is basically the last time the planner has the opportunity to make any major changes without disrupting the facility because once an event is in progress, it is very difficult and potentially costly to make major changes. If the planner decides one hour before a session that the room should be set with only chairs rather than with tables and chairs as listed on the Function Setup Order, it can cause havoc. Additional staff may be needed to remove the tables, and the planner may be charged for the labor. Sometimes the last-minute request of a planner cannot be fulfilled; for example, if fifty tables, are requested just prior to an event, the hotel may not have them available or may not have scheduled staff for setup.

POSTCONVENTION MEETING

At the conclusion of a major meeting, the meeting planner will create a written document to record all key events of the meeting. This is used for planning the next meeting and also serves as a "report card" for the facility and the meeting manager. It will include what went right as well as what went wrong. Then a postconvention (postcon) meeting is held. It is smaller than the pre-con and may include the planning staff, the CSM, the food and beverage director, the audiovisual manager, and a representative from the accounting department. This is the time to address any billing discrepancies, service failures, and other problems and to praise facility staff for a job well done. Most major meetings will have a post-con; smaller meetings may not. In some cases, the planner is just too mentally and physically exhausted to conduct a post-con meeting immediately following the event—a good night's rest and some peace and quiet may be needed first.

Summary

Education has replaced recreation as the driving force for most meetings; however, people like to be entertained as well as educated, so the planner must attend to all the needs of the attendees and provide both. The format of the education sessions as well as the setup of the meeting space should be appropriate to the objectives of the meeting. Program content should be designed with both a track and a level that will target the majority of the attendees. Housing and registration are important components in implementing the plan for a meeting or event. Both paid and voluntary speakers can be utilized—each has positives and negatives. Planners should utilize speaker guidelines to assist speakers in designing program content that will be of interest. Care must be taken to ensure that speakers are adequately prepared to address the group and are contractually obligated to perform. Finally, ancillary activities such as shopping trips, tours, child care, and other services that enhance an attendee's meeting experience should be planned thoughtfully so as not to interfere with the scheduled programming.

Key Words and Terms

For definitions, see the Glossary or go to http://glossary.conventionindustry.org.

Accepted Practices Exchange (APEX)

Ancillary activity

Annual meeting

Break-out session

Concurrent session

Convention services manager (CSM)

Cutoff date

Destination management company (DMC)

Early bird rate

General session

Housing bureau

Keynote address

Level

Plenary session

Poster session

Preconvention session

Presenter contract

Room block

Room list

Roundtable session

Speaker bureau

Speaker guidelines

Speaker ready room

Specification guide

Track

Workshop

Review and Discussion Questions

1. Why would a planner hire a high-paid nationally known speaker for the keynote address?
2. What is the purpose of using program formats, tracks, and levels in designing effective meeting programming?
3. What is the purpose of using speaker contracts?
4. What are the benefits and challenges of using volunteer speakers compared to paid speakers?
5. Why are speaker guidelines used, and what should be included?
6. What are the benefits and challenges of providing ancillary activities?
7. What are the benefits and limitations of outsourcing components of a meeting such as housing or registration?

8. How can planners use registration data before, during, and after a convention?

9. How does preregistration assist the planner in planning a meeting?

10. Describe the four different methods of housing.

11. What is the purpose of a specification guide? What information should it contain?

12. Explain the benefit of having a pre-con and post-con meeting.

About the Chapter Contributor

Curtis Love, Ph.D., is an associate professor and graduate coordinator in the Tourism and Convention Administration Department at the William F. Harrah College of Hotel Administration at the University of Nevada–Las Vegas. His teaching and research concentrations are in the area of meetings, conventions, and exhibitions. Prior to joining UNLV, he was the vice president of Education for the Professional Convention Management Association.

CHAPTER 11

Food and Beverage

An attended buffet gives elegance to a food and beverage function.
Dorling Kindersley Media Library

Chapter Objectives

This chapter provides the reader with an understanding of the following:

- Types of catering operations and types of caterers
- Relationships between the catering department and other hotel departments
- Purposes of the meal function
- Types of meal functions, menu planning, menu design, and pricing
- Types of beverage functions, beverage menu planning, and pricing
- Liquor laws and third-party liability
- Space requirements and room setup

Chapter Outline

Introduction

Food and beverage is an area that many meeting planners shy away from by outsourcing its planning and negotiation to third-party planners. It is often a mystery to many planners as to what is negotiable, how caterers price their services, and where caterers will make concessions.

The Convention Industry Council (CIC) has a glossary that provides the following definition:

Caterer. (1) A food service vendor. The term is often used to describe a vendor who specializes in banquets and theme parties. (2) An exclusive food and beverage contractor within a facility.

The quality of the food and beverage **functions** can impact the overall impressions of a meeting. While many simply see food as fuel, for others it is an important component of the overall experience. From planning menus to negotiating prices, catering is one area not to leave to chance. It is one of the major expenses of a meeting and an area where Murphy's Law prevails. Further, the importance of cuisine must be emphasized. The choices and preparation of food have changed dramatically over the past few years; organic, ethnic, and vegetarian menus are examples. It is posited that food revenue is increasing steadily due to the choice of cuisine, but beverage revenue may be declining because sponsors of events do not want to assume liability for alcohol consumption. (*Source:* Angelo Camillo Ph.D., San Francisco State University)

Here are some questions to ask when planning for food and beverage:

1. Whom will I work with planning the event?
2. Who will be on site during the event?
3. When can I expect your written proposal?
4. What is your policy regarding deposits and cancellations?
5. When is the final payment due?
6. Are there other charges for setup, delivery, overtime, etc.?
7. Do you take credit cards? Do you take personal checks?
8. When must I give you my final guarantee?
9. What percentage is overset above the guarantee?
10. What is the sales tax, and what are your gratuity and/or service charge policies?
11. What are the chef's best menu items?
12. What are your portion sizes?
13. Will wine be poured by the staff or placed on the tables?
14. How many staff will be working the event?
15. What are your substitution policies for vegetarian plates and special meals?
16. Could you pass wine or champagne as guests arrive?

17. How many bartenders will be used during the cocktail hour?
18. Do you provide table numbers?
19. What size tables do you have?
20. What are the options for linen, chair covers, china, stemware, flatware, and charger plates?
21. What decorations do you provide for tables, buffets, and food stations?
22. Are you compliant with the Americans with Disabilities (ADA) Act?
23. Can you provide a podium, mike, and overhead projector?

Catered Events

Catered events generally have one host and one bill, and most attendees eat the same meal. (Exceptions would be if attendees arranged for vegetarian, low-fat, or other special meals.) A mandatory gratuity is added to the check that can range from 15% to 22% of the total bill, and taxes can add another 5% to 9%. The distribution of this gratuity varies widely among companies: In some companies, the gratuity goes exclusively to the servers and bartenders; in other venues, a portion goes to management, such as the catering manager or the convention services manager (CSM). A gratuity differs from a tip because a tip is voluntary and is given at the discretion of the client for service over and above expectations. Service charges are a murky area, but they generally do not go to the service personnel. The lesson here is, when in doubt, ask.

Catered events can be held in just about any location. **Off-premises catering** transports food—either prepared in advance or prepared on site—to a location such as a tented area, museum, park, or attraction. Sometimes food is prepared in a kitchen and transported fully cooked to the event site; at other times food is partially prepared in a kitchen and is finished at the site, or everything can be prepared from scratch at the site. Mobile kitchens can be set up just about anywhere by using generators and/or propane and butane as fuel to heat cooking equipment. Caterers also usually must rent equipment, including tables, chairs, chafing dishes, plates, flatware, and glassware.

On-premises catering is done in a facility that has its own permanent kitchens and function rooms, such as a hotel, restaurant, or convention center, which allows the facility to keep permanent furniture, such as banquet tables and solid banquet chairs, in their inventory. Meeting planners are usually locked into using the catering department of the hotel at the site of the meeting. In a citywide convention, one hotel is usually named the host hotel and holds most of the food functions, although some events often move attendees to a variety of venues. However, many meetings have at least one off-premises event, often the opening reception, the closing gala, or a themed event. Attendees want to experience some of the flavor of the destination, and they often get "cabin fever" if they never leave the hotel. Events can be held at an aquarium, a museum, a winery, or a historic mansion; for example, in Dallas, many events are held at Southfork Ranch, site of the television show *Dallas*.

OFF-PREMISES CATERING

In Orlando, it is much easier logistically to transport a 20-person board of directors dinner to a local restaurant than to transport 1,000+ attendees to Disney World. As a meeting planner, you may be responsible for simultaneously coordinating both off-premises catering events. In this case, a shuttle bus system must be set up to transport attendees back and forth, which can be expensive.

Many notable and excellent restaurants have banquet rooms, and bigger restaurants have banquet sales coordinators. Arnaud's in New Orleans has a six-person sales staff, so banquets are big business. In Las Vegas, a trend in recent years has celebrity chefs creating their own signature restaurants within the hotel, separate from the hotel's own food service operations. These restaurants, such as Spago in the Forum Shops at Caesar's Palace or Delmonico's at the Venetian, also have their own banquet sales staff. The Web has made it easy to research what local restaurants have to offer. The MIM List (at http://www.mim.com), a free e-mail listserv for meeting planners sponsored by *Meeting News* magazine, is a great place to ask for suggestions and advice. For an off-premises event, the first step for a meeting planner would be to create a request for proposal (RFP) and send it to event managers or caterers in the area. The RFP would include basic information, such as the objective of the event, information on the company, workable dates, number of attendees, and approximate budget, as well as any special requests, such as the need for a parade area. Many catering companies have online RFPs. Once the planner has had the opportunity to review the proposals, an interview and (if possible) a site inspection would follow. During the site inspection, look at the ambiance of the space, the level of cleanliness and maintenance, and other necessary amenities, such as parking and restrooms.

In many cases, off-premises events will be outsourced with a destination management company (DMC). DMCs are familiar with the location and have relationships established with unique venues in the area. For example, in Las Vegas the Liberace Mansion is available for parties; in New Orleans, Mardi Gras World, where the parade floats are made, is an outstanding setting for a party. Just about every destination has some distinctive spaces for parties: Southfork in Dallas, the Rock and Roll Hall of Fame & Museum in Cleveland, the Getty Museum in Los Angeles, and so on.

DMCs also know the best caterers, decorators, shuttle companies, entertainment, and any other product or service you may require. While DMCs charge for their services, they often can get quantity discounts because of the volume they purchase throughout the year. And if there is a problem with the product or service, the DMC can usually resolve it faster because of the amount of future business that would be jeopardized.

Two of the challenges with off-premises events are transportation and weather. Shuttle buses are an additional expense for the meeting. Weather can spoil the best-laid plans, so contingency measures must be arranged. Backup shelter should be available, whether it is a tent or an inside function room. For example, outdoor luaus in Hawaii are frequently moved inside at the last minute because of the frequent tropical storms that pop up there.

During the initial site inspection, obtain a copy of the facility's banquet menus and policies. Do they offer the type of menu items that would be appropriate for your group? Are they prepared to handle custom menus if you decide not to use their printed offerings? When planning custom menus, always check the skill level that is in the kitchen and the availability of special products that may be required.

Other important considerations include the demographics of the group. Menu choices would be different for the American Truck Drivers Association and the International Association of Retired Persons. The typical truck driver would probably prefer a big steak, while a retired person would likely prefer a smaller portion of chicken without heavy spices. You need to consider gender, age, ethnic background, profession, and so on.

ON-PREMISES CATERING

Most meals are catered on the premises during a meeting. Serving attendees all at once prevents strain on the restaurant outlets, keeps attendees from leaving the property, and ensures that everyone will be back on time for the following sessions.

Conference centers offer a complete meeting package, which includes meals. Breakfast, lunch, and dinner are generally available in a cafeteria-type setup at any time the group decides to break. This keeps the group from having to break just because it is noon if they are in the middle of a productive session. If more than one group is in the facility, they will each be assigned different areas of the dining room. Refreshments are usually available at any time as well, allowing breaks at appropriate times. Conference centers can also provide banquets and receptions on request.

Convention centers and stadiums usually have concession stands open. More and more, trade shows are holding their own opening reception or providing lunch on the show floor to attract attendees into the exhibits. Most convention centers are public entities, and the food service is contracted out to companies such as ARAMARK or Sodexho. These contract food service companies often have exclusive contracts; other vendors or caterers are not allowed to work in the facility.

The above venues generally also have full-service restaurants on the property. If the group will use the restaurant, check the capacity and hours relative to the needs of the group. For example, the Council on Hotel, Restaurant, and Institutional Education (CHRIE) held its annual convention at a major hotel in Palm Springs, California, during late July. They attracted about 700 attendees and were virtually the only people in the 1,500-room hotel. CHRIE felt that the five freestanding restaurants would be more than adequate to meet the dining needs of the group (dining off site was not a practical option). This would normally be true; however, since it was low season for the hotel, all but two of the restaurants were closed, with the result that CHRIE convention attendees were faced with waits of over two hours to be seated for dinner.

Meeting planners also need to stay abreast of current food trends. They do so by reading trade journals, such as *Meeting News*, *Successful Meetings*, *Convene*, or *Meetings & Conventions*. Many of the event and food trade publications, such as *Event Solutions*, *Special Events, Hotel F & B Director*, and *Catering*, are wonderful resources. Online versions are linked on the Web page http://tca.unlv.edu/pub. BizBash (at http://www.bizbash.com) is a great site to see creative things that others are doing.

TABLE 11–1	Types of Functions
Continental Breakfast	This meal is typically a bread or pastry, juice, and coffee, although it can be upgraded with the addition of sliced fruit, yogurt, and/or cold cereals. Most are self-service, although table service is an option.
Full (Served) Breakfast	This would be plated in the kitchen and would normally include some type of eggs (such as eggs Benedict), a meat (such as bacon or sausage), a potato item (such as hash browns), fruit, and coffee.
Breakfast Buffet	An assortment of foods with a variety of fruits and fruit juices, egg dishes, meats, potatoes, and breads would be served.
Refreshment Break	This is often beverages only but may include snacks such as cookies, bagels, or fruit.
Brunch	This is a late-morning meal and includes both breakfast and lunch items. A brunch can be a buffet or a plated (served) meal.
Buffet Lunch	This can be a cold or hot buffet, with a variety of salads, vegetables, meats, etc. A deli buffet can include a make-your-own sandwich area.
Box Lunch	This meal is made to carry away from the hotel and eat in a remote location. It can be eaten on a bus if there is a long ride to a destination (such as a ride from San Francisco to the Napa Valley for a day's activities) or eaten at the destination (such as a picnic area to hear the Boston Pops Orchestra). Box lunches can also be provided to attendees at a trade show.
Full (Served) Lunch	This is a plated lunch, usually a three-course hot meal, and often includes a salad, a main course, and a dessert. A one-course cold meal, such as chicken salad served in a pineapple half, is sometimes provided.
Reception	This is a networking event where people stand up and mill around. Food is usually placed on stations around the room on tables and may be butlered. There are often bars. Light receptions may only include dry snacks and beverages and often precede a dinner; heavy receptions would include hot and cold appetizers and perhaps a meat-carving station, and they are often planned instead of a dinner.
Dinner Buffet	This would include a variety of salads, vegetables, meats, desserts, and beverages. Often meats are carved and served by attendants.

(continued)

TABLE 11–1	Types of Functions (*continued*)
Full (Served) Dinner	This could be a three- to five-course meal, including an appetizer, soup, salad, main course, and dessert. Food can be pre-plated in the kitchen (American service) or served from trays to guests at the table (banquet French service).
Off-Site Event	This is any event held away from the host hotel. It could be a reception at a famous landmark, such as the *Queen Mary* in Long Beach, or a picnic at a local beach or park.
Theme Party	This is a gala event with flair. It can be a reception, buffet, or served meal. Themes can run the gamut; for example, it might have an international theme, with different stations set up with food from Italy, China, Japan, Mexico, Germany, etc.

Styles of Service

There are many ways to serve a meal, from self-service to VIP white-glove service. The White House protocol is also being followed in this book. The White House publishes the *Green Book*, which explains how everything is to be done for presidential protocol. However, because of confusion in this area, it is important to be sure that the planner and the catering representative agree on what the service styles mean for the event. (Unfortunately, the *Green Book* is not available to the public, as it also includes info on presidential security, etc.) While there is some disagreement on a few of the following definitions, these are based on the CIC's Glossary:

Buffet. For a **buffet,** food is attractively arranged on tables, and guests serve themselves and then take their plates to a table to sit and eat; beverages are usually served at the tables. Buffets are generally more expensive than plated, served meals because there is no portion control, and surpluses must be built in to ensure adequate supplies of each food item. Be sure to allow adequate space around the table for lines to form. Consider the flow, and do not make guests backtrack to get an item. For example, place the salad dressings after the salad so that guests do not have to step back toward the guest behind them to put dressing on their salad. Provide one buffet line per 100 guests, with 120 being the break point.

Attended Buffet/Cafeteria. With an attended buffet or cafeteria style, guests are served by chefs or attendants. This is more elegant and provides better portion control.

Combination Buffet. Inexpensive items, such as salads, are presented buffet style, where guests help themselves. Expensive items, such as meats, are served by an attendant for portion control.

Plated Buffet. A selection of pre-plated foods is set on a buffet table for guests to choose from. This is helpful for portion control.

Action Stations. Sometimes referred to as performance stations or exhibition cooking. **Action stations** are similar to an attended buffet, except food is freshly prepared as guests wait and watch. Some common action stations include pastas, grilled meats or shrimp, omelets, crepes, sushi, flaming desserts, Caesar salad, Belgian waffles, and carved meats.

Reception. At receptions, light foods are served buffet style or are passed on trays by servers (**butler service**). Guests usually stand and serve themselves and do not usually sit down to eat. Receptions are often referred to as "Walk and Talks." Plates can add as much as one-third to food cost because people heap food on the plates. Some receptions serve only finger food (food eaten using the fingers), while others offer fork food (food eaten using a fork).

Family Style/English Service. For family style and **English service,** guests are seated, and large serving platters and bowls of food are placed on the dining table by the servers; guests pass the food around the table. A host often will carve the meat. This is an expensive style of service because surpluses must be built in.

Plated Style/American Service. For plated style and **American service,** guests are seated and served food that has been preportioned and plated in the kitchen. Food is served from the left of the guest, the meat or entree is placed directly in front of the guest at the six o'clock position, and beverages are served from the right of the guest. When the guest has finished, both plates and glassware are removed from the right. American service is the most functional, most common, most economical, most controllable, and most efficient type of service. This type of service usually has a server to guest ratio of 1:32, depending on the level of the hotel.

Preset Service. With **preset service,** some foods are already on the table when guests arrive. The most common items to preset are water, butter, bread, and appetizer and/or salad. At luncheons, where time is of the essence, the dessert is often preset as well. These are all cold items that hold up well.

Butler Service. At receptions, the term "butler" refers to having hors d'oeuvres passed on trays and the guests help themselves. At dinner, butlered is an upscale type of service, with food often passed on silver trays. Guests use serving utensils to serve themselves at the table from a platter presented by the server. (This is similar to and often confused with Russian service.)

Russian Service. There are two types of **Russian service.** With banquet Russian service, the food is fully prepared in the kitchen and all courses are served from either platters or an Escoffier dish. Tureens are used for soup and special bowls for salad. The server places the proper plate in front of the guest, who is seated. After the plates are placed, the server returns with a tray of food and, moving counterclockwise around the table, serves the food from the guest's left with the right hand. With this style of service, the server controls the amount served to each guest. With restaurant Russian service, guests are seated and foods are cooked tableside on a *rechaud* (portable cooking stove) that is on a *gueridon* (tableside cart with wheels). Servers place the food on platters (usually silver), and then guests serve themselves. Service is from the left.

Banquet French Service. For **banquet French service,** guests are seated while platters of food are assembled in the kitchen. Servers take the platters to the tables and serve from the left, placing the food on the guest's plate using two large silver forks or one fork and one spoon. Servers must be highly trained for this type of service. The use of the forks and spoons together in one hand is a skill that must be practiced. Many hotels are now permitting the use of silver salad tongs.

Cart French Service. Less commonly used for banquets (except for small VIP functions), **cart French service** is used in fine restaurants. Guests are seated, and foods are prepared tableside using a rechaud on a gueridon. Cold foods, such as salads, are prepared on the gueridon, sans rechaud. Servers plate the finished foods directly on the guest's plate, which is then placed in front of the guest from the right. Bread, butter, and salad are served from the left, while beverages are served from the right. Everything is removed from the right.

White-glove service.
Getty Images, Inc.

Hand Service. With hand service, guests are seated; there is one server, who wears white gloves, for every two guests. Foods are pre-plated. Each server carries two plates from the kitchen and stands behind the two guests assigned to him or her. At a signal from the room captain, all servings are set in front of all guests at the same time. This procedure can be used for all courses, just the main course, or just the dessert. This is a very elegant and impressive style of service used mainly for VIP events because the added labor is expensive.

A la Carte Service. For a la carte service, guests are given a choice of two or three appetizers and main courses (in the case of a steak main course, guests can order steak well done, medium, or rare). The service, however, can only be done for up to about 500 people.

Waiter Parade. The waiter parade is an elegant touch, with white-gloved servers marching into the room and parading around the perimeter carrying food on trays, often to attention-getting music and dramatic lighting. This is especially effective with a flaming baked Alaska dessert parade. The room lighting is dimmed, and a row of flaming trays carried by the waiters slowly encircles the room. When the entire room is encircled, the music stops and service starts. Guests are usually applauding at this point. (Flaming dishes should never be brought close to a guest. In this case, after the parade, the dessert would be brought to a side area, where it would be sliced and served.)

The Wave. The wave does not use servers assigned to workstations or tables; instead, all servers start at one end of the room and work straight across to the other end—for both service and plate removal. All of the servers are on one team, and the whole room is the station. This is a quick form of service—not classy, but functional when you want fast service or the servers are inexperienced. Guests do not receive individualized attention. This style is only appropriate with pre-plated foods.

Mixture of Service Styles. You can change service styles within the meal—the whole meal does not have to conform to one type of service. For example, you can have your appetizer preset, have the salads "Frenched" (dressing added after salads are placed on the table), have the main course served American, and end with a dessert buffet.

Menus

In times past, menus rarely changed. Today, change is necessary to keep pace with the changing tastes of the public. Most food trade journals run features on "What's Hot and What's Not." Table 11–2 lists some items that are generally always "hot."

Food Consumption Patterns

The most important information in deciding how much food to order is the history of the group: Who are they? Why are they here? A pretty good determination can be made based on previous years. If this is a new group or the history is not available, then consider the demographics of the attendees. Another consideration is any menu restrictions based on the guests' dietary needs.

TABLE 11–2	"Hot" Menu Items
Seasonal Foods	Locally grown produce, in season, was first popularized some years ago by Chef Alice Waters. These items include foods at their peak flavor.
Ethnic Foods	With the influx of peoples from other cultures into the United States has come unique cuisines from many areas of the world. The American palate has grown beyond the ethnic foods of the past, such as Italian, Chinese, and Mexican, to include the foods of many Asian countries, the Middle East, and South America.
High-Quality Ingredients	People may pinch pennies at the grocery store, but when they eat out at a banquet, they want the best. No longer satisfied with frozen, sweetened strawberries, they want fresh Driscoll strawberries on their shortcake. They want giant Idaho baked potatoes and Angus beef.
Fresh Ingredients	Frozen, canned, and dried foods, once seen as the newest, greatest technology, have worn out their novelty. The loss of flavors during preservation of these foods has made fresh food highly prized.
New and Unusual Ingredients	With the increased means of transportation in recent years, new foodstuffs have appeared in marketplaces that were previously unknown to most Americans. These include kiwifruit, lemongrass, Uglis, star fruit, Yukon Gold potatoes, purple potatoes, and blood oranges.
Safe Foods	Organic foods and foods free from pollution and pesticides are considered safe.
Highly Creative Presentations	Plate presentations are increasingly important. We eat with our eyes before anything hits our taste buds.
Excellent Service	Food served promptly (while still hot) and friendly, courteous service are important considerations in the enjoyment of a meal.

TABLE 11–3	Food Consumption Guidelines

Type of Reception	Amount Based on Type of Guests	Hors D'Oeuvres Needed Per Person
Two hours or less	Light	3–4 pieces
Dinner following	Moderate	5–7 pieces
	Heavy	8+ pieces
Two hours or less	Light	6–8 pieces
No dinner	Moderate	10–12 pieces
	Heavy	12+ pieces
Two to three hours	Light	8–10 pieces
No dinner	Moderate	10–12 pieces
	Heavy	16+ pieces

SOME GENERAL GUIDELINES

Guests will eat an average of seven hors d'oeuvres during the first hour because they will generally eat more at the beginning of a reception, but the amount of food consumed does depend on demographics (blue-collar, white-collar, or pink-collar guests).

White-collar workers are business types who usually wear suits and white shirts, and blue-collar workers are characterized as those who wear uniforms or work attire other than suits; pink-collar workers are females in the workforce. It is safe to assume that a group of typical truck drivers would eat more (and differently) than a group of typical secretaries.

The amount of food consumed may also depend on how many square feet of space is available for guests to move around in (smaller equals less consumption).

MENU RESTRICTIONS

Banquet servers should know the ingredients and preparation method of every item on the menu. Many attendees have allergies or are restricted from eating certain items such as sugar or salt due to health concerns. Others do not eat certain foods due to their religious restrictions, and some are vegetarians who do not eat meat. There are three basic types of vegetarians:

1. Vegetarians who will not eat red meat but will eat chicken and fish
2. Lacto-ovo vegetarians who will not eat anything that has to be killed but will eat animal by-products (cheese, eggs, milk, etc.)
3. Vegans who will not eat anything from any animal source, including animal by-products such as honey, butter, and dairy

When in doubt, assume attendees who identify themselves as vegetarian are vegans. To serve a vegan a plate of vegetables with butter and/or cheese would not be appropriate.

Other dietary restrictions are necessary for people who are lactose intolerant, which means they have difficulty digesting anything containing milk or milk products. Today, people have imposed dietary restrictions on themselves in an effort to eat in a more healthy fashion and may choose low-carbohydrate diets, high-fiber diets, etc. Religious restrictions may also impact food and diet. For example, people who maintain a kosher diet will not eat anything that is not blessed by a rabbi, will not mix dairy products with meat products, and will keep separate kitchens for dairy and for meat, so if one is catering to a kosher clientele, bacon and eggs would not be served for breakfast (or anytime for that matter).

It is a good idea to have attendees fill out a form indicating if they have any menu restrictions. This information can then be communicated to the catering manager, who will ensure that the proper number and type of alternative menu items are available. At meetings of the National Association of Catering Executives, attendees are provided with complete menus of every event, along with a form where they can indicate which meals they need to have changed.

Food and Beverage Attrition

Most planners do not like **attrition** clauses, although they benefit both planner and hotel because they set down legal obligations for both sides and establish liability limits. When a contract is signed, both parties want the food and beverage guarantee to be met, but caterers want long lead times and specificity, while planners want to wait until the last minute to give the final guarantee. If the guarantee is too high, the planner might have to pay for it in the form of attrition.

Attrition hits the planner in the pocketbook if the **guarantee** is not met. The planner agrees in the contract to buy a specific number of meals or to spend a specific amount of money on group food and beverage; the caterer's obligation is to provide the service and the food. If the guarantee is not met, the planner must pay the difference between the guarantee and the actual amount or an agreed-on percentage of the actual amount (see chapter 12 on legal issues for more information on attrition).

The planner may also lose concessions that he or she has negotiated. Function space often is provided free of charge because of the revenue the group brings into the hotel through sleeping rooms and catered events. If the revenue does not come in, the hotel can charge for services that normally would have been complimentary, such as labor; the hotel could also reassign or reduce space being held for the planner if minimums are not met.

Catering sales managers must strive to maximize revenue per available room, so they need a way to guarantee that money when booking a group. Meeting planners should know how much revenue their meeting produces before negotiating an attrition clause. Caterers should pin down how much money the group will be spending on catering instead of getting a head count, since food prices fluctuate.

When using a dollar amount guarantee, provide some flexibility as to how the money may be spent. For example, the contract could indicate that food and beverage fees would be reduced if the catered event is replaced with other business.

Amenities and Gifts

Many hotel CSMs, the DMC, and so on like to say "Thank you for your business" with a token of appreciation, which may be an in-room amenity. The meeting planner may also be offered the opportunity to send in-room amenities to meeting VIPs. When sending an in-room gift during the meeting, do not just send the customary fruit and wine basket—give some thought to the person and what he or she might like. Sending a bottle of wine to the room of a recovering alcoholic or a big box of chocolate truffles to a diabetic would be a bad move. However, something that shows the planner gave some thought to the gift will impress a VIP, so if a VIP likes a particular wine, be sure that same wine is placed in his or her room.

Cut fruit and cheese do not last, so only send whole fruit and small packaged cheeses. In areas of high humidity, open crackers go stale quickly; just include small packages. Bottled water is always appreciated. If the sender knows nothing about the client's tastes, a gift certificate for room service would give the client choices, and room service may be a luxury not normally indulged in. Or you may give the client a certificate for a massage or for the gift shop (so he or she can take items back home). Flowers are pretty, but attendees do not enjoy them because they spend little time in their rooms and flowers do not fare well on an airplane.

Beverage Events

PURPOSES

Beverage events are popular and include refreshment breaks and receptions. Beverage breaks not only provide liquid repasts and possibly a snack but also allow the attendee to get up, stretch, visit the restroom, call the office, and possibly move into another room for the next break-out session.

Receptions are slightly different because most include alcohol and probably a larger variety and quantity of food options. Purposes for receptions include:

Socializing. To loosen guests up—it is easier to sell to a relaxed potential client.

Networking. To look for a job or business leads.

CATEGORIES OF LIQUOR

The three categories of liquor are beer, wine, and spirits. Beer and wine are considered soft liquor, and spirits are considered hard liquor. There are three categories of spirits—**well brands, call brands,** and **premium brands:**

1. Well brands are sometimes called "house liquors." This is less expensive liquor, such as Kentucky Gentleman Bourbon. Well brands are served when someone does not ask for a specific brand.
2. Call brands, such as Jim Beam Bourbon or Smirnoff Vodka, are priced in the midrange and are generally asked for by name.
3. Premium brands are high-quality, expensive liquors, such as Crown Royal, Chivas Regal, or Grey Goose Vodka.

SELLING METHODS

Per Bottle   Selling per bottle is common for open bars, and poured wine at meal functions. The planner pays for all of the liquor bottles that are opened. A physical inventory is taken at the beginning and end of the function to determine liquor usage. Most hotels charge for each opened bottle, even if only one drink was poured from it. This method saves money but is inconvenient to monitor and calculate because the planner will not know the final cost until the event is over. Usually, the group's history will give some indication of how much consumption to expect. Open bottles may not be removed from the property, and unopened bottles may not be removed either unless the hotel has an off-sale liquor license. You can, however, have them delivered to a hospitality suite or to the room of a VIP to use during the meeting.

Per Drink   The per drink method is typical for a cash bar and uses tickets or a cash register for control. Normally, the price per drink is high enough to cover all relevant expenses (limes, stirrers, napkins, etc.). Individual drink prices are set to yield a standard beverage cost percentage set by the hotel, which is the amount of profit the hotel expects to make from the sale of the liquor. Cost percentages range from 12% to 18% for spirits and usually around 25% for wine. The planner will not know the final cost until the event is over.

Per Person   The per person method, which usually includes food and is common for open bars, is more expensive for the planner but involves less work and hassle. The planner chooses a plan, such as premium liquors for one hour, and then tells the caterer how many people are coming (for example, $25 per person times 500 guests equals $12,500). Costs are known ahead of time—no surprises. Tickets are collected from attendees at the door, so the guarantee is monitored.

Per Hour   The per hour method, similar to the per person method, often includes a sliding scale, with a higher cost for the first hour because guests usually eat and drink more during the first hour then levels off. You must provide a firm guarantee before negotiating a per hour charge, or you can combine per person with per hour. For example, if the charge is $25 per person for the first hour and $20 per person for the second hour, hosting 100 guests for a two-hour reception would cost $4,500 ($25 times 100 equals $2,500 and $20 times 100 equals $2,000, for a total of $4,500). No consideration is given for those who arrive late or leave early; the fee is $45 per person, regardless.

Flat Rate   The host pays a flat rate (similar to payment per bottle) for the function based on the assumption that each guest will drink about two drinks per hour for the first hour and one drink per hour thereafter. (Be sure to check the history and demographics of your group.) Costs will vary based on the number of guests who will attend; whether well, call, or premium brands are poured; and the type of food that is served.

Open Bar   With an open bar (also called a host bar), guests do not pay for their drinks; a host or sponsor pays for them. Guests usually drink what they want and as much as they want. Liquor consumption is higher because someone else is paying. The sponsor can be the meeting itself, an exhibitor, a similar organization, and so on; for example, at the Super Show, which features sporting goods, Nike may sponsor an open bar.

Cash Bar   With a cash bar (also called a no host bar), guests buy their own drinks, usually purchasing tickets from a cashier to exchange with a bartender for a drink. At small functions, the bartender may collect tickets and serve drinks, eliminating the cost of a cashier. Cashiers are usually charged as extra labor because they provide better control and speed up service, and bartenders do not have to handle dirty money and then handle glassware.

Combination Bar   When using a combination bar, a host purchases tickets and gives each attendee a certain number (usually two). If the guest wants a third drink, he or she must purchase it. Or the host can pay for the first hour, and the bar reverts to a cash bar for the second hour. This method provides free drinks to guests but retains control over costs and potential liability for providing unlimited drinks.

Limited Consumption Bar   A limited consumption bar prices by the drink, using a cash register. The host establishes a dollar amount, and when the cash register reaches that amount, the bar is closed. The host may decide to reopen as a cash bar.

Calculate Total Cost to Determine the Best Option

If the hotel charges $80 for a bottle of bourbon that yields twenty-seven 1 ¼ ounce drinks, each drink costs the client $2.96. Guests are expected to drink two drinks per hour, and there is a one-hour reception for 1,000 people.

If bourbon is purchased by the bottle, the group would cost $6,000.

If bourbon is purchased by the drink, at $4 per drink, the same group would cost $8,000.

If the event is priced at $10 per person (no food), it would cost $10,000.

As you can see, the hotel makes more money selling per person.

LABOR CHARGES

Extra charges are usually levied for bartenders and/or barbacks, cocktail servers, cashiers, security, and **corkage.** A barback is the bartender's helper—restocking liquor, keeping fresh ice, clean glasses, and so on—at the bar so the bartender will not have to do it during service hours. Corkage is the fee added to liquor brought into the hotel rather than purchased from the hotel. The hotel charges this fee to cover the cost of labor, use of the glasses (which must be delivered to the room, washed, and placed back in storage), mixers, olives, lemon peels, and so forth. Prices for the servers, cashiers, and corkage are negotiable, depending on the value of the business. For example, if a bar sells over $500 in liquor, the bartender charge may be waived.

One bar or bartender per every 100 guests is standard. If all guests are arriving at once or if there is concern about guests standing in long lines, one bar or bartender for every 50 or 75 guests can be used. Unless yours is a very lucrative group, the hotel passes on the labor charges to you.

SPIRITS

All premium brands are available in 750-milliliter and 1-liter bottles. One 750-milliliter bottle equals 20 (1 ¼ ounce) servings; a 1-liter bottle equals 27 (1 ¼ ounce) servings. Consumption will average three drinks per person during a normal reception period.

TABLE 11–4	Number of Drinks per Bottle			
		1 Ounce	**1¼ Ounces**	**1½ Ounces**
Liter	33.8 ounces	33	27	22
Fifth (750 milliliters)	25.3 ounces	25	20	16

WINE

All premium brands are available in 750-milliliter bottles and/or 1.5-liter bottles (magnums):

One 750-milliliter bottle equals five 5-ounce servings.

One 1.5-liter bottle equals ten 5-ounce servings.

Consumption will average three glasses per person during a normal reception period, assuming that 50% of the people will order wine. You should order thirty 750-milliliter bottles for every 100 guests.

Champagne should be served in a flute glass instead of the classic "coupe" because there is less surface exposed to the air and the bubbles do not escape as fast, causing the champagne to go flat (Figure 11–1).

Hospitality Suites

Hospitality suites are places for attendees to gather outside of the meeting events. These suites are normally open late in the evening, after 10:00 P.M., but occasionally around the clock. There are three types of hospitality suites:

1. Morning—continental breakfast
2. Afternoon—snacks and sodas
3. Evening—liquor and snacks

Some suites offer a full bar, others beer and wine only; some have lots of food, others only dry snacks. There may be desserts and specialty coffees. Consider ordering more food if the attendees have had an open evening.

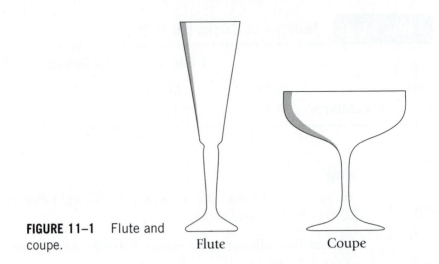

FIGURE 11–1 Flute and coupe.

Flute   Coupe

Hospitality suites usually are held in a client's suite on a sleeping room floor, are handled by room service, and are sold by catering. Sometimes they are held in a public function room and are both sold and serviced by catering. Hospitality suites can be hosted by the sponsoring organization, a chapter of the organization, an exhibitor, a nonexhibiting corporation, an allied association, or a person running for an office in the organization.

Watch for "underground hospitality suites" where unofficial parties pop up. In these types of hospitality suites, you only gain liability and lose revenue. The court case resulting from the Tailhook scandal, in which a female was groped in a hallway at a military meeting at the Las Vegas Hilton, set a precedent that a hotel can no longer claim that it does not know what is going on within the property.

Another factor to keep in mind is that liquor laws vary from state to state and county to county. You should always check the laws in your specific location, as these examples show:

- In Las Vegas and New Orleans, liquor can be sold 24/7.
- In California, liquor cannot be sold between 2 A.M. and 6 A.M.
- In Atlanta, liquor may not be served until noon on Sundays.
- In some states, liquor may not be sold at all on Sundays.

But there are generally four types of illegal liquor sales wherever you are located:

1. Sales to minors
2. Sales to intoxicated persons
3. Sales outside legal hours
4. Sales with an improper liquor license

There are on-sale licenses, off-sale licenses, and beer and wine licenses, and licenses stay with the property. For example, if your hotel has a liquor license, it is not valid in the public park across the street; the caterer would need to obtain a special temporary permit.

Planners who wish to bring their own liquor into an establishment must check local laws and be prepared to pay the establishment a per bottle corkage fee.

Rooms

SETUPS

Room setup is a critically important area to be familiar with. How the room is set up can affect the flow of service, the amount of food and beverage consumed, and even the mood of the guests. The ambiance can make or break a meal function—be it a continental breakfast or a formal dinner (Figure 11–2).

Room setup includes tables, chairs, décor, and other equipment, such as portable bars, stages, and audiovisual equipment. It is essential that you communicate *exactly* how you want the room to be set to the banquet setup manager. This is done by filling out the banquet event order (BEO) form and by using room layout software, which allows you to place tables, chairs, and other equipment into a meeting room plan. Free room layout software demos can be downloaded from the following sites:

* Meeting Matrix—http://www.meetingmatrix.com
* Optimum Settings—http://www.ceosoft.com
* Room Viewer—http://www.timesaversoftware.com

Grand Hall

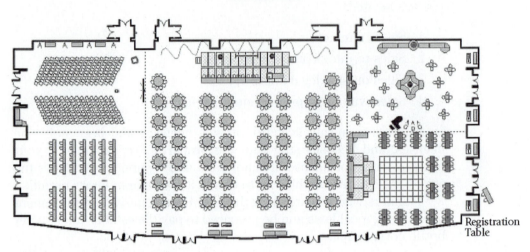

Registration
Table

FIGURE 11–2   Sample room layout.

RENTAL CHARGES

Can rental charges be waived? It varies, depending on the venue. If the event is part of a meeting with room nights, it is easier to negotiate with the hotel about dispensing with the room charge. When undertaking catering events at hotels that are handled by the catering department rather than the sales department because there are no room nights involved, a planner rarely encounters a rental fee for the space; instead, there will be a minimum sales amount on the room. The group may have to spend $50,000 to secure a ballroom for an event, which frequently means that guests eat *very* well. However, in event venues (otherwise known as off-premises venues), it depends on how the venue has set up its charge/profit schedule. Most off-site venues charge some type of fee: Some charge a rental fee, some charge an admission fee per guest, and a few charge both and then add on catering, rentals, and service costs. Which type of charge is used almost always depends on how big or profitable the event is. Everything is negotiable. At several venues, it may be possible to negotiate removing the rental charge when bringing a large or highly profitable event to the property; it varies depending on the venue. If the event is part of a meeting with room nights, there sometimes is no charge from the hotel.

SPACE REQUIREMENTS

Aisle Space   Aisles allow people to move easily around the room without squeezing through chairs and disturbing seated guests.

Banquet room set with tables for a function.
Used by permission of Paradise Light & Sound, Orlando, Florida

They also provide a buffer between the seating areas and the food and beverage areas. Aisles between tables and around food and beverage stations should be a bare minimum of 36 inches (3 feet) wide, but it would be preferable to have 48 inches. Also, leave a 3-foot (minimum) aisle around the perimeter of the room; cross aisles should be 6 feet wide. Check with the local fire marshal for local rules and regulations. Because of the major hotel fires in Las Vegas in the early 1980s, the local fire marshal must check and approve any layout for 200 or more people.

Tables   Allow 10 square feet per person at rectangular banquet tables and 12.5 square feet per person at round tables. This assumes the facility is using standard 20-inch by 20-inch chairs.

Remember to deduct space taken up for furniture before calculating the number of people. Include large sofas (found in many hospitality suites), buffet tables, portable bars, plants, décor and props, check-in tables, and so forth; also, allow 3 square feet per person for dance floors. Always remember to check local fire codes.

TABLE 11–5	Space Requirements

Space Requirements for Tables

Rounds	60 inches around	5 feet in diameter	Seats 8
	72 inches around	6 feet in diameter	Seats 10
	66 inches around	5.5 feet in diameter	Seats 8–10
Rectangle	6 feet long	30 inches wide	Seats 6
	8 feet long	30 inches wide	Seats 8
Schoolroom or classroom	6 or 8 feet long	18 or 24 inches wide	
Half-moon table	One-half round table		
Serpentine	One-quarter hollowed-out round table		

Space Requirements for Receptions

Minimum (tight)	5 ½ to 6 square feet per person
Comfortably crowded	7 ½ square feet per person
Ample room	10+ square feet per person

SERVICE REQUIREMENTS

One bartender per every 100 guests is standard. If guests will arrive all at once or if you do not want long lines, you could have one bartender for every 50 or 75 guests, but there may be an additional labor charge.

Service is critical—many excellent meals are ruined by poor service. Meal service levels can run from 1 server per 8 guests to 1 server per 40 guests. Most hotel staffing guides allow for a ratio of 1:32, but most meeting planners want 1:20 or 1:16 with either poured wine or French service.

Savvy meeting planners negotiate for the following:

General Service

Rounds of 10; 1 server for every 2 tables

Rounds of 8; 1 server for every 5 tables

1 bus person for every 3 servers

Poured Wine or French Service

Rounds of 10; 2 servers for every 3 tables

Rounds of 8; 1 server for every 2 tables

Buffet Service (1:40 Ratio)

1 bus person for every 4 servers

1 runner per 100–125 guests

French or Russian Service

Rounds of 8 or 10

1 server per table

1 buser per 3 tables

In terms of supervision, there should be one room captain as well as one section captain for every 250 guests (25 rounds of 10). The overset guarantee, which is the percentage of guests the hotel will prepare for beyond the guarantee in case additional (unexpected) people show up, is negotiable. Average overset is 5%, but you must look at the numbers, not just the percentages:

Up to 100 guests equals 10% overset

100–1,000 guests equals 5% overset

Over 1,000 guests equals 3% overset

Cocktail Servers   Cocktail servers can only carry from 12 to 16 drinks per trip. Counting the time to take the order, the time to wait for the drinks at the service bar, and the time to find the guest and deliver the drink, it takes at least 15 minutes per trip to the bar, which makes it possible to serve 48 to 64 drinks per hour. Cocktail servers are usually only used at small or VIP functions.

Service Timing   Fifteen minutes before you want to start serving, dim the lights, ring chimes, start music, open doors, and so on to get the guests to start moving to their tables.

The salad course should take from 20 to 30 minutes, depending on dressing or style of service. The main course should take from 30 to 50 minutes from serving to plate removal, and dessert should take from 20 to 30 minutes. A typical luncheon would take 1 hour and 15 minutes, while a typical dinner would take 2 hours.

TABLESCAPES

The tabletop is the stage—it sets expectations and should reflect the theme of the event. Once the guests are seated, the focus is mainly on the table, so it is imperative that it not be overlooked. The centerpiece can be low or high, with a Lucite or slender pole in the middle portion, but should not block sight lines for people sitting across the table from each other.

The term "cover" refers to the place setting and includes the placement of flatware, china, and glassware. "Napery" is the term used for all table linens, including tablecloths, overlays, napkins, and table skirting. Other décor may include ribbons, greenery, or items related to the theme of the meal. Following are some tablescape options:

Trailing flower garlands or ribbons between place settings

Different colored napkins at each cover

Different napkin folds at each cover

Creative centerpieces

Edible centerpieces (such as a basket of bread)

A garland of flowers set off this coffee station.
Dorling Kindersley Media Library

Major props for tablescapes can be rented from prop houses, service contractors, or party stores or be provided by the hotel or club. Small decorative props can be found in many places:

Junk, Goodwill, or antique shops

Auto supply stores

Toy or crafts stores

Garage sales or flea markets

Garden centers

Ethnic food stores or import shops

Travel agencies (destination posters)

Sports clubs or sporting goods stores

Medical supply stores

Military surplus stores

Summary

Food and beverage is an integral part of most meetings. Astute planning can save a tremendous amount of money; knowing what is negotiable and how to negotiate is critical. Food and beverage events create memories and provide a necessary service beyond being a refueling stop. While most attendees do not specify food and beverage events as a reason for attending a meeting, when asked later about a meeting, they will often rave (or complain) about these events based on the food and beverage. Catered events can set the tone of the meeting and create great memories that can result in future business, not only from the planner but also from every guest in attendance.

Key Words and Terms

For definitions, see the Glossary or go to http://glossary. convention industry.org.

Action station	Banquet French service
American service	Buffet
Attrition	Butler service

Call brand	Off-premises catering
Cart French service	On-premises catering
Catered event	Premium brand
Corkage	Preset service
English service	Room setup
Function	Russian service
Guarantee	Well brand

Review and Discussion Questions

1. What is the first step for a meeting planner when planning for an off-premises event? List five types of functions and give a brief description of each.
2. Describe how family style/English service and plated/American style service differ.
3. What is the most important information to consider when deciding how much food to order for a group?
4. What is the average number of hors d'oeuvres a guest will eat during the first hour of an event?
5. What are the three categories of liquor?
6. What is the function of a hospitality suite, and what are the three types?
7. What important aspects of an event are affected by how the room is set up?
8. When catering an event at a hotel and no room nights are involved, which department handles the booking of the event?
9. Why is it imperative that the tabletop not be overlooked?

About the Chapter Contributor

Patti J. Shock is a professor and chair of the Tourism and Convention Administration Department in the Harrah College of Hotel Administration at the University of Nevada–Las Vegas. She has written three textbooks on catering and teaches catering online as well as on campus. She was named one of the "25 Most Influential People in the Meetings Industry" by *Meeting News* magazine in 2002 and one of the "10 Most Powerful Women in the Convention Industry" by *Successful Meetings* in 2002.

CHAPTER **12**

Legal Issues in the MEEC Industry

Knowledge of legal issues will help to keep MEEC organizers out of court.

Dorling Kindersley Media Library

Chapter Objectives

This chapter provides the reader with an understanding of the following:

- Fine points of negotiation between the sponsor or organizer and suppliers
- Concept of risk management and ways to deal with risk
- Taxation
- Employment laws
- Concept of intellectual property and how it relates to MEEC
- Ethics and unique applications in MEEC

Chapter Outline

Introduction

Negotiation

   Information

   Flexibility

Contracts

   Negotiations

   Attrition Clauses

   Cancellation Provision

   Termination Provision

Risk

Americans with Disabilities Act

Intellectual Property

   Recording or Videotaping of Speakers

Labor Issues

Ethics

   Supplier Relations

   Intellectual Material

   Gifts

Introduction

Whether we like it or not, we live in a very litigious society. Thus, legal issues are becoming increasingly important, especially in the meetings, expositions, events, and conventions (MEEC) industry. There are legal aspects or issues in almost everything we do as meeting planners and organizers. Contracts are a part of virtually every event and have become increasingly complex—mere humans have difficulty reading them! We enter into negotiations regardless of whether we are the buyer (e.g., event sponsors, organizers) or suppliers (e.g., hotels, destination management companies, caterers). We have to be concerned about risks such as acts of God, injuries to people, and failures to perform; we also have to be concerned with national, state, and local laws that impact how we put on an event, whom we employ, and the entertainment we use. In this chapter, we delve into many of these issues and provide some insight into this important area. Remember that this chapter does not take the place of consulting with an attorney who is knowledgeable about MEEC and licensed to practice in your jurisdiction.

Negotiation

Negotiation is the process by which a meeting planner and a hotel representative (or other supplier) reach an agreement on the terms and conditions that will govern their relationship before, during, and after a meeting, convention, exposition, or event. While many believe that the goal of a negotiation is to create a win-win situation (one in which both parties feel satisfied about the outcome), in fact the real "winner" may be the party who is better prepared entering the negotiation and who has a good idea of what he or she wants. In this regard, hotel representatives generally have an advantage over a planner, since they usually know more about a planner's organization than the planner knows about the lodging industry or the specific hotels under consideration.

Many hoteliers, particularly those who have been in the industry for many years, sum up meeting negotiations with this simple maxim: "**Dates, rates, and space**—you can only have two." Following this maxim, the planner can get the dates and meeting space he or she wants for a meeting but may have to give a little on the rate.

In reality, what is negotiable includes not only space, room rates, and meeting dates but also such things as complimentary room ratios, cutoff dates, rates after cutoff, attrition or cancellation clauses, meeting or exhibit space rental, comp suites, staff rates, limo service, audiovisual rates, VIP amenities, parking fees, and food and beverage provisions. In short, *everything* about a hotel (supplier) contract is negotiable.

There are almost as many approaches to negotiating strategy as there are negotiators. One negotiator has offered these tips:

- *Do Your Homework.* Develop a game plan of the outcomes sought, and prioritize your needs and wants. Learn as much about the other side's position as you can.
- *Keep Your Eyes on the Prize.* Do not forget the outcomes sought.

Negotiating is a difficult and oftentimes frustrating experience.
Dorling Kindersley Media Library

- *Leave Something on the Table.* When everything can't be finalized, it may provide an opportunity to come back later and renew the negotiations.
- *Do Not Be the First One to Make an Offer.* Letting the other person make the first move sets the outside parameters for the negotiation.
- *Bluff, But Do Not Lie.* When negotiating, you can bluff, but you must tell the truth.
- *When There Is a Roadblock, Find a More Creative Path.* Thinking outside the box often leads to a solution.
- *Timing Is Everything.* Remember that time always works against the person who does not have it and that 90% of negotiation usually occurs in the last 10% of the time allocated.
- *Listen, Listen, Listen . . . and Do Not Get Emotional.* Letting emotions rule a negotiation will cause one to lose sight of what result is important.

If a meeting planner is going to successfully negotiate with a hotel, the planner should:

- Understand the competitive marketplace in which the hotel operates, for instance, its strengths, weaknesses, and occupancy patterns.
- Understand how a hotel evaluates business.
- Position the meeting in its best perspective, using detailed information to support this approach.

To understand how a hotel approaches a meeting negotiation, the planner must first know about the hotel. Some of the necessary information is obvious:

- *Location*. Is the hotel downtown, near an airport, or close to a convention center?
- *Type*. Is the hotel a resort with a golf course, tennis court, and other amenities? Is it a convention hotel with a great deal of meeting space or a small venue with limited meeting facilities?

However, some of the information that is important to know is not so obvious and may in fact change depending on the time of year. For example, it is important to know the mix between the hotel's transient business (that derived from individual business guests or tourists) and groups; within the group sector, it is valuable to know how much business is derived from corporate, government, and association sources. It is also important to know what the hotel regards as high season, when room demand is highest, and low season, when demand is at its annual low. This information is important because it helps the planner understand the hotel's position in the negotiation process, and it may provide some helpful hints in structuring a proposal to meet the hotel's needs.

Seasonal fluctuations may be driven by outside factors, such as events in the city in which the hotel is located. For example, an informed planner will know that it is difficult to book rooms in New Orleans during Mardi Gras or during that city's annual Jazz Fest (in late April and early May) because hotels can sell their rooms to individual tourists at higher rates than to groups. Many hotels in Palm Springs, California, are heavily booked during spring break; therefore, favorable meeting rates may be difficult to obtain then.

The arrival and departure patterns of the majority of a hotel's guests are also important for a planner to know. For example, a hotel in Las Vegas is generally difficult to book for weekend meetings, since

Jazz Fest draws upwards of 100,000 attendees per day to New Orleans in late April.
Photo by George G. Fenich, Ph.D.

that city attracts large numbers of individual visitors who come to spend the weekend. A hotel that caters to many individual business guests may have greater availability on Friday and Saturday nights, when business travelers are not there. Nationally, occupancy for typical hotels is lowest on Sunday evenings and highest on Wednesdays.

While hotels generate revenue from a variety of sources—and recently have become more sophisticated in analyzing these "profit centers"—the primary source of hotel income is sleeping room revenue; one industry research report estimates that, on the whole, more than 67% of all hotel revenue is generated from sleeping rooms. Sleeping room revenue is also profitable, with more than 73% of the income going to the hotel's bottom line as gross profit. This profit figure does not take into account expenses for marketing, engineering, general and administrative overhead, or any items related to debt service, such as mortgage payments and insurance. While food and beverage operations are the second largest source of revenue, this source is far less profitable, with about 25% being recorded as profit.

Hotels set their sleeping room rates—at least the published or so-called **rack rates**—in a number of ways. First, the hotel wants to achieve a total return on its investment. However, since nearly 50% of all rooms in all hotels are sold at less than rack rate, hotels vary their actual rates depending on a number of supply and demand factors, including time of year (which is a function of demand).

Most hotels have adopted the concept of **yield management,** also called revenue management, pioneered by the airline industry. In this approach, hotels are able to vary their rates almost daily, depending on the actual and anticipated demand for rooms at a particular time. This yield management concept may have some negative impact on meeting planners. For example, a planner who books a meeting fifteen to eighteen months in advance may find that as the meeting nears, total hotel room utilization is lower than the hotel anticipated, so the hotel (hoping to generate additional revenue) starts to promote special pricing; this may result in rooms costing less than the price offered to the meeting sponsor. A contractual provision prohibiting this practice—which many hotels will not agree to—or at least giving the meeting sponsor credit toward his or her room block for rooms booked at these lower prices can help take the sting out of yield management practices. When negotiating with a meeting planner, a hotel sales representative keeps in mind the hotel's booking criteria and then considers the potential business as a "package," that is, the total revenue that a meeting or event can generate for the hotel and the cost of generating that income.

Some meetings are space intensive—in other words, a significant number of meeting or function rooms are needed. That may be acceptable to a hotel if the meeting is going to utilize all or a major share of available sleeping rooms, but it may not be acceptable if the sleeping room block is too small in relation to the meeting rooms used. This, in effect, prohibits the hotel from using its available meeting rooms to entice other group business. This rooms-to-space ratio is one of the more important measures that a hotel uses to evaluate potential business.

While sleeping room utilization generates the major share of hotel revenue, a food and beverage function is also important, but only if it is the "right" kind of food and beverage function, since not all functions are equal in value. For example, a seated dinner for 100 people is worth more to a hotel—in revenue and profit—than a coffee break or continental breakfast for the same number of people.

Hotels also factor into their evaluation the type of organization sponsoring the meeting. For example, the hotel knows from experience that certain types of meeting attendees are likely to spend more on hotel restaurant meals than other types of attendees, who may venture outside the property for meals at more expensive restaurants. From experience, a hotel is also able to estimate the number of attendees who will not show up or who will check out early. This deprives the hotel of revenue that on the face of the contract it might have expected to generate. A meeting planner who wishes to strengthen his or her negotiating position with a hotel should keep two words in mind: information and flexibility.

INFORMATION

As indicated, a hotel may base its evaluation of a meeting, especially one it has never hosted before, on its perception of the industry or profession represented by the meeting sponsor. Thus, the sponsor can counter any negative impressions, or buttress positive ones, by providing the hotel with as much information as possible on the sponsor's meeting history.

Data pertaining to previous meeting room blocks and subsequent room utilization, total spending on sleeping rooms or on food and beverage, or utilization of ancillary services such as telephones and in-room movies is especially helpful. The hotel where the meeting is conducted can supply this information; the best way to ensure that it is provided at the conclusion of a meeting is to indicate in the meeting contract that the sponsor's master account will only be paid when the requested information is supplied.

When analyzing how much a meeting is worth from a financial standpoint, many planners overlook "in conjunction with" activities, which technically are not part of the meeting but would not occur if the meeting did not take place. For example, some vendors rent suites for hospitality purposes during a meeting; while these do not appear on a master account, they represent a portion of the total meeting package just as much as a sponsor-hosted event. The planner should be sure to include in his or her contract a requirement that the hotel provide this information after a meeting so that the requirement can be utilized for future events. Thus, the planner should indicate in the contract all the activities directly and indirectly associated with the event. These can include:

- Sleeping rooms
- Meeting rooms
- Catered events
- Equipment rental

Suites like this one are sometimes rented by exhibitors and vendors to host parties for clients.

PhotoLibrary.com

- Business services
- Recreational events
- Historical information on group (food, drink, and entertainment)

Data comes in two forms: hard and soft. Examples of **hard data** include financial information and room usage; examples of **soft data** include **profiles** of attendees. A meeting of meeting planners, for which a hotel can showcase itself to others for the possibility of future business, may be worth more than a meeting of building engineers, who are not in a position to utilize the hotel for later meetings.

FLEXIBILITY

A planner can also gain some bargaining leverage with a hotel by being flexible in his or her requests. For example, if a planner understands that the meeting's space-to-rooms ratio is greater than customary, the planner can help his or her position by altering the program format, eliminating 24-hour holds on meeting or function space and allowing the hotel to sell the space in unused hours.

Changing arrival and departure dates to more closely fit the hotel's occupancy pattern can also lead to a successful negotiation. Moving the meeting forward or backward one or more weeks can also result in savings, especially if the preferred time coincides with a period of high sleeping room demand.

Contracts

In far too many instances, **contracts** for meetings, conventions, and trade shows—and the ancillary services provided in connection with these events—contain self-serving statements, lack specificity, and fail to reflect the total negotiation between the parties. This is understandable since neither meeting planners nor hotel sales representatives generally receive training in the legal rules governing these agreements.

Before one can understand the nuances of meeting contracts, it is important to learn the basic elements of contract law. By definition in *The Meeting Planner's Legal Handbook* (Goldberg, 2003), first-year law students learn that a contract is

> [a]n agreement between two or more persons consisting of a promise or mutual promises which the law will enforce, or the performance of which the law recognizes as a duty. (p. 1-1)

A contract need not be called a contract but can be referred to as an agreement, a letter of agreement, a memorandum of understanding, and sometimes a letter of intent or a proposal. The title of the document or understanding is not important—its contents are. For example, if a document called a proposal sets forth details of a meeting and contains the legal elements of a contract, it becomes a binding contract when signed by both parties.

Following are the essential elements of a contract:

- An offer by one party
- The acceptance of the offer as presented
- The **consideration** (the price negotiated and paid for the agreement)

Although consideration is usually expressed in monetary terms, it not need be—for example, mutual promises are often treated as consideration in a valid contract.

Offers can be terminated prior to acceptance in one of several ways:

- At the expiration of a specified time (e.g., "This offer is only good for 24 hours.")
- At the expiration of a reasonable time period
- On specific revocation by the offeror (in this case, however, the revocation must be communicated to the offeree to be effective)

A rejection of the offer by the offeree or the proposal of a counteroffer terminates the original offer, but a request for additional information about the offer is not construed as a rejection of the offer. For example, if an individual responds to an offer by saying, "I accept, with the following addition," that is not really an acceptance but the proposal of a counteroffer, which the original offeror must then consider and either accept or reject.

Often, a meeting contract proposal from a hotel will contain a specified termination period for the offer. These offers are usually couched in the phrase "tentative first option" or in similar wording. Because the meeting sponsor pays or promises nothing for this "option," it is (in reality) nothing more than a contract offer, which must be specifically accepted by the meeting planner. There is no legal obligation on the part of the hotel to keep the option or offer open for the time period stated.

In a meeting context, the hotel or other venue is usually the offeror—that is, the written agreement is generally proposed—after some preliminary negotiation by the hotel. The meeting sponsor becomes the offeree, but typically a counteroffer is made.

In order for an offer to be accepted, the acceptance must be unequivocal and in the same terms as the offer. Any deviation from the offer's terms is not acceptance; it is a counteroffer, which must then be accepted by the original offeror in order for a valid contract to exist.

Acceptance must be communicated to the offeror using the same means as the offeror used. In other words, if the offer is made in writing, the acceptance must be in writing. Mere silence on the part of the offeree is never construed as acceptance, and an offeror cannot impose an agreement on the other party by stating that the contract will be assumed if no response is given by a specified date.

As indicated, consideration is the price negotiated and paid for the agreement. While consideration generally involves money paid for the other party's promise to perform certain functions—for example, money paid to a hotel for the provision of sleeping rooms, meeting space, and food and beverage functions—it could also be an exchange of mutual promises, as in a barter situation.

Consideration must be what the law regards as "sufficient," not from a monetary standpoint but from the standpoint of whether the act or return promise results in a benefit to the promisor or a detriment to the promisee. The fairness of the agreed exchange is legally irrelevant; thus, the law is not concerned about whether one party overpaid for what he or she received. One need not make an affirmative promise or payment of money; forbearance—for instance, not doing something that someone is legally entitled to do—can also be consideration in a contract. It is important that both promises must be legally enforceable to constitute valid consideration. For example, a promise to commit an illegal act is not consideration because the law will not require one to commit an illegal act.

Although a contract does not have to be in writing to be enforceable, every law student learns that it is better to have a written document because there can be less chance for a misunderstanding about the terms of the agreement. Under what is called the Statute of Frauds, however, some contracts must be in writing to be enforceable. This statute was first passed in England in 1677 and in one form or another has become a part of the law of virtually every state in the United States. The exception is Louisiana, where law is based on French Napoleonic code.

Among the agreements that must be in writing are contracts that are for the sale or lease of real estate and contracts that are not to be performed within one year of the agreement. The latter includes contracts for meetings and other events that are to be held more than one year in the future; the former could also include a meeting contract since the agreement might be construed as a sponsor's "lease" of hotel space. The law requires these contracts to be in writing because they are viewed as more important documents than "ordinary" agreements. However, as indicated, planners are strongly encouraged to put all contracts in writing to avoid the possibility of misunderstandings.

A valid written contract must contain the identity of the parties, an identification or recitation of the subject matter and terms of agreement, and a statement of consideration. Often, where the consideration may not be obvious, a contract will state that it is entered into for "good and valuable consideration, the receipt and sufficiency of which are acknowledged by the parties."

When a contract is in writing, it is generally subject to the so-called parol evidence or four corners rule of interpretation. Thus, where the writing is intended to be the complete and final expression of the rights and duties of the parties, evidence of prior oral or written negotiations or agreements or contemporaneous oral agreements cannot be considered by a court charged with interpreting the contract. Many contracts contain what is often called an "entire agreement" clause, which specifies that the written document contains the entire agreement between the parties and supersedes all previous oral or written negotiations or agreements.

Parol evidence (evidence of an oral agreement) can be used in limited instances, especially where the plain meaning of words in the written document may be in doubt. A court will generally construe a contract most strongly against the party that prepared the written document, and if there is a conflict between printed and handwritten words or phrases, the latter will prevail.

Many contracts, especially meeting contracts, contain addenda prepared at the same time or sometimes subsequent to the signing of the contract. In cases where the terms of an addendum differ from those of the contract, the addendum generally prevails, although it is a good idea when using an addendum to specifically provide that in the event of differences, the addendum will prevail.

Planning and executing a meeting may involve the negotiation of several contracts. Obviously, the major—and perhaps most important—agreement is the one with the hotel and/or trade show facility. However, there can also be agreements covering a myriad of ancillary services, such as temporary employees, security, audiovisual equipment, destination management companies (e.g., tours and local transportation), entertainment, outside food and beverage, exhibitor services or decorating, and housing bureaus. Moreover, agreements may be negotiated with "official" transportation providers such as travel agencies, airlines, and rental car companies.

NEGOTIATIONS

When negotiating meeting contracts—or any agreements—it is wise to keep some general rules in mind. While a good contract negotiation is a win-win situation, providing something for each party, the real "winner" in a negotiation is usually the one who is best prepared and/or the one who has the best bargaining leverage. The following general rules will help with the negotiation of a meeting contract:

- *Go into the Negotiations with a Plan.* A skilled negotiator knows his or her bottom line, that is, what is really wanted and what proposals can be given up to reach a compromise result.
- *Always Go into a Contract Negotiation with an Alternative Location or Service Provider in Mind.* Bargaining leverage is better if the other party knows you can go somewhere else with your business.
- *Be Thorough.* Put everything negotiated in the contract, and do not be afraid to utilize an addendum, provided that it is referred to in the body of the contract. Develop your own contract if necessary.
- *Do Not Assume Anything.* Meeting industry personnel change frequently, and oral agreements or assumptions can be easily forgotten or misunderstood.
- *Be Specific.* For example, do not state "Food and beverage prices will be guaranteed (or negotiated) 12 to 18 months out." Instead, specify that "Food and beverage prices will be guaranteed (or negotiated) 12 months prior to the meeting."
- *Beware of Language that Sounds Acceptable But Is Not Specific.* For example, what does a "tentative first option" mean? Words such as "reasonable," "anticipated," and "projected" should be avoided, since their meaning is different for different people.
- *Do Not Accept Something Just Because It Is Preprinted on the Contract or the Proposal Is Given to You by the Other Party.* Everything is negotiable.
- *Read the Small Print.* For example, the boilerplate language about indemnification of parties in the event of negligence can make a major difference in the resolution of liability after an accident or injury.
- *Look for Mutuality in the Contract's Provisions.* For example, do not sign a contract in which the "hold harmless" clause protects only one of the parties—such provisions should be applicable to both parties. And never give one party the unilateral right to do anything, such as change the location of the meeting rooms without consent of the meeting sponsor.

In addition to these general rules applicable to all contract negotiations, there are some special rules about hotel contracts that should also be kept in mind:

- Remember that a meeting contract provides a "package" of funds to a hotel. Think in terms of overall financial benefit to the hotel (its total income from room rates, food and beverage, and so on), and allocate this to the organization's benefit.
- Never sign a contract in which major items (e.g., room rates) are left to future negotiation. Future rates can always be set as a percentage of then-current rack rates or as a predetermined increase over existing rates (such as the Bureau of Labor Statistics Consumer Price Index, officially called the "Consumer Price Index for All Urban Consumers," or CPI-U). You may provide for a decrease in rates if the market falls, although that may be unlikely. Also indicate the specific date when final rates are to be determined. For example, a contract could indicate that the room rate (if not guaranteed) is to include the increase over the CPI-U, a certain percent off the then-current rack rate, or 5% per year over the current group rate, whichever is less.
- Specify special room rates—such as for staff and speakers—and indicate any upgrades for them. Indicate whether these are included in the complimentary room formula, and specify what that formula is.
- Remember that while it is preferable to have specific meeting and function rooms designated in the contract, they should be assigned at least six to nine months prior to the meeting, depending on the time of the first promotional mailing. Do not permit a change in assigned meeting rooms without approval of the meeting sponsor.
- Provide the ability to cancel a meeting without penalty or damages if:
  - Hotel ownership, management, or brand affiliation (often called the "flag") is changed.
  - The meeting outgrows hotel space or substantially shrinks in size.
  - The hotel does not perform satisfactorily at an earlier meeting (e.g., in the event of a multiyear contract with the same property).

- There is an adverse change in the hotel's quality rating, as measured by the American Automobile Association or the Mobil Travel Guide.
- Specify the payment in dollars (not percentages of something) and base it on the hotel's lost profit rather than lost revenue if a cancellation clause will trigger a monetary payment to the hotel. When lost room revenue is involved, make sure to measure lost sales against the normal occupancy for the particular time of the year, not against the hotel's capacity. Damages should not be payable if the hotel resells the space. While many contract drafters strive for mutuality in provisions, there is a difference of opinion with regard to specified damages in a contract for cancellation by the hotel. Some believe this is important; others point out that it only provides the hotel with a predetermined figure that it can use to buy out of a deal and that it may not actually reflect the true damages to the meeting sponsor of hotel cancellation.
- Do not agree to any changes that are not spelled out either in the contract or in a later addendum. If an addendum is used, make sure it references the underlying agreement; if it is signed at the time of the agreement, make sure the agreement references the addendum. Be sure that all documents are signed by individuals who are authorized to bind the parties.

One of the most frequently overlooked yet most important parts of a hotel contract is the names of the contracting parties. While the meeting's sponsor is listed (an independent planner should always sign as agent for the sponsor or have an authorized representative of the sponsor sign), the name of the hotel is (in almost all cases) simply listed as the name on the hotel marquee (e.g., Sheraton Boston). But the hotel's name is merely a trade name—that is, the name under which the property's owner or management company does business. In today's hotel environment, it may actually be a franchise of a national chain operated by a company that the planner has never heard of. For example, one of the country's largest hotel management companies is Interstate Hotels & Resorts, Inc. Included in the more than 300 hotels it manages are properties operating under the following chain names: Marriott, Holiday Inn, Hilton, Sheraton, and Radisson. Thus, if a contract with one of Interstate's properties simply states that it is with the "Gaithersburg (MD) Marriott," the planner might never know that the actual contracting party is Interstate Hotels & Resorts.

Every meeting contract should contain the following provision, usually as the introductory paragraph:

> This Agreement dated_____ is between (official legal name of entity), a (name of state) (corporation) (partnership) doing business as (name of hotel) and having its principal place of business at (address of contracting party, not hotel) and (name of meeting sponsor), a (name of state) (corporation) (partnership) having its principal place of business at (address of meeting sponsor).

Attrition, cancellation, and termination provisions for a hotel are frequently confusing. If not carefully drafted, a written agreement can lead to many problems (and much expense) when a meeting sponsor does not fill its room block or wishes to change its mind for some reason.

ATTRITION CLAUSES

Clauses dealing with **attrition** (sometimes also referred to as performance or slippage clauses) provide for the payment of damages to the hotel when a meeting sponsor fails to fully utilize the room block specified in the contract. Most hotels regard the contracted room block as a commitment by the meeting sponsor to fill the number of room nights specified. However, in at least one case, a court determined that the room block did not represent a commitment by the meeting sponsor; that decision was predicated, in part, on contract language that indicated that room reservations would be made by individuals and not the meeting sponsor.

A well-written attrition provision should provide the sponsoring organization with the ability to reduce the room block by a specified amount (e.g., 10%–20%) up to a specified time prior to the meeting (e.g., six to twelve months) without incurring damages. Thereafter, damages should accrue only if the sponsor fails to occupy a specified percentage (e.g., 85%–90%) of its adjusted (not the original) room block. Occupancy should be measured on a cumulative room night basis, not on a night-by-night basis.

Because hotels sometimes offer rates to the general public that are lower than those available to the meeting attendees as part of special promotional packages, it is important that the meeting room pickup be measured by all attendance, regardless of the rate paid. This may involve some extra work on the part of the hotel and the meeting sponsor, but the result could save the organization money, especially if the meeting attendance is not as good as expected. For example, the meeting contract could include language similar to the following:

> Group shall receive credit for all rooms used by attendees, regardless of the rate paid or the method of booking. Hotel shall cooperate with Group in identifying these attendees and shall charge no fee for assisting Group.

Using this language, an organization would submit its meeting registration list to the hotel and ask that the hotel match the list against those guests who are in-house at the time. An alternate approach, which many hotels reject, is to have the hotel give the group its in-house guest list and have the group do the matching.

Damages triggered by the failure to meet a room block commitment should be specified in dollars, not measured by a percentage of some vague figure such as "anticipated room revenue." The latter may provide the hotel with an opportunity to include estimated spending on such things as telephone calls and in-room movies. The specified damages should be based on the hotel's lost profit, not its lost revenue. With sleeping rooms, for example, the average industry profit margin is 75%–80%, so the per-room attrition fee should not exceed 80% of the group's single room rate; the industry standard for food and beverage profit is 25%–30%. In any event, damages for failure to meet a room block commitment should never be payable if the hotel is able to resell the rooms. The contract should impose a specific requirement on the hotel to try and resell the rooms and, if possible, require the hotel to resell the rooms in the organization's room block first.

Attrition clauses often appear in the portion of a contract that discusses meeting room rental fees, with the contract providing that meeting room rental fees will be imposed, typically on a sliding scale basis, if the room block is not filled. If the clause appears in conjunction with meeting room rental, it should not also appear somewhere else, resulting in a double charge, and language should be inserted making it clear that the meeting room rental fee is the only charge to be imposed in the event that the room block is not completely utilized.

Some meeting sponsors have attempted to insert a provision that is, in essence, the reciprocal of an attrition clause. Such a provision would state that if the group exceeds its room block by a specified percentage (usually the same as the attrition percentage), the hotel would provide a monetary payment of a specified amount to the sponsor's master account, recognizing the additional revenue generated by the larger than anticipated attendance. Hotels, however, have been generally reluctant to agree to such a provision, even though it can be argued that it is merely the reciprocal for damages for failure to fill a room block.

CANCELLATION PROVISION

The cancellation provision provides for damages should the meeting be canceled for reasons other than those specified, either in the same clause or in the termination provision. More often than not, this provision in a hotel-provided agreement is one-sided—it provides damages to the hotel in the event the meeting sponsor cancels. A properly drafted agreement should provide for damages in the event that either party cancels without a valid reason. However, as indicated previously, some contract drafters believe damages should not be specified in the event of a hotel cancellation because it provides the hotel with an amount that it can use to buy out of an agreement.

The meeting sponsor should not have the right to cancel solely to book the meeting in another hotel or another city, and the hotel should not cancel and then book another, more lucrative meeting in place of the one contracted for. However, a meeting sponsor should be able to cancel, without payment of damages, if the hotel ownership, management, or brand affiliation changes; if the meeting size outgrows the hotel; if the hotel's quality rating (as measured by the American Automobile Association or Mobil Travel Guide) changes; or if there are other reasons that make it inappropriate or impractical to hold the meeting there. The latter language should be broad enough to cover so-called boycott situations, where a group decides not to hold a meeting in a particular location because of action taken by the state legislature. As an example, the sponsor of a major shooting sports trade show (SHOT) canceled the event after the sponsoring city sued gun manufacturers that were the show's major exhibitors. In some cases, cancellation is provided without damages as long as it is done within a specified time (e.g., two to three years) prior to the meeting. This gives the hotel ample opportunity to resell the space.

The damages triggered by a cancellation are sometimes stated on a sliding scale basis, with greater damages being paid the closer to the meeting date the cancellation occurs. Damages should be expressed as "liquidated damages" or a cancellation fee, not as a penalty, since the law generally does not recognize penalty provisions. As with damages in an attrition clause, damages should be expressed in dollar amounts, not room revenue (so that sales tax can be avoided) and should be payable only if the hotel cannot resell the space.

TERMINATION PROVISION

Sometimes called a **force majeure** or **act of God** clause, the termination provision permits either party to terminate the contract without damages if fulfillment of the obligations imposed in the agreement is rendered impossible by occurrences outside the control of either party. This usually includes such things as labor strikes, severe weather, and transportation difficulties. This provision sometimes contains the "inappropriate or impractical" situation referred to in the discussion of cancellation provisions. However, many hotels seek to limit termination to situations where performance becomes illegal or impossible, so some negotiation is usually required.

Contracts provided to planners by hotels generally vary significantly from property to property, even within the same chain. Some of the variance can be attributed to the fact that some chain properties are managed by outside parties, making standardization difficult. Often, however, it has been the result of a lack of attention to the meeting contracting process by the chains themselves. Some hotels have resisted development of standard contracts, saying that all meetings are different and thus one contract cannot fit all. More recently, though, most major hotel chains have adopted or are considering standard agreements, even though some of the provisions contain multiple options for use by sales representatives.

Because there are differences in contracts supplied by hotels and because it is often so easy for planners (even experienced ones) to overlook key elements of a contract, some meeting sponsors are developing their own standard contract. While many meeting sponsors may be unsure of the costs involved in having a competent attorney prepare this type of document, such costs are minimal when compared with the time (and therefore expense) involved in reviewing each and every contract proposed by a hotel, whether the review is conducted by legal counsel or by a meeting planner or by another staff member.

A sponsor's development of its own contract will ensure that its particular needs are met and will minimize the chances of subsequent legal problems caused by a misunderstanding of the terms of the agreement. No matter how carefully a contract is written, disputes may occur either because the parties might disagree as to their individual rights and obligations or because one of the parties may perform less than had been promised. These controversies seldom involve precedent-setting legal issues; rather, they concern an evaluation of facts and interpretation of contract terms. When these differences arise, parties often prefer to settle them privately and informally in the kind of business-like way that encourages continued business relationships.

Sometimes, however, such resolution is not possible. This leaves the aggrieved party with three options: forget the possibility of reaching a solution and walk away from the problem, go to court and sue, or resolve the dispute through other means. Going to court can be an expensive and time-consuming proposition, with crowded court dockets delaying a decision for several months or (in some cases) several years. Counsel fees can mount up quickly, especially if extensive pretrial proceedings are involved. Depending on the court's location, one of the parties may have to expend additional fees for travel expenses. Since court cases are matters of public record, potentially adverse publicity may result.

For this reason, arbitration is gaining favor as a means of settling disputes. Arbitration is defined as "settlement of a dispute by a person or persons chosen to hear both sides and come to a decision" (*Webster's New Universal Unabridged Dictionary*). Under rules administered by the American Arbitration Association, arbitration is designed for quick, practical, and inexpensive settlements. It is, at the same time, an orderly proceeding, governed by rules of procedure and standards of conduct prescribed by law. Either party can utilize lawyers, but there is a minimum of pretrial procedures. If arbitration is chosen as the dispute mechanism procedure in the contract, the parties also generally agree that the results are binding, that is, the decision cannot be appealed to a court of law. The contract should also specify the location of the arbitration. Arbitration is not generally a matter of public record, so all of the proceedings can remain private. For this reason, arbitration, often called alternative dispute resolution, is favored by many hotels.

While the filing fee required to commence an arbitration proceeding is generally higher—often considerably higher—than that required to begin litigation in the courts, the overall cost of arbitration is frequently significantly lower because there is no extensive pretrial maneuvering and because attorneys are often discouraged or even prohibited from participating as representatives of the parties. The downside to arbitration is that some believe arbitrators may often "split the difference" in a dispute, seeking an equitable solution rather than following the letter of the law.

If the parties choose arbitration as a means of settling disputes, the choice should be made before disagreements arise and language governing the arbitration option should be included in the meeting contract. The contract should include the location of the arbitration proceeding. If arbitration is not selected, the contract should spell out which state's law (e.g., where the meeting took place or where the meeting sponsor is located) will be utilized to resolve a court dispute. Under the American system of justice, each party to a court suit or an arbitration proceeding is required to bear the costs of its own attorneys unless the agreement provides that the winning party is entitled to have the loser pay its attorneys' fees and costs.

Finally, a well-drafted contract should specify the damages to be awarded in the event of a breach by either party. Such an approach takes the decision out of the hands of a judge or an arbitrator and leaves the dispute resolver to determine only whether a breach of the agreement occurred. Damages are typically stated as "liquidated damages," that is, damages that the parties agree in advance will be the result of a breach. Courts will generally not honor a contract provision that imposes a "penalty" on the one breaching the agreement, so that term should be avoided.

Risk

All meetings involve an element of risk. The best way for a planner to manage this is to first understand what types of risk are faced. In general, all risk falls into the following four categories:

1. *Contractual Risk.* The planner voluntarily and willingly undertakes contractual risk by signing an agreement that calls for certain tasks to be performed.
2. *Operational Risk.* This operational risk occurs as a result of conducting a meeting or event and includes such areas as liquor and host liability.
3. *Negligent Occurrence.* Something that happens because one party did (or did not) take a certain action would be a negligent occurrence.
4. *Act of God.* Damages that occur because of tornadoes, hurricanes, earthquakes, and other natural disasters are the result of acts of God.

After one understands what might happen, the risk can be managed in a number of ways. First, the risk can be avoided; for instance, the planner simply decides that conducting a risky endeavor is simply not worth the benefit that might accrue. Second, the risk can be transferred to another party involved in the transaction. This occurs when, for example, a planner states in a contract that the hotel is responsible for compliance with all state laws involving alcohol beverage service and will indemnify (to protect against or keep from loss, damage, and so on) the planner for any violation that results in an injury. Finally, the

An Unusual Risk

A number of years ago, an interesting "risk" situation developed. A company sponsored a Christmas party at a hotel and alcohol was served. The company went so far as to provide comp rooms to attendees so that they would not "drink and drive." A male and female employee each consumed enough alcohol to become inebriated and, with their moral guard down and a hotel room available, decided to engage in sexual relations. The woman became pregnant as a result and sued the employer company for contributing to the pregnancy by allowing her to become intoxicated. The court agreed with the woman, and the company was held liable!

risk can be insured, which is a form of transference, using an insurance company's money to pay any damages.

While not all risk can be insured against, there are several types of insurance policies available to minimize the sponsor's liability. Workers' compensation and comprehensive general liability are two types of insurance:

- Workers' compensation insurance is mandatory in all states. It provides coverage for employees who are injured on the job. While most states permit employers to either self-insure or purchase coverage from private companies, a few states (e.g., Nevada) require employers to purchase this insurance only through a state fund. This could cause a problem if an organization holds a meeting in Nevada and hires temporary employees to perform services at the meeting. To avoid this problem, organizations should utilize only independent contractors for temporary staffing or hire individuals provided by a temporary agency.

- **Comprehensive general liability (CGL)** policies are the commercial equivalent of a homeowner's policy. They protect the organization against personal injury claims and loss (including theft) or damage to the insured's property as well as the property of others. Although these policies are designed to cover all risk, they frequently have exclusions, so it is important to carefully review what is not covered as well as what is included in the policy's scope.

It is not clear from many of these policies whether they insure against events that occur outside of the organization's premises, such as at meetings, conventions, and trade shows. If they do not cover these types of events, they should be amended to cover them or additional insurance should be secured. Further, many general liability policies may not cover liability resulting from alcoholic beverage service without a specific amendment. Athletic events, such as "fun runs," may also be excluded from coverage without a specific endorsement. In addition, it is important to be sure that the policy specifically refers to and covers contractual liabilities, like those that would be incurred under a meeting contract.

Another coverage that should be checked as part of any CGL policy is alcohol server liability. Serving alcoholic beverages at an event, especially if the guests are going to drive home afterward, can subject the sponsoring organization to the risk of litigation if an attendee becomes intoxicated at the event and then is involved in an automobile accident. Such an occurrence led to a lawsuit in Washington, DC, against a company holding a holiday party for its employees at an off-site location.

Planners should review the definition of who is the "insured" under the policy, since it may be important to extend coverage to the organization's employees and volunteers as well as the organization itself. Frequently, a hotel or convention center will require that it be designated as an "additional named insured"; this is easily done through the insurance broker who procured the policy.

How much insurance to carry is also a concern for planners. While multimillion-dollar awards are all too common in liability cases, the typical general liability policy has coverage limits of $1 to $2 million. If additional coverage is desired, it is relatively easy to obtain an "umbrella" policy that provides coverage in the $2–$10 million range.

- **Association professional liability (APL)** policies protect the organization and its officers, directors, staff, and volunteers against personal liability arising from their official actions. This type of policy is broader than a traditional directors and officers (D&O) liability policy in that it covers the organization as an entity as well as covering individuals.

  Unlike many other forms of insurance, APL policies issued by different companies vary greatly, and organizations may find that certain coverages, such as antitrust or libel protection, may not be available from a particular company. Therefore, it is important to obtain several sample policies and premium quotations in order to properly evaluate options. The lowest-cost policy may not always be the best.

The APL policy generally does not protect the organization against the kind of liability that is covered by the CGL policy. APL premiums are generally considerably higher than those for general business liability, although some carriers are attempting to cut premiums by writing APL policies in conjunction with CGL coverage.

- Convention cancellation policies are a specialized form of protection, insuring against unforeseen circumstances, such as labor disputes, inclement weather, or damage to the convention or meeting facility; the failure of a featured speaker or entertainer to appear may or may not be included in the coverage. These policies often cover the organization's personal property (such as computers and other equipment) utilized at the convention or meeting and the loss or theft of on-site convention receipts. However, this coverage is generally in excess of any other existing personal property or loss of money coverage that an organization may carry. It is not intended to be used as a "first dollar" coverage against loss to personal property and/or money and receipts.

  Planners should seek to include coverage for reduced attendance as well as total cancellation at an event, although most policies will not protect against lack of attendance for reasons other than unforeseen circumstances. Many policies will include so-called remedial action taken by a meeting sponsor, such as purchasing fans to deal with a failed air conditioning system. Additionally, some policies will provide automatic coverage for smaller meetings (e.g., under $50,000 budgeted gross revenue) when an organization's major meetings are covered. This coverage only applies to the period of time the coverage is in force for major meetings. These policies also do not protect against liability to third parties.

- Exhibitor liability policies provide protection to the organization for damage caused by exhibitors. In addition, these policies generally protect the organization for loss or damage that it causes as part of its convention or meeting management; many policies also provide host liquor liability coverage. For example, one company quotes a premium on the basis of $50 per exhibitor, with a $500 minimum. This type of coverage may not be necessary if all exhibitors are major companies and the exhibitor contract includes a provision requiring indemnification of the organization for damage caused by the exhibitor's negligence.

Americans with Disabilities Act

Federal legislation makes it illegal to discriminate against or fail to accommodate people with disabilities. The legislation resulted in passage of the **Americans with Disabilities Act (ADA),** which places responsibility on the owners and operators of public facilities to make reasonable accommodations for people with many types of disabilities. This can include people in wheelchairs as well as those with visual impairments, hearing impairments, and food intake restrictions.

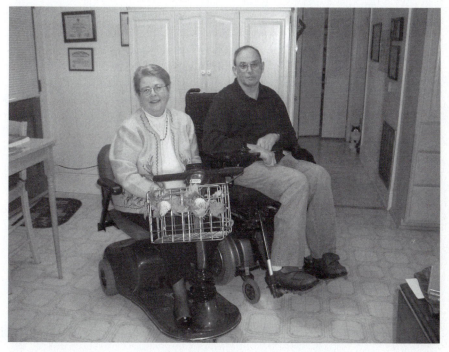

Anne Jakob, CMP, and her husband, Bob, both require special accommodations because they use motorized wheelchairs.
Photo by George G. Fenich, Ph.D.

Guidelines for Addressing ADA

Listed below are some general areas covered in the ADA:

- Providing staff training:
  - Etiquette
  - Language
  - Role play

- Providing opportunities for persons with disabilities to identify them-selves and request accommodation:
  - Membership applications
  - Meeting registrations
  - Certification process applications

- Providing accommodations for blind and visually impaired attendees:
  - Technology orientation
    - Mobility specialists
    - Tactile maps
    - Scribes or readers

- Providing accommodations for individuals who are deaf or hard of hearing:
  - Technology
    - Relay service
    - TDD/TTY
    - E-mail
    - Captioning
      - Real time
      - Open or closed
  - Interpreters
    - American Sign Language (ASL)
    - Pidgin Sign English (PSE) and Signing Exact English (SEE)
    - Oral interpretation
  - Boards and committees

- Providing minutes and documents in alternative media:
  - Braille
  - Text files
  - E-mail

- Providing help during voting:
  - Visual signals
  - Auditory signals

- Providing chat rooms or video for conference calls

- Providing access at social functions

Some of the other tasks a planner should consider are:

- At least one staff member should be designated as the contact person for disability accommodations. That person should coordinate with the housing venues regarding those with disabilities who might identify themselves on one form but not on the other.
- Put together a list of vendors who could provide support for people with disabilities at the conference site.
- Registration forms for the meeting or event should include places for people with disabilities to identify themselves and request accommodations.
- Be sure that disability accommodations are included in the meeting budget. At least 7%–10% of the budget should be allocated for accommodating people with disabilities.

Source: Critta P., and D. Hulse. 2003. "Becoming an Advocate for All Attendees," *Convene*, February, pp. 48–49.

Following are the four stated purposes of ADA:

1. To provide a clear and comprehensive national mandate for the elimination of discrimination against individuals with disabilities
2. To provide clear, strong, consistent, enforceable standards addressing discrimination against individuals with disabilities

3. To ensure that the federal government plays a central role in enforcing the standards on behalf of individuals with disabilities

4. To invoke the sweep of congressional authority, including the power to enforce the Fourteenth Amendment and to regulate commerce, in order to address the major areas of discrimination faced day-to-day by people with disabilities

Source: The Americans with Disabilities Act of 1990, Titles I and V, The U.S. Equal Employment Opportunity Commission.

This act applies to meeting planners and organizers. They must (1) determine the extent to which attendees have disabilities and (2) make reasonable efforts to accommodate the special needs of those attendees at no cost to the attendees. As a result, we now see sections on registration forms asking if the attendee has any special needs. One of the most common relates to dietary needs, such as the individual who is lactose intolerant (cannot drink milk or consume milk products), but the planner would not have to provide milk substitutes for that attendee because the situation does not impair a major life function. Another example is the attendee who is hearing impaired, and the planner would have to provide a sign language interpreter. Readers may have seen these interpreters in class or during important speeches. For those with vision impairment, the planner may have to provide documents with extra large type or with text in Braille. Failure to accommodate attendees with disabilities can result in legal action and fines. Further, the accommodations requirement is not limited to attendees— it applies to employees as well.

The planner must be aware of the ramifications of the ADA and be sure that all facilities used meet the standards. The planner must also be sure that the activities and programs meet the guidelines set forth in the act. Be aware, however, that this act applies only to events and meetings in the United States; Canada does not have the equivalent of the ADA, and many of its facilities do not meet the standards put forth in the act. Accessibility and accommodation of those with disabilities vary significantly from country to country.

Intellectual Property

Many meetings and trade shows feature events at which music is played, either by live musicians or through the use of prerecorded CDs.

Music may be provided as a background (such as at a cocktail reception) or as a primary focus of attention (such as at a dinner-dance or concert). At trade shows, individual exhibitors as well as the sponsoring organization can provide music.

Regardless of how music is provided, it is important to remember that under the federal **copyright** act, the music is being "performed," and according to many court decisions, the organization sponsoring the event is considered to be controlling the "performance," even if that "control" means only hiring an orchestra without telling the conductor what to play. The only recognized exemption to the "performance" rule is for music played over a single receiver (radio or TV) of a type usually found in the home.

The **American Society of Composers, Authors, and Publishers (ASCAP)** and **Broadcast Music, Inc. (BMI)** are membership organizations that represent individuals who hold the copyright to approximately 95% of the music written in the United States. ASCAP and BMI exist to obtain license fees from those who "perform" copyrighted music, including radio stations, retail stores, hotels, and organizations that sponsor meetings, conventions, and trade shows. A 1979 decision of the U.S. Supreme Court conferred on ASCAP and BMI a special limited exemption from normal antitrust law principles, and this decision has enabled them to develop blanket licensing agreements for the various industries that utilize live or recorded music.

Following negotiations with major meeting industry organizations (such as the International Association of Exhibition Managers and the American Society of Association Executives) in the late 1980s, both ASCAP and BMI developed special licensing agreements and fee structures for meetings, conventions, trade shows, and expositions. These special agreements were designed to replace earlier agreements under which hotels paid licensing fees for meetings held by others on the property. Although the negotiated agreements technically expired at the end of 1994, ASCAP and BMI have extended them on a year-to-year basis, with slight increases in licensing fees. (Copies of the current ASCAP and BMI music licensing agreements may be obtained from ASCAP at http://www.ascap.com or from BMI at http://www.bmi.com.) Under court decrees, ASCAP and BMI are forbidden to grant special deals to individual meetings, so the agreements, which must be signed, are the same for all meetings and cannot be altered to meet the needs of a particular meeting. Failure to sign these agreements—and agreements with *both* organizations must be signed—could subject a meeting or trade show sponsor to costly and embarrassing litigation for copyright infringement.

Under copyright law, an organization cannot meet its obligation by requiring the musicians performing the music or the booking agency or hotel providing the musicians to obtain ASCAP and BMI licenses. The organization sponsoring the event must obtain the requisite licenses.

The applicability of the music licensing requirement to a trade show is a controversial one. Both ASCAP and BMI have pressured trade show operators to obtain the license, noting that organizations sponsoring trade shows or expositions at which exhibitors play live or recorded music need only obtain one license each from ASCAP and BMI to cover the entire show; if this is done, individual exhibitors are not required to obtain licenses. Some trade show sponsors charge slightly higher fees to exhibitors who use music to offset the license fee, but others prefer to absorb the fee as a cost of running the trade show or exposition. If an organization's meeting or show features hospitality suites at which music might be played, the organization's license with ASCAP and BMI can be written to cover the suites as well.

If a trade show operator is going to allow exhibitors to play music or is going to "perform" music itself, it would appear that the preferable course of action is to obtain a license covering the entire trade show, since the fees paid would be less than would be the case if individual exhibitors obtained the necessary ASCAP and BMI licenses.

RECORDING OR VIDEOTAPING OF SPEAKERS

An organization sponsoring a meeting will often want to make audio or video recordings of certain speakers or programs, either for the purpose of selling copies to those who could not attend or for archival purposes.

Speakers or program participants have a common law copyright interest in their presentations, and the law prohibits the sponsoring organization from selling audio or video copies of any presentation without obtaining the written permission of the presenter. Many professional speakers who also market books or recordings of their presentations frequently refuse to provide consent to be recorded by the meeting sponsor.

Permission can be obtained by having each speaker whose session is to be recorded sign a copyright waiver, a simple document acknowledging that the speaker's session is going to be recorded and giving the sponsoring organization permission to sell the recordings made of the speaker's presentation. If the recording is to be done by a commercial audiovisual company, a sample waiver form can usually be obtained from that company.

Labor Issues

Preparation for on-site work at meetings and trade shows often involves long hours and the use of individuals on a temporary or part-time basis to provide administrative or other support. It is therefore important for organizations to understand how federal employment law requirements impact these situations.

The federal Fair Labor Standards Act (FLSA), adopted in 1938, is more commonly known as the law that prescribes a minimum wage for a large segment of the working population. Another major provision of the FLSA, and one frequently misunderstood, requires that all workers subject to the law's minimum wage coverage *must* receive overtime pay at the rate of one and a half times their regular rate of pay *unless* they are specifically exempted by the statute.

There are many common misconceptions (all of which are *not* true) that employers have about the FLSA's overtime provisions:

- Only hourly employees (not those paid on a regular salary basis) are eligible for overtime.
- Overtime pay can be avoided by giving employees compensatory time off instead.
- Overtime need be paid only to those who receive advance approval to work more than forty hours in a week.

Over the years, Department of Labor regulations and court decisions have made it clear that overtime pay cannot be avoided by a promise to provide compensatory time off in another workweek, even if the employee agrees to the procedure. According to the Department of Labor, the only way so-called comp time is legal is if it is given in the same week that the extra hours are worked or in another week of the same pay period and if the extra time off is sufficient to offset the amount of overtime worked (i.e., at the time and a half rate).

The use of comp time is probably the most common violation of FLSA overtime pay requirements, and it occurs frequently because many employees, particularly those who are paid by salary, would rather have an extra day off from work at a convenient time to deal with medical appointments, holiday shopping, or simply "attitude adjustment." Compensatory time is also frequently—but not legally— provided when a nonexempt employee works long hours in connection with a meeting or convention and then is given extra time off in some later pay period to make up for the extra work.

Overtime cannot be limited only to situations where extra work is approved in advance. The law is also clear that premium pay must be paid whenever the employee works in excess of forty hours per week—or is on call for extra work—even when the extra effort has not specifically been approved in advance. Thus, if a nonexempt employee works a few extra hours in the days prior to a meeting to complete all assignments for that meeting, the employee must be paid overtime.

Overtime pay is not limited to lower-salaried employees or those paid on an hourly basis. The FLSA requires *all* employees to receive overtime unless they fall under one of the law's specific exemptions. The most generally available exemptions are the so-called white-collar exemptions for professional, executive, and administrative employees.

In order to determine whether an employee falls within one of these exemptions, one should review the FLSA and applicable regulations and interpretations carefully. It is also most important to remember that the exemptions apply only to those whose actual work activity falls within the definitions; job titles are meaningless in determining whether an employee is exempt. Below is simply a summary:

- The professional exemption is available only to those whose job requires that they possess a skill obtainable only through an advanced degree. This is generally limited to lawyers, physicians, architects, and some engineers. An employee whose employer prefers, or even requires, an advanced degree cannot be exempt from overtime unless the actual job being performed—such as general counsel—requires such an education.

- The executive exemption is available only to those whose primary duty is management and who regularly supervise the work of two or more full-time employees (or their part-time equivalents). Thus, someone who has the title "Director" but who only supervises an administrative assistant or secretary is not exempt from overtime under this category.

- The administrative exemption is probably the most difficult to understand, although it may be available to those employees who cannot qualify under either of the other two white-collar exemptions. According to Labor Department regulations, an administrative employee is one whose primary duty is the performance of

Doctors are exempted from FSLA overtime regulations.
Dorling Kindersley Media Library

nonnmanual (i.e., office) work directly related to management policies and who, in the course of that work, generally exercises discretion and independent judgment. The regulations make clear that an administrative assistant is not exempt from overtime merely because he or she exercises discretion over such things as what office supplies to order or how to process meeting or convention registrations. These decisions are viewed as merely carrying out established management policy.

It is important for all employers to know which of their employees are exempt from overtime pay requirements and which are not. This is especially significant when employees are asked to work long hours at meetings or conventions, particularly those held out of town, or to pitch in and help complete a large mailing or project. When in doubt about overtime, an organization should review job descriptions with a competent human resources professional or experienced legal counsel.

To provide on-site logistical support, such as assistance with registrations, organizations that hold meetings (particularly large ones) frequently hire individuals to work on a temporary full- or part-time basis. There is often a question as to whether these individuals are employees or independent contractors. The distinction is an important one, for if the individuals are employees, the hiring organization must withhold federal (and perhaps state) income taxes and Social Security (FICA) payroll taxes; there may also be implications for the organization's benefit programs. On the other hand, the hiring organization has no such financial obligation to an independent contractor.

Unfortunately, there is no "bright line" distinction between the two types of relationships. The Internal Revenue Service (IRS) itself considers twenty factors, enumerated in Revenue Ruling 87–41 (1987–1 C.B. 296), to assist it in making the determination. The essence of the IRS test is control—the more control exercised by the hiring organization (in terms of such matters as setting hours of work and determining the manner in which work is to be done), the greater is the likelihood that the relationship is one of employer–employee.

If one hired to provide temporary help at a meeting is determined to be an independent contractor, the hiring organization must file a Form 1099 for the individual at the end of the year, provided the amount paid is greater than $600. In addition, the organization should be aware that many states include the compensation paid to an independent contractor within the organization's wage base for determining unemployment compensation taxes.

Ethics

The preceding part of this chapter deals with legal issues, and the planner can look to legislation or legal advisors for assistance in dealing with them. There are many other issues, actions, and activities in MEEC that may be legal but may raise questions of ethics. *Webster's New Universal Unabridged Dictionary* (1972) defines ethics as "(1) the study of standards of conduct and moral judgment; moral

Getting Cozy with a Caterer

The conference center at a university only allows approved caterers to supply food and beverage for events at the center. There are five approved caterers. One of the sales managers was heard saying that he tries to steer all of the clients with whom he interacts to one particular caterer, even though this caterer is the most expensive. When asked why he tries to influence his clients in this way, he said that this caterer provides the best products and service, which would be expected from the most expensive caterer. He went on to say he has become a friend of this caterer and that the caterer regularly gives him tickets to sporting events, the theater, and so on. Is this behavior ethical?

philosophy, (2) the system or code of morals of a particular philosopher, religion, group, profession, etc." Ethics guide our personal and professional lives. Further, the issue of ethics has come to center stage with the unethical practices of Enron, Imclone, Martha Stewart, and others, and ethics are addressed on the evening news and on the front page of newspapers today. The MEEC industry, by its very nature, offers a multitude of opportunities for unethical behavior or practices.

William Brown said in a series of articles in *Convene* (June 1998, July 1998, September 1998) that there is "no right way to do the wrong thing" as it relates to ethics. He goes on to stress the importance of harmonizing ethics at three levels—personally, interpersonally, and professionally. How someone responds to an issue regarding ethics is personally and culturally based. What is ethical behavior in one community or society may be considered unethical in another. Loyalty to personal friends versus an employer is another ethical consideration faced in the MEEC industry. Ethical issues and personal conduct are important aspects of any industry, including MEEC. The topic cannot possibly be covered in a few paragraphs; thus, readers are encouraged to seek additional sources of information on this topic.

SUPPLIER RELATIONS

Many planners feel suppliers are out to make a buck and will do anything they can to get the contract for an event. Some believe suppliers and vendors will promise anything but may not deliver on their promises. While promising more than can be delivered or embellishing their abilities may be legal, it may not be ethical. On the other hand, many suppliers and vendors feel meeting planners tend toward over-statement, for example, in estimating the number of rooms they will use in a hotel and the amount their group spends on food and bever-age. This too is an ethical question. The solution to these issues is to put everything in writing, preferably in the contract.

Even with a contract, the buyer (planner, organizer, or sponsor) and the seller (vendor or supplier) should be as open, forthright, and honest as possible in dealing with each other. A relationship not built on trust is a fragile relationship, at best. Further, given the increasing importance of relationship marketing, honest and ethical behavior can lead to future business.

INTELLECTUAL MATERIAL

Still another ethical issue deals with the ownership and use of intel-lectual material. Destination management companies (DMCs) in particular often complain that meeting planners submit requests for proposals (RFPs) to many suppliers while the DMCs spend quite a bit of time, energy, and money to develop creative ideas and programs to secure the planners' business. However, there are many cases in which a planner will take the ideas developed by one DMC and have another implement them, or the planner may then carry out the ideas on his or her own. Is this legal? Yes. Is it ethical? No.

GIFTS

Still another issue for suppliers concerns the offering of gifts. Should a DMC employee or sales representative accept gifts and privileges from a supplier or vendor? If amenities are accepted, is there some obligation on the part of the salesperson to repay the supplier by steer-ing business in the supplier's direction? When does one cross the line from ethical to unethical behavior? Is it proper to accept a Christmas gift but not proper to accept football tickets when offered?

Another ethical question regards so-called fam (familiarization) trips. Fam trips bring potential clients on an all-expenses-paid trip to a destination with the hope that they will bring their business to the community. But what if a planner or sponsor is invited on a fam trip to a destination but has no intention of ever holding a MEEC gathering in that location? Should the planner accept the trip? If accepted, is there some implicit expectation that the planner *will* bring business to the locale? Although it is perfectly legal to accept a trip with no intention of bringing business to the locale, is it ethical?

The planner or sponsor of a large MEEC gathering has significant clout and power based on the economic and social impact of the gathering and may ask for special consideration or favors based on this power. It may be ethical to exert this influence on behalf of the group, such as when negotiating room rates, catering rates, and comp services, but is it ethical for the planner or sponsor to request personal favors that only benefit him- or herself? Is it ethical for the planner to accept personal favors from a supplier or a community?

Examples of ethical issues and questions abound in the MEEC industry. An individual must adhere to a personal code of ethics, and many industry associations have developed their own code of ethics to which members must adhere. Colleges and universities have recognized the need to address ethics by implementing courses on the subject. The discussion of ethics in this chapter is meant to make readers aware that ethics are an important aspect of the study of the MEEC industry, but it is not meant as a comprehensive treatise.

Summary

Legal issues are an increasingly important factor in the MEEC industry. This chapter is meant to provide insights into some of these issues, such as negotiation, contracts, labor, and intellectual property. There are other issues that were not discussed, and entire books are devoted to them. Readers are reminded to seek legal counsel whenever appropriate.

Key Words and Terms

For definitions, see the Glossary or go to http://glossary.convention industry.org.

Act of God

American Society of Composers, Authors, and Publishers (ASCAP)

Americans with Disabilities Act (ADA)

Association professional liability (APL)

Attrition

Broadcast Music, Inc. (BMI)

Comprehensive general liability (CGL)

Consideration   Negotiation
Contract   Parol evidence
Copyright   Profile
Dates, Rates, and Space   Rack rate
Force majeure   Soft data
Hard data   Yield management

Review and Discussion Questions

1. Discuss the negotiation process. What are the important points for each party to be aware of?
2. Define a contract.
3. What laws are important to know with regard to contracts?
4. Discuss negotiating contracts.
5. Discuss attrition.
6. What is the difference between cancellation and termination with regard to events?
7. Discuss the different types of risk a planner may face and how to deal with them.
8. What is the ADA, and how does it impact events and gatherings?
9. What is intellectual property, and why should a planner or sponsor be aware of it?
10. What are some of the labor issues unique to MEEC?

About the Chapter Contributor

James M. Goldberg is a principal in the Washington, DC, law firm of Goldberg & Associates, PLLC. His practice focuses on the representation of trade associations and professional societies as well as independent meeting and event planners and other providers of services to the association community.

A frequent writer and speaker on association and hospitality industry legal issues, James is the author of *The Meeting Planner's*

Legal Handbook, a widely distributed publication also used as the text for his course "Meeting and Exhibition Law and Ethics," taught each fall at Northern Virginia Community College in Annandale, Virginia. The book is also used as required or recommended reading for meeting planning courses offered by George Washington University, Metropolitan State College (Denver), and the University of Georgia's Gwinnett Center.

James is a charter member of the Academy of Hospitality Industry Attorneys and a member of the Legal Advisory Council of the Convention Industry Council's APEX initiative. He is also an active participant in the District of Columbia Bar's Committee on Tax-Exempt Organizations.

He has an undergraduate degree in journalism from Syracuse University and a law degree from George Washington University.

Contact Information

Goldberg & Associates, PLLC
(A Limited Liability Company Including Nonlawyers)
Suite 1000
1101 Connecticut Avenue, NW
Washington, DC 20036
Phone: 202-628-2929
Facsimile: 202-463-4545
E-mail: jimcounsel@aol.com
Internet: http://www.assnlaw.com

CHAPTER 13

Technology and the Meeting Professional

Satellite technology is used to beam MEEC programming to remote locations.
Dorling Kindersley Media Library

Chapter Objectives

This chapter provides the reader with an understanding of the following:

- Ways that technology currently impacts the site selection function
- New technologies that support meeting networking
- Critical technology terms that apply to the hospitality industry
- Best web portals that are used for researching industry information
- Technology that is used in the seven types of Web-based gatherings
- Ways that technology impacts convention centers

Chapter Outline

Introduction
Before the Event
Desktop Applications
Virtual Site Selection and Research
  Online Request for Proposals (RFPs)
  Open Bidding
  Virtual Tours
  Industry Information Portals
Marketing and Communications
  Web Sites and Strategic
    Communications
  E-Marketing
  Room Design Software
  Sales of the Show Floor
  Attendee Networking (Pre-Event)
  Online Registration
During the Event
Technology Infrastructure
  Bandwidth
  Wired versus Wireless

Digital Recording and Streaming
    Media
To VoIP or Not to VoIP?
Radio Frequency Identification
    Device (RFID)
Lead Retrieval System
Audience Response System (ARS)
Blogs
Mobile Technologies
Virtual Gatherings
Postconference Technology
    Applications
  Evaluations and Surveys
  Media for Marketing Purposes
Twenty-First-Century Convention
    Centers
  Use of Technology
  Types of Technology
  Access to Technology
  Green Technology

Whether it's to increase service speed and reliability, cut cost through automation, find new markets, or add value to products, every business, including exposition management, must use technology to stay current.

Sam Lippman

Introduction

Imagine a meeting where name badges communicate seamlessly with one another, an event where networking begins months before your attendees ever arrive at the conference, a conference whose specification (spec) sheet includes 3D floor plans that showcase the actual room utilized—perhaps even an event where on-site registration is primarily handled at kiosks. No, this isn't a vision of the future; it is the present, one where the meeting professional embraces available technologies to enhance and support the goals of the organization and the attendees.

The meeting planning industry, like many others, has taken its time in adopting technology to support meetings, and that is not necessarily a bad approach. As any gadget purchaser knows, the version 1.0 of any product can be filled with bugs and problems, and newer products often have higher price tags. It may make some sense to wait before adopting any new technologies.

Although we also struggle with the blending of technology into our everyday professional lives, we are at a stage where the two are beginning to meet quite nicely. The current meeting professional's job is, in part, to understand and embrace new technologies so that the ever-changing demands of attendees can be met. This chapter will examine new (and not so new) technologies that meeting planners need to be familiar with today to better plan conferences and events.

Before the Event

The technology-savvy meeting professional has more tools than ever before to help research, promote, and organize their event. It could be said that technology applications are the most supportive to the conference planner in this phase of the event's life cycle. From desktop uses to virtual site selection support to ubiquitous Web-based marketing tools, meeting planners now have plenty of choices to make the planning process work for them.

Desktop Applications

While there are dozens of industry-specific software packages on the market, the clear leader in the industry is still the basic Microsoft Office Suite. With Word, Excel, Access, and PowerPoint, the meeting professional's desktop has the tools to manage all components of any event. However, this general software package does not fill every need. Many planners, especially in organizations with noncentralized meeting departments, need tools that allow information to be shared across the organization. The industry has a number of other tools that foster better information centralization.

At the core of this need to centralize information is the need for organizations to get a handle on the amount of purchasing leverage they have. Individuals planning a small meeting within a large organization are at a disadvantage in negotiating, unless they can combine their hotel room contracting with others within the organization. This is where third-party software tools can have a significant advantage over the MS Suite. More expensive third-party software tools such as Scan*Star, Ethereal, and PortMon frequently provide exceptional cross-organization value by allowing organizations to bundle their purchasing needs.

As it relates to technology, the Technology Advisory Council of the **Accepted Practices Exchange (APEX)** has created APEX Office Ready for Meeting and Event Planning. It is a series of templates throughout Word, Excel, and PowerPoint that help the user manage information utilizing a common format, which is the core of the APEX initiative.

Virtual Site Selection and Research

ONLINE REQUEST FOR PROPOSALS

As the World Wide Web developed in the mid to late 1990s, some of the first tools available, both through convention and visitor bureau (CVB) Web sites and through hotel and third-party planning sites, were those allowing the planner to create an efficient online **request for proposal (RFP)**, the tool many planners use to distribute information to hotels about potential meetings. While the model of RFPs has evolved from a fee-based to a free approach, the idea remains the same: Online RFPs allow the planner to input specifications (specs) easily and allow the Web to be the conduit for distributing the information to potential cities and hotels.

Without standardization, each RFP would have its own nuances, which could cost the meeting planner time in completing each one. Planners still need to determine which vehicle (CVB-based, hotel-based, or third-party-based) is best to distribute their meeting specifications.

Some planners eschew the RFP forms and just use e-mail and the Internet to save time by allowing an office-based spec sheet to be distributed via e-mail. Regardless of how one looks at it, technology is saving significant time in helping planners distribute their meeting requirements.

OPEN BIDDING

The Web has enabled another approach to site selection—open bidding, often referred to as the meeting auction. Here, planners can post their needs on a third-party site and invite suppliers to bid on the business. This controlled model works within a specified time frame, helping to expedite the process and to eliminate some of the tedious negotiations by creating a framework for an agreement at the end of the bidding cycle.

A reverse process is also available. In that instance, a hotel may have space that is available (possibly due to a cancellation). The hotel posts the critical information (dates, number of room nights) on the Web site and then allows planners to bid on it in a specific period of time. Once again, the exact framework of an agreement is established through the winning bidder. While neither of these approaches has dominated the meeting industry, they do provide another example of how technology can support the RFP and site selection process.

VIRTUAL TOURS

Industry statistics have estimated that over one-half of all meetings are booked without a formal site inspection. While there is no substitution for visiting a venue, the Web's visual capabilities have allowed planners to at least get a sense of a facility if time or budgetary restrictions prevent their inspection. Almost ubiquitous at the moment are sites (hotel and third-party) that post not only photographs but 360-degree panoramic tours of meeting space and sleeping rooms. The planner who cannot visit the site can get a better sense of its look and feel by viewing these videos. There are a number of Web sites that actually stream video promotions of hotels (and even cities) for planners and travelers to view.

The next wave in virtual tours is being showcased by Virtual Visit (http://www.virtualvisit.ca). This hotel-directed site visit is a tool that allows the hotel to literally walk the planner through the space, focusing on areas of interest to both parties. This tool is ideal for remote site inspections but can also be used in tandem with a traditional site visit, perhaps in conjunction with a laptop personal computer (PC), where the planner can call up alternate room setups and capacity information with a single click.

INDUSTRY INFORMATION PORTALS

Less elegant, but still enormously useful and currently thriving, are industry information **portals.** While search engines are incredibly useful for general research, our industry also has a great deal of information available at the fingertips of savvy Web users, who can find resources and tools at their disposal in a few clicks of the mouse.

Any discussion of information portals for the hospitality industry should begin with the Web site of Corbin Ball (http://www. corbinball. com). From the home page, linking to the "favorites" page presents the viewer with nearly 3,000 industry-related Web sites, all organized categorically.

CVB pages are also rich with information for planners to plan their meetings. Electronically based information, available through dropdown menus on CVB sites, has replaced the more archaic printed city meeting planning guides. The only difficulty with the CVB sites is finding the web address (URL); sometimes they are obvious, but not always. When you don't know them, it is good to know the site of the Destination Marketing Association International (http://www.destinationmarketing.org). Formerly the International Association of Convention and Visitor Bureaus (IACVB), this site has resources that include a listing of CVBs from the United States and over twenty countries worldwide.

For nearly a decade, many meeting professionals have expedited their site inspection research with a trip to the "mpoint" (http://www. mpoint.com). Now part of the OnVantage brand, mpoint provides planners with an industry-specific search engine that allows planners to quickly identify properties that meet certain criteria, including location, number of sleeping rooms, and amount of meeting space. While a number of other players provide similar services, mpoint has been at or near the top for the past decade.

Marketing and Communications

If the advent of the Web has done one thing exceptionally well for planners and suppliers, it has transformed how they market to and communicate with their customers. Long gone are the days of multiple expensive direct-mail printings and postage issues. In their place is the capability for immediate and current communication with clients and colleagues. The cost savings of not having to print expensive four-color brochures and mail them to every potential customer is enormous—it could be the greatest cost transformation that Web technology has provided.

However, while technology has had a tremendous impact on cost savings, it has also basically changed how planners market and communicate. Because of the immediacy of technology tools, how they communicate (and how much competition they have) has exponentially increased. In fact, many of the old rules (such as "Just send as many and as often as you can afford") no longer bring the required results. Today's technology-savvy meeting professional must do a far better job of identifying potential customers, and communicate with them in a way that does not end up in a junk mail folder.

WEB SITES AND STRATEGIC COMMUNICATIONS

Form over function is a battleground. Ask some people about what a great Web site is and they gush over cool flash animations, dancing icons, and eye-popping colors. Ask marketers if those cool features are the hallmarks of an effective meeting Web site and they might tell you differently. It is clear that some rules have changed—but some rules haven't changed:

- You need clear, easy-to-find information.
- You should focus on the 5 W's (who, what, where, when and why) of the conference.
- You need to be able to get to the point of making a sale (e.g., the payment process on the registration form) in a way that doesn't scare away the customer.

Creating an efficient, customer-friendly Web site is clearly one critical issue when discussing strategic communications with clients and customers. Additionly, technology has provided many more tools and options to create better clarity in communications with everyone.

E-MARKETING

The Web site is only one facet of the e-marketing strategy of the technology-savvy meeting professional. Four other areas of importance include e-blasts, really simple syndication, blogging, and podcasting.

E-Blasts   Twenty years ago, a planner could (and would) send out as many direct-mail pieces as frequently as the budget would allow, since it was thought that the more information that landed on the desk of the buyers, the greater the likelihood they might attend the function. Fast forward to today. If the planner were to use the same strategic approach to marketing via direct e-mail, he or she may not get nearly the same results, but it's an alluring consideration: Since a multiple e-mail marketing barrage is so cheap, the planner might begin sending out notices every day to tens of thousands of potential customers.

However, as we stated earlier, the rules have changed. People are so inundated with spam e-mail (some experts have estimated the percentage of spam received to be as high as 85% of daily e-mail) that multiple unsolicited e-mails are having the reverse effect—people are tuning out all e-mail communications from a spam sender, once that sender is identified.

Instead of just blasting the audience with e-mail after e-mail, the planner may be wise to heed a different set of marketing rules to best promote the conference to the audience:

- *Opt In*. Just because you have obtained an e-mail address, it is not an open invitation to commence spamming. In fact, the technology-savvy approach would be to establish a dialogue and confirm that the recipient wants to be included in future mailings. This way, not only will those e-mails get to the people who may actually wish to attend, but they won't have the effect of designating you as a spammer (which could put all of your mailings at risk).

- *Don't Overdo It*. Once you've received the okay to e-mail, don't begin a barrage of mindless communications. The end result of too many e-mails from a single person or organization is the tuning out of all of them. People get hit with far too many communications on a daily basis, so they're looking for ways to reduce the number on which they need to focus. Better to spend time creating useful messages that are sent occasionally than to create mindless reminders that are sent repeatedly.

- *Use the What's in It for Me (WIIFM) Perspective*. Why would your customers want to read your e-mails? If all you are doing is sending information about the conference, it will look just like a continuous hard sell. Since this is a marketing medium (as well as one that can finalize the sale), use the technology to create a dialogue about important information with your customers: Give them educational information, inform them of useful tools to help them become better at their job. Oh yes, you can also tell them about your conference's benefits, but that information is better received in an environment of trust than one of constant sales.

- *Keep It Simple.* Don't write your novel in every e-mail. Over the past generation, people have become more accustomed to sound bites, and people don't have time to read lengthy pieces (you can always give visitors access to those, but allow them to venture down that path themselves). Keep your messages easy to read and as short as possible. And if you're providing any links, make sure they work.

Really Simple Syndication (RSS)   Possibly the most important approach to the Web today is in the use of **really simple syndication (RSS).** This is a tool where a Web site creates or gathers a feed of information about a specific topic and publishes it as an RSS feed. This information is changed continuously, so it always has up-to-date content. (For an excellent example of a generic RSS feed, Google News is a great site: http://www.news.google.com.) This feed could be the cornerstone of a well-designed topical Web site, or it could be gathered and read by recipients in their own RSS reader.

The Web site that provides topical RSS feeds is one that is constantly providing the reader with pertinent information. Imagine if a planner runs the conferences for a National Widget Association. Why would the association's members want to go to his or her Web site? They would go because the information on the site is useful, but once they've been there, the only reason to return is if the information is updated. And that's what a successful RSS feed can do to enhance a Web site—provide a steady stream of continuously updated content, making the Web site the place to return for information that helps them do their job.

Currently, some organizations have chosen to create their own custom RSS feed and place it on their Web site. By locating sources of information and designing their own Web site RSS feed (at a cost), they can cull the best information available and provide it to their clients and customers on a 24/7 basis—the value is enormous!

In addition to streaming RSS onto their Web site, many knowledgeable users maintain their own ability to read RSS feeds. Both Google and Yahoo have personal services (free of charge) to gather and customize a home page to provide news of importance to each reader. Plus, there are dozens of free RSS reader products on the market that provide the same service.

If you believe the adage that, on a Web site, "Content is king," how much better is it to provide a stream of current information (at little to no expense), all of which gets the potential attendee to want to return? And when they do return, they may just see the link to your conference and choose to learn more about other ways your organization can help them.

Blogging   The blog, or web log, is an online diary that is posted to the Web. Part of the social networking fabric of the World Wide Web, **blogging** allows anyone to become part of the Web by posting anything that is on their mind. (A 2005 survey by *Blogpulse*, at http://www.blog.blogpulse.com, identified more than 10 million active blogs.) Blogging inherently is a two-way medium, as most blogs allow people to respond and further the discussion on the posted blog.

The use of the blog in marketing a conference is very similar to the concept of RSS—in fact, many blogs contain RSS feed information, as the concept of the Internet as a web of information is what gives the Internet such rich content. A planner might post a regular blog about the widget industry as a way to reach out and communicate with a large number of peers (and importantly, many *younger* users, as blogs and social networking sites have been adopted much quicker by those who grew up with the technology). Maintaining an ongoing dialogue with your peers is critical to understanding the needs of your community as well as keeping your organization in the front of the minds of your potential customers.

Podcasting   Here's a quick quiz. The MP3 player is:

- A way cool music player.
- A 30+ GB backup hard drive for your files.
- The future of distance learning.

The answer is all of the above. For now, let's focus on the distance learning aspect. Wikipedia (http://www.wikipedia.org) defines **podcasting** as "the method of distributing multimedia files, such as audio or video programs . . . for playback on mobile devices and personal computers." Consider Jane Planner's boss's blog. Well written and informative, it provides a great tool to communicate with colleagues . . . as long as they are at their computer. But how about that long morning and evening commute? By creating podcasting content, many organizations have taken blogs and other information and enabled users to listen to the information anytime on their MP3 player.

Clearly, podcasting has more uses. Imagine live podcasts from your event, streaming information to people who cannot attend. How about podcasts (both audio and video) of the keynote speaker and general session?

ROOM DESIGN SOFTWARE

Certain aspects of your event (themed parties, banquets, or just unique setups) are not efficiently communicated by the written word. In these cases, planners use computer-aided design (CAD) **room design software** to enhance communications. The meeting planning industry has many versions of this type of software, which tends to be simple to use but can greatly range in price. Some work better for meetings; others focus on special events. Two products that provide this capability include Meeting Matrix (http://www.meetingmatrix.com) and Vivien (http://www.cast-soft.com).

The latest in room design enhancements is the 3D room tour. Once you create your room setup, a click of a button transforms it into a virtual 3D tour, with the room setup precisely as you diagrammed it. In some cases, the hotel can enhance that by providing the actual room images (carpeting, windows, lighting, sconces) as part of the 3D walkthrough. In fact, you may not even be sure if the image is real or virtual.

SALES OF THE SHOW FLOOR

Another way technology is enhancing event marketing and communications is by assisting the trade show manager in selling the show floor. Traditional exhibit sales were focused on a document called the exhibit prospectus, along with a generic layout of the show floor. By posting the show floor diagram on the Web and using its interactivity, the trade show manager can now offer potential buyers a better look at where they might want their booth. Advantages of this include providing updated layouts (as the show floor diagram is frequently modified when exhibitors buy space) as well as helping the buyer locate a floor space that is either near or far away from competitors (depending on the buyer's approach). The use of colors to represent booths can help differentiate which ones are available as well as the ones where premium costs apply.

Almost every trade show now uses some kind of virtual enhancement in the trade show floor selling process. These sites also include a downloadable version of the exhibit prospectus, as well as other information of use to exhibitors. We will discuss **virtual trade shows** in more detail in the section titled "Virtual Gatherings," where we can discuss how the actual event can be an online experience for the attendee and exhibitor.

ATTENDEE NETWORKING (PRE-EVENT)

One of the latest enhancements for the attendee is the ability for him or her to meet other attendees before they even arrive at the conference. Once again, in the category of enhanced social networking, these Web-based networking tools are in use for meetings of varying sizes.

The attendees, as they pre-register, are asked to answer a few questions about the meeting as it relates to their needs. These questions are customized for each group but frequently include the objectives of the conference, their critical reasons for attending, and the types of individuals with certain skill sets with whom they hope to meet and network.

As the attendees complete this information, the Web-based tools post it in a secure environment. By allowing individuals to see who else has similar interests and then to communicate directly with them (though no e-mail addresses are distributed without both parties' agreement), these tools can greatly enhance the experience and the results of a conference for the attendees. Two such tools that are on the market include IntroNetworks (http://www.intronetworks.com) and Leverage Software (http://www.leveragesoftware.com).

ONLINE REGISTRATION

A few years ago, in discussions of event technology, the topic of online registration would dominate the conversation. One of the first critical benefits of technology to the meetings industry was the ability to register for events online, which truly enhanced the marketing and communications of the event organizers.

Currently, online registration is a relatively mature technology, and most planners who need to use it do so. It is interesting to note that all meetings do not use online registration. Many meetings, especially internal meetings where attendance is mandatory, should not incur the expense of establishing a professional online registration presence but should use more traditional approaches or simple e-mail messages to handle meeting registration.

With this said, there are still a number of issues that confront planners when establishing the online registration process—the largest one for many planners being the integration of data. If planners conceptually agree that even in the best of circumstances, 100% of the attendees will not use the online approach, the planners' challenge is to make sure that when they integrate the data, there are no inaccuracies or duplication of records. Ensuring that the online service can properly export into the tool you are using to maintain the remaining records (such as Excel) is a critical area that needs to be addressed when considering which companies to use.

Another issue that is raised by organizations using online services is unexpected added expenses. One particular area of concern is in the creation of additional reports. The planner has two approaches to offset this issue: One is having an understanding of the reports that online services might require, and having this discussion negotiated into the purchase of the service; the other, more technology-savvy approach is to learn how to use the report writing feature of online services. Many online registration services use the product Crystal Reports to generate reports for the client.

There are many online resources that can perform the online registration service. Research using an industry portal such as Corbin Ball (http://www.corbinball.com) and his industry favorites will give the user a plethora of options from which to choose.

During the Event

You've created the ideal Web site and used tools to efficiently communicate and market to your prospective attendees and exhibitors. You've also established an ongoing dialogue with your constituents using RSS, blogging, and podcasting. Is your use of technology complete? Of course not.

Even before you go on site with the meeting, you need to be considering how you want technology to support your goals and objectives at the conference. From your setup work to your awareness of the devices to complement your (and your attendees') goals, technology is playing an enormous role in creating a successful conference experience for all of the shareholders—planners, exhibitors, and attendees.

Technology Infrastructure

The meeting professional understands the importance of negotiations with hotels. From rates, dates, and space to every other aspect of the event, the planner, armed with knowledge and information about his or her event and the destination, can have a productive give-and-take discussion with the hotel to create a win-win event.

However, many planners, fearful about or unaware of the uses for technology, leave out any discussion of technology during this part of the planning process—and this can be a very expensive omission. Technology-savvy planners, however, understand enough about the technology that supports their event that they know what they need to plan for (even negotiate) during the initial stages of meeting planning.

Planners also need to think about bandwidth, and how they will use the Internet and other technologies to support their goals. Additionally, the technology-savvy planner will think about how attendees will want to use different technologies to enhance their meeting experience. While a planner may not be able to implement all of these technologies, he or she can identify which ones are most critical (and useful) to successfully meet everyone's goals, thereby allowing those technologies to play a spectacular supporting role in the success of the conference.

BANDWIDTH

Bandwidth is the amount of information that can pass through a communications line. As it relates to the Web, bandwidth comes in two basic "flavors": dial-up and high speed. Dial-up is nowhere near adequate in handling the online and streaming needs at a conference; high speed (also referred to as broadband) is required.

But how much bandwidth is needed? Here is where planners may need help, and it can come from their own information technology (IT) personnel, but only if they understand and plan for their on-site needs. Here is a partial list of tasks where the planner needs to use bandwidth (and understand how much bandwidth to use) at the event:

- Registration networking
- Attendee e-mail kiosks
- Attendee message centers (incorporation of e-mail access for phone and other message services)
- Office and press room bandwidth for communications
- Speaker Internet access for presentations
- Live **Web conferencing** (streaming audio and video) for sessions

So how much bandwidth will you need? That depends on the answers to these (and other) questions. Having that dialogue with your IT staff (or a third-party organization with which you contract to support your on-site technology setup) before the contract is signed will enable you to ensure that the facility can meet your needs and will allow you to negotiate costs to a more reasonable level.

WIRED VERSUS WIRELESS

Many attendees will want to access their e-mail wherever they go in the venue. A truly wireless property can support that goal (though not without cost to either the attendee or the sponsoring organization). Whether attendees are in their sleeping room, public space, or meeting space, space that is wirelessly accessible is of enormous value to them.

If you have connected to a wireless network, you know that it is not always a panacea: Wireless network signals are not always as strong as you need them to be; many of them have the tendency to drop out (always at the most inopportune moment). Even in guest rooms, the strength of the wireless signal is not always sufficient to allow the guest to adequately check e-mail, let alone browse the Web.

The wireless standard is an engineering specification named **80211.** This spec, adopted in the late 1990s, defines how a wireless interface between clients and access points is constructed. However, there are a number of flavors of 80211, each one providing a different amount of potential bandwidth to the user: Talk to your IT department about the limitations of 80211b, 80211g, and 80211n standards.

Many speakers who require high-speed access for the success of their presentation prefer hardwired (an Ethernet cable directly attached to their computer) as opposed to wireless high-speed connectivity. As the MEEC industry progresses to create a more seamless broadband experience, wireless may (and should) become the standard; however, a good planner will at least have a hardwired backup in case the wireless signal is not an adequate solution.

DIGITAL RECORDING AND STREAMING MEDIA

The general session is a critical part of any annual meeting or conference. The marketing success of many conferences depends on the quality (and often name recognition) of the keynote speakers, who establish the tone of a conference.

However, there are many people who cannot attend and who would like to watch or hear the speaker(s), either in real time or on an archived basis. The organization can offer access to the keynote addresses (as well as other meeting components) to those who cannot attend by digitally recording the event and streaming it over the Internet (frequently referred to as **webcasting**). If you have never done this at a meeting, be aware that a lot of extra coordination and support are required. You'll need to have cameras (and video/audio engineers) in the session to ensure that the recorded material is of good quality; you'll also require a company to digitize the video into a format that can be electronically distributed, and you will need to determine whether the event should be streamed live (always a more risky proposition) or archived. Another question: Will people have free access to the webcast, or will the organization charge a fee for people to attend virtually on the webcast?

An excellent resource for the planner initially foraying into this is on the Web site of MAP Digital (http://www.mapdigital.com). From its Planner's Guide to its Digital Events link, the site answers the questions planners need to ask and discusses the practices they need to know in order to better understand and plan for this level of live connectivity.

While learning about the technical side, the planner must also understand a great deal about the audience and what the attendees might want to view online. Age and demographics certainly play a role in whether an entire session or just highlights should be digitized. The adage "Know your group: Who are they? Why are they here?" applies to all aspects of meeting planning, even the technological side.

TO VOIP OR NOT TO VOIP?

Many people recognize **voice over Internet protocol (VoIP)** by another name—digital telephone. VoIP is the more accurate term used for your high-speed Internet connection to make and receive phone calls. This technology may ultimately replace traditional telephone service, due to its significantly cheaper calling costs. In fact, many Fortune 500 companies have switched their telephone infrastructure to a VoIP system. This affects the meeting planner in numerous ways. If the hotel/facility has changed over to a VoIP system, decreases in charges may be realized (depending on how the facility cares to share that savings).

The planner can also choose to establish VoIP as his or her main approach in making phone calls while at the event. Anywhere there is a strong broadband signal is a place where VoIP service can work. The planner must be aware that the service is not fully mature, and numerous VoIP customers have indicated service does occasionally cut off a call (if the high-speed signal fails, so does the phone service using VoIP).

Some mobile phone manufacturers have begun to package VoIP software with their phones; Skype (at http://www.skype.com) is one of the leading consumer VoIP products. Planners and suppliers in the future may need to do nothing more than use their mobile phone to access the VoIP service.

RADIO FREQUENCY IDENTIFICATION DEVICE (RFID)

Possibly the hottest technology in the marketplace today is the **radio frequency identification device (RFID)** tag. Attached to a product or device, this tag emits a short-distance signal that allows the user to accurately track information. In our everyday lives, these miniscule devices are attached to many products, from electronic toll boxes that allow drivers to avoid stopping at toll booths on the road (EZ-Pass) to products in a company's warehouse that enables the company to better track its inventory. RFIDs are also finding a use in the meeting planning industry, as many services (covered in the following sections) are popping up at many events and conferences.

Interactive Name Tags   Perhaps the most common use of RFID is on **interactive name tags.** Either attached to a slim piece of paper behind a badge or as part of a slightly larger wearable name tag, the RFID-based service offers better networking and interactivity among conference attendees as well as between attendees and vendors.

One of the top RFIDs in the industry is made by nTag (http://www.ntag.com), whose wearable badge/device allows attendees to identify things of interest to them. When the attendee approaches another attendee wearing the badge (who has also identified interests), the two badges communicate with one another, with the digital display showing any commonality between the attendees.

In addition to enhancing live networking, RFID name tags frequently contain program contents, surveys, instant messaging capabilities, and other interactive tools for the attendee to utilize while at the event. The badge is now a communication device and a program (as well as a name tag) for the duration of the event. The interactive RFID name tag has two more meeting-specific uses:

- *CEU Tracking.* Many organizations need to track attendance at each educational session, in order to provide continuing education units (CEUs) for the attendee. (In many industries, these units are critical to maintain certification required for employment.) The RFID-based tag, coupled with readers in each room, can automatically track attendance so that proper CEUs can be awarded. Medical and scientific meetings are examples of

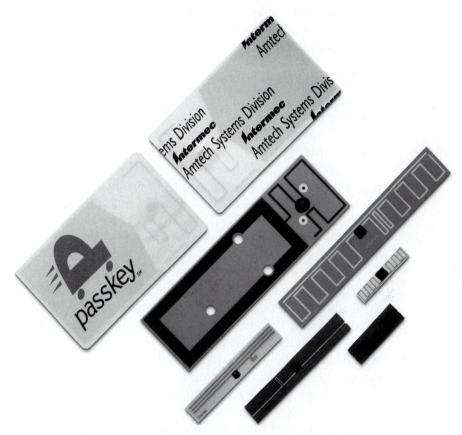

RFID tags.
Intermec Technologies Corporation

conferences where significant value is placed on tracking attendance because it allows the individual to obtain the required
CEUs.

- *Interactive Message Centers.* Conference message centers have
previously consisted of a phone (and a hired attendant to take
messages), along with a cork board and push pins. Today's
RFID-based system can provide an electronic board that, as you
walk past the board, will display your name and will indicate
whether you have any messages waiting—a far cry from cork
board and push pins!

When thinking about the networking advantages of RFID devices,
don't forget about the pre-event networking options discussed earlier

in the chapter. Today's attendee, when supported by a technology-savvy meeting professional, can truly take advantage of the enormous benefits of conference networking by using these systems.

LEAD RETRIEVAL SYSTEM

For many years, trade shows and exhibits have used **lead retrieval systems** to help capture customer information. The process begins with the meeting organizer asking questions during the registration process that will help identify information of importance to the exhibitor. These questions often include the attendees' purchasing responsibility as well as the nature of products and services in which attendees may have an interest. The information is coded into a badge, though it needn't be an RFID—many groups still use a simple bar coding on the badge (or even a credit card–based system) that can contain this information.

When the attendee enters the trade show floor and interacts with an exhibitor, the exhibit staff member can ask to swipe the badge with the lead retrieval device. Typically, these are rented to the exhibitor for the duration of the show by a vendor who is supporting the meeting. Once the badge is swiped, the information now resides in the attendee's handheld lead retrieval device. At day's end, the exhibitor can download this information to a spreadsheet or database and then have customized thank-you notes e-mailed to the attendee before work for the day is complete. Also, the exhibitor now has excellent information about prospective clients.

The planner's job in this process is to identify and select a system or service that can support the lead retrieval process. Since exhibitors require this level of information to determine whether exhibiting at a function will potentially help their business, lead retrieval systems are primarily used for trade shows; however, these systems have also been used to help facilitate attendee surveying using automated kiosks around the event.

AUDIENCE RESPONSE SYSTEM (ARS)

If you've ever watched audience participation game shows, you've seen the host poll the audience to determine their opinion about a question. The audience is outfitted with small keypads that allow them to answer questions quickly and have their data tallied immediately. This is the essence of an **audience response system (ARS).**

The ARS can be implemented online as an electronic survey or poll or on site during a presentation. In a meeting room, the ARS is typically a radio frequency device (as is an RFID). These devices do not need a clear line of sight to function, making them easier to use. Additionally, radio frequency devices have a greater transmission range than other types of transmissions, such as infrared, which makes them more appropriate for an ARS.

An ARS typically comes with predefined polling questions but also allows for modification and editing. It also provides instant information (demographic or otherwise) about attendees, which can be used to customize content and direction of educational sessions. Many ARSs seamlessly integrate into the speaker's PowerPoint presentation, allowing for feedback to be integrated on the fly. One company, Turning Point Technologies (http://www.turningtechnologies.com), has such a product available.

BLOGS

Blogging can enhance attendee communications while at an event. The meeting professional's responsibility in facilitating attendee blogging is to provide wireless broadband connectivity in meeting rooms and pre-function spaces. Though this can carry a significant cost, it allows attendees to utilize their computers in sessions. Some speakers find this can be a distraction while giving their presentation, but in spite of these concerns, there are benefits to attendee blogging. For example, if a speaker makes a remark that would be of interest to an attendee's colleague who did not attend the event, the attendee can post a blog when the remark is made and the colleague in the office can read the information and instantly ask a question to the attendee to clarify a point.

Conference blogs extend the audience of an event to anyone interested in the conference. Currently, many technology organizations are finding these blogs invaluable. In 2004, the U.S. political conventions had to provide over 20,000 square feet of space for the event bloggers who were read by hundreds of thousands of interested readers.

MOBILE TECHNOLOGIES

In addition to RFID, lead retrieval systems, and ARS, other technologies are available to enhance attendees' on-site experience. Here are a few more mobile devices that have been infiltrating into conferences.

Smart Phone   Today's mobile phone is far more than it was just a few years ago. Once the domain of voice-only communication, **smart phones** (most new phones fall into this classification) support not only voice but high-speed data transmission. This allows for services

The Treo is one example of a smart phone.

Jae C. Hong, AP Wide World Photos

that are becoming standard today: web browsing, e-mail access, and audio/video streaming, among others.

Imagine a conference program sent to the attendee's smart phone (or 3G phone) prior to the event. Perhaps the very near future will allow smart phones to interact with the hotel's or the meeting planner's registration kiosk to facilitate a completely automated registration experience, or perhaps these devices will be used as the keypads for the ARS at the event.

The possibilities are limitless. Technology-savvy planners who understand their group's needs (who they are and why they are attending) will be able to continually add services that provide extra value to both meeting organizers and conference attendees.

Personal Digital Assistant (PDA)   A few years ago, some technology pundits may have hyped the **personal digital assistant (PDA)** as the complete future of mobile communications. Now a more mature technology (though still expanding), the PDA, at its core, is a device that provides individuals with most of their critical needs (such as calendars and contacts) in a handheld device. The PDA can also be integrated with smart phone technology, blurring the distinction between these items. The PDA tends to be a slightly larger device than the mobile phone, so it frequently provides a slightly larger typing area and screen size, which can allow the PDA to better read web pages and other information that take up more screen size.

In the section titled "Virtual Gatherings" below, we discuss how an interactive floor plan can assist all participants. The PDA-based setup is one approach. A number of companies, including NearSpace (http://www.nearspace.com), are providing conference organizers with a PDA/smart phone–based downloadable version of the program. This can include not only session information but a floor plan of the exhibits. By selecting a company name, the attendee can locate its booth; by highlighting space on the show floor, the attendee can find out which exhibitors are in that area.

Let's look at another use for the PDA (or smart phone—remember that these lines are blurry). Many meeting planners, especially those managing larger shows, have traditionally produced a daily conference newspaper for distribution every morning to attendees; these dailies serve to enhance yesterday's experience and promote what's on the schedule for today. However, instead of delivering thousands of papers to everyone's sleeping room (the current mode), what if the technology-savvy planner beamed this information to everyone's PDA on a daily basis? What if everyone doesn't have a PDA or doesn't want to read it for that purpose? These are proper questions, as PDAs might not be appropriate for many groups, but we can't discount what might be the future of the electronic meeting journal simply because it's not a staple today.

Bluetooth   The PDA/smart phone also allows communication via **Bluetooth** technology, a telecommunications standard that allows mobile devices to communicate with each other. This is a short-distance communication, with most devices capable of utilizing

Bluetooth at a distance of no more than thirty feet. The most-used Bluetooth device is the mobile phone, working with the hands-free headset.

How can Bluetooth work in the meeting environment? How about setting up printing stations for attendees to wirelessly send documents to print? What about Bluetooth chats, where people can discover other nearby users and initiate live chats on their mobile devices? Perhaps another future use for Bluetooth is the interaction of the smart phone device with the registration kiosk to create name badges on site. Since its range is short, Bluetooth will probably not replace other technologies such as RFID; however, it will probably maintain a very usable place in the technology-savvy planner's (and attendee's) toolbox.

Virtual Gatherings

A special use of event-based technology is the purely virtual meeting. Many smaller meetings where stakeholders cannot afford the time or money to travel can be run virtually. The generic term "e-conferencing" is used to describe the online services that allow audio and/or video content to be delivered over the Internet.

Planners must be careful when and how they use these tools. Typically, an attendee will not sit at his or her desk all day long to view a conference, so content and visuals must be focused for this medium. Interactivity, while a cornerstone of many webcasts, can be more challenging to achieve than in a live environment. Cost can also be a major issue for some groups.

E-conferencing comes in many different forms. A few basic terms to know are listed below:

Web Conferencing. Web conferencing is a catch-all term to describe the various types of e-learning options available to the planner and attendee.

Teleconference. Also referred to as audio or voice conferencing, teleconferencing strictly uses the telephone as the medium for conversation. No Web-based environment is needed, though many Web-based tools also use an audio conference to enhance their content discussion and delivery.

Videoconference. As the name indicates, a **videoconference** uses video (and typically audio) to send content to and from facilities. Traditionally, videoconferencing is not Web-based; it uses production facilities to both upload and download the information. Some organizations and facilities have videoconferencing capabilities in-house, while many other groups must outsource this process. With the advent of webcasting, videoconferencing became a less used tool because it's much more expensive.

Webcasting. Webcasting includes streaming audio and video and use of the Web as the tool to deliver content to individuals. In a conference, organizers frequently choose to videotape certain keynote sessions. The organizers then have choices to make about the delivery of this information: It can be live or archived, can be free or pay-per-view, and can include virtual audience interactivity (typically with live webcasts). Many planners use the virtual material to add educational (and marketing) content to their Web sites. This can also be a moneymaking endeavor, although there are many expenses (hidden and otherwise) associated with this process.

Virtual Trade Show. Different from the process of selling the show floor (see earlier section titled "Sales of the Show Floor"), the attendee-based virtual trade show is an online experience where the individual can "walk the floor" and "visit booths" without leaving his or her home or office. Varying styles of interactivity and graphics are used in this approach, but whichever format is used, the main benefit of a virtual trade show is that it greatly extends the trade show from the two or three days of live exhibits to potentially a year-round buying and selling marketplace.

Podcasting. As mentioned earlier, podcasting can be used to post entire meetings for select or interested attendees to download.

Online Meeting. For small groups, **online meetings** can be an enormous time and money saver. Using a Web-based service such as WebEx (http://www.webex.com), which is one of the larger players, participants can virtually meet, using tools such as shared desktops, PowerPoint presentations, Instant Messaging (IM), chatting, as well as voice conferencing to structure the event. Many smaller committee meetings within organizations are successfully held using these tools.

The best place to learn more about videoconferencing is ConferZone (http://www.conferzone.com). Explanations, vendors, and services in this category are all available through this portal.

Postconference Technology Applications

Technology has clearly served a great purpose in the marketing and operation of a meeting, and it continues to be a useful tool once a meeting is completed. From the postconference evaluation process to the digital highlights (which weave into the marketing for the next conference), there is more to review regarding technology applications in our industry.

EVALUATIONS AND SURVEYS

Many organizers have begun to move the meeting evaluation from a paper-based process on site (it can be digitized as well) to a postconference online approach. There is debate over whether postconference evaluations provide the best accuracy of information or the highest quantity of completed evaluations. Regardless of their position, many planners use an online system. In fact, Web-based tools, such as Zoomerang (http://www.zoomerang.com), are becoming increasingly popular for this process. The Web-based services not only distribute the evaluations but tally them and provide planners with an easy-to-read analysis of the questions they posed to the attendees.

This process should not be limited to conference evaluations. Any meeting professionals who are involved in the programming process understand that learning about the needs of their audience is one of the best tools to identify program elements that create greater value for the attendee. The online survey, independent of the conference evaluation, can provide significant support to that process.

MEDIA FOR MARKETING PURPOSES

The essence of postconference technology is to extend the event past the traditional time boundaries. A conference is no longer bound to a Monday through Thursday time frame but can begin with attendee networking months prior to the opening session (using the tools previously discussed). After the conference, the planner can provide content to those who didn't attend or those who wish to view it again.

As the planner makes arrangements to videotape and stream conference activities, the wheels are put in motion to consider how to deliver this information, and issues of cost and delivery are a significant part of the conversation. Regarding cost, will planners charge for virtual attendance? Will they provide complimentary video clips of the event on their Web site either to enhance purchasing or to help the marketing of future events? As for delivery (especially in a live environment), the planner needs to make certain that the servers and technology (including bandwidth) are available so that whoever wishes to log on and view the event can do so without the signal degrading or breaking up.

The planner's best marketing tool is the success of the previous event. The digitization and distribution of this content are an absolutely critical tool for not only generating revenue from this year's event but continuing to attract attendees in future years.

Twenty-First-Century Convention Centers

Technological advances have impacted not only meetings and events but convention facilities as well. Earlier in the chapter was a discussion about various technologies that might be found in hotels. Now we move to convention centers. For a convention center to survive well into the twenty-first century, technology will be needed to ensure its competitive advantage in the future. It is important that managers understand and market technology as part of their product. For example, Price Waterhouse research (1998 Convention & Congress Center Annual Report) delineates how technology has impacted convention centers:

- Cities, CVBs, and convention centers are utilizing the Internet to market themselves to prospective clients.
- Conferencing tools allow event planners to work online with suppliers and CVBs as well as to coordinate events.
- Show managers provide online registration for exhibitors and attendees to secure Web sites for capturing credit card information.
- Development of the "smart card," a data storage device, facilitates meeting planning and security. It also provides centers and associations with valuable attendee information (e.g., registration, session attendance, purchases of products or publications, and evaluations of meetings and the center).
- User requirements for information technology services include fiber-optic and broadband data and voice and video transmissions, allowing exchanges of information with outside parties.

The following section discusses existing technology, improved service, and recommendations. This information is used to determine future needs in order to achieve a competitive advantage for facilities.

USE OF TECHNOLOGY

Having information online, through teleconferencing and videoconferencing, is highly recommended by the Convention & Congress Center's annual report. Convention center bureau information, bookings, procurement management, floor plans and setup, and even accommodations (such as hotels and restaurants near the convention center) were mentioned there. Other recommendations were copper Category 5 wiring, fiber optics, Internet access, digital and analog setups, and a variety of data lines, such as Integrated Services Digital Network (ISDN), network setup, switch 56K, and cable modems.

TYPES OF TECHNOLOGY

Most centers have a network setup and ISDN lines. Cellular and wireless technology availability is very important in properly marketing the convention center. Another recommendation is the use of access cards for security; a conference center also needs a business center offering computers, fax service, phone service, e-mail access, and Internet access. Along with the technical services, a very strong information technology support system is required to handle any problems that could arise.

ACCESS TO TECHNOLOGY

Access to technology, an aspect of customer service, is critical for attendees to communicate outside the property. Customer service and support will continue to gain emphasis in the future with attendees' desire for faster and more reliable services. There are many good convention facilities and a flood of new facilities being built across the country, but to obtain and maintain business, facilities need to make sure customer service is a number one priority. As an example, the Washington State Convention and Trade Center in Seattle initiated a service plan that is essential among all employees who work in the facility—the vision is to "provide ordinary service in an extraordinary manner." This statement says that details, no matter how small, are of great importance. This is an example of a corporate culture that can and will compete in the marketplace throughout the twenty-first century.

GREEN TECHNOLOGY

Not only does the David L. Lawrence Convention Center boast state-of-the-art technology, but it also can claim it is the first environmentally smart convention center using green technology in the United

Pittsburgh Convention Center

The city of Pittsburgh constructed a new convention center, the David L. Lawrence Convention Center, that tripled the size of its exhibit space from the previous building. The facility became fully operational in 2003. Architect Rafael Vinoly, who was inspired by the suspension bridges that connect the city to its neighbors, was the lead project designer. He imitated the bridge design by creating an upward swooping roofline that flows with the bridges. The structural plans received input from civic leaders in the fields of hospitality, planning, architecture, and economic development as well as input from the local arts community.

This $331 million center is an outstanding example of form and function. Being merged with the cultural district and business district allows a perfect setting for diversity. Visitors will find points of interest that are appealing while attending functions within the convention center. The Lawrence Convention Center boasts the following:

- Prefunction area facing the Allegheny River
- About 330,000 square feet of exhibit space
- Column-free exhibit space of 250,000 square feet
- Roughly 80,000 square feet in a secondary hall
- Ballroom with 34,000 square feet of space
- Two 175-seat lecture halls and fifty-three meeting rooms, totaling nearly 90,000 square feet
- Main kitchen with 12,000 square feet
- Thirty-seven highly accessible loading docks
- About 750 parking spaces
- Roughly 3,000 available hotel rooms in downtown business district
- New adjoining hotel in development
- State-of-the-art teleconferencing and telecommunications capabilities
- Internet access throughout
- Pedestrian walkway to river and riverfront trail

The building's technology is at the forefront of modern architectural design (it has been wired with category 6 cables). Convention goers are able to hook up to the Internet, use videoconferencing, and access wireless technology in the building—there are no dead spots for wireless users in the building.

A shadowed image of the David L. Lawrence Convention Center.
Used with permission from the David L. Lawrence Convention Center

States. The goal of the design team was to receive a gold rating under the U.S. Green Building Rating System. The center estimated that 30%–50% could be obtained in energy savings.

Water for the convention center is taken from an aquifer that exists under the city (an aquifer is a formation of permeable material that yields a sufficient amount of water to wells and springs). This water is used to reduce the energy consumption for heating and cooling. All the plants and landscape around the center are native, so there is no need for water sprinklers around the facility, thus conserving water.

Energy conservation is helped by the design of the sloped roof; it pulls up cool breezes off the water, creating the first naturally ventilated exhibit hall of its size in the United States. Natural lighting is used throughout the building, and blackout shades are available to darken rooms or to control temperatures. The convention center used materials in the building that emit fewer toxins. Also, 25% of the building was constructed with recycled material, and local materials were used in order to cut down transportation costs.

This was a new direction for convention centers, and Pittsburgh took the lead and ran with it—from the superior technology that the center was wired with to a new green technology that was just on the horizon. These complement the award-winning service the Greater Pittsburgh Convention and Visitor Bureau team has provided for years.

Buildings that merit the gold rating from the U.S. Green Building Rating System are at the forefront of an innovative way of constructing new buildings. The issues of protecting the environment and conserving resources have helped the world to see that a more environmentally friendly building can be constructed that is also a much more efficient and cost-effective building. In fact, the Environmental Protection Agency (EPA) recently put forth guidelines regarding "green meetings" to be used by all government meeting planners (*New York Times*, April 18, 2007).

Summary

Today's technology-savvy meeting professional has an arsenal of tools at his or her disposal to enhance an organization's event, from the point of both the attendee and the organization. Since time, money, and objectives don't require every technology to be integrated, the true role of planners today is to identify and determine those tools that add the greatest value to their meetings while continuing to learn about other technologies that could also impact their organization. The same holds true for facility designers and operators—the future of their business is dependent on the successful use and integration of technology.

Key Words and Terms

For definitions, see the Glossary or go to http://glossary.convention industry.org.

80211

Accepted Practices Exchange (APEX)

Audience response system (ARS)

Bandwidth

Blogging

Bluetooth

Interactive name tag

Lead retrieval system

Online meeting

Personal digital assistant (PDA)

Podcasting

Portal

Radio frequency identification device (RFID)

Request for proposal (RFP)

Room design software

Really simple syndication (RSS)

Smart phone

Videoconference

Virtual tour

Virtual trade show

Voice over Internet protocol (VoIP)

Web conferencing

Webcasting

Review and Discussion Questions

1. How can technology impact site selection?
2. List three new technologies that support meeting networking.
3. What are the seven types of Web-based gatherings?
4. How is third-party software used, and what is its advantage?
5. Why has the Web become so important to meeting planners and suppliers?
6. What are the five facets of the e-marketing strategy of the technology-savvy meeting professional?
7. In addition to enhancing live networking, RFID name tags frequently contain what other interactive tools?
8. What is the major benefit of attendee blogging during a session?
9. List four types of e-conferencing and discuss each.
10. What are some of the benefits of using online evaluations?
11. What is the main benefit of a virtual trade show?

12. What is green technology?
13. What are some of the uses of technology employed in the convention center in Pittsburgh?

About the Chapter Contributor

James Spellos, CMP, is the president of a company called Meeting U.

The convention center section of the chapter was contributed by:

Denis P. Rudd, Ed.D., CHA, FMP, PTC, is a professor and director of Hospitality and Tourism Management at Robert Morris College, Coraopolis and Pittsburgh, Pennsylvania.

Kathleen Taylor Brown holds a bachelor's degree from Lock Haven University and a master's in liberal studies from Duquesne University. Kathleen has taught part-time at Robert Morris College in Pennsylvania since 1997.

CHAPTER 14

International Issues in MEEC

MEEC organizers must be prepared to work with diverse people and cuisines.
Merrill Education

Chapter Objectives

This chapter provides the reader with an understanding of the following:

- Ways trade fairs and exhibitions vary around the world
- Status of the trade fair industry in different regions
- Terminology and protocol differences across cultures
- Aspects to consider before commitment to an international trade fair

Chapter Outline

Introduction

How Does MEEC Vary around the Globe?

    Europe

    Asia

    Africa

    Middle East

    Latin America

Ownership, Sponsorship, and Management Models

    Professional Congress Organizer (PCO)

World Trade Centers Association

International MEEC Considerations

    Lessons to Be Learned

    Methods of Exhibiting

    Terminology

    Contractual and Procedural Issues

    Customs Clearance

    Protocol

    Decision to Participate

    Other Considerations

Trade Fair Certification

Introduction

The growth of international communications and travel has brought about phenomenal changes in how the world does business. Twenty-five years ago, only the largest companies were considered "international." Today, there are few large companies that do not have an international presence. Consequently, the meetings, expositions, events and conventions (MEEC) industries have expanded internationally. In this chapter, we look at how the international scope of meetings and exhibitions has evolved and how it differs in various parts of the world.

The 69th Union of International Fairs (UIF) Congress held in October 2002 in Munich, Germany, announced some incredible statistics about the international trade fair industry. Dr. Hermann Kresse,

Report from CeBIT 2006

CeBIT is the world's largest trade fair showcasing digital IT and telecommunications. Deutsche Messe AG has organized CeBIT in Hannover each spring
since 1986. Over 6,200 exhibitors from 70 countries and some 480,000 visitors
from around the world attended the 2005 CeBIT. According to an interview
with Safak Alpay, general manager of Hannover Fairs Interpro, a subsidiary of
Deutsche Messe AG, Germany, at the 2006 CeBIT Bilisim Eurasia, 142,889
visitors were registered during the six-day event. A total exhibitor staff of
10,276 persons was deployed, 1,804 journalists were represented, and 952
companies from 19 different countries exhibited.

Source: http://www.cebit.de/7588?x=1

AUMA CEO, announced that the economic impact of trade fairs in
Germany was 23 billion euros and employment reached 250,000 full-
time jobs in the exhibition industry. The UIF has produced an updated
edition (June 2006) of its research study of the trade fair market in Asia.
The research and analysis were undertaken for UIF by Business
Strategies Group (BSG) in Hong Kong: "The report shows that the overall Asian exhibitions market grew over 12% in 2005 in terms of actual
space sold by organisers. Exhibition sales topped 10 million square
metres in the year according to the UIF/BSG research. China remains
the top market with almost 40% of space sales in the region, followed
by Japan in second place and South Korea in third." Regardless of the
location, the purposes of international meetings and exhibitions
remain the same—communication, learning, and marketing.

How Does MEEC Vary around the Globe?

Despite similarities of purpose, cultural and business influences have created different models for the MEEC industry in various parts of the world.
In this section, we survey the types of meetings and exhibitions held in
different regions of the world, how they differ in scope and operation, and
what areas of the world are embracing **trade fairs** as a primary method
of marketing. At the end of this chapter is a compilation of international
trade fair organizations with their corresponding Web addresses.

EUROPE

The trade fair industry's roots are in Europe. During the Middle Ages, the concept began with farmers and craftsmen bringing their products and wares to the town center to link with their customer base. Although the world wars of the twentieth century devastated European industry, today Europe is the focal point of international trade fairs and **trade exhibitions.**

There are two primary reasons for this. First is location—Europe has always been the crossroads of the world. International hub airports in Frankfurt, London, Amsterdam, Paris, and Rome enable visitors and

The Grassmarket has been a focal point in the Old Town for 500 years and a trading place since the beginning of the city of Edinburgh, Scotland.
Getty Images, Inc.–Hulton Archives Photos

Largest Exhibition Venue

Hannover, Germany, is the model for government and private industry working together to create a successful trade fair venue with an unparalleled economic impact on a region. Managed by Hannover Messe A.G., Hannover Fair, the world's largest exhibition venue, consists of over 5 million square feet of indoor exhibit space and 1 million square feet of covered outdoor space, restaurants, warehouses, and meeting facilities. More importantly, the regional government and the management company have worked together to establish excellent transportation and lodging facilities. Local companies have also contributed to making this facility the best in the world.

cargo to easily arrive from all parts of the world. In addition, a superlative network of rail transportation within Europe enables many cities to be within a day's transportation of one another. The second reason for the growth of trade fairs is Europe's industrial base. With reconstruction help from the United States, Europe was able to recover its manufacturing and distribution base within a few decades of World War II. With the help of their governments, European industrial centers develop trade fair facilities that are unrivaled in other parts of the world.

Germany is usually thought of as the center of industry and trade fairs in Europe. Trade fairs and exhibitions are a $10.5 billion business in Germany alone. Over 165,000 exhibitors participate in 133 international events each year; over 40% of trade fair exhibitors in Germany are from countries not in the European Union. Four of Europe's top five trade fair facilities are located in Germany (Hannover, Frankfurt/Main, Cologne, and Dusseldorf). In addition, five of the world's top international trade fairs and exhibitions are held in Germany:

1. Hannover Fair—Industrial; over 7,000 exhibitors
2. CeBIT—Information technology; over 8,000 exhibitors
3. Domotex—Flooring; over 3,000 exhibitors
4. Frankfurt Book Fair—Over 4,000 exhibitors
5. Biotechnology—Over 3,000 exhibitors

Italy is another center of international trade fair activity. Milan is the fashion trade fair center of the world and attracts buyers from

Hannover Fair—Statistics 2006

There was brisk exhibitor participation from outside Germany. Out of a total of 5,175 exhibitors, 2,322 foreign companies came from 66 different nations to exhibit in Hannover, Germany, in 2006—a turnout which is about 5% greater than in 2004. And the total amount of display space occupied by foreign exhibitors (around 45,250 square meters) was also up by more than 20% as measured against the last directly comparable show back in 2004, further confirmation of an upward trend in foreign participation at Hannover Messe. The largest foreign delegation came from India—this year's Partner Country—(343 exhibitors), followed by China (250), Italy (210), Switzerland (138), and Turkey (103). Exhibitors from other European nations were particularly gratified at the quality and international mix of trade visitors. They detected an optimistic mood and a palpable sense of an economic upswing. For the majority of Central and Eastern European exhibitors as well, Hannover Messe remains an absolute must. Numerous businesses there have recorded full order books and are already requesting stand space for the coming year.

The high level of participation on the part of Asian exhibitors also underscores the significance of Hannover Messe as a gateway to international markets. The Chinese contingent—the second-largest group of foreign exhibitors after Partner Country India—indicated extreme satisfaction with the results of their trade fair appearance.

around the world for its almost constant fashion-related trade fairs. Rome hopes to rival Hannover and Dusseldorf for industrial trade fairs. Many trade fairs and exhibitions in Italy are sponsored by the strong network of world trade centers in cities across the country.

The nations of the United Kingdom host over 1,800 exhibitions, attracting 17.3 million visitors to over 450 venues. Top exhibitions include:

- Birmingham Spring Fair
- World Travel Market (London)
- Furniture Show (Birmingham)
- Birmingham Fall Fair
- Security Solutions (Birmingham)

The Benelux nations also have a strong trade fair program. Excellent facilities exist in downtown Amsterdam and at Schipol airport, Rotterdam, and Brussels; new Congress facilities in Paris are attracting new trade fairs as well. Again, world trade centers in these cities are the focal point of promotion and operation of trade fairs.

Perhaps the greatest growth of trade fairs in Europe is occurring in the countries of Eastern Europe. New facilities are opening in Zagreb, Belgrade, Warsaw, and (most recently) Moscow.

It is anticipated that the growth of the European Union, common currency with the euro, and removal of trade barriers and tariffs will only make the European trade fair and exhibition industry continue to grow.

ASIA

The growth of trade fairs and exhibitions in Asia has been phenomenal over the past fifteen years. New facilities and government promotion have taken the industry from its infancy to world class in little more than a decade. Primarily, Asian trade fairs focus on high technology, consumer electronics, and food; however, all types of manufacturing and service industries are well represented. Asian trade fairs and exhibitions are sponsored by either trade organizations, such as the world trade centers, or individual governments.

Taiwan and Singapore have been the backbone of Asian trade fairs and exhibitions. Taiwan has excellent facilities and routinely sponsors trade fairs in the semiconductor, consumer electronics, and food industries and is also the world's leader in exhibiting at trade fairs and exhibitions in North America and Europe.

Singapore is a major destination city and consequently attracts many visitors to its textile, fashion, food, and electronics trade fairs. It has multiple facilities all linked to world-class shopping and entertainment complexes. Singapore is also attractive because it provides excellent transportation facilities, with its world-class airport serving every continent, and every facility and attraction in the city are generally within walking distance or a short taxi ride from each other. The government of Singapore is very active in promoting exhibitions. The Singapore Trade Development Board is the lead agency for marketing Singapore as an international exhibition city and provides financial and marketing support for trade fairs of both Singaporean and international organizers; it also chairs the Exhibition Management Services Council, a public/private partnership of government agencies, industry associations, chambers of commerce, and exhibition companies.

Travel and Tourism Trade Fair in Moscow

DATES AT A GLANCE

Date:
19–22 September 2006
Venue:
IEC "Crocus Expo"
143400 Moscow, Russia
Exhibition Space:
20,000 sqm
Registration Deadline:
1 July 2006

Otdykh-Leisure 2006 is held in combination with Mibex Russia/MICE Moscow 2006

International Trade Fair for Meetings,
Incentives, Conferences, Events, and Business Travel
19–21 September 2006
IEC "Crocus Expo"

Luxury Leisure 2006

International Trade Fair for Luxury Travel
19–21 September 2006
IEC "Crocus Expo"
including

SPA & HEALTH Moscow Forum for Health Tourism, Resorts, and Spa

LEISURE MOSCOW 2005

Otdykh-Leisure is the main International Autumn Trade Fair for Tourism in Russia and CIS and marks the beginning of the winter season.

   11th International Trade Fair for Tourism Otdykh-Leisure took place 21–24 September 2005 in SC "Olympiisky" and again proved its role as the main and most important autumn travel and tourism event in Russia and CIS bringing together key players of Russian and international tourism industry.

EXHIBITORS FROM ALL OVER THE WORLD

Otdykh-Leisure 2005 welcomed **967 exhibitors** (562 international, 405 Russian) from **67 countries**—among them 38 national tourism authorities. The

(continued)

Travel and Tourism Trade Fair in Moscow (*continued*)

show featured the entire product range of tourism—from city and sightseeing trips, winter holidays, winter-sun and long distance destinations to adventure and safari tours, wellness and educational holidays as well as MICE and VIP tourism.

A QUALIFIED AUDIENCE

About **58,500 visitors** attended **Otdykh-Leisure 2005**, including **85% trade visitors**. As always, the majority of trade visitors were decision makers of the Russian travel industry who met international experts to learn about new destinations and programmes, establish new business contacts, and sign contracts for the coming season.

OTDYKH-LEISURE 2005 REFLECTED THE LATEST DEVELOPMENTS IN THE RUSSIAN TRAVEL SECTOR

This year MSI Fairs & Exhibitions successfully launched two new projects dedicated to the most rapidly growing sectors of the travel industry:

MICE MOSCOW at LEISURE Workshop and Conference on 20 September SPA & HEALTH MOSCOW at LEISURE Workshop and Conference on 21 September.

TESTIMONIALS

Thanks to MSI Fairs & Exhibitions, Otdykh-Leisure has proved to be an excellent tool for developing tourism in South America as it has been bringing a daily increase in the number of visitors to our country through the contacts made there.

We will continue taking part in all future Otdykh-Leisure fairs as they are an excellent way to initiate and maintain international business relationships.

Abraham Peczenik
Tours Brasil
Rio de Janeiro, Brasil

We were very pleased with our participation and the response from both trade visitors and consumers at Otdykh-Leisure 2005. We made use of several possibilities of intensifying our presence at this event. The dance performances organised in Moscow during Otdykh-Leisure were a huge success as well, as this was the very first time that SLTB organised such an event in Russia.

Sri Lanka Tourism also got involved in agents' briefing sessions where over 60 Russian travel agents were briefed on the current situation in Sri Lanka.

Numerous trade visitors from Sri Lanka participated together with Sri Lanka Tourism at Otdykh-Leisure, and they were able to make new contacts at the stall and meet some interesting media representatives.

Otdykh-Leisure is currently one of our most successful presentation platforms on the Russian market.

Channa Jayasinghe
Director
Sri Lanka Tourism
Central European Office

Otdykh - Leisure Moscow 2006

China, as it opens up to international trade, is expanding the number and quality of its trade fairs and exhibitions. Major new facilities have been built in Hong Kong, Shanghai, and Beijing. The Shanghai International Exhibition Corporation facility covers over 1.5 million square feet. Recent trade fairs have focused on consumer goods, food, and electronics. In Hong Kong, there are more than thirty fair organizers belonging to the Hong Kong Exhibition and Convention Organizers and Suppliers Association, which includes for-profit companies, associations, and government agencies.

Thailand is a major center for clothing and textile trade shows. Excellent transportation facilities in Bangkok make it easy for visitors to arrive from around the world. Other countries nurturing trade fair programs with government promotion include Vietnam, Malaysia, and India. In these countries, the facilities are usually owned and operated by the government, and promotional activities are sponsored by various government agencies. Vietnam has taken a strong position in clothing and food trade fairs, while India is at the forefront of Asian information technology and software shows.

AFRICA

Both Cairo and Johannesburg are heavily promoting continental trade fairs with new facilities and incentives for international exhibitors. Because Johannesburg is relatively difficult and expensive to travel to, the government of South Africa works with major trade organizations and other countries to provide incentives for regional and country pavilions. The U.S. Department of Commerce

The Merlion is the symbol of Singapore. It is half fish and half lion.

Photo by George G. Fenich, Ph.D.

is providing specialized assistance to companies that plan to exhibit at African trade fairs. Special rates for participating in the U.S. pavilion and assistance from trade professionals from the Department of Commerce help make it easier for U.S. companies to exhibit in Africa. In addition, the new National Exhibition Centre in Johannesburg offers almost 500,000 square feet of covered exhibit space.

MIDDLE EAST

Trade fairs and exhibitions in the Middle East are concentrated in Dubai and Abu Dhabi in the United Arab Emirates. This concentration is the result of excellent government promotion, new facilities, and ease of travel access. Both Dubai and Abu Dhabi host international airports with service to every continent. This crossroads concept, as well as the fact that exhibition facilities are located at or near the international airports, is emphasized heavily in promotional materials. For example, both Dubai and Abu Dhabi strongly promote the duty-free zones near their airports and the extensive duty-free shopping available at their facilities. In addition, the regional market for consumer goods is very strong and puts the focus of trade fairs on items such as furniture, automobiles, and consumer electronics.

LATIN AMERICA

The huge population base of Latin America makes it well suited for trade fairs and exhibitions. Until recently, most of the Latin American trade fairs and exhibitions were regional; however, new facilities and promotional efforts have set the stage for a growth in international exhibitions. New facilities in Sao Paulo, Brazil; Santiago, Chile; and Mexico City are the hubs for this activity. The Feria International de Santiago contains over 1 million square feet of covered exhibition space and almost the same amount of open-air space. The Las Americas Exhibition Center in Mexico City provides the latest in technology to support exhibitors and attendees. Additionally, the center is built within an entertainment complex that includes a horse racing track, restaurants, hotels, and a shopping center.

Ownership, Sponsorship, and Management Models

In the United States, many trade shows are adjuncts to association meetings and are owned by the associations; others are sponsored by private entrepreneurial companies and operated on a for-profit basis. Ownership and management are usually accomplished by two companies working for the success of the show. Other service companies support the industry by helping both the trade show management company and the exhibitors.

This U.S. model is not typically followed in other countries. For their international trade fairs and exhibitions, associations do not play a major role in the organization and sponsorship. Often governments, in collaboration with organizing companies, plan and operate the trade fairs. For example, the government of China plays a major role in the sponsorship of most trade fairs presented in Beijing, Hong Kong, and Shanghai.

PROFESSIONAL CONGRESS ORGANIZER (PCO)

According to Wright, in the United States, organizers and sponsors of MEEC events will typically work with a convention and visitors bureau (CVB) and /or a destination management company (DMC). Outside the United States, there is an alternative: the professional congress organizer (PCO). The PCO represents the client in dealing with the CVB, DMC, hotel, restaurant, transportation company, and other suppliers and will negotiate with vendors on behalf of the client. PCOs tend to charge a flat fee rather than use a sliding scale or per-person basis as found at DMCs; they also tend to be more familiar with international issues such as customs, taxation, and government regulations. The PCO may even handle financial transactions, letters of credit, and foreign bank accounts. PCOs have their own association called the International Association of Professional Congress Organizers (IAPCO), and the association has a Web site: http://www.iapco.org/. (*Source: Wright. 2005. The Meeting Spectrum: An Advanced Guide for Meeting Professionals*. Amherst, MA: HRD Press.)

World Trade Centers Association

The **World Trade Centers Association** was created in 1970 as an apolitical not-for-profit organization to promote the concept of world trade centers worldwide and to encourage reciprocal programs among all of its members. Today, there are more than 300 world trade centers in 100 countries servicing more than 750,000 international businesses (go to its Web site for more information: http://world.wtca.org).

The purpose of a world trade center is to bring together businesses and government agencies involved in international trade. Most world trade centers provide business services, such as support and meeting facilities, videoconferencing, secretarial services, and translation capabilities, to their member companies. Many also conduct group trade missions to help businesses explore new markets.

Many world trade centers have also found the benefits of trade fairs and exhibitions appealing to their member companies, so most of the world trade centers have built exhibition centers as part of their facilities. Throughout the year, the centers sponsor trade fairs and events that showcase their members' products. World trade centers also sponsor trade meetings and educational events open to businesses both in their area and internationally.

International MEEC Considerations

LESSONS TO BE LEARNED

It is important for trade fair, event, and exhibition managers to learn the reasons for success in different aspects of the international marketplace. For example, North American trade show managers can learn from their European colleagues in three areas:

1. *Excellence of Infrastructure.* Few American facilities rival those of Germany; in addition, public transportation systems in Europe provide excellent support of trade fairs and exhibitions. We have already discussed the case of Hannover, Germany, earlier in this chapter. Other European cities, including Dusseldorf, Berlin, Cologne, and Rome, are following that model. Berlin has invested heavily in infrastructure to support its facilities.

2. *Logistics.* International trade fair organizers are, by necessity, experts in logistics. Because the lifeblood of many international shows is the international exhibitor, many have specialized departments devoted to helping exhibitors overcome obstacles for exhibiting in their countries. Shipping and storage procedures are simplified and expedited by these agencies to help make exhibiting in their countries as easy as possible.

3. *Support Organizations.* In America, many trade shows are sponsored and organized by associations. Even though they may be very successful, trade shows are often a secondary mission of associations. In other parts of the world, trade fairs and exhibitions are sponsored and organized by trade promotion organizations, such as the world trade centers or government agencies.

By the same token, many international trade fairs can also learn some tips from North American trade shows. For example, although the typical trade show staff in America can use additional boothmanship training, this is a dire need in most other countries. What American exhibitors consider "sins," such as smoking in a booth or leaving a booth unattended, are commonplace in other countries.

METHODS OF EXHIBITING

There are a number of differences between exhibiting at an American trade show and at an international trade fair or exhibition. These differences need to be a part of the basic research before initiating an international trade fair program. Typically, companies have choices in how they will exhibit at an international trade fair or exhibition. The U.S. government sponsors U.S. pavilions at many trade fairs, and a U.S. company can work through the government to be part of the U.S. exhibit. If a company does decide to be a part of the exhibit, the U.S. Department of Commerce can provide significant help.

Another option is to exhibit under the auspices of another company that is organizing a pavilion. This is similar to U.S. government sponsorship except that a private company may be the main interface and contractual arrangements are made with its staff. Companies should fully investigate this type of situation to ensure that the organizing company is reputable and has experience in the host country and with the desired trade fair.

Joint ventures can also be formed between companies, particularly when one has experience exhibiting at a certain trade fair. In this case, it is important that companies be sure that their products or services do not compete with each other. This type of arrangement works best when the two companies' products complement each other, and it is an excellent way for a company to enter the international trade fair marketplace and gain valuable experience.

Going it alone is another option for companies entering the international trade fair arena. Many large companies choose this route because they have the budget and staff to support the complexities of international exhibiting. Smaller companies must ensure that they have a clear understanding of all the requirements, costs, and scheduling before committing to this route; for example, smaller companies must factor in all the personnel time and costs involved in verifying that all tasks are completed. Assuming that the preparation time for an international trade show is the same as that for a domestic trade show can be a very costly mistake.

TERMINOLOGY

In many parts of the world, an exhibit is not called an exhibit or even a booth; rather, it is called a **stand.** And this is only the beginning of the differences in terminology. Depending on where the trade fair is being held and who is managing it, participating companies must be familiar with those differences.

For example, in Germany the following terms must be understood:

Ausstellung—Consumer show

Congress—Meeting or convention

Gesellschaft—Company or society

GMBH—Limited liability company

Messe—Trade fair

Messegelande—Fair site

PLC—Public limited company

Trade exhibition—Trade show

CONTRACTUAL AND PROCEDURAL ISSUES

In addition to terminology differences, contractual and procedural differences abound. Labor rules in the United States are very different from those in Europe or Asia. In Asia, there are few unions and no jurisdictional issues. Exhibitors have much more freedom in what they can do within their exhibit. In Europe, although there are unions, they are much more flexible than many in the United States.

Companies should not assume that setup or logistical contracts read the same as those in their home country. Substantial differences exist from country to country and from trade fair to trade fair. Companies should read each contract closely and adhere to all the requirements. If something is not understood, it should be brought to the attention of show management immediately.

CUSTOMS CLEARANCE

Exhibition organizers at international shows provide access to experienced international freight forwarders, who also act as custom brokers, to ensure that everything is in order and arrives on time. The freight forwarders are knowledgeable about the custom regulations for the host country and take action to ensure exhibitors know of every requirement and deadline.

Typically, goods can be temporarily imported to an international show site without having to pay duties or taxes, using either a **carnet** or a **trade fair bond.** A carnet can be very complicated to obtain, and a hefty bond must often be established. However, most trade fair venues offer trade fair bonds, which are simple to arrange. Again, the international freight forwarders are the point of contact for trade fair bonds. Be sure to inquire about host country rules on giveaways and promotional materials. In some countries, a duty is charged when the value is above a certain limit; in others, a duty is not charged for materials used for this purpose.

Freight forwarders are also cognizant of the estimated time for materials to clear customs, and they factor these times into the schedules that they provide to exhibitors. Companies fully adhere to these schedules to ensure that their materials arrive on time. Countries vary widely in the amount of time to clear customs, so be very aware of the differences if you are exhibiting in more than one country. Do not assume that because it takes only one day to clear customs in Paris or Frankfurt that it will be the same in Dubai or Taipei.

PROTOCOL

It is the responsibility of the company trade fair manager to research the business customs of the host country and the individual trade fair. Staff should then be thoroughly trained in these differences before departing for the trade fair. Always remember that what is acceptable in one country or at one trade fair may very well be offensive in the next country or at another trade fair. Although English is normally the "official" language of international trade fairs, it is not safe to assume that all attendees or other exhibitors speak English. The wise company will ensure that at least some of the staff are bilingual, particularly in the host country's language.

Exhibit staff members will be greeting people from many countries at their international exhibit, so it is imperative that they be familiar with the appropriate greetings for different cultures and the acceptable forms of address. Although most visitors will not be offended if protocol is not strictly followed, it does give visitors a positive impression if their cultural standards are observed. It is also important for visitors to be aware of negative gestures in various cultures—what is a normal gesture in one culture may be extremely offensive in another. Gift giving and invitations are other areas that require research and training before embarking on an international trade fair program. Staff should also be aware of other cultural factors concerning dining and traveling

First International Trade Show

At one point before joining academe, Dr. George G. Fenich had the job of running all the marketing and trade shows for a company. The first international show in which the company participated was held in Innsbruck, Austria. The equipment to be displayed was air freighted well in advance of the trade show, and the written material and brochures were sent later but with ample time to clear customs. Dr. Fenich sent one of his technical representatives to man the booth. On arrival, the tech rep frantically called Dr. Fenich. Although the crate was delivered to the booth and appeared in good order, when the container was opened, it was found that a critical high-tech component was missing, and in its place was a box of inexpensive nails. Some time during shipment, probably while waiting to clear customs, thieves had opened the box and stolen the equipment. They replaced it with the box of nails so that the weight of the container would remain the same and not draw suspicion. There was no time to get another piece of high-tech equipment to Austria before the show closed.

On another occasion, the tech rep arrived at a trade show the day before it was to open only to find that the written materials and brochures had been lost. He called the company and asked that a new set of brochures be sent "overnight express" to be there in time for the opening of the show. The problem was that while the shipment could get there overnight, it would take three or four days to clear customs, and the trade show would have ended.

in the host country. If spouses are traveling to the host country, they should be given briefings on the host country and its cultural expectations as well. Cultural differences and expectations vary widely:

Examples
- In Indonesia, greetings are stately and formal; do not rush. Hurried introductions (which commonly occur in trade fair settings) show a lack of respect.
- In the Netherlands, always avoid giving an impression of superiority. Egalitarianism is a central tenet of Dutch society. Everyone in a Dutch company, from the boss to menial laborers, is considered valuable and worthy of respect.
- When interacting with French visitors to an exhibit, never use first names until you are told to do so.

- Germans generally take a long time to establish a close business relationship and may appear cold in the beginning, but this will change with time.
- Be very careful regarding what your exhibit staff wear. What is the customary business dress for the host country? What colors should not be worn? For example, avoid wearing yellow in Singapore; it is the color worn at funerals.
- At a business meeting in Saudi Arabia, coffee is often served toward the end of the meeting as an indication that the meeting is about to end.
- Also, in most Arabic countries, the left hand is considered dirty, so you should never eat or accept anything with this hand. Be sure when giving gifts or promotional materials that you do so with the right hand.
- When giving away gifts in Switzerland, avoid giving away knives—it is considered bad luck.
- If a Japanese person gives you a gift, do not throw away the wrapping or tear it up. It is considered part of the gift.
- Aside from handshakes, there is no public contact between the sexes in many countries. Do not kiss or hug a person of the opposite sex in public—even if it is your spouse. On the other hand, in some countries contact is permitted between people of the same sex. Men may hold hands with men and even walk with arms around each other; this is interpreted as nothing but friendship.
- Westerners frequently find Arabic names confusing. The best solution is to request the names of anyone you meet, speak to, or correspond with. Find out their full names (for correspondence) as well as how they are to be addressed in person.
- Understand the hierarchies of doing business within a foreign country. For example, the managing director in England equates to the CEO in an American firm.
- Keep in mind that the English do not consider themselves European. This is vital when discussing issues regarding the European Union.
- In many European countries, employees get four or five weeks of summer vacation. Many countries virtually shut down for the month of August.
- Eye contact among the French is frequent and intense—often this is intimidating to U.S. visitors.

- When negotiating in China, always give many alternatives so the Chinese negotiators have room to negate several options with dignity. Also, always keep the same negotiating team throughout the process.
- The traditional Chinese greeting is a bow. When bowing to a superior, you should bow more deeply and allow him or her to rise first.
- In many Asian countries, it is not appreciated to pat people on the shoulder or initiate any physical contact.
- When negotiating in Italy, a dramatic change in demands at the last minute is often a technique to unsettle the other side. Be patient—just when it appears impossible, the situation will clear itself.
- In Japan, the host will always treat when you are taken out. Allow your host to order for you. Be enthusiastic while eating and show great thanks afterwards.
- Also in Japan, business cards are presented after a bow or hand-shake. Present your card with the Japanese side facing your colleague so that it can be read immediately. Handle cards very carefully, and do not put them in your pocket or wallet. Never write on a person's business card in his or her presence.
- Age and rank are very important in Korea, so it is usually easiest to establish a relationship with a businessperson of your own age.
- The Swedes tend to be very serious, and humor is not part of the business environment.
- Hospitality is very important in Taiwan. Expect to be invited out every night after hours. This will entail visiting local nightspots and clubs, and outings may last until the wee hours of the morning.
- Avoid pouring wine at a social occasion in Argentina. There are several complex taboos associated with wine pouring that a foreigner can unknowingly violate. For example, pouring with the left hand, a common practice in the United States, is a major insult in Argentina.
- In the United States, the hand gesture where the thumb and forefinger are forming a circle with the other three fingers raised is considered the "OK" sign.
    - In Brazil, it is considered a vulgar or obscene gesture.
    - In Greece and Russia, it is considered impolite.
    - In Japan, it signifies money.
    - In southern France, it means zero or worthless.

Japanese persons exchanging business cards.
Stock Boston

- In the United States, waving the hand back and forth is a means of saying hello.
  - In Greece, it is called the *moutza* and is a serious insult—the closer the hand is to the face of the other, the more threatening it is.
  - In Peru, waving the whole hand back and forth can signal "no."
- In most of the world, making a fist with the thumb raised means "OK."
  - In Australia, it is a rude gesture.

These are simply a few of the cultural issues that foreign businesspeople must face. Before traveling to any country, it is wise to consult as many sources as possible to learn the appropriate business and social behaviors for the culture. Take the time to learn the appropriate behavior in the host country and the greeting expectations for potential visitors to the trade fair.

The following are some Web sites that deal with international protocol:

- eDiplomat: Global Portal for Diplomats at http://www.ediplomat.com/

- U.S government site at http://www.state.gov/s/cpr
- Central Intelligence Agency World Fact Book at http://www.cia.gov/cia/publications/factbook/
- Executive Planet at http://www.executiveplanet.com/

Below are some other differences between international trade fairs and U.S. trade shows (keep in mind that these are generalizations and do not apply to all situations):

- Hospitality events are generally held on the exhibit floor, with many companies providing food and beverage as a matter of course in their exhibit.
- Height restrictions may be nonexistent. Many large exhibits may be two or three levels.
- Rules on smoking in the exhibit hall may not exist, and many exhibitors and attendees may smoke in the exhibits.
- Some trade fair organizing companies may not offer "lead retrieval" systems that U.S. companies are accustomed to. It is always wise for a company to bring its own method of capturing leads.
- International trade fairs are often longer in duration than U.S. trade shows and often are open on weekends as well. Although in Europe the show may run from 9 A.M. to 6 P.M., in Brazil or other Latin American countries it is common for trade fairs to open at 2 P.M. and run until 10 P.M. or 11 P.M.
- Be aware that most of the world outside the United States is metric. Voltages may differ, and exhibitors may need plug-in adaptors or transformers. The video format may be different, so the electronic media you carry to the show may be worthless if the television only accepts Phase Alternating Line (PAL) format.

DECISION TO PARTICIPATE

Because exhibiting at an international trade fair or exhibition is a significant investment, it is important that companies seriously consider whether this move makes good business sense. First, consider the following top-level questions:

- Would international trade fair exhibiting support your business objectives?
- Who is your international audience that can be reached through a trade fair program?

- What trade fairs or exhibitions are available in your industry?
- What is the audience profile for each potential trade fair or exhibition?
- Do you have a system in place to determine your return on investment?

If these questions support a company's decision to initiate an international trade fair program, the following questions help analyze the situation before making a final decision:

- What are the costs associated with exhibiting at each potential trade fair or exhibition? Companies must be sure to calculate the costs for travel, shipping, translated materials, and other items that are not a normal part of domestic exhibiting.
- What are the cultural consequences of exhibiting at each potential trade fair or exhibition? Investigate how the fair operates and what cultural rules may apply. Provide training for all staff who will participate.
- Does the company have the personnel resources to support adding international trade fairs to its marketing mix? International trade fairs are often longer than domestic trade shows and therefore may require more staff.
- What type of participation is best for the company? Explore the options that are available: U.S. pavilion? Joint venture? Going it alone?
- Have all the requirements for each trade fair been identified and analyzed? Every trade fair is different, and an exhibiting company must be clear on all requirements before committing funds and resources.
- Does senior management support an international trade fair program? An international trade fair or exhibition is a serious investment—one that should require commitment from the highest levels of company management.
- Are the logistic requirements fully understood? Although trade fair management companies generally provide detailed instructions to exhibitors, it is imperative that key people in the company understand all the requirements, especially deadlines, for shipping materials.

OTHER CONSIDERATIONS

There are many other considerations when a company is determining whether to participate in an international trade fair:

- Visas may be required for entry and exit.
- Items that Americans take for granted may have to be declared upon entry to a country. For example, brochures and written materials must be declared and taxes paid on them
- Many international destinations require payment of departure taxes.
- Most countries require that payment be made to ensure that goods exhibited at a trade show are exported and not sold within the country. A freight-handling company can arrange a bond as security.
- Not only is the language in a foreign country likely to be different, but so is the electrical current (120 volts in the United States compared to 220 volts elsewhere), recording media and playback mechanisms, television/VCR monitor protocols, and measurement (meters, not feet/inches).

Trade Fair Certification

The U.S. Department of Commerce has developed a program to promote exports of U.S. products and services abroad. The **Trade Fair Certification Program** endorses independent and association show organizers who manage and organize overseas events. The certification helps trade fairs attract more exhibitors, provides additional support and value-added services for exhibitors, and promotes the event through a variety of publications and sources. Requirements that trade show organizers must meet for Department of Commerce Trade Fair Certification are shown in Figure 14–1.

To receive certification, trade associations:

- Must have either a U.S. pavilion or a commitment to attract at least ten U.S. exhibiting companies.
- Must have a U.S. office or agent.
- Must have exhibited before.

FIGURE 14–1   Trade Fair Certification.

Source: http://www.usatrade.gov/Website/Website.nsf/WebBySubj/TradeEvents_TradeFairCertification

Summary

The growth of international trade fairs and exhibitions has been phenomenal over the past ten years. Europe, the historical home of trade fairs, continues to strengthen its hold on the world's largest trade fairs and those with the most significant economic impact. Asia has made great strides by building state-of-the-art facilities and promoting its efforts throughout the world. The Middle East, Africa, and Latin America all have strong efforts under way to capture a larger piece of the international trade fair and exhibition market.

Worldwide communications, easy travel access, and open markets have been a boon to the international trade fair and exhibition industry. Few large companies can afford not to be in the international marketplace today. What was once the playground of only the world's largest companies is now a necessity for most companies of any size. Trade fairs and exhibitions are the easiest method for these companies to enter the marketplace and meet their potential customers.

Exhibiting at international trade fairs is not easy. Cultural and business differences present a new set of problems for the exhibitor, along with more complex logistics and travel procedures. Companies must seriously analyze all factors before committing to an international trade fair program.

Key Words and Terms

For definitions, see the Glossary or go to http://glossaryconvention industry.org.

Ausstellung	PLC
Carnet	Stand
Congress	Trade exhibition
Gesellschaft	Trade fair
GMBH	Trade fair bond
Messe	Trade Fair Certification Program
Messegelande	World Trade Centers Association

Review and Discussion Questions

1. List some ways that international trade fairs may differ from U.S. trade shows.
2. What are two reasons for Europe's strength in the international trade fair industry?
3. What is the purpose of the World Trade Centers Association?
4. What are some of the complexities that a company must consider before exhibiting at an international trade fair or exhibition?
5. What options does a company have for participating in an international trade fair or exhibition?

References

Web Sites

Association of Exhibition Organisers (U.K.)	http://www.aeo.org.uk
Union des Foires Internationales	http://www.ufinet.org
Association of German Trade Fair Industry	http://www.auma-fairs.com

Canadian Association of Exhibition Management	http://www.caem.ca
Scandinavian Trade Fair Council	http://www.fairlink.se
Hong Kong Exhibition and Convention Organisers and Suppliers Association	http://www.exhibitions.org.hk
InterEXPO	http://www.inter-expo.com
Singapore Association of Convention Organisers and Suppliers Association	http://www.saceos.org.sg
Thailand Tradeshow Organization	http://www.thaitradeshow.org
China Council for Promotion of International Trade	http://www.ccpit.org
China Events	http://dcoem.com
European Major Exhibition Centres Association	http://emeca.com
Association des Expositions, Foires et Salon Wallonie	http://www.fil.be
Federation Belge des Activites de l'Expos	http://www.exobel.be
Federation des Foires et Salons de Belgiq du Grand-Duche de Luxembourg	http://www.febelux.be
Federation Française des Métiers de l'Exposition	http://www.ffme.org
France-Congres	http://www.francecongres.org
Foires Salons et Congres de France	http://www.foiresaloncongres.com
Fachverband Messen und Ausstellungen	http://www.fama.de
FAMAB Design-Exhibition-Event	http://www.famab.de
Forum Marketing-Eventagenturen	http://www.fme-net.de
German Convention Bureau	http://www.gcb.de
Interessengemeinschaft Deutscher Fachmesse Ausstellungsstadte	http://www.idfa.de
Associazione Promozione Mostre	http://www.assoexpo.com
Associazione Enti Fieristici Italiani	http://www.aefi.it

Associazione Nazionale Aziende Allestrici Fieristici Mostre	http://www.federlegno.it
Feram I&CT	http://www.feram.org
European Arenas Association	http://www.eaaoffice.org
Exhibition Services Association Holland	http://www.esah.nl
Branchevereniging voor Beurzen & Evenemen	http://www.fbtn.nl
Netherlands Convention Bureau	http://www.nlcongress.nl
Netherlandse Vereniging van Beursoorganisato	http://www.nvbo.nl
Asociacion de Ferias Espanolas	http://www.afe.es
Schweizerische Zentrale Fur Handelsforderung	http://www.osec.ch
Switzerland Convention & Incentive Bureau	http://www.myswitzerland.com
Swiss Expo & Event Makers	http://www.expo-event.ch
Vereinigung Messen Schweiz	http://www.messenschweiz.ch
British Exhibition Contractors Association	http://www.beca.org.uk
Exhibition Venues Association	http://www.exhibitionvenues.com
National Arena Association	http://www.primary.uk.com/naa
European Federation of Conference Towns	http://www.efct.com
European Society of Association Executives	http://www.esae.org
European Tourism Trade Fair Association	http://www.ettfa.org
Europaischer Verband der Veranstaltungs	http://www.evvc.org
Associated European Exhibition Organization	http://www.xmeurope.com
Asociacion de Ferias Internacionales de Am	http://www.afida.com
Association Internationale des Palais de Congres	http://www.aipc.org
Bureau International des Expositions	http://www.bie-paris.org

Confederation of Organisers of Packaging Expositions	http://www.cope.org.uk
International Association of Assembly Managers	http://www.iaam.org
International Association of Convention and Visitor Bureaus	http://www.iacvb.org
International Association of Professional Congress Organizers	http://www.iapco.org
International Chamber of Commerce	http://www.icc.org
International Congress and Convention Association	http://www.icca.nl
International Exhibition Logistics Associates	http://www.iela.org
International Exhibit System Association	http://www.iesaj.org
International Federation of Exhibition Services	http://www.ifesnet.org
Union des Associations Internationales	http://www.uia.org
World Council for Venue Management	http://www.venue.org
World Trade Centers Association	http://www.wtca.org

About the Chapter Contributor

Ben McDonald is the vice president of BenchMark Learning, Inc. Founded in 1995, BenchMark Learning assists businesses with training and development solutions primarily in the sales and business development areas. The company has since expanded its services and partnerships to include the full spectrum of sales solutions, business development, benchmarking, and competitor analysis in order to provide clients with a total solution for increasing revenue.

CHAPTER 15

Putting It All Together

MEEC events are like puzzles—eventually they must be put together.
Dorling Kindersley Media Library

Chapter Objectives

This chapter provides the reader with an understanding of the following:

• Key tasks in creating a citywide meeting
• Method to create a statement of conference objectives
• Ways to identify budget expenses and income sources
• Timetable for implementation of different meeting planning tasks
• Process of conducting a site inspection
• Assessment of success of the meeting

Chapter Outline

Introduction

Many books contain a concluding chapter that repeats and summarizes the elements of the earlier chapters. In this textbook, a fictitious case study of a citywide convention serves the same purpose. The goal of this case study is to bring together all the previous chapters. Throughout this text, you have read about the tasks associated with meeting planning. Through this case study, you will learn more about topics from the previous chapters and how they apply to a citywide annual conference for 3,000 attendees. The objective of this case study is to help you understand the various tasks a planner must complete in order for a meeting, exposition, event, or convention to be successful. In addition, this case study will help you to understand the complexities of the budget and timetable, as well as the many people with whom a planner must communicate.

This case study uses a three-year planning timetable for one citywide conference. The meeting planning cycle is continuous, and it is important to understand that two of the key skills a planner must possess are the abilities to organize and to multitask. Planners typically work on three to five meetings or events simultaneously, each in different stages of development.

As you review the budget portion of the case study, it is important to understand that many variables, including the time of year the meeting is held, the planner's ability to negotiate, the value of the business to the facility, and the trade-offs, will affect the budget. This budget is broad and was created to highlight the many details the planner must consider.

The Association

As a meeting or event planner, it is important to understand your audience—the attendees of the event. For association meeting planners, this is critical as they market the conference to association members and to potential members. The meeting planner must also communicate information about his or her association members to suppliers for the convention. The better a supplier understands the audience of the meeting planner, the better the supplier can serve them. For example, if a hotel knows that the majority of the people attending a meeting are women, the hotel might add products that women use, such as hand cream or shower caps, to the room amenities.

The American Small Animal Association (ASAA) is an example of a typical association in the United States. The ASAA is an 8,000-member nonprofit association whose members are veterinarians from throughout the United States who specialize in care for small animals. The ASAA was founded ten years ago by a group of veterinarians who saw the need to update research and to network with

AMERICAN SMALL

ANIMAL ASSOCIATION

Logo for the (fictitious) American Small Animal
Association.

other veterinarians specializing in small animal care. Over 60% of
the organization's membership operates independently owned
veterinary clinics; the remainder of the association members are
suppliers to the veterinary industry. The suppliers include pharmaceutical companies, prescription food companies, and product suppliers. Although the number of women members is increasing, 70%
of the members are male; 60% of the members are Caucasian, 30%
African American, and 10% a mix of Latino, Asian, and Native
American. It is important to know the makeup of the organization so
that the event can meet its wants and needs. The planner or
organizer must ask two questions: Who is the group? Why are its
members here?

An executive committee and a board of directors operate the ASAA, while the executive director and seven committee members oversee the day-to-day operations of the association. Members of the board of directors are elected from seven established regions and serve two-year terms. All board elections take place during the annual meeting and are announced during the final night.

Sue Rodriguez is the director of meetings for the ASAA and is a full-time employee. Sue is one of the five full-time employees and is responsible for coordinating the seven regional meetings and the annual conference; she reports directly to the executive director. Planning for the annual conference begins three years in advance of the meeting date. For the past five years, attendance at the annual conference has increased 5% per year, and last year, 37% of the membership attended the meeting. This increase is attributed to the success of the trade show portion of the conference that was added five years ago.

GOALS

To begin preparation for the annual conference, Sue reviews past annual conference evaluations from attendees and members of the board of directors. The board of directors wanted to save money by cutting down on the cost related to networking activities, but the members indicated how important it is to have time to meet other professionals from around the country. The board also would like to see the money collected from this conference increased by 10% because other than membership dues, the annual conference is the largest revenue source for the association. Last year, the ASAA created the Small Animal Preventive Disease Certificate (SAPDC). During the annual convention, veterinarians earn five continuing education units (CEUs) and learn about the preventive medicines that can be used to save the lives of small animals.

To help focus her thoughts, Sue reads the ASAA mission statement: The mission of ASAA is to provide an educational forum for members to exchange ideas and develop ways to ensure the health of small animals. This mission is accomplished by providing quality education for its members, offering assistance to new veterinarian clinics, and providing a forum for members to meet and to assist each other with emerging technologies.

To help Sue measure **return on investment (ROI),** she creates operational and educational objectives. The operational objective for this conference is to increase meeting profits by 5% over last year's conference. Sue works with the program committee to create the educational objective for this meeting, which is to increase the number of attendees enrolled in SAPDC classes by 10% and to provide additional networking opportunities. Sue hopes to meet these objectives by offering a four-day conference focused on education and networking that will result in an increase of conference profits by 5%.

BUDGET

To create the budget (see Tables 15–1 and 15–2), Sue reviews the past meeting budgets. For her expenses, she includes the cost of marketing materials, the convention center, host hotel, decorator, audiovisual equipment, speakers, entertainment, and staff. In addition, Sue must consider operational objectives for the meeting. To locate income sources, Sue looks at past meeting **sponsors** and exhibitors.

The hotel budget will include meeting room rental, food and beverage, staff sleeping rooms, and service charges and gratuities. In creating the budget, Sue knows that she will have some negotiation opportunities based on the ASAA sleeping and meeting room usage ratios. The better that the ASAA's use of meeting rooms to sleeping rooms will match the hotel's ideal sleeping room to meeting room ratio, the better the rate that can be negotiated. To assist in managing the hotel blocks, Sue uses a housing bureau and includes that cost in the hotel expense item.

The convention center expenses will include the cost of space for meeting rooms, exhibit hall, electricity, Internet connection, garbage pickup, security, and staffing for coffee and food stations. To maximize dollars, Sue plans the majority of her educational events at the convention center. This not only enables her to use the daily rate for the rooms at the convention center but also is a selling point for the exhibitors who want attendees near the trade show.

Sue will need to identify an **exposition service contractor (ESC)** to provide decorations and to set up the trade show. She will also need to assess audiovisual needs for both the hotel and convention center. The ESC will provide staging for the reception, general session, trade show, and awards night; and the **audiovisual (AV) company** will provide sound and light. In order to provide an accurate quote, the ESC must be given information on carpeting requests, number of trade show booths, estimated freight use, and types of staging needed for the opening session, general session, and awards dinner.

TABLE 15–1	Budget Income		
Budget		**Income**	**Registration**
			3,000 attendees
Members			1,680 attendees
	early (at 60% = 1,008 people)	$600 p/p	$604,800
	late (at 40% = 672 people)	$800 p/p	$537,600
Nonmembers			
	early (at 50% = 300 people)	$700 p/p	$210,000
	late (at 50% = 300 people)	$900 p/p	$270,000
Student	(at 5% = 120 people)	$100 p/p	$12,000
Speakers	(100 people)	$300 p/p	$30,000
Exhibitors		Included in exhibit fee	
Registration Total			**$1,664,400**
SAPDC	(500 people)	$100 p/p	$50,000
Exhibitors	(500 exhibitors)	$3,000 p/exhibit	$1,500,000
Sponsors			$120,000
Extended Learning			$10,000
Other			$5,000
Total Income			**$3,349,400**
Expenses			$1,881,438
Net Income			**$1,467,962**

The AV company will need to know the sound and lighting needs for each venue and the type of production for the general session, opening reception, and awards dinner. The general session will be sent via webcast to members unable to attend, so Sue lists this as a separate expense (see Table 15–2).

To budget transportation, Sue looks at past budgets to determine how many attendees used the shuttle service for airport transfers, but she knows this expense will vary greatly depending on the existing

TABLE 15–2	Budget Expenses

Budget	Expenses
Convention Center	$350,000
Host Hotel	$212,643
Decorations	$102,245
Signage	$80,000
Audiovisual Equipment	$125,000
Webcasting	$60,000
Pressroom	$50,000
Transportation	$18,250
Off-Site Venue	$50,000
Golf Event	$150,000
Marketing Committee	$185,000
Program Committee	$10,000
Speakers	$52,000
Entertainment	$17,000
Security	$180,000
Insurance	$100,000
Special Services	$5,000
News Delivery	$30,000
Temporary Staff	$67,200
Tote Bags	$30,000
Site Visits	$2,100
Other	$5,000
Total Expenses	**$1,881,438**

transportation options in a given city. At this point, she includes full shuttle service for each day of the conference, VIP transportation, and transportation to the off-site events and the golf tournament. In addition to ground transportation, Sue's transportation budget includes air transportation for staff and VIPs as well as freight shipping. Of the transportation items budgeted, freight shipping is the least expensive;

due to the large shipping volume of exhibitors, the ASAA is charged a minimum for association shipping needs. The budget for the off-site golf tournament will vary depending on the conference location. To include these items, Sue uses the amount from the last meeting and increases the cost by 5%.

Reviewing the budget history is also a good starting place when Sue allocates funds for marketing. With a minimum of five marketing pieces being created, this can become very expensive; however, with the increased use of the Internet, more money is being spent on Web development rather than large marketing brochures.

Of the speakers for the ASAA, 75% are members presenting research papers. To encourage members to make presentations, the ASAA offers presenters a 50% discount on the early registration fee. The majority of the money allocated for speakers actually is used for a keynote speaker and entertainment. To locate the keynote speaker and entertainment, Sue uses a speaker's bureau; the speaker's bureau's fee is included in this expense item.

In order to have a smooth meeting, Sue will need to hire temporary staff. This budget item includes the cost for registration personnel, staff for on-site assembly of attendee packets, room monitors, and staff to distribute evaluations and carry out other duties. Sue will need to bring in temporary staff one day prior to the meeting for training and will pay staff for their time.

Security is an ongoing expense that the ASAA must include in its budget. Because the ASAA is increasing its involvement in new research for small animals and this new research is both confidential and controversial, more security will be needed.

Insurance is another increasing expense. Sue includes insurance to cover attrition and loss of revenue due to acts of God, terrorism, and liability. The $100,000 budgeted represents 5% of the cost to host this meeting.

To cover expenses for attendees with special needs, Sue includes a special services item in the budget, which will be used for members who identify themselves as needing translators, written material to be published in Braille, sign language interpreters, special accommodations for Seeing Eye dogs, and so on. For example, Sue knows that one of her key sponsors is legally blind and has a Seeing Eye dog. To accommodate him, Sue makes sure that water and dog food are available. Five of the ASAA members are hearing impaired, so for these members, Sue arranges for sign language interpreters to be on site to escort them throughout the conference.

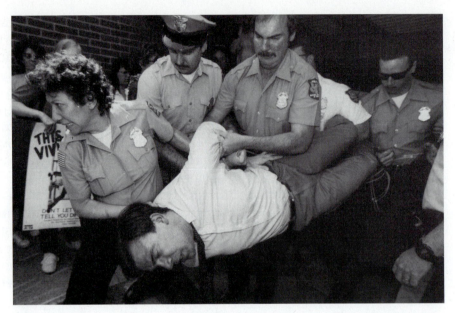

Sammy Busby, a member of People for the Ethical Treatment of Animals, was arrested during protests at the National Institutes of Health in Bethesda, Maryland. Several people were arrested while demonstrating against the use of animals for experimentation as part of World Laboratory Animal Liberation Day.

AP Wide World Photos

When Sue creates the budgets, she contacts city officials where the meeting will be held. As a nonprofit, the ASAA is exempt from most city and state taxes, but she must file the documents to ensure the exemption. Furthermore, Sue will need to bring forms proving that the ASAA is a not-for-profit organization; the forms will also be filed with suppliers.

Sue includes some expenses in the budget even though she knows that these expenses will be picked up by sponsors. Each year, Sue has no problem finding a company to sponsor tote bags given to all attendees, the on-site newspaper, transportation, the meal for the opening reception, and the entertainment for the VIP dinner. It is important that Sue includes these items in the budget to document these expenses.

To allow for unexpected expenses, Sue creates an "Other" expense category, which is used to cover additional expenses that do not occur every year or that are not planned for. For example, if the cost of stamps increases, this contingency would be covered.

INCOME

The income (see Table 15–1) will offset the expenses for the meeting. Estimated expenses for this meeting are $1,881,438. To reach the financial objectives and make a profit, Sue must not only pay all expenses but also build in a profit.

In determining the income, Sue starts with income generated from the registration fees. She first takes the expected attendance of 3,000 and subtracts 500 exhibitors whose registration fee is included in the exhibitor fee and then subtracts the 100 speakers who will pay a reduced registration. The ASAA has three registration fee categories: members, nonmembers, and students. Convention history shows that 70% are members, 25% nonmembers, and 5% students. In order to reduce attrition fees, Sue creates an early registration fee and a late fee for members and nonmembers. Typically, 60% of the members and 50% of the nonmembers will register early. Sue estimates that if registration alone will cover expenses, she must charge $629 per person. With this in mind, Sue's registration fee structure is $600 for an early member, $700 for an early nonmember, $800 for a late member, and $900 for a late nonmember. Students only pay $100, thus encouraging them to join when they are employed in the field. Sue estimates her registration income to be $1,664,400.

Following the income generated from registration fees, the exhibitors are the largest single source of income for the ASAA. It will cost the ASAA approximately $10 per square foot for the convention space, ESC, and audiovisual equipment. The ASAA will sell this trade show space for $30 per square foot. History shows a steady 10% increase in exhibitors per year; at the last conference, about 450 companies ordered booths. Sue estimates exhibitor income for this year to be $1,500,000 (500 exhibitors spending $3,000 each for a ten-foot by ten-foot booth).

Other sources of income that Sue will include in the budget are rebates generated from hotel rooms, the transportation company, and the ESC. Rather than accept commissions for these items, the ASAA negotiates a rebate per room night that becomes an income stream. There is a small amount of money raised by the sale of extended learning products, including DVDs, CDs, books, and audiotapes.

Income from the SAPDC is $100 per person, in addition to the registration. Last year, the ASAA charged $200 per person—the cost is low to encourage attendees to take classes toward certification.

Request for Proposal (RFP)

Once the meeting objectives are laid out and a budget determined, Sue creates a **request for proposal (RFP).** In creating the RFP, Sue wants to include accurate information to help hotels and cities submit good proposals. She includes meeting specifications on the ASAA and explains that the RFP is sent three years prior to the annual conference date. Sue collects proposals and reviews them with Dave Rogers, executive director, and Elizabeth Rice, a board member serving as the convention chair. Sue, Dave, and Elizabeth will choose two cities to visit in order to conduct an initial site inspection. After the initial site inspections to all selected cities are complete, a decision will be made, and Sue and Dave will conduct a second site inspection to the chosen city to begin contract negotiations. In order to avoid any bias, the ASAA will pick up the cost of the site inspection with the understanding that when a city is selected, the host city will rebate the cost of the site inspection.

The RFP will include a list of cities under consideration and the preferred dates. Although the dates may vary between the months of March and April, the days of the week must be Thursday to Sunday. The annual conference is held around the country, primarily in large cities near places where members of the board of directors reside.

Sue's RFP includes a detailed grid of her meeting room needs. She includes special requests; for example, her classroom sets require two chairs per six-foot table and a water station set in the back of the room. She also includes a food and beverage summary that notes special dietary needs of attendees. Her meeting room grid includes the event, number of attendees, and room set.

The ASAA prefers to use no more than five hotels in a given city. A grid is created requesting the number of suites, single rooms, and double rooms that the ASAA anticipates using at each hotel. In considering a city, Sue looks for downtown hotel properties that offer a wide range of room prices, but the hotels need to be in close proximity to each other. The host hotel must be willing to block a minimum of 900 rooms; in addition to the sleeping room block, the host hotel will be the site of the opening night reception and break-out rooms for special-interest groups.

A detailed history, in the form of a grid of the last three years, is included in the RFP. The history grid shows the peak room nights, meeting room block, sleeping room block, pickup for the host hotel and the room block, and pickup at each of the nonhost hotels. She also includes a food and beverage section showing reported use. The ASAA reports a 10% increase in meeting attendees per year over the last two years and has an attrition rate of only 2%.

The final portion of the RFP is a two-page questionnaire for the hotel to complete and submit with the proposal. Questions include comp room policy, deposit policy, definition of "sold out," attrition policy, master accounts, split folios, shuttle service availability, tax rate, nonprofit tax policy, gratuity distribution, Internet connection, phone charges, and fitness facilities. Sue also includes questions about how the hotel handles "in conjunction withs" (ICWs) and exhibitor room blocks and whether the hotel will work to create priority housing for members over non-members. Sue found that this form provides a quick way for her to compare hotels.

The RFP is sent to the destination marketing organization (DMO) **convention and visitors bureau (CVB)** for distribution to appropriate hotels. Included in the RFP is a questionnaire for the DMO to complete. The questionnaire includes questions regarding state, local, and hotel room taxes as well as holidays, union contracts, special venues, DMO services, and citywide events or holidays that take place during the ASAA meeting dates.

First Site Inspection

Sue, Dave, and Elizabeth have reviewed the proposals and identified two cities with available dates to host the ASAA citywide: Chicago and Dallas. Sue calls the DMOs in those cities to arrange to spend three days in each city and explains to them that the team plans to conduct a detailed site inspection to look for hotels, off-site venues, and golf courses. She sends the site inspection form that the team will use to evaluate the city and properties, explaining that the team will stay at the hotels under consideration as host properties and will conduct short tours of nonhost hotels under consideration. For the nonhost properties, the team only needs to meet with the hotel sales contact, see a standard room, and tour the outlets.

DAY ONE

Mark Tester, vice president of sales, Chicago CVB, meets Sue, Dave, and Elizabeth at Chicago's O'Hare airport. On arrival, Mark gives a driving tour of downtown, passing by all the hotels under consideration.

They have lunch at the Chicago Museum of Art, where they are joined by Kesha Evans, owner of Windy City, a **destination management company (DMC).** Kesha explains the various services she can provide, including transportation and arrangements for off-site events, spouse tours, and private dining. Tom Delaney, catering manager at the Chicago Museum of Art, introduces himself and takes the group on a tour of the private function areas of the museum and recommends the best area for an off-site event. He gives Sue a sales packet with sample menus and pricing.

After lunch, Mark takes the inspection team to the Hyatt Regency McCormick Place to meet with its sales manager, Bob Taylor, and its general manager, Larry Rose. They tour the property, looking at sleeping rooms, suites, singles, and doubles as well as the meeting rooms and ballrooms for possible locations for the opening reception, special-interest group meetings, and available outlets. After the tour, they meet in one of the conference rooms to discuss available dates and rates.

Then Sue, Dave, and Elizabeth meet at 6 P.M. in the hotel restaurant for dinner. During dinner, they make observations, noting how the guests are treated, what the quality of the food is, the time food is served, and whether the wait staff are attentive. They order different entrées to sample the many types of food their attendees might order if they stay at this hotel. After dinner, Sue walks the meeting space, looking into the meeting rooms to see how the rooms are set.

DAY TWO

At 8:30 A.M., Mark meets the team members, who have already eaten breakfast and checked out of the hotel. Mark has arranged for a 9:00 A.M. meeting with Randy Moses, senior sales manager of McCormick Place Convention Center. Randy gives a tour of the facility, taking time to show them what he sees as the best locations for their functions, loading docks, and shuttle drop-off and pickup, as well as the areas where sponsored items such as banners are allowed. Sue asks about available dates, food and beverage concession hours, taxes, union rules, and contract renewal dates. Randy provides this information and discusses the security and the medical and emergency procedure guidelines. Both Mark and Randy explain to Sue, Dave, and Elizabeth how the CVB and convention center work as a team to help market the Chicago meeting to attendees. They discuss marketing options, including premailers and on-site promotions the year prior to coming to the host city.

For lunch, Mark takes the group to the Golden Princess, a luxury yacht owned by ABC Charters, a company that provides dinner tours of Lake Michigan. Rich Cunningham, general manager of ABC Charters, meets with them. Today, they are having a special lunch for meeting planners to sample the menu and enjoy a mini-charter experience. The president of Chicago DMC Services, Deborah Adams, explains her services and has photos showing other off-site locations Sue may want to consider.

The afternoon is spent making contacts and touring the hotels under consideration. Mark arranges thirty-minute tours of each non-host hotel and explains to the hotel sales contact that they only want to see sleeping rooms and restaurant areas.

By 4 P.M., Sue, Dave, and Elizabeth are ready to check into the Hyatt Regency Chicago, the second hotel under consideration as the headquarters hotel. Rachel Monroe introduces herself as the association sales manager and begins the tour. She is excited about a new ballroom that was recently added and explains how the ballroom could be used for the opening reception. After the tour, Richard Moore, the general manager, joins the group to look at available dates and rates.

Sue, Dave, and Elizabeth take an hour break and meet in the restaurant for dinner. During dinner, they review all notes from the past two days. After dinner, Sue takes her tour of the meeting rooms.

DAY THREE

The team checks out early and waits in the hotel lobby. They notice a line forming as people check out of the hotel. They take mental notes, observing how long the checkout time is and how courteous the employees are at the front desk and bell stand. Mark arrives at the hotel and takes the group to the first stop, Harborside International Golf Center, a four-star course only twelve miles from downtown Chicago. The group meets with the special events manager of the Harborside to discuss the optional golf outing that is part of the ASAA event. The tournament is held Thursday afternoon, prior to the opening reception. Mark takes the group to one more golf course and on two more hotel site inspections before they depart for the airport.

Sue, Dave, and Elizabeth thank Mark for his time and inform him that they will be touring Dallas next month and plan to make a decision in two months. After the Dallas site inspection, the ASAA will make its decision and will contact the bureau regarding that decision.

One month later, Sue, Dave, and Elizabeth go to Dallas for another three-day site inspection. Patty Towell, the sales manager of the Dallas CVB, arranges for the group to meet with staff from the hotels, the convention center, and the off-site locations.

After both site inspections conclude, the inspection team reviews their notes. Due to the conflict of dates with other industry meetings, they decide to meet on St. Patrick's Day. In evaluating Chicago, they are concerned about room availability, the renewal dates for some union contracts, and the fact that the cost to hold the meeting in Chicago is 25% more than in Dallas. This increase in cost might be off-set by the number of attendees who prefer to meet in Chicago over Dallas, but this meeting will attract more attendees seeking the SAPDC—thus location will not be as much of an issue. Dallas is selected for the annual conference. Sue calls Mark from the Chicago CVB, expresses their concerns, and explains why Dallas was selected. Sue reminds Mark that they have not held a meeting in Chicago in five years and would like to look there again in the future.

Second Site Inspection

DAY ONE

Sue sends Patty Towell, at the Dallas CVB, a letter of intent to hold the conference in Dallas and contacts her to help arrange a second site inspection. This second site inspection will include only Sue and Dave and will be for three days. The goal is to finalize nonhost prop-erties, select off-site venues and a golf course, select the DMC and transportation company, and begin contract negotiations. When Sue and Dave arrive in Dallas, they rent a car and take a self-guided tour of the city. They check in at the Hyatt Regency Downtown, the loca-tion of the headquarters hotel for the meeting.

At the Hyatt Regency in downtown Dallas, Sue and Dave meet with Nancy Simonieg, the senior sales manager, and Rizwan Naqvi, CMP, LES, the **convention services manager (CSM)**. Once the contract is signed, Sue will work with the CSM for the remainder of the meeting. During this meeting, Sue and Nancy will begin negotiations for sleep-ing rooms, meeting rooms, shuttle service, and so on.

After the meeting with the hotel staff, Sue meets Sonja Miller, sales manager of the Dallas Convention Center; Erika Bondy, CMP, senior event coordinator; and Bill Baker, director of catering. Once the con-tract is signed, Sue will work with Erika on all her meeting details and with Bill on meeting food and beverage requirements. Today, Sue begins negotiating rates with the Dallas Convention Center; at the meeting, she will review her needs and see what is the best win-win situation for her attendees and the convention center.

Sue and Dave have lunch at the Dallas Museum of Art and meet with the catering sales manager, Cindy Hartman, to review rates for having the VIP dinner in the restaurant. Carolyn Petty, president of EMC (a DMC), joins Sue and Dave for lunch to discuss what the DMC can provide for the ASAA meeting, including gift baskets and general transportation needs.

In the afternoon, Patty has arranged for Sue to meet with two of the nonhost hotels under consideration in the city for sleeping room space; at each hotel, Sue meets the sales manager to negotiate the rates and amenities. For dinner, Patty takes Sue and Dave to a small Mexican restaurant that is a favorite of the locals. At dinner, Patty discusses the services the bureau can assist with, including registration personnel, marketing, slides, leads for suppliers, transportation, Internet services, and on-site brochures. She will staff a promotional booth at the meeting prior to the one in Dallas.

DAY TWO

The morning is spent touring and reestablishing contact with the remainder of hotels that will provide sleeping rooms. Sue and Dave have lunch at the Dallas World Aquarium because they are looking for a fun site for the VIP meeting; they meet with Jose Lopez, sales manager, for a tour and a discussion of possible dining options. Although this is an option, it might be too casual for the group. Jose brings a portfolio with pictures of events held at the aquarium, and Sue's concerns dissipate.

In the afternoon, Sue and Dave tour two golf courses. For each course, Sue makes contacts, has the event sales manager take them on a nine-hole tour, and begins discussing rates. Sue pays attention to where the group might meet before and after the tournament to determine if there is an area where the group might meet as they finish playing golf.

Her evening is free to review her notes. Sue will catch up on e-mails missed during her day of meetings and will carefully look at all the brochures she is given. She really likes the idea of having the VIP dinner in an unusual location.

DAY THREE

Sue and Dave begin the day meeting the ESC contact, Jack Boyd, account executive for the Freeman Companies, and Darren Temple, vice president of sales, AVW TELAV Audio Visual Solutions, an AV company that is part of the Freeman Companies. Jack, Darren, Dave, and Sue meet first at the Dallas Convention Center and then at the Hyatt Hotel to discuss ESC and audiovisual equipment needs. They tour each venue, discussing specific staging, setup, and other needs for each event. Sue realizes the impact that the ESC and the AV company have in making a meeting successful. Sue takes the time to review all meeting details. For example, since this is a medical meeting and attendees will receive CEUs for poster session presentations, the poster session must be set up at least four feet from any exhibitor. Once all the details of each venue are known, the ESC and the AV company can provide an accurate estimate of expenses. When all the details are wrapped up, Sue and Dave catch their flight home.

Marketing Committee

ASAA has both an in-house marketing department and an outside advertising agency, and they work together to create the marketing pieces for the annual conference. After Sue returns home from the second site inspection, she meets with George Day, the ASAA director of marketing, and Julie Love, the account manager for Idea Maker, Inc., an advertising company. Sue discusses the convention location and the meeting objectives and also explains how important promoting the new SAPDC is for this conference.

After two weeks, Sue meets with George and Julie again. Julie brings theme ideas and visuals for the marketing pieces. After reviewing several themes, "Power of Prevention" is selected. The visual will be the skyline of Dallas with the Hyatt Regency Hotel ball of lights brightly shining on the downtown area, with the ball of lights representing the power and the light shining on the city showing its power.

After reviewing the success of past marketing pieces, it is decided that four marketing tools will be used. A four-color postcard-size mailer will be developed as a teaser and mailed to all past conference attendees and targeted to potential members; this teaser will also be used as an advertisement that will be placed in industry newsletters and magazines. The second piece will be a magazine-style brochure to be sent to all association members. This brochure will include a convention agenda giving dates, times, and speakers; a program-at-a-glance grid; current sponsors; and convention and housing registration forms. Idea Maker, Inc., designs web pages and maintains ASAA's e-mail newsletter. The third marketing approach will be a web page that will serve as an electronic brochure, allowing people to register for the meeting and make hotel reservations online. The final approach is the e-newsletter that will feature convention information and will include testimonials from people who have earned their SAPDC.

In creating the meeting program to be given to attendees on check-in, Sue meets with George and Dave to discuss content of the program. Dave is concerned that attendees will take the wrong class because they will not understand the level of instruction. George assures Dave that each session will be color-coded to provide easy identification of the education level and that this color-coded scheme will be repeated in the program. Among topics discussed are the size of sponsors' ads and the amount of copy for educational event descriptions. All agree that to support the objective, the SAPDC should receive a full-page description in the front of the program.

During each conference, a new board of directors is introduced, awards are given, and important announcements must be made. Sue, George, and Dave meet to discuss the types of presentations that will be made and the scripts that George and his team will write. Sue is responsible for arranging rehearsal time for each presentation.

The marketing committee is responsible for creating press releases that will be sent to professional publications. For each conference, a new piece of research is featured, and the marketing committee works to promote this research to the public.

Creation of the Program

When Sue returns from the Dallas site inspection, she meets with the program committee to begin creating the educational content of the meeting. Serving on the program committee is Doug Walker, board member and chair of the SAPDC; Dan Dearing, chairman of the board of directors of the Program Committee for the Power of Prevention annual convention; and his appointed committee members Liz Stewart and Mark Collins, along with Donna Smith, ASAA administrative assistant. These five people and Sue will work together to create the content of the meeting.

Sue begins the meeting by giving each committee member a notebook with responsibilities of the committee members, past convention notes, and the meeting theme, the "Power of Prevention." Sue wants to make sure the committee members understand the objective of the meeting: to increase the number of member attendees taking the SAPDC by 10% by offering a four-day conference that is focused on education which will increase meeting profits by 5%.

The committee agrees to follow the same meeting agenda as in the past: opening reception, general session, awards dinner, and poster session (which runs at the same time as the trade show). The conference will include an ASAA VIP dinner, a golf tournament, and a total of 120 ninety-minute education sessions in two days. The one change in the schedule is to add 2 four-hour segments for the SAPDC class. The committee will locate speakers for SAPDC classes and all break-out sessions. ASAA members will present 100 of the 120 educational sessions. To help the program committee, a separate committee—called the paper review committee—is created that will issue the call for papers, grade and evaluate papers, and inform the program committee of its final selection for presentations and poster session. Sue will use a speaker's bureau for the opening reception, general session, awards dinner, ASAA VIP dinner, and all entertainment.

Sue reviews the time line with the committee. The paper review committee will begin the call for papers one year prior to the meeting; six months prior, the paper review committee will provide the program committee with the final selection, and the program committee will make initial contact with presenters and speakers. The committee will recommend speakers for all sessions. Once speakers and backup speakers have been identified, Sue will send out invitation letters, in which she will ask the speaker to sign a commitment sheet and will require the speaker to provide an abstract of the presentation and his or her biography.

The committee will be responsible for contacting all the speakers and following up with those not responding. There will also be a point person for all speaker questions. Once speakers have been selected, Sue's role is to collect information, assign time slots, and correspond with the speakers, including letters of acceptance and a reminder letter.

One key feature in the conference is the exhibitors. Jill Kochan, ASAA staff, is the ASAA trade show manager for the conference. Jill is responsible for all communications with the exhibitors and the ESC as they set up the trade show. Jill will work closely with Sue to communicate exhibitor needs and will meet with the ESC to create specifications for the exhibitor prospectus.

Partnerships

As Sue prepares for this meeting, she knows the importance of her meeting partners. Throughout the conference, Sue depends on many companies to provide excellent service and to create a memorable experience for the ASAA members. She reviews her contact list, looking at the many companies she will partner with for the upcoming conference.

Although most housing bureaus can provide a complete housing package, including hotel selection, negotiation, and contract, Sue prefers to work with the housing bureau after she has selected the hotels. Once the selections have been made, the housing bureau will manage the hotel room block. The housing bureau will create a web link for attendees to book rooms online and a paper form for attendees to complete and fax. Once an attendee selects a hotel, the housing bureau will send a confirmation letter. One of the best aspects about Sue's partnership with the housing bureau is room block management: Rather than call all the hotels being used, Sue calls the housing bureau for monthly, weekly, and daily rooming reports as needed and depends on the housing bureau to manage the exhibitor room block.

Sue likes to partner with a local DMC for the annual conference. For this conference, Sue uses the DMC for arranging the airport transfers, VIP transportation, and shuttle service from hotels to the convention center. The DMC made all logistical arrangements for the VIP dinner, which allowed Sue to concentrate on VIP invitations and content of the event. Sue also appreciates the fact that a DMC normally has access to many motor coach suppliers because transportation is always an area of concern for Sue. Once, in Washington, D.C., Sue contracted with a motor coach company, and one of the motor coaches broke down with all her attendees in it. The company had no back-up motor coaches, so her attendees waited almost an hour to be rescued and taken to the event.

For key speakers and entertainment, Sue uses a speaker's bureau because she does not have the time to research the many speakers and entertainers who could speak to ASAA members. The speaker's bureau will make recommendations on the best speakers and entertainers, and once Sue makes her selection, the speaker's bureau will handle all arrangements. It will ensure that the speakers are at the meeting on time, and if something happens, the speaker's bureau can quickly arrange for a backup speaker.

Sue selects an online registration company to help with the many attendees who prefer this registration method. The designated registration company will accept registrations electronically, automatically send attendees a confirmation letter, and store the registrations for easy retrieval to create name badges at the meeting site.

Sponsors are important partners for the ASAA conference. Sue will work with all the sponsors to ensure that they receive exposure to members in exchange for their financial and/or in-kind support. Sue realizes that without annual conference sponsors, the ASAA would not reach its financial objectives for the convention.

The ASAA has always included meeting security for attendees' safety and exhibitor products, but for this conference, Sue will increase security. An animal rights association contacted the ASAA and plans to protest a new test being conducted on laboratory rats. Sue realized that she must allow this group to protest, but she wants to ensure that they protest peacefully and do not disturb meeting attendees.

Key partners in making the conference a success are the ESC providing the decorations and the AV company supplying the electronic equipment. Sue considers the ESC as the partner that brings the theme to life, so the decorations must wow attendees visually. Sue recognizes the important role the ESC plays in keeping the exhibitors happy in addition to pleasing the conference attendees. This is important to the ASAA, as the exhibitors generate 44% of the revenue for the conference.

Sue loves to work with the AV company because this partner is crucial for every meeting event. Without proper projection and sound, the attendees would not be able to learn. Sue works closely with its staff during the meeting. One burned-out light bulb or malfunctioning microphone can ruin a break-out session.

In selecting an ESC and an AV company, Sue chooses the Freeman Companies. Unlike other ESCs and AV companies, the Freeman Companies offers both ESC and AV supplier services under one company. This makes communications run more smoothly. Additionally, the organizational structure of the Freeman Companies allows Sue to have one contact from sales to service of the meeting.

In order to keep things running efficiently at the conference, Sue hires temporary staff and builds a partnership early with these people. They will be part of the team and will represent the ASAA during the conference.

"The Total Show" is a promotional concept used by the Freeman Companies.
Photo by George G. Fenich, Ph.D.

CONTRACTS

Sue has a contract for each convention partner and every service provider. Each contract specifies the exact services that are expected and the penalties if the expectations are not met. Early in Sue's career, she worked with an association that signed a contract that did not include a realistic attrition clause. The association did not meet its room block and paid the hotel over $10,000 for unused rooms. At least one year out, Sue reviews each contract carefully. Before the meeting begins, Sue will have contracts finalized with the host hotel, housing bureau, airlines, off-site venue, golf course, speaker's bureau, security, AV company, DMC, ESC, and many others.

One-Year to Six-Month Countdown

Sue looks at her **meeting time line** and realizes that she is eighteen months away from the Power of Prevention annual conference. She takes out her meeting resume and reviews all contracts. She meets with George and Julie from the marketing committee to look at the blue line of the marketing pieces and the first draft of the program. The blue line, or "proof" as it is also called, is the final copy that will be reviewed before the marketing piece is printed. If Sue and her team miss an educational session or a grammatical error, then that is the way it will be printed. If the mistake is important enough, the marketing piece will be reprinted and the expenses added to the cost of the conference.

She arranges a meeting with Doug and Dan from the program committee to select the speakers for the convention. On selection, Sue mails out the acceptance letter to the speakers; in her letter, Sue requests that the speaker confirm his or her commitment by sending a speaker biography, presentation abstract, and audiovisual needs form. Sue makes a point to contact the speaker's bureau to check the status of the motivational speaker and entertainment. She requests that all electronic equipment needs are identified one year prior to the meeting. By doing this, Sue is able to have a more accurate budget item for the equipment and can spot any potential fire hazards associated with its usage.

Sue secures ten sponsors for the meeting, including Small Vets Pluss, a company that supplies the vaccines for small animals, for the tote bags; Houver Pharmaceutical, a small-animal antibiotic producer, for transportation; LabSmlab, a provider of medical instruments used in animal surgery, for the opening night reception; Mix-a-vet, developer of special food for small animals, to sponsor the newspaper; and Smalco, a pet store featuring small-animal products. Small Vets Pluss will cosponsor the VIP entertainment and the awards dinner. Sue will contact each sponsor to confirm the commitment and sign the contract. In her conversation, Sue reminds sponsors that she needs to have them return a form with the exact spelling of their company name and the design of their signage or logo.

The trade show floor plan for the Dallas conference was created and approved fourteen months prior to the Dallas meeting. Exhibit space for the Power of Prevention conference was sold on site at the ASAA conference prior to Dallas—the ASAA has an 87% exhibitor retention. Nine months out, the ESC updates the floor plan and mails exhibitor packets to potential exhibitors.

In addition to the trade show, Sue works with the ESC in finalizing the setup for the opening reception, general session, and awards dinner. She determines where the media center and the registration area will be located. Sue depends on the ESC to recommend the best location to place sponsor banners and signage. Most convention centers have strict rules regarding banner and signage placement, and ESCs that work with convention centers frequently know the rules and have great ideas on how sponsors can be recognized.

Six Months to Day of the Meeting

Fast forward to the six-month countdown for the Power of Prevention conference. The marketing committee writes and sends press releases. If timed correctly, the press releases will be published within a month of when the convention ads are scheduled to run.

Early registration forms begin to arrive within weeks after being sent. In reviewing the registration forms, Sue notices that three of the attendees indicated that they have mobility disabilities and will need special accommodations. In compliance with the Americans with Disabilities Act (ADA), Sue will work with all meeting partners to ensure that these attendees are able to fully participate in the conference. She needs to arrange for handicapped rooms and notes that the meeting rooms will need to be set with aisles to accommodate these attendees.

Sue receives the menus from the hotel catering manager and selects the meals. She makes a special note informing catering that she will require five special meals for attendees with dietary needs.

She contacts the host hotel and convention center to get the names of the meeting rooms that will be used for the Power of Prevention conference. It is important for Sue to get the name of the location of the meeting rooms so that this information can be added to the convention program. Hotels and convention centers rarely want to give this information out early, as they do not want to commit to a particular meeting room that might be sold to another planner, so good communication and flexibility are important.

Sue works with the DMC to review the menu and with the ESC for the VIP dinner at the Dallas World Aquarium. The DMC located a florist that will create floral arrangements that look like coral reefs on the sea bottom. The entire event is designed to make attendees feel like they are underwater.

Sue contacts Larry Grant, the event organizer at Tennison Golf Course, to finalize tournament rules. It looks like this will be a great year for this event—ten people are already registered for this event. Sue gives Larry the names and handicaps.

During this time, Sue will also contact the DMC to finalize shuttle routes to all events, enabling her to begin ordering signage for transportation. Sue learns each year how even highly educated people get lost at meetings—it baffles her that veterinarians cannot read the location material in their program. Sue must clearly list all the events, their locations, and the shuttle service times. Signage is very important in the total conference experience.

MONTH FIVE

Five months prior to the meeting, Sue sends out reminders to all speakers, and she works with the marketing committee to finalize and send the marketing brochure and the e-mail announcement. After some quiet time to proofread the meeting program, she creates a detailed work schedule for staff, temporary employees, and volunteers. Sue orders meeting name badges and meeting supplies and then calls the security company to review her needs.

MONTHS FOUR AND THREE

During the fourth and third months prior to the meeting, Sue monitors registration on a weekly basis. At the third month, Sue reviews registration and makes adjustments to her room block (she negotiated this option in her hotel contract as a way to control attrition).

Sue looks at her initial room block and compares it with current hotel registrations. Convention history shows that 60% of the people register early, indicating that in a perfect world, the host property would have 600 rooms reserved and the remaining properties would have 300 each. In looking at the actual hotel registrations, Sue notices that all rooms have been filled at the Fairmont, but she is unable to get additional rooms so will need to close reservations for the Fairmont. The Wyndham and W Hotel are right on schedule and will require no changes. The Holiday Inn is 200 rooms less than what it should be; Sue reduces the block by 40% and is now obligated for 300 rooms rather than 500. She has the opposite problem with the Hyatt Regency, the host hotel—the host property is 100 rooms over what she expects, so she conservatively increases the block by 5% and is obligated for 1,050 rooms.

In addition to the room block adjustments, she has received calls from the convention center to move the location of meeting rooms and calls from speakers needing to cancel. These changes affect the information in the program, so it must be revised. She sees this as a time of many changes, but these changes are all part of Sue's job. The work

TABLE 15–3	ASAA Hotel Room Blocks				
Hotel	**Hyatt Regency Downtown Dallas**	**Fairmont**	**Wyndham Anatole**	**W Hotel**	**Holiday Inn**
Initial Room Block	1,000	500	500	500	500
90-Day Room Block Review	700	500	300	300	100
Room Block Adjustment	Over—will add +50 rooms	No change	On schedule	On schedule	Under—will remove 200 rooms
New Room Block	1,050	500	500	500	300

she did a year ago is paying off. A speaker cancels, so she contacts the program committee to see who they have planned as a backup.

MONTH TWO

At two months out, Sue arranges another trip to Dallas. Patty, CSM of the Dallas CVB, arranges for Sue to meet with all the key contacts to make the Power of Prevention conference a success. Rizwan, the CSM at the Hyatt Hotel Downtown, meets with Sue to conduct a property walk-through, and he will introduce Sue to the catering manager to review the menu, the accounts receivable contract to explain the bill review process, the front desk manager to confirm pre-key guests and the check-in and check-out process, and the director of security and medical staff to review emergency procedures. The CSM explains that he is the hotel contact and will assist Sue in providing information needed from the hotel, from room pickup to bill review. Rizwan and Sue will work closely together.

At the Dallas Convention Center , Sue will meet with Erika Bondy, senior event coordinator, to conduct a walk-through and invites the ESC and the AV contacts to join her. By doing this, Sue has many eyes looking for potential problems that might occur. She will also spend time with the catering manager to review the menu for lunch and awards dinner.

Sue meets with the DMC representative to walk through hotel transportation routes and finalize menus, decorations, and entertainment for the VIP dinner at the Dallas World Aquarium. Sue then meets with the event coordinator at the Tennison Golf Course to update the player list and review pairings.

When Sue returns from Dallas, she makes final changes to the program and sends it to the printer. She also ships material to the convention site, works with the marketing committee on the final scripts, and reviews her staging guide that has all her contacts, the time line, contracts, menus, and notes for her to review.

MONTH ONE

One month prior to the meeting, Sue continues weekly monitoring of the registrations and sends reminder letters to all the speakers. She works with the advertising firm to approve press releases to announce research findings that will be presented at the Power of Prevention conference; she also works with the staff to finalize work schedules, marketing, scripts, and rehearsal times. Sue will create a checklist and pack her convention material. She is a good planner and has thought about backup plans for her activities; for example, if the golf tournament is rained out, the group will spend the morning on a sports tour of Dallas.

Sue likens the month before the meeting to a tennis match. Emergencies—which feel like five to ten tennis balls coming across the net at her at the same time—can hit her, so Sue knows she must be ready with her racket in hand to successfully hit those balls back over the net and be ready for the next barrage of balls.

PREMEETING ACTIVITIES

Three days prior to the meeting, Sue and her staff arrive in Dallas to set up the meeting headquarters. She is happy to see that all her convention material arrived safely. Sue meets all contacts to finalize meeting plans and arranges a walk-through of the host hotel and the convention center with her staff, temporary employees, and volunteers. The host hotel arranges a pre-con meeting where everyone working on the meeting will get together and review the meeting resume for any changes or concerns.

Sue monitors the setup of all meeting events and conducts on-site troubleshooting. Something always needs to be changed; it might be a sponsor sign with an error that needs to be redone by calling the ESC or a more complicated situation like the space for the registration being too small. This is a time of constant problem solving.

Sue joins George and the marketing staff as they rehearse for the general session, set up the pressroom, and conduct a press conference. George takes time to review the press list with Sue because she needs to know the names of press attendees to ensure that when they arrive, someone from the ASAA staff can quickly assist them. Good publicity can ensure the success of future conferences.

MEETING DAY ACTIVITIES

The meeting begins, and Sue is busy working with the staff to ensure all meeting rooms are set up properly and that all speaker materials and evaluations are ready. Her role is to work behind the scenes to make the attendees' experience perfect. She is the first one to arrive on site and will be the last person to leave. The day is filled with questions that she must clarify or problems that need to be solved. This is the time that excites Sue—the time when she sees all her hard work become a reality. She uses the contacts she made to quickly solve problems. For example, the equipment in one of the rooms is not working, so Sue calls the AV company and the problem is quickly solved. At the beginning of each day, Sue meets with the hotel CSM and the accounts receivable department to conduct a bill review. She also checks with the housing bureau to follow up on a comparison of the ASAA registration with the in-house guest list to ensure that ASAA attendees are properly coded to the ASAA block, which helps with future event accommodations.

A special ASAA exhibitor headquarters office opens at the convention center. Jill, the ASAA's trade show manager, will remain in this office to handle any problems that might occur during the trade show and to accept exhibitor bookings for next year's ASAA conference.

After the Meeting

IMMEDIATE POSTMEETING ACTIVITIES

A tired Sue sips coffee and takes a moment to review the successes and the areas of opportunity of the Power of Prevention conference. Before leaving Dallas, Sue will facilitate a post-con meeting to evaluate this year's conference, where people who attended the pre-con meeting will be present to discuss the conference and answer questions: What were the problems? What could be done to improve this situation for future conventions? She will work with the hotel and vendors to reconcile registration numbers, review all pickups, and estimate ancillary business.

Planning a convention is a team event. Sue takes time to thank all speakers, sponsors, committee members, and facilitators for helping with the conference—she also rewards her staff by giving them a free day in Dallas to relax.

TWO-MONTH POSTMEETING ACTIVITIES

After the statistics and evaluations have been reviewed, Sue begins her report to the executive director and to the board of directors regarding conference ROI. It is important after each conference that an evaluation is conducted. In creating this conference, Sue and her team set the convention objectives: to increase the number of attendees taking the SAPDC by 10% by offering a four-day conference that is focused on education and networking which will increase conference profits by 5%. What is the point of having a convention if the success is not measured? Part of the meeting planner's job is to demonstrate how a convention or meeting helps achieve organizational goals. By establishing objectives and reviewing ROI, a planner can show his or her role in supporting company objectives and the bottom line.

Sue is excited about the Power of Prevention convention. The industry press gave excellent premeeting coverage, with over $50,000 tracked as nonpaid advertising. Sue believes this third-party endorsement definitely increased attendance. The meeting objectives were met: 500 people took the classes for SAPDC (a 10% increase from the 454 who took SAPDC classes last year), and meeting profits grew from $1,393,297.60 to $1,462,962.50 (a 5% increase).

Sue finishes her report and takes a call from the Orlando Convention Center, the location for next year's annual conference. She is twelve months away from the conference and is receiving the names of the meeting rooms that will be used . . . and the meeting cycle continues.

Summary

In this chapter, you have learned about the process of creating a city-wide meeting. This is a large task for one person and requires many partners to make the conference successful. Through this case study, you have been able to see a day in the life of a meeting planner on a site inspection and have looked at the many tasks leading up to the conference. The chapter began with creating conference objectives and budgets, and it ended with evaluating ROI to determine the success of the meeting.

Key Words and Terms

For definitions, see the Glossary or go to http://glossary.convention industry.org.

Audiovisual (AV) company

Convention services manager (CSM)

Convention and visitor bureau (CVB)

Destination management company (DMC)

Exposition services contractor (ESC)

Meeting time line

Request for proposal (RFP)

Return on investment (ROI)

Sponsor

Review and Discussion Questions

1. Who is the group in this chapter? Why are they here?
2. Where else has the group met?
3. What are the steps Sue goes through to plan this meeting?
4. Whom does Sue work with on her staff?
5. Whom does Sue work with in the city where the meeting is being held? Which suppliers or vendors?
6. What does Sue do after the meeting is over?

About the Chapter Contributor

M. T. Hickman, CTP, CMP, is the head of the Travel, Exposition, and Meeting Management program at Richland College in Dallas, Texas. She began her career at the Irving, Texas, CVB, where she worked in many departments, including tourism sales, convention sales, and special events. Over the years, she has worked as director of marketing for the National Business Association and as a proposal writer for WorldTravel Partners. She is active in the meeting and exposition planning associations, including MPI, PCMA, and IAEM.

Other Chapter Contributors

Erika Bondy, CMP, Senior Event Coordinator, Dallas Convention Center

David Gisler, Director of Sales and Training, Total Show University, Freeman Companies

Dana Nickerson-Rhoden, CMP, CMM, Manager of Scientific and Corporate Meetings, American Heart Association

Nancy Simonieg, Senior Sales Manager, Hyatt Hotel Downtown Dallas

Patty Towell, Sales Manager, Dallas Convention and Visitor Bureau

APPENDIX

This appendix includes a detailed example of a Site Selection Sample Request for Proposal (RFP). It is used with permission of the originator, Joan L. Eisenstodt.

Forms for Use in Requesting a Proposal and On-Site Selection

The sections that follow provide a number of forms, or frameworks, that are used by meeting professionals. Studying and reviewing these documents will help provide the reader with a better understanding of the myriad of details that a meeting professional must deal with.

Site Selection—Sample Request for Proposal (RFP)(v. 18b)

Group or Meeting Sponsor: Full name of organization (acronym in parentheses)

Contact Information: Name(s) including alternate contacts, title(s), address(es), communication numbers (phones, fax, email, tdd/tty), and contact times and time zones

Organization: Provide brief organizational description—structure, mission, purpose.

The Meeting: Provide brief description—purpose, goals and objectives, general format, and audience profile.

History: Provide up to 2 years of meeting history—dates, attendance, hotel(s) used, rooms blocked and picked up, and range of rates.

Schedule for Future Meetings; Future Years for Meeting

Considerations for This Meeting:

Destination(s) and site(s)

Dates (acceptable and unacceptable)

Rates

Special requirements/information (transportation, attractions/restaurants, quirks)

References: Request for meetings of similar size, focus/scope, held in last 6 to 12 months

Proposals Due/Decision Process: Provide date by which proposal must be received and what collateral materials should be included. Describe decision process and date by which decision is expected.

Meeting Specifications:

Sleeping Room Block: Describe day-by-day, including early arrivals/late departures; bed and room types; suites.

Meeting Space: Provide day-by-day description of the program, including meeting/ conference office space, speaker ready room, lounges, and times needed.

Exhibit/Display Space: For literature tables, other displays or exhibits and the times the space is needed. Include move-in and move-out times.

<u>Site Selection</u>
<u>Request for Proposal</u>
Organization Name
Attachment A

If you plan to submit a proposal, please keyboard all information and upload these forms to (*e-mail address*).

Property name _____ *City/State* _____

Property contact name/title/e-mail and phone _____

Year property built _____ Last building inspection and results _____

Number of floors _____ Total number of rooms _____ suites _____

Single/one-bedded rooms _____ Double/two-bedded rooms _____

Number of nonsmoking rooms _____ Number of disability-accessible rooms _____

Year of last guest room renovation _____ Year of last public space renovation _____

<u>Scope of Planned Renovation and Schedule:</u>

Type of property

      ☐ *meeting/convention*   ☐ *resort*   ☐ *full service*   ☐ *limited service*

<u>Market tier:</u> ☐ *luxury*   ☐ *upscale*   ☐ *moderate*

<u>Property location:</u> ☐ *suburban*   ☐ *downtown/city center*

<u>Property ownership & management</u>

Chain owned? (Y/N) _____ If no, name of owners. _____

Management Company _____

Franchise? (Y/N) _____

Owner's company is at least 51% owned, controlled, and operated by an American citizen minority? (Y/N) _____

Owner's company is at least 51% owned, controlled, and operated by an American citizen nonminority woman? (Y/N) _____

<u>Site Selection</u>
<u>Request for Proposal</u>
Organization Name
Attachment A

If you plan to submit a proposal, please keyboard all information and upload these forms to (*e-mail address*).

Property name _____ *City/State*_____

Property contact name/title/e-mail and phone _____

Rating

| AAA Diamonds | 1 | 2 | 3 | 4 | 5 | not rated |
| Mobil Stars | 1 | 2 | 3 | 4 | 5 | not rated |

Other rating(s) (specify) _____

Outlets

Name _____ Location _____ Hours _____

Full or Ltd. Service _____ Nonsmoking?_____

Transportation and Parking

Airport One

Name _____ 3-Letter code _____

Distance from property _____ miles

      Minutes/rush hour _____ Minutes/nonrush hour_____

Complimentary shuttle (Y/N) _____

Estimated taxi charge (each way) _____

Alternate mode of transportation _____ Cost each way _____

Driving directions (attach)

Airport Two

Name _____ 3-Letter code _____

Distance from property _____ miles

      Minutes/rush hour _____ Minutes/nonrush hour _____

Complimentary shuttle (Y/N) _____

Estimated taxi charge (each way) _____

Alternate mode of transportation _____ Cost each way _____

Driving Directions (attach)

Number of parking spaces at property _____ Charge for self-park _____

Charge for valet park _____

Identify facility's parking capacity for large trucks, semitrailers, etc.: _____

Taxes, service, and/or gratuity charges

The current rooms tax is ____% plus $____ occupancy tax.

    → There is ___ is not ___ a ballot initiative in the next election to raise those taxes.

There is a ____ gratuity or a ____ service charge of _____% on group food and beverage.

    → This is taxed at _____%.

Site Selection
Request for Proposal
Organization Name
Attachment A

If you plan to submit a proposal, please keyboard all information and upload these forms to (*e-mail address*).

Property name _____ *City/State* _____

Property contact name/title/e-mail and phone _____

Facilities/Services on Property (check all that apply)

☐ Cocktail lounge
☐ 24-hour room service OR
   ☐ Room service Start time _____ End time _____
☐ Safety deposit boxes/lobby area
☐ Express check in and out   ☐ Video review/check out
☐ Full business center   Hours _____ A.M. to _____ P.M.   Days of the week _____
☐ Gift/newsstand   Hours _____ A.M. to _____ P.M.   Days of the week: _____
☐ Full-service health club   Hours ___ A.M. to ___ P.M.   Days of the week: _____
☐ Laundry/valet service (circle applicable responses)

Circle one: On property or *Sent out*

   Circle service: 5 days/week   *6 days/week*   *7 days/week*   *overnight service*
☐ Shoe shine service
☐ Indoor pool   ☐ outdoor pool
☐ Airline desk(s)   (specify) _____, _____
☐ ATM (Current use fee is $ ____.____.)
☐ Car rental desk(s)   (specify) _____, _____
☐ Evening turndown service   ☐ All guests   ☐ VIPs only
☐ Golf course
☐ Tennis court(s)
☐ Racquetball courts
☐ Other (specify) _____

Guest Rooms

☐ In-room safe   ☐ No charge   ☐ Charge to use ($_____/day)
☐ Working desks with outlets above floor
☐ Voice mail   ☐ Personalized voice mail
☐ 2 line phones/all rooms   ☐ 2-line phones/concierge/specialized rooms only
☐ Data ports on all phones   ☐ Digital or analog phone lines
☐ Phone in bathroom   ☐ bathroom phone/concierge or specialty rooms only
☐ Access charge for local phone calls _____ Access charge for toll-free calls _____
☐ AM/FM radio   ☐ with cassette player   ☐ with CD player
☐ Color TV
☐ Remote control TV   ☐ Cable TV   ☐ Satellite TV
☐ All news cable channel   ☐ Weather channel
☐ Other special channels (specify) _____
☐ In-room movies on demand
☐ Closed-circuit television (CCTV)

Site Selection
Request for Proposal
Organization Name
Attachment A

If you plan to submit a proposal, please keyboard all information and upload these forms to (*e-mail address*).

Property name _____ *City/State* _____

Property contact name/title/e-mail and phone _____

Guest Rooms (cont.)

☐ In-room video players
☐ Iron/ironing board
☐ Mini-bar   ☐ Refrigerator on request
☐ Coffee/Tea maker   ☐ Daily complimentary coffee/tea
☐ Working desk/desk lamp
☐ Free **daily** paper delivered to room   ☐ Paper/**weekdays only**

Reservations and Check-in/out

☐ Reservations may be made through a toll-free number.
   ☐ That number is _____   ☐ Number is accessible throughout United States.
   ☐ A number that can be used for those residing in the state in which the reservations department is located:
   ☐ A reservation number for those outside the United States is ( ) _____.
   ☐ The TTY/TDD number is ( ) _____.
   ☐ The fax number for reservations is ( ) _____.
   ☐ Reservations may be made on line at http://www._____,
   ☐ or by email to _____.
☐ All rooms in a group's block are released to the toll-free number.
☐ The property has an in-house reservations department.
☐ The reservations department is located off-site.

Check-in time is _____. Check-out time is _____.

☐ The facility will audit the room reservations using a group's registration list.

Site Selection
Request for Proposal
Organization Name
Attachment A

If you plan to submit a proposal, please keyboard all information and upload these forms to (*e-mail address*).

Property name _____ *City/State* _____

Property contact name/title/e-mail and phone _____

Safety and Security (check all that apply)

☐ Smoke detectors in all guest rooms   Hardwired?   Y/N _____
☐ Smoke detectors in hallways   Hardwired?   Y/N _____
☐ Smoke detectors in public areas   Hardwired?   Y/N _____
☐ Audible smoke detectors   ☐ Visual alarms for people with hearing impairments
☐ Sprinklers in all guest rooms   Sprinklers in hallways
☐ Sprinklers in public areas
☐ Fire extinguishers in hallways
☐ Automatic fire doors
☐ Auto link to fire station
☐ Auto recall elevators
☐ Ventilated stairwells
☐ Emergency maps in guest rooms/hallways
☐ Emergency information in all guest rooms
☐ Emergency lighting
☐ Safety chain on door   ☐ Doors with viewports ("peep holes")
☐ Deadbolts on all guest room doors
☐ Restricted access to guest floors
☐ Property has AEDs (automatic external defibrillators)
    ☐ Staff has been trained to use defibrillators   *Per shift* _____
☐ Staff trained in CPR   CPR-trained staff *per shift* _____
☐ Staff trained in first aid   *Per shift* _____
☐ Secondary locks on guest room glass doors
☐ Room balconies accessible by adjoining rooms/balconies
☐ Primary guest room entrance accessible by interior corridor/atrium
☐ Guest room accessible by exterior entrance only
☐ Guest room windows open
☐ Uniformed security
☐ 24-hour security throughout facility   Number of staff ___
☐ Public address system
☐ Video surveillance in public areas/elevators
☐ Video surveillance at entrances
☐ Video surveillance in hallways
☐ Staff trained in issuance of duplicate keys/cards
☐ Emergency power source: _____
    ☐ SOPs for power outages _____

Food Safety:
Detail the frequency of inspection by county or city health inspectors and the results of the last three (3) inspections.

> Site Selection
> Request for Proposal
> *Organization Name*
> *Attachment A*

If you plan to submit a proposal, please keyboard all information and upload these forms to (*e-mail address*).

Property name _____ *City/State* _____

Property contact name/title/e-mail and phone _____

Emergency call response time (for fire, police, EMTs) in minutes to your property _____
Does property have an emergency evacuation plan? (Y/N) _____
    How often does property conduct emergency evacuation drills? _____
Nearest police station (blocks/miles) _____ Nearest hospital (blocks/miles) _____
Does facility comply with all country/state/local fire laws? (Y/N) _____

Please describe

—The actions your facility took beginning 9/11/01 for the safety and comfort of your guests:

—Any change of policies governing safety/security instituted or reinstituted since 9/11/01.

—The communication tree among your property and local/state/federal emergency management officials.

—Any policies in effect that govern "containment" of guests in the property for issues of bioterrorism? Inability to travel because of airport closures?

"Oversold/Underdeparted" ("Walk") Policies or Guidelines
☐ Property will arrange accommodations at comparable or superior property within 10 minutes of this property.
☐ Property will pay directly for one room night and tax at comparable property.
☐ Traveler will be provided with transportation.
☐ Traveler will be reimbursed for (number) _____ of phone calls to home and/or office.
☐ Other (specify) _____

<u>Site Selection</u>
<u>Request for Proposal</u>
Organization Name
Attachment A

If you plan to submit a proposal, please keyboard all information and upload these forms to (*e-mail address*).

Property name _____ *City/State* _____

Property contact name/title/e-mail and phone _____

Staff and Staffing
☐ Average length of employment at this property:
  Management staff _____ years   line staff _____ years
☐ Staff organized for the purpose of collective bargaining (List unions and staff positions, contract renewal dates on separate sheet.)

Policies and Miscellaneous Charges
☐ Credit cards are charged when reservation is made.
　☐ If charged, is it for _____ first night _____ last night _____ all nights
☐ Guest may cancel guaranteed reservations without penalty/charge
　　　_____ to 4 P.M./day of arrival　　_____ to 6 P.M./day of arrival　　_____ 24 hours
　　　_____ 48 hours　　　　　　　　_____ 72 hours　　　　　　　　_____ other
☐ Guest substitutions are allowed, at any time, without penalty or charge to group and/or individual.
☐ Guest substitutions are not allowed without a charge to group and/or individual.
☐ Extended stays (based on availability) are allowed at no charge.
☐ Early checkouts incur a charge of $_____ if the front desk is not notified at check-in.
☐ The property charges $____/page for receipt of faxes.
☐ The property charges $___/page to send faxes.
☐ There is a charge of $_____ for receipt of packages.
☐ There is a charge of $_____ for property to send packages.
☐ There is a charge of $_____ to deliver packages to individual or group.

Site Selection
Request for Proposal
Organization Name
Attachment A

If you plan to submit a proposal, please keyboard all information and upload these forms to (*e-mail address*).

Property name _____ *City/State* _____

Property contact name/title/e-mail and phone _____

Policies and Miscellaneous Charges (cont.)

☐ Is a resort or hotel or other fee added to the room rate? Y/N _____

   ☐ If so, the current amount per room (or per guest) per night is $_____ which is/is not taxed.

      ☐ This covers:

   ○ Contractual issues that must be included in our contract are attached to this document.

Energy Issues

☐ The property does charge an energy surcharge of $_____ per room per night. This charge is or is not taxed. (Is ____ Is not ____) If taxed, it is at _____%.

☐ The power supply for the property is from _____.

☐ Describe the property's backup power source(s):

☐ Describe the property's emergency procedures for brownouts and blackouts:

☐ Describe the property's backup systems for water and phones:

☐ Define any charges for use of electrical outlets for meetings and/or in public space and/or in guestrooms:

Environmental Issues

○ Our property recycles the following materials:

   _____ paper   _____ plastic   _____metal/tin/aluminum

○ The method by which guests may recycle is:

○ We ask guests to advise us by use of a card if they want their towels and/or bed linens changed every day.

○ Other areas we protect the environment are:

<u>Site Selection</u>
<u>Request for Proposal</u>
Organization Name
Attachment A

If you plan to submit a proposal, please keyboard all information and upload these forms to (*e-mail address*).

Property name _____ *City/State* _____

Property contact name/title/e-mail and phone _____

Other Groups
During the group's preferred dates, the other events confirmed in the city, including conventions, festivals, other public and private events that are known to the bureau or the facility, are:

During the group's preferred dates, the other events confirmed in the facility are:

City/County Labor Issues
Note any groups organized for the purpose of collective bargaining in the city or county whose contract deadlines are 2 months on both side of preferred dates, and their history of labor actions:

<u>Audio Visual Equipment</u>
The in-house or recommended company is _____.

The facility has the ability to negotiate prices on behalf of the AV company. (Y/N) ____

A discount of ____% off list prices can be offered for AV equipment for the meeting.

The service charge is ____%. It is taxed at ____%. It is not taxed. ____

If an outside AV company is brought in by our organization, there is ____ is not ____ a fee.
    If there is a fee, it is _____.

<u>Electricity Supply/Vendor</u>
Electricity (for exhibits and meeting space) is provided to the facility by _____ in-house or _____ external vendor. (If external, specify _____.)

The facility has the ability to negotiate prices for meeting and exhibit electrical service.
    (Y/N) ____

Electricity is available to the outdoor portions of the facility (for outside exhibits).
    (Y/N) _____

A discount of ____% off list prices can be offered for meeting room and exhibit electricity for the meeting.

<u>Site Selection</u>
<u>Request for Proposal</u>
Organization Name
Attachment A

If you plan to submit a proposal, please keyboard all information and upload these forms to (*e-mail address*).

Property name _____ *City/State* _____

Property contact name/title/e-mail and phone _____

Operations and Technology

☐ *Our sales/convention services staff use* _____ *word processing software, version*
_____.

☐ *Sales and convention services personnel use e-mail.* _____ *yes* _____ *no*
  E-mail addresses are:
    ☐ *Sales* _____
    ☐ *Convention/Catering services* _____
    ☐ *Reservations* _____
☐ *Sales and convention services have Web access.* ___ *yes* ___ *no*
☐ *Reservations is fully automated and can respond by e-mail.* ___ *yes* ___ *no*
☐ *Our Web site address is* _____.
☐ *Group/Meeting reservations can be made on line.*
    ☐ *If reservations may be made on line, please specify information that must be included in any published URLs and any restrictions and/or policies.*

NATIONAL SALES RESPONSE FORM
(year/meeting) Site Selection
Request for Proposal: (name of organization)

Please complete and return this form <u>after</u> reading the RFP. To allow us to track proposals, please advise to which properties in which cities you will send the RFP. **Please upload this to** (*e-mail address*), **or fax this form to** (*name, fax number*) **to be received by** (*day, date, time/time zone*).

Please print or type in black:

Company _____

Contact name/title _____

Direct phone no. _____

Direct fax no. _____

E-mail address _____

The RFP is being sent to the following properties:

_____/City _____

_____/City _____

_____/City _____

_____/City _____

_____/City _____

_____/City _____

Comments:

CVB RESPONSE FORM
(Year/Meeting) Site Selection
Request for Proposal: (Organization/Meeting Name)

Please complete and return this form <u>after</u> reading the RFP. To allow us to track proposals, please advise to which properties you will send the RFP, keeping in mind that it should only be sent to properties not represented by the companies noted in the cover note and only to those that meet the criteria. If responses are received by properties that do not meet the criteria, or by vendors for whom we do not need services, we will reject the proposals.

Please upload this to (*e-mail address*), **or fax this form to** (*name, fax number*) **by** (*day/date/time/time zone*).

Please print or type in black:

CVB _____

Contact name/Title _____

Direct phone no. _____

Direct fax no. _____

E-mail address _____

The RFP is being sent to the following properties:

                    _____

                    _____

                    _____

                    _____

                    _____

                    _____

Comments:

Property RESPONSE FORM
(Year/Meeting) Site Selection
Request for Proposal: (Organization/Meeting)

Please complete and return this form <u>after</u> reading the RFP but before sending a proposal. There is no need to send a follow-up letter or e-mail, or to call once this form has been sent. **Please upload this to** (*e-mail address*), **or fax to** (*organization/fax number*) **to be received by** (*day/date/time/time zone*).

Full proposals and collateral are due by (day/date/time/time zone).

Please complete and return this information <u>whether or not</u> a proposal is being submitted. If completing by hand, please use black ink.

Property name/City _____

Contact name/Title _____

Direct phone no. (_____)_____

Direct fax no. (_____)_____

E-mail address _____

URL *http://www.*_____

Check/complete all applicable responses:

_____ We will send proposal and collateral to be received by (*due date*).
_____ Dates noted on first option basis are being held for this group.
_____ Dates will *not* be held until a contract is signed.

Dates available/First option   Dates available/Second option

_____   _____
_____   _____
_____   _____
_____   _____

_____ We regret we are *unable to send a proposal* for the following reason(s):
_____ None of preferred dates available.
_____ Meeting space and/or sleeping rooms not appropriate for meeting.
_____ Unable to meet rate parameters.
_____ Other (specify):

_____
_____

Comments:

Glossary

Definitions are taken from the chapters or from http://glossary.conventionindustry.org.

80211: Engineering specification for the wireless standard. This defines how a wireless interface between clients and access points is constructed.

Accepted Practices Exchange (APEX): Initiative of the meetings, expositions, events, and conventions industry managed by the Convention Industry Council (CIC). APEX develops and manages the implementation of accepted practices (voluntary standards) for the industry.

Act of God: Extraordinary natural event such as extreme weather, flood, hurricane, tornado, earthquake, or similar natural disaster that cannot be reasonably foreseen or prevented and over which a contracting party has no reasonable control. It makes performance of the contract illegal, impracticable, or impossible; thus the parties have no legal responsibility to continue performance of the contract.

Action station: Place where chef prepares foods to order and serves them fresh to guests. Popular items for action stations include pasta, grilled meat or shrimp, carved meats, sushi, crepes, omelets, flaming desserts, Caesar salad, etc. *Also called* performance stations or exhibition cooking.

Agenda: List, outline, or plan of items to be done or considered at an event or during a specific time block and may include a time schedule.

Amenity: Complimentary item in sleeping rooms such as writing supplies, bathrobes, fruit baskets, shower caps, shampoo, and shoe shine mitts provided by the facility for guests.

American service: Serving style where guests are seated and served food that has been preportioned and plated in the kitchen.

American Society of Association Executives (ASAE): Membership organization and voice of the association profession. Founded in 1920, ASAE now has more than 22,000 association CEOs, staff professionals, industry partners, and consultant members.

American Society of Composers, Authors, and Publishers (ASCAP): Membership organization that represents individuals who hold the copyrights to music written in the United States and that grants licensing agreements for the performance of that music.

Americans with Disabilities Act (ADA): U.S. legislation passed in 1992 requiring public buildings (offices, hotels, restaurants, etc.) to make adjustments meeting minimum standards to make their facilities accessible to individuals with physical disabilities.

Amphitheater: Outdoor facility with a flat performance area surrounded by rising rows of seats or a grassy slope that allows the audience to view the performance. The seating area is usually a semicircular shape or adapted to the surrounding landscape.

Ancillary activity: Event-related support services within a facility that generate revenue.

Annual meeting: Meeting that takes place once a year.

APEX Initiative: Industrywide task force formed to begin a codification of definitions and standardized practices, policies, procedures, and terminology.

Arena: Facility featuring a large, flat main floor surrounded by fixed seats in a sloping oval or modified oval shape, much steeper than the typical theater. Some are arranged in two or more tiers. Sight lines are nearly always designed for events the size of a hockey floor, circus, ice show, or basketball court.

Association: Organized group of individuals and/or companies that band together to accomplish a common purpose, usually to provide for the needs of its members. It is usually a nonprofit organization.

Association professional liability (APL): Policy that protects the organization and its officers, directors, staff, and volunteers against personal liability arising from their official actions. This type of policy is broader than a traditional directors and officers (D&O) liability policy in that it covers the organization as an entity as well as individuals.

Attrition: Difference between the actual number of sleeping rooms picked up (or food and beverage covers or revenue projections) and the number or formula agreed to in the terms of the facility's contract. Usually there is an allowable shortfall before damages are assessed.

Audience response system (ARS): System in which the audience is outfitted with small keypads that allow them to answer questions quickly and have their data tallied immediately.

Audiovisual (AV) company: Supplier of technical staff and audiovisual equipment (e.g., projectors, screens, sound systems, video, and staging).

Ausstellung: German term for consumer show.

Awards ceremony: Event (usually formal) to honor outstanding performance.

Bandwidth: Amount of information that can pass through a communications line. As it relates to the Web, bandwidth comes in two basic flavors: dial-up and high speed.

Banquet Event Order (BEO): Form most often used by hotels to provide details to personnel concerned with a specific food and beverage function or event room setup.

Banquet French service: Serving style where platters of food are composed in the kitchen. Each food item is then served from the guests' left by the server from platters to individual plates. Any course can be "Frenched" by having the dressing put on the salad or having sauce added to an entrée or dessert after it has been placed in front of the guest.

Blogging: Online diary that is posted to the Web.

Bluetooth: Telecommunications standard that allows mobile devices to communicate a short distance with each other. Most devices are capable of utilizing Bluetooth at a distance of no more than thirty feet.

Board meeting: Meeting of the Board of Directors of an organization that is usually small in size.

Boardroom: Room set permanently with a fixed table and suitable seating.

Boardroom setup: Seating arrangement in which rectangle- or oval-shaped tables are set up with chairs on both sides and ends. It is often confused with hollow square setup.

Bonding: Purchase, for a premium, of a guarantee of protection for a supplier or a customer. In the hospitality industry, certain bonding programs are mandatory.

Break-even point: Figure calculated by the CIC manual as the total fixed cost divided by the contribution margin (the registration fee minus the variable cost).

Break-out room: Small function room set up for a group within an event as opposed to a plenary or general session.

Break-out session: Small-group session, panel, workshop, or presentation offered concurrently within the event, formed to focus on specific subjects. The event is separate from the general session but is held within the event format. The sessions can be arranged by basic, intermediate, and advanced levels or divided by interest areas or industry segments.

Broadcast Music, Inc. (BMI): Music licensing organization that represents individuals who hold the copyrights to music written in the United States. It grants licensing agreements for the performance of music.

Buffet: Assortment of foods offered on a table and self-served.

Butler service: (1) Style of service that offers a variety of both hot and cold hors d'oeuvres on platters to guests at receptions. (2) Style of table service where guests serve themselves from platters presented by the server. (3) Specialized in-room service offered by a hotel.

Call brand: Brand of liquor, distinguished from the house brands, selected by a customer according to personal preference. It is usually of a higher quality than house brands.

Carnet: Customs document permitting the holder to carry or send merchandise temporarily into certain foreign countries (for display, demonstration, or similar purposes) without paying duties or posting bonds. *Also called* trade show bond.

Cart French service: Style of service that involves use of serving pieces (usually silver); heating and garnishing of food tableside by a captain; and serving of food on a heated plate, which is then served to the guest by a server. Plated entrées are usually served from the right, bread and butter and salad from the left, and beverages from the right. All are removed from the right.

Catered event: Event that generally has one host and one bill. Most attendees eat the same meal.

Center for Exhibition Industry Research (CEIR): Member of the Convention Industry Council (CIC).

Certified meeting professional (CMP): The foremost certification program of today's meetings, conventions, and exhibitions industry. The CMP program recognizes individuals who have achieved the industry's highest standard of professionalism.

Citywide event: Event that requires the use of a convention center or event complex as well as multiple hotels in the host city.

Clear span tent: Tent that has a strong roof structure so it is possible to hang lighting from the beams by using special clamps.

Community infrastructure: Those facilities and companies in a locale that support the MEEC industry.

Complete meeting package (CMP): All-inclusive plan offered by conference centers that includes lodging, all food and beverage, and support services, including audiovisual equipment, room rental, etc.

Comprehensive general liability (CGL): Policy that is the commercial equivalent of a homeowner's policy. It protects the organization against personal injury claims and loss (including theft) or damage to the insured's property as well as the property of others. Although these policies are designed to cover "all risks," they frequently have exclusions, and it is important to carefully review what is not covered as well as what is included within the policy's scope.

Concessionaire: Person or company that operates the concessions.

Concessions: All-inclusive plan offered by conference centers that includes lodging, all meals, and support services.

Concurrent session: One of multiple sessions scheduled at the same time. Programs on different themes or subjects are offered simultaneously.

Conference: (1) Participatory meeting designed for discussion, fact-finding, problem solving, and consultation. (2) Event used by any organization to meet and exchange views, convey a message, open a debate, or give publicity to some area of opinion on a specific issue. No tradition, continuity, or periodicity is required to convene a conference. Although not generally limited in time, conferences are usually of short duration with specific objectives and are on a smaller scale than congresses.

Conference center: Facility that provides a dedicated environment for events, especially small events. It may be certified by the International Association of Conference Centers (IACC).

Congress: (1) Regular coming together of large groups of individuals, generally to discuss a particular subject. A congress will often last several days and have several simultaneous sessions. The length of time between congresses is usually established in advance of the implementation stage and can be either pluri-annual or annual. Most international or world congresses are of the former type, while national congresses are more frequently held annually. (2) Meeting of an association of delegates or representatives from constituent organizations. (3) European term for convention. *See* Conference and Convention.

Consideration: Cause, motive, price, or impelling influence that induces a contracting party to enter a contract.

Continuing education unit (CEU): Requirement of many professional groups by which members must certify participation in formal educational programs designed to maintain their level of ability beyond their original certification date. CEUs are nonacademic credit. One CEU is awarded for each ten contact hours in an accredited program.

Continuing medical education (CME): Requirement for doctors to retain their medical license. They must take a certain amount of CME courses to keep current with innovations in health care.

Contract: Agreement between two or more parties that creates in each party a duty to do or not do something and a right to performance of the other's duty or a remedy for the breach of the other's duty.

Convention: Event where the primary activity of the attendees is to attend educational sessions, participate in meetings/discussions, socialize, or attend other organized events. There is a secondary exhibit component.

Convention and visitor bureau (CVB): Not-for-profit organization charged with representing a specific destination and helping the long-term development of communities through a travel and tourism strategy. CVBs are usually membership organizations bringing together businesses that rely on tourism and events for revenue. For visitors, CVBs are like a key to the city. As an unbiased resource, CVBs can serve as a broker or an official point of contact for convention and event planners, tour operators, and visitors; they assist planners with event preparation and encourage business travelers and visitors alike to visit local historic, cultural, and recreational sites.

Convention Industry Council (CIC): Federation of national and international organizations representing individuals, firms, or properties involved in the meetings, conventions, exhibitions, and travel and tourism industries. Formerly the Convention Liaison Council.

Convention services manager (CSM): Person whose job is to oversee and arrange every aspect of an event. The CSM can be an employee or hired ad hoc to plan, organize, implement, and control meetings, conventions, and other events.

Copyright: Federal law that allows for the ownership of intellectual property (writings, art, music). Copy-written material cannot be used without the owner's permission or the payment of royalty fees.

Corkage: Charge placed on beer, liquor, and wine brought into the facility but purchased elsewhere. The charge sometimes includes glassware, ice, and mixers.

Corporate meeting: Gathering of employees or representatives of a commercial organization. Usually, attendance is required and travel, room, and most meal expenses are paid for by the organization.

Corporation: A group of people who obtain a charter granting them (as a body) legal power, rights, privileges and liabilities of an individual but distinct from those individuals making up the group.

Cutoff date: Designated date when the facility will release a block of sleeping rooms to the general public. The date is typically three to four weeks before the event.

Dates, rates, and space: Words that begin the maxim "Dates, rates, and space–You can only have two," which is used by hoteliers to sum up meeting negotiations. The meaning is that the planner can get the dates and meeting space he or she wants for a meeting but may have to give on the rate.

Destination: City, area, or country that can be marketed to groups or individuals as a place to visit or hold an event.

Destination management company (DMC): Professional services company possessing extensive local knowledge, expertise, and resources and specializing in the design and implementation of events, activities, tours, transportation, and program logistics. Depending on the company and the staff specialists in the company, a DMC offers, but is not limited to, the following: creative proposals for special events within the meeting; guest tours; VIP amenities and transportation; shuttle services; staffing within convention centers and hotels; team building, golf outings, and other activities; entertainment, including sound and lighting; décor and theme development; ancillary meetings for management professionals; and advance meetings and on-site registration services and housing.

Destination Marketing Association International (DMAI): World's largest resource for official destination marketing organizations (DMOs) dedicated to improving the effectiveness of DMOs in more than twenty-five countries. DMAI provides members with educational resources, networking opportunities, and marketing benefits worldwide.

Destination marketing organization (DMO): *See* CVB.

Destinations showcase: Fast-paced and productive one-day exhibition and conference sponsored by the International Association of Convention and Visitor Bureaus (IACVB) where qualified meeting professionals attend valuable education sessions, network with industry leaders and peers, and explore a full range of destinations from throughout the world.

DMAI online RFP: Service provided by the DMAI where the meeting professional can visit and select the cities he or she is interested in and either fill out the RFP form provided or attach an already prepared RFP. Go to http://www.destinationmarketing.org for more information.

Drayage: Delivery of exhibit materials from the dock to an assigned exhibit space, removal of empty crates, return of crates at the end of the event for recrating, and delivery of materials back to the dock for carrier loading.

Early bird rate: Lowered rate offered as an incentive for attendees to send in registration before a pre-definite date. *Also called* early bird discount.

Education session: Time period during which information or instruction is presented.

English service: Style of service where guests are seated and large serving platters and bowls of food are placed on the dining table by the servers. Guests pass the food around the table.

Exclusive: Agreement that limits who may provide specific products or services under certain conditions to only one party. A general service contractor, for instance, may have an exclusive in a particular facility, meaning that no other contractor is allowed to provide the same services or products in that facility.

Exclusive contract: Contract between a facility and a service provider designating that provider as the only provider of specific services or products in that facility.

Exclusive service: Service that is provided only by the official service contractor.

Exhibit hall: Area within a facility where the exhibition is located.

Exhibition: (1) Event at which products and services are displayed. The primary activity of attendees is visiting exhibits on the show floor. These events focus primarily on business-to-business (B2B) relationships. (2) Display of products or promotional materials for the purposes of public relations, sales, and/or marketing.

Exhibition management company (EMC): Company or individual who designs and/or builds exhibits. The EMC may also provide other services.

Exhibition service contractor (ESC): Organizer or promoter of an exhibition responsible for rental of space as well as financial control and management of the exhibition. Sometimes an agent can act in this capacity.

Exhibitor-appointed contractor (EAC): Company other than the designated "official" contractor providing a service to an exhibitor. EACs are a subset of service contractors that work for the exhibiting company and travel throughout the country setting up and dismantling their booths rather than working from one city or location.

Exhibitor service manual: Manual or kit, usually developed by the service contractor for an event, containing general event information, labor/service order forms, rules and regulations, and other information pertinent to an exhibitor's participation in an exhibition.

Expenditure Impact Study (ExPact): Study that updates the International Association of Convention and Visitor Bureaus (IACVB) delegate, exhibitor, and event organizer spending information for meetings, conventions, and trade shows. Additionally, ExPact provides an estimate for the economic impact that this industry has on the United States and Canada. Formerly known as the Convention Expenditure and Impact Study.

Exposition: (1) Event at which products and services are displayed. The primary activity of attendees is visiting exhibits on the show floor. These events focus primarily on business-to-business (B2B) relationships. (2) Display of products or promotional material for the purposes of public relations, sales, and/or marketing.

Exposition management company (EMC): Company that is in the business of owning and managing trade shows and expositions. EMCs both develop and produce shows that profit their companies as well as produce events for a sponsoring corporation, association, or government client.

Exposition service contractor (ESC): *See* General Service Contractor (GSC).

Fair: (1) Enterprise principally devoted to the exhibition of products of agriculture or industry. Typically, fairs also provide entertainment activities such as rides, games, and food concessions. (2) Exhibition of products or services in a specific area of activity held with the objective of promoting business.

Fam trip: Familiarization trips. Method of promoting a destination or particular facility to a meeting planner. Fam trips are a no- or low-cost trip for planners to personally review sites for their suitability for a meeting. These trips may be arranged by a local community or by a hotel directly.

Festival: A special celebration usually involving a community.

Field staff: Staff that are responsible for handling the installation and dismantling of freight, drayage, carpentry, electrical equipment, and plumbing and the oversight of iron workers, riggers, and maintenance crews.

First-tier city: City that is notoriously expensive based on the average year-round cost for one night—single room, corporate rate, plus three meals per day, and taxes—at a first-class hotel. *See* Second-tier City.

Fixed costs: Expenses incurred regardless of the number of attendees.

Force majeure: Event (e.g., war, labor strike, extreme weather, or other disruptive circumstances) or effect that cannot be reasonably anticipated or controlled. *Also called* fortuitous event. *See* Act of God.

Frame tent: Tent that is set up on the grass. It is one of the simplest of all meeting venues and requires little advance planning beyond making sure the tent rental people can get set up in time. *Also called* open-sided tent.

Function: (1) Organized occasion that contributes to a larger event. (2) Activity or role assigned to an event planner (or other industry professional).

General service contractor (GSC): Organization hired by the show manager to handle the general duties necessary to produce the show on site, providing a wide range of services. *Also called* official show contractor. *See* Exposition Service Contractor (ESC).

General session: Meeting open to all those in attendance at a event. *See* Plenary Session.

Gesellschaft: German term for company or society.

GMBH: German term for a limited liability company.

Guarantee: Amount of food that the planner has instructed the facility to prepare and that will be paid for.

Hard data: *See* Quantitative Data.

History: Record of an event over time.

Hotel: A type of accommodation where one pays for the service.

House brand: Brand of wine or distilled spirits selected by a hotel or restaurant as its standard when no specific brand is specified. *Also called* well brand.

Housing bureau: Third-party outsourced company that handles all hotel arrangements for a fee (that may be paid by the local convention and visitor bureau).

IACVB Resource Center: Online center that is a new and developing industry resource and that houses valuable information for CVB professionals. As the center continues to grow, a wealth of resources, such as sample bureau operations documents and bureau research statistics, will be provided. The IACVB Resource Center will also strive to act as a referral source for other industry-related information.

Incentive event: Reward event intended to showcase persons who meet or exceed sales or production goals. *Also called* incentive program.

Incentive trip: Travel reward given by companies to employees to stimulate productivity.

Indirect costs: Costs that are listed as overhead or administrative line items in a program budget. These are organizational expenses not directly related to the meeting, such as staff salaries, overhead, or equipment repair.

In-line exhibit: Exhibit space with exhibit booths on either side and back.

Interactive name tag: RFID either attached to a slim piece of paper behind a badge or made part of a slightly larger wearable name tag device.

The RFID-based service offers better networking and interactivity between conference attendees as well as between attendees and vendors.

International Association of Conference Centers (IACC): Association in which member facilities must meet a list of over thirty criteria to be considered an approved conference center.

International Association of Convention and Visitor Bureaus (IACVB): Member of the Convention Industry Council (CIC). Now DMAI.

Island booth: Booth/stand space with aisles on all four sides.

Keynote address: Session that opens or highlights the show, meeting, or event.

Lead retrieval system: Process used to capture customer information. The process begins with the meeting organizer asking questions during the registration process that will identify information of importance to the exhibitor.

Level: (1) Level of audio volume. Level refers to the power magnitude in either electrical watt or acoustic watts but is often incorrectly used to denote voltage. (2) The relative depth of knowledge of attendees.

Local event: Event, such as a graduation ceremony or a local festival, that draws its audience primarily from the local market. Typically 80% of attendees reside within a 50-mile (80-km) radius of the event site. Local audiences typically do not require overnight accommodations.

Loss leader: Item offered by a retailer at cost or less than cost to attract customers. *Also called* price leader.

Material handling: Services performed by general service contractor (GSC) that include delivery of exhibit materials from the dock to assigned space, removal of empty crates, return of crates at the end of the event for recrating, and delivery of materials back to the dock for carrier loading. It is a two-way charge, incoming and outgoing. *See* Drayage.

MEEC: Meetings, expositions, events, and conventions.

Meeting: Event where the primary activity of the attendees is to attend educational sessions, participate in meetings/discussions, socialize, or attend other organized events. There is no exhibit component to this event.

Meeting event order (MEO): Specifications for each function that is part of the overall meeting or event

Meeting event specification guide: Document used by a planner to communicate specific requirements for a function. It includes a general overview of the event, a timetable outlining all functions that compose the overall event, and specifications for each function that is part of the overall event.

Meeting Industry Network (MINT): Online information network tracking historical and future site/booking information. MINT is provided by the International Association of Convention and Visitor Bureaus (IACVB) to its members. Formerly the Convention Industry Network (CINET).

Meeting professional: Person whose job is to oversee and arrange every aspect of an event. This person can be an employee or hired ad hoc by large companies, professional associations, or trade associations to plan, organize, implement, and control meetings, conventions, and other events.

Meeting Professionals International (MPI): Member organization of the Convention Industry Council (CIC).

Meeting time line: Schedule that includes each task to be accomplished. It is the core of the program plan.

Messe: German term for trade fair.

Messegelande: German term for fair site.

Multilevel exhibit: System often used by large companies to expand their exhibit space without taking up more floor space. The upper floor may be used for special purposes, such as meeting areas, private demonstration areas, or hospitality stations.

Needs analysis: Planning tool used to determine the client's needs and expectations for a meeting.

Negotiation: Process by which a meeting planner and a hotel representative (or other supplier) reach an agreement on the terms and conditions that will govern their relationship before, during, and after a meeting, convention, exposition, or event.

Network: (1) Two or more computers or peripherals that are linked together for the purpose of sharing data. (2) Two or more people gathering in an informal setting.

Nonprofit association: Association whose members may not benefit financially from its net proceeds.

Not-for-profit: Organization that exists with the intention of providing a service for its members.

OfficialTravelGuide.com: Official Web site of the International Association of Convention and Visitor Bureaus (IACVB) that links consumers and meeting professionals directly to the CVBs and tourist boards. On this site, there is official information for 1,000+ destinations, including information on hotels, conference centers, convention centers, attractions, and activities.

Off-premises catering: Foods that are usually prepared in a central kitchen and transported for service to an off-site location.

Online meeting: Web-based service where participants meet virtually, using tools such as shared desktops, PowerPoint presentations, IM/chatting, and voice conferencing.

On-premises catering: Meals that are catered on site during an event.

Opening ceremony: Formal general session at the beginning of a congress or convention.

Operations and production: Performance of the practical work of operating a program. It usually involves the in-house control and handling of all phases of the services, both with suppliers and with clients.

Outlet: Restaurant, lounge, or retail store within a facility.

Outsourcing: Hiring of an outside firm or individual to perform a task instead of using in-house staff or subcontracting of a task or responsibility to a third party.

Parol evidence: Evidence of an oral agreement that can be used in limited instances, especially where the plain meaning of words in the written document may be in doubt. A court will generally construe a contract most strongly against the party that prepared the written document; if there is a conflict between printed and handwritten words or phrases, the latter will prevail.

Peninsula booth: Exhibit with aisles on three sides.

Per diem rate: Rate paid per day. Some event attendees, such as government employees, have a limited amount of money (a daily allowance) they can spend per day on food, lodging, and other expenses.

Permit: License required by many local governments to use parks or even private property for special events. The police, the fire department, and (in many places) the building code officer must be notified when a permit is desired.

Personal digital assistant (PDA): Mobile communications device that provides individuals with most of their critical needs, such as calendars and contacts, in a handheld device.

PLC: German term for public limited company.

Plenary session: General assembly for all participants.

Podcasting: Method of distributing multimedia files, such as audio or video programs, for playback on mobile devices and personal computers.

Pole tent: A temporary fabric-covered shelter that is supported by one or more poles in the middle of the area.

Portal: An electronic access point.

Postconvention meeting: Meeting held after an event to address any billing discrepancies, service failures, and other problems or to praise facility staff for a job well done.

Poster session: (1) Display of reports and papers, usually scientific, accompanied by authors or researchers. (2) Session dedicated to the discussion of the posters shown inside the meeting area. When this discussion is not held in a special session, it can take place directly between the person presenting the poster and interested delegate(s).

Preconvention session: Meeting at the primary facility at which an event will take place just prior to the event beginning. Attendees generally include the primary event organizer and/or representatives of the final adjustments as needed. *Also called* pre-con meeting.

Prefunction space: Area adjacent to the main event location often used for receptions prior to a meal or coffee breaks during an event.

Premium brand: Higher-quality, higher-priced spirits (hard liquor).

Preregistration: Process of registering attendees weeks or months in advance of an event. This benefits the planner in several ways.

Presenter contract: Contract for the person explaining a given topic in an informational session.

Preset service: Style of service that puts plated foods on banquet tables prior to seating guests.

Profile: Detailed information about a traveler and/or a company kept on file by a travel management company.

Program: Schedule of events that gives details of times and places.

Promotional mix model: Mix that includes four elements: advertising, sales promotion, publicity and/or public relations, and personal selling. However, this author views direct marketing as well as interactive media as additional major elements in a promotional mix model.

Proposal: (1) Plan put forth for consideration or acceptance and (2) Communication sent by a supplier to a potential customer detailing the supplier's offerings and prices.

Public show: Exhibition that is open to the public, usually requiring an entrance fee. The attendees are basically defined by their interests and geographic proximity to the show location.

Qualitative data: Descriptive information that is a record of what is observed, presented in narrative by the respondent. *Also called* soft data.

Quantitative data: Information that is represented numerically, that can be assigned ranks or scores, and that can be used to determine averages and frequencies. *Also called* hard data.

Rack rate: Facility's standard preestablished guest room rates.

Radio frequency identification device (RFID): Tag attached to a product or device that emits a short-distance signal that allows the user to accurately track information.

Really simple syndication (RSS): Tool by which a Web site creates or gathers a feed of information about a specific topic and publishes it as an RSS feed. This information is updated continuously.

Request for proposal (RFP): Document that stipulates what services the organization wants from an outside contractor and requests a bid to perform such services.

Return on investment (ROI): Net profit divided by net worth. This financial ratio indicates the degree of profitability.

Risk management: Recognition of and plan for the possibility of injury, damage, or loss as well as the means to prevent it or provide insurance.

Room block: Number of rooms guaranteed by the event planner. These rooms are subtracted from the hotel inventory as attendees make reservations.

Room design software: Computer-aided design (CAD) that is applicable to room design. This software is used to enhance communications between the venue, the meeting planner, and the client.

Room list: Listing that is compiled as attendees reserve rooms with their organization and then given to the hotel. In the case of a small high-profile event, the room list includes the type of room and special requests.

Room setup: Physical arrangement of a room, including the layout of tables, chairs, and other furniture.

Roundtable session: Group of experts who meet on an equal basis to review and discuss specialized professional matters, either in closed session or (more frequently) before an audience.

Russian service: Style of service where foods are cooked tableside on a rechaud (portable cooking stove) that is on a gueridon (tableside cart with wheels). Servers place the food on platters and then pass the platters at tableside. Guests help themselves from the platters.

Sales and marketing: Process of identifying human wants and needs and developing a plan to meet those wants and needs. It encompasses everything involved with convincing an attendee to come to the event and also refers to providing information to support the exhibit sales function.

Schedule: Listing of times and locations for all functions related to an event. This information should be included in the specifications guide for an event.

Schedule of events: Timetable that outlines all functions that compose the overall meeting or event.

Seasonality: Period of time when the demand for a certain supplier's product or service is usually high, low, or neither. For example, winter in Florida is high season, while summer is low season.

Second-tier city: Destination city that is often more affordable than major cities. It is more likely to negotiate the best prices for accommodations and services. *See* First-tier City.

Service contractor: Outside company used by clients to provide specific products or services (e.g., pipe and drape, exhibitor manuals, floor plans, dance floors, or flags).

Shoulder: Beginning and ending days of a room block when fewer rooms are contracted.

Shoulder season: Period when the demand for a supplier's product or service is neither high nor low.

Showcase: Event to preview/highlight someone or something.

Signing authority: Person from the sponsoring organization who has the authority to make additions or changes to what has been ordered.

Site inspection: In-person on-site review and evaluation of a venue or location for an event. *See* Fam Trip.

Site selection: Process of deciding the physical location for the event, the type of facility to use, the transportation options, and many other meeting components.

SMART: Acronym for the critical components of a well-written objective: Specific, Measurable, Achievable, Relevant, Time.

Smart phone: 3G phone that supports not only voice but high-speed data transmission. This allows the smart phone to be used for services such as web browsing, e-mail access, and audio/video streaming.

SMERF: Acronym for certain categories of meeting market segments: Social, Military, Educational, Religious, and Fraternal.

Social event: (1) Event with the purpose of facilitating pleasant companionship among attendees or (2) Life cycle celebration (e.g.. wedding, bar/bat mitzvah, anniversary, birthday).

Soft data: *See* Qualitative Data.

Speaker bureau: Professional talent broker who can help find the perfect speaker to match the event objectives as well as the budget.

Speaker guidelines: (1) Instructions regarding the specific expectations for a speaker at an event. Usually outlined is the required format for presentations, AV request procedures, travel and accommodations instructions, etc. (2) Instructions regarding the required format to be used for the written preparation of a speech.

Speaker ready room: Area set aside for speakers to meet, relax, test audiovisual equipment, or prepare prior to or between speeches. *Also called* ready room and try-out room.

Special event: One-time event staged for the purpose of celebration; unique activity.

Specialty service contractor: Supplier that deals with a specific area of show production or event service, such as photography, furniture rental, audiovisual equipment, or floral decoration.

Specification Guide: Spec Guide. The industry preferred term for a comprehensive document that outlines the complete requirements and instructions for an event. This document is typically authored by the event planner and is shared with all appropriate vendors as a vehicle to communicate the expectations of services for a project. *Sometimes called* Staging Guide, Resume, Bible.

Sponsor: (1) Person or company underwriting all or part of the costs of an event. Sponsors may or may not participate in any of the profit from the event. (2) Individual who assumes all or part of the financial responsibility for an event or commercial sponsor that provides financial backing for an aspect of an event and in return receives visibility, advertising, or other remuneration in lieu of cash.

Sporting event: Event where athletes compete and spectators view the athletic activities and ceremonies.

Stadium: Facility that is usually designed for baseball or football as a primary function and that may be domed or open. It is sometimes difficult to distinguish a stadium from a large arena.

Stand: European term for booth or exhibit. *See* Standard Booth.

Standard booth: One or more standard units of exhibit space. In the United States, a standard unit is generally known to be a 10-foot by 10-foot space (one standard booth/stand unit equals 100 square feet). However, if an exhibitor purchases multiple units side by side or back to back, the combined space is also still referred to as a booth or a stand. It is a specific area assigned by management to an exhibitor under contractual agreement. *See* Stand.

Theater: Facility with fixed seats, usually on a sloped floor, with sight lines focused on a permanent stage. Typically, a stage box is located behind the proscenium, which contains the performance area and the fly loft.

Theme party: Event at which all foods, beverages, decorations, and entertainment relate to a single theme.

Track: Separation of programming into specific genres, such as computer skills, professional development, marketing, personal growth, legal issues, certification courses, and financial issues.

Trade exhibition: *See* Trade Show.

Trade fair: International term for an exhibition.

Trade Fair Certification Program: Program developed by the U.S. Department of Commerce to promote exports of U.S. products and services abroad. The Trade Fair Certification Program endorses independent and association show organizers who manage and organize overseas events. The certification helps trade fairs attract more exhibitors, provides additional support and value-added services for exhibitors, and promotes the event through a variety of publications and sources.

Trade show: Exhibition of products and/or services held for members of a common or related industry that is not open to the general public.

Trade show bond: Method used so that goods can be temporarily imported to an international show site without having to pay duties or taxes. *See* Carnet.

Variable costs: Expenses that vary based on the number of attendees.

Venue: (1) Site or destination of meeting, event, or show. (2) Location of a performance, such as a hall, a ballroom, or an auditorium.

Videoconference: Conference that uses video (and typically audio) to send content to and from facilities. Traditionally, videoconferencing is not Web-based; it uses production facilities to both upload and download the information.

VIP services: Services provided to a very important person who has a special function at the event (speaker, dignitary, etc.) and who should be treated with special care and attention.

Virtual tour: Technology tool that is ideal for remote site inspections but that can also be used in tandem with a traditional site visit (perhaps used with a laptop or personal computer), where a planner can call up alternate room setups and capacity information at a single click.

Virtual trade show: Attendee-based trade show that is an online experience where the individual can "walk the floor" and "visit booths" without leaving his or her home or office. Varying styles of interactivity and graphics are used in this approach.

Voice over Internet protocol (VoIP): Digital telephone that is used with a high-speed Internet connection to make and receive phone calls.

Webcasting: Streaming audio and video, using the Web as the delivery tool to deliver content to individuals.

Web conferencing: Catch-all term to describe the various types of e-learning options available to the planner and attendee.

Well brand: Brand of wine or distilled spirits selected by a hotel or restaurant as its standard when no specific brand is specified. *Also called* house brand.

Workshop: (1) Meeting of several persons for intensive discussion. The workshop concept has been developed to compensate for diverging views in a particular discipline or on a particular subject. (2) Informal and public session of free discussion organized to take place between formal plenary sessions or commissions of a congress or of a conference, either on a subject chosen by the participants themselves or on a special problem suggested by the organizers. (3) Training session in which participants, often through exercises, develop skills and knowledge in a given field.

World Trade Centers Association: Association created in 1970 as an apolitical not-for-profit organization to promote the concept of world trade centers worldwide and to encourage reciprocal programs among all of its members. Today, there are more than 300 world trade centers in 91 countries servicing more than 750,000 international businesses.

Yield management: Computer program that uses variable pricing models to maximize the return on a fixed (perishable) inventory, such as hotel rooms, based on supply-and-demand theory.

Index